LEABHARLANN

HARLANN

UNSPEAKABLE

UNSPEAKABLE

The Autobiography

John Bercow

WEIDENFELD & NICOLSON

First published in Great Britain in 2020
by Weidenfeld & Nicolson

1 3 5 7 9 10 8 6 4 2

A CIP catalogue record for this book
is available from the British Library.

HB ISBN 9781474616621
eBook 9781474616652

Typeset by Input Data Services

Printed in Great Britain by Clays Ltd, Elcograf SpA

MIX
Paper from
responsible sources
FSC® C104740

Weidenfeld & Nicolson

The Orion Publishing Group Ltd
Carmelite House
50 Victoria Embankment
London, EC4Y 0DZ
An Hachette UK Company
www.weidenfeldandnicolson.co.uk
www.orionbooks.co.uk

Dedication

First, from the bottom of my heart, I thank my wife of seventeen years and friend for thirty, Sally, together with our wonderful children, Oliver, Freddie and Jemima. They have given me encouragement, made me laugh, filled me with pride and kept me sane. Second, the book is dedicated to all who believe that Parliament's duty is not to bend the knee to the government but to exercise scrutiny of it. That was my overriding mission as Speaker.

Contents

Prorogue

It is 11.30 a.m. on Wednesday 25 September 2019. Unexpectedly, the House of Commons is sitting again. It ceased to do so on 9 September and had not thought it would resume until a State Opening on 14 October. Without a doubt, it is the most peculiar atmosphere I have known in the Chamber in my more than twenty-two years as a Member of Parliament.

The expressions on government ministers' faces range from affronted dignity to sheepish embarrassment to world-weary resignation. Opposition Members, meanwhile, are jubilant. Surveying the scene from my vantage point of the Speaker's Chair, I began proceedings on this extraordinary day with a gentle but clear signal of contentment that the government's plan to close down or 'prorogue' Parliament for five weeks at the height of the unresolved Brexit crisis had been foiled.

'Colleagues, welcome back to our place of work.'

I went on to confirm to MPs that the Supreme Court had sensationally ruled the previous day that Parliament 'had not been prorogued' and that I and my opposite number in the House of Lords should take 'immediate steps to enable each House to meet as soon as possible'.

In Parliament, naturally and properly, everything said is recorded and published verbatim. An accurate historical record is crucial. I therefore agreed with the senior Clerks that the citation for the Supreme Court judgment should be entered in the Journal of the House; and the item relating

to the prorogation of Parliament in the Journal of Monday 9
September should be *expunged*. I almost competed with the
clerks in fondness for that word 'expunged', conveying as it
does the image of a forceful and decisive scrubbing away of a
dirty imposter. The House would instead be recorded as having
'adjourned' at the close of business on Monday 9 September.

It might have struck viewers as inexplicable, reprehensible
or simply quaint that, having just returned to our business,
there was no Ministerial Question Time that day, including no
Prime Minister's Question Time. In order to explain this apparent anomaly I pointed out that questions had to be tabled
three sitting days in advance. As colleagues had not known
that the House would sit today, they could not possibly have
done so. However, I stressed that there was scope for Urgent
Questions, Ministerial Statements and other business.

It seemed apposite that we began with an Urgent Question that I had granted to the SNP's Joanna Cherry to ask the
Attorney General, Geoffrey Cox, about his legal opinion on
the advice given to the Queen to prorogue Parliament. There
was a piquancy about the question coming from her – she was
her party's spokesperson on legal and constitutional matters
but, perhaps more importantly, she had actively supported
the legal case brought against the government on prorogation
in Scotland and England. The Attorney General knew that.
While legitimately seeking to draw Geoffrey Cox on what his
legal advice had been, she was also twisting the knife in the
government's gut.

Predictably, and perfectly properly, the Attorney General
said that he was bound by the long-standing convention that
the views of the law officers are not disclosed outside the government without their consent. This refusal to disclose advice
will not have surprised Cherry or any other Member of Parliament. In reality, Opposition Members simply wanted to exploit
government embarrassment. Accordingly, Cherry hailed the
Supreme Court ruling for asserting the rule of law and the

separation of powers, arguing that it 'restored democracy'. Yet she claimed that what she was really interested in was how the attempted prorogation was ever allowed to happen.

Although the exchanges on the Urgent Question lasted for forty minutes there was no dramatic revelation. The Attorney General honestly believed that the government was entitled to ask the Queen to prorogue Parliament as the existing session had lasted over two years and the government wished to open a new session to unveil the legislative and policy priorities of the new, Boris Johnson-led administration.

Geoffrey Cox was both the best and the worst representative to pop up for the government that day. The best – I am being generous here – in that he is supremely articulate, opinionated, tough-minded and ready to bat for the government without the slightest hint of embarrassment or self-doubt. I have no reason to suppose that he did not believe every word he spoke. Yet if he didn't, such was his thespian quality that he carried it off with shameless aplomb. The best in terms of playing to the gallery of shocked Tory MPs and the extreme Brexiteers of the media was also the worst to those not signed up to the message that anyone seeking to stop Brexit was somehow an enemy of the people.

Though his eloquence was almost flawless, and his baritone strangely sonorous, Geoffrey Cox appeared before his peers in two guises – law officer and politician. As the former, he was a model of courteous but unmistakable legal clarity. Responding to his colleague, the ex-minister Rory Stewart, he declared, 'The Supreme Court invoked the principle of parliamentary sovereignty and the convention of ministerial accountability to Parliament as a justification for making justiciable the decision to prorogue. That is what it was entitled to do, and it effectively amounts to converting a political convention into a legal rule. That, traditionally, was not thought to be possible. The Supreme Court has decided that it is and I certainly do not complain in any way with its right to do so.'

In that same answer to Stewart, lip-service to the Court's right having been paid, Cox then turned his machine-gun fire upon Parliament. Becoming more florid of face, hyper in tone and undilutedly pompous, he thundered, 'We now have a wide number in this House setting their face against leaving [the EU] at all. When the government draw the only logical inference from that position, which is that we must leave therefore without any deal at all, they still set their faces, denying the electorate the chance of having their say in how this matter should be resolved.'

At this point, on the flicking of a mental switch, the studied and elaborate courtesy which had long been a hallmark of a Cox performance in Parliament gave way to a wild and un-stoppable rant reminiscent of a *Monty Python* sketch.

'This Parliament is a dead Parliament,' he roared. 'It should no longer sit. It has no moral right to sit on those green benches . . . They don't like to hear it, Mr Speaker . . . This Parliament is a disgrace.'

The man had worked himself up into a frenzy which oscil-lated between the comic and the terrifying. Visibly enjoying his sense of moral outrage at the activities of his opponents, Cox began to rotate at the despatch box, swivelling round to rouse his Conservative colleagues to paroxysms of righteous indignation at the Remainer enemy. Turning his back on the House was both mildly 'disorderly', in parliamentary parlance, and very unpopular. I therefore intervened good-naturedly, saying, 'I do not normally offer stylistic advice to the Attorney General, but his tendency to perambulate while prating is disagreeable to the House. He should face the House with confidence and assurance and an acknowledgement that the House wishes to hear his every utterance.'

'I wonder if you, Mr Speaker,' Cox replied, 'in a well-earned retirement, would like to give lessons to frontbenchers. It could be the beginnings of a new and very glorious – or even more glorious – career.'

If Cox wound himself up, he wound up his opponents too. Barry Sheerman, for forty years the Labour Member for Huddersfield, was enraged by Cox, launching into a tirade and, momentarily I feared, into orbit. Claiming that he had come into the Chamber feeling sorry for the Attorney General, Sheerman appeared shocked and disgusted that Cox had showed 'no shame at all'.

'The fact is,' Sheerman protested, 'that this government cynically manipulated the prorogation to shut down this House, so that it could not work as a democratic assembly.' Warming to his theme, indignant and by now frenetically finger-wagging at the Attorney General, he declaimed at still higher volume, 'He knows that that is the truth and to come here with his barrister's bluster to obfuscate the truth, and for a man like him, a party like his, and a leader like this Prime Minister to talk about morals and morality is a disgrace!'

Cox brushed off the attack, arguing that the Opposition should be seeking a general election if it so disapproved of the government. But I noticed he was much less comfortable when challenged as to why the government did not file a witness statement attesting to its claim that prorogation was merely the standard prelude to a new session of Parliament. Citing legal privilege as the reason not to answer that question, Cox insisted that the government's position was set out clearly in argument before the Court. It was, but one might have assumed that senior government officials would have been asked to offer sworn witness statements. If they were not – or were, but declined to do so – that seemed odd.

The suspicion was that no such statements were made for one simple reason: they would have had to concede that limiting parliamentary debate on Brexit was part of the rationale for the advice to the Queen to prorogue, thereby gravely undermining the government's case. The alternative would have potentially incriminated officials who had argued for prorogation with that in mind. Committing perjury was obviously out of the question.

Not for the first time, the Labour MP for Rhondda, Chris Bryant, asked a pertinent question, one which had also been in my mind for some weeks. He asked the Attorney General whether it might be a good idea if, in the future, prorogation were only allowed to proceed if there had been a vote in the House in favour of it. Intriguingly, Cox ducked the question, perhaps because he privately agreed with Bryant or perhaps because he just did not judge it necessary to engage with the argument. Historically, of course, prorogation has been undertaken without seeking the mandate of a parliamentary vote. But most governments have had a majority and would have won such a vote. This government did not and would not.

As if the government's embarrassment was not sufficiently acute, Geoffrey Cox then made the situation worse. The Labour MP Clive Efford asked when the Attorney General first became aware that the advice given to the Queen and others about the reasons for prorogation was not true. Cox's reply was pithy but, politically, not savvy at all. In his words: 'In advocacy terms, that is what we used to call a "when did you stop beating your wife?" question. I do not accept the premise of the question. There is no question that the Supreme Court found in any way that any advice that had been given was consciously or knowingly misleading.'

The reference to the 'when did you stop beating your wife?' question rightly went down extremely badly in the House, especially but not only with female colleagues. Sure enough, it is an old legal adage but a cannier politician and someone more evidently abreast of twenty-first-century mores would not have committed such a blunder. It reinforced the sense that Cox was not altogether comfortable with the modern world but, rather, a man born in 1960 at the age of sixty. When Labour's Emma Hardy rose on a point of order to complain that the Attorney General should learn to moderate his language and not make jokes about domestic violence, Cox was sensibly conciliatory. 'If I have given offence, I apologise,' he declared.

After the Urgent Question to Geoffrey Cox, we turned to other business. Layla Moran queried the government about Hacker House, a company owned by Jennifer Arcuri, Boris Johnson's friend, and which had received a grant of £100,000 from public funds; there was a statement from the Transport Secretary, Grant Shapps, about the collapse of the tour operator Thomas Cook; and Michael Gove delivered a statement entitled 'Brexit readiness: Operation Yellowhammer', covering the government's preparations for a no-deal Brexit. As always, Gove was immensely competent, though equally oleaginous, but the statement had the ring of propagandistic filler about it. Colleagues weighed in as if to make up for our fortnight's absence and to demonstrate that they had points to raise, so I called all eighty-seven backbenchers who wished to ask a question, meaning that the Gove grilling lasted over two hours.

A further hour or so was required for a statement by the Foreign Secretary, Dominic Raab, about Iran before we reached the headlining, best gig of the day – or worst, depending on your assessment of its quality – in the form of a statement by the Prime Minister.

I won't describe the atmosphere as electric – that would be too kind, suggestive of excitement, tension and, perhaps, the constructive direction of power. It was worse, far worse, than that. The atmosphere was one of raw, intense, undiluted anger on both sides of the House of Commons, made more alarming by the direction of the anger. It was not aimed at the culprits for an external event such as a terrorist attack. Rather, the anger was that of the Prime Minister towards the Opposition benches; to opponents on his own; the Supreme Court and, to a degree, me, as the person who had enabled opponents to express their objections to the attempted prorogation of Parliament, which I had myself publicly deplored.

In more than two decades in the House, a period that included the most high-octane debates over the Iraq War, I had never known a mood so toxic. The Prime Minister's statement lasted fourteen minutes, during which I had to call for order four times. As we had not sat for over two weeks I was determined that every MP should question the Prime Minister, however long it took – which in the end was three hours and eleven minutes, featuring no fewer than 111 backbench inquisitors and a total of 21 interventions by me to call for order.

The Prime Minister set the tone. In his second sentence, he referred to 'this paralysed Parliament'. Barely three minutes later he referred to the European Union (Withdrawal) (No. 2) Act, commonly known as the Benn Act, which required the Prime Minister to seek an extension to the Brexit withdrawal date in certain circumstances, as the 'Surrender Act'. Shortly afterwards he declared that he thought that the Supreme Court 'was wrong to pronounce on what is essentially a political question' – adding that it had done so at a time of great national controversy. The Prime Minister was visibly angry with the Supreme Court and with his political opponents, saying of the latter that 'they ran to the courts'. In turn, the Opposition – and some rebels on the government benches – were patently angry with him and rightly so. His central demand was that the House should enable him to 'get Brexit done' by 31 October or agree to a general election so that the people could give their own verdict on whether he and his party should govern and resolve Brexit, or his opponents should do so.

Answering Jeremy Corbyn, the Prime Minister again referred to the 'Surrender Act' which, he added pointedly, 'he [Corbyn] passed'. Of course, it was passed not by one person or by one party but by Parliament, following a vote for the legislation supported by several parties and a number of dissident members of the Prime Minister's own. Boris Johnson knew that perfectly well but he was out to personalise the matter and to demonise Corbyn. Answering the Democratic Unionist Party leader in the Commons, Nigel Dodds, the Prime Minister again referred to the 'Surrender Act', justifying his description by saying 'that is what it is, because it would require us to take "no deal" off the table'. Perhaps concerned that he had not made his point with sufficient force or frequency, the Prime Minister went on to use the phrase 'Surrender Act' four more times in replies to other colleagues.

Intriguingly, Alison McGovern raised the issue of 'political culture' in a very measured manner. Describing that culture as 'toxic' and the Prime Minister's language as 'violent', she asked him to 'promise to change'. Johnson conceded that 'tempers have become very ragged across the country' but argued that 'the best way to sort this out' – presumably the issue of ragged tempers – 'is to get Brexit done'. McGovern had referred to the murder of her friend, Jo Cox, and the need for a change in political culture, but the Prime Minister chose not to engage directly with that point at all.

Answering the former Conservative Cabinet minister Justine Greening, who had said that to call a Bill passed by the House a 'Surrender Bill' was 'deeply disrespectful' to the Commons, the Prime Minister was openly contemptuous.

The atmosphere was appalling. I gently but firmly underlined the premium placed by *Erskine May* (the bible of parliamentary procedure) on moderation and good humour in the use of language. Immediately afterwards, the Prime Minister referred to the 'Surrender Act' yet again. Paula Sherriff, constituency neighbour of the late Jo Cox, appealed to the Prime Minister not to resort to the use of 'offensive, dangerous or inflammatory language' about legislation that he did not like. His initial response was to say that he had 'never heard such humbug' in all his life. This prompted outrage and fury on the Opposition benches. I intervened to appeal for calm, after which the Prime Minister explained why he described the Benn Act as he did, deploying the word 'surrender' twice more in the process. In response to further questions the Prime Minister again repeated the word 'surrender' of the Benn Act, adding in for good measure the words 'capitulation' and 'humiliation'.

Obviously the language that produced such upset was no accident. It was deliberate and calculated to press home his 'Parliament versus the People' narrative, plainly to be used intensively in an upcoming election campaign. Buoyed by innate self-confidence, full-throttle roars of support from most Conservative MPs and the belief that he had a winning message, Johnson did not hold back. He rammed home his script with unremitting vigour.

In the short term, however, there was a downside to his aggressive and adversarial approach. He was at that point still in need of support from Opposition MPs to back any deal he might strike with the EU. Such a rabidly confrontational tone and demeanour was not likely to garner him that support.

Immediately after the exchanges on the Prime Minister's statement, several MPs leapt to their feet to raise points of order. I did not know exactly what they would be but I had been told that they related to the Prime Minister and his statement. I suggested to Johnson that it would be a courtesy to stay for the first, from the Shadow Chancellor, John Mc-Donnell. Initially, he seemed minded to do so. I suggested that he go and sit down for the purpose but he had a change of heart and left. Later, he texted me to say that he intended no discourtesy but simply decided to stick to his original plan to leave straight after questioning on his statement had finished. Frankly, that was disingenuous of him. The truth was that he had had enough. He didn't care a damn what I or anyone else thought about him departing the Chamber. It was not a good look for the Prime Minister but, in the grand picture, it was a minor matter.

To his credit, Jeremy Corbyn said later that day that we had to put out a message that we would treat each other with respect. If not, people minded to be violent would be emboldened. He urged that I convene a meeting of party leaders in order to produce a joint declaration. I agreed and subsequently hosted a cross-party gathering in Speaker's House – attended by Jeremy Corbyn, Ian Blackford, Jo Swinson, Nigel Dodds, Anna Soubry, Liz Saville-Roberts, Caroline Lucas and, for the Conservatives, the Chief Whip Mark Spencer – after which the declaration was issued.

By the end of that fateful day of 25 September, I had chaired the business of the House from 11.30 in the morning to just before 11 p.m. without a break. It was my privilege. Yet the atmosphere was worse than I had ever known it. Rancour, demonisation and contempt for opponents' views were apparent on both sides of the House.

The following day, I told colleagues that we had not shown ourselves to advantage and should do better. I had not liked the Prime Minister's language of 'surrender' and 'capitulation' at all, but it was not 'disorderly'. Free speech matters. I do not believe that Johnson sought to incite violence or disorder. Rather, his was a ruthless bid to whip up support for Brexit, for his party and, last but by no means least, for himself. His entire approach to Brexit may be wrong-headed, irresponsible and damaging to the UK national interest, in my view, but that was no reason to censor him from the Chair. I could appeal for restraint and I did. But I could not insist on it.

* * *

Such was the culmination of the furious row over prorogation. Neither Geoffrey Cox at the start of proceedings nor Boris Johnson towards their close offered the slightest scintilla of contrition or remorse. If anything, they were even less conciliatory than they would have been if they had won the court case. The country saw a replay of an old truth: people are angrier and more resentful when they lose.

The saga had begun weeks before. At the end of August I was on holiday in Turkey with my wife Sally and our three children when I first saw online the suggestion that the government would seek to prorogue Parliament some time between 9 and 12 September. The House was due to return for two sitting weeks as usual in September, before a recess for party conference season. The expectation in Westminster was that the government would look to resume the sitting of Parliament on Monday 7 or Tuesday 8 October. Yet there were well-founded rumours that dissident Conservative backbenchers and the Opposition would seek to amend this timetable so that Parliament could come back immediately after the Conservative Party Conference in order to legislate against a no-deal Brexit.

Now, suddenly, at the back end of August, with Parliament on its summer break, the government was announcing that it intended the September sitting to be cut, indeed potentially halved, not resuming until 14 October. The State Opening of a new session of Parliament would take place that day with no scope for votes until the following week, some days *after* the EU Council on 17–19 October at which the government needed to get a Brexit deal if the UK was to leave the EU in an orderly fashion on 31 October.

The official Opposition was not consulted. To my knowledge, no other party was consulted. I was certainly not consulted. By summary announcement, the Prime Minister was indicating that he intended to shut down Parliament for five weeks and to resume only days before the EU Council but with no opportunity for MPs to debate and vote on Brexit before that historic summit. Only a government that had come to hold Parliament as an institution, and large numbers of Members as individuals, in abject contempt could possibly believe that this was a proper way to conduct the affairs of State. It was a disgrace.

Speakers of the House of Commons do not regularly issue

press releases. We say what we have to say to the House. That was my normal approach too. However, the House was in recess. These were abnormal times. I did not think it right to allow that arbitrary edict from 10 Downing Street, aimed at Parliament and deliberately fired off to wrong-foot it when it was not sitting, to go unchallenged. Before going to lunch with my family, I penned a statement for immediate release to the Press Association:

> I have had no contact from the government, but if the reports that it is seeking to prorogue Parliament are confirmed, this move represents a constitutional outrage. However it is dressed up, it is blindingly obvious that the purpose of prorogation now would be to stop Parliament debating Brexit and performing its duty in shaping a course for the country. At this early stage in his premiership, the Prime Minister should be seeking to establish, rather than undermine, his democratic credentials and indeed his commitment to parliamentary democracy.

My reaction, that the government's move was designed to stymie Parliament in debating and deciding an approach to Brexit, was widely echoed. As we have seen, the government denied that the intended prorogation had anything to do with Brexit, the Prime Minister arguing that it was purely about opening a new session of Parliament to unveil fresh policies following the long session since June 2017.

Although Johnson said that there would be time to debate Brexit before the EU Council, it was clear there would be no opportunity for actual votes on Brexit in the days in October running up to the EU Council, even though the House might want to send a clear signal as to its wishes. There was, though, a chance for the House to debate Brexit and even to seek to legislate in the first week of September. MPs from across the Commons sought my agreement to ask the House to allow them to provide parliamentary time to introduce a Bill to block a so-called cliff-edge, no-deal exit from the EU. The request was legitimate under Standing Order 24 which allowed for emergency debates. I granted the request. Those MPs won the vote, introduced the so-called Benn Bill and Parliament passed it so that it became an Act.

It might be argued that, as the government did not prorogue to deny Parliament that first week in September to debate and – as it transpired – to legislate on Brexit, that proves that ministers were not in fact seeking to stymie Parliament on Brexit. But in my view it merely proves they made a tactical error, didn't have the balls to shut down Parliament at once and wrongly thought that opponents would not get their act together in time.

They probably calculated that a complete shutdown at once would have been harder to pass off as having nothing to do with Brexit. That's true. But as hampering the Commons on Brexit was very much their purpose, it would have been straightforward. However, it would have provoked a still bigger uproar and they must have baulked at the prospect.

The weakness in the government's approach was exposed when Gina Miller and others brought their court cases against prorogation. Ministers had said that the rationale for prorogation was nothing to do with Brexit and that the ongoing debates formed no part of the advice to the monarch. Yet no government minister or official provided a witness statement to the Supreme Court. As we have seen, this fuelled the widespread suspicion that ministers and officials did not want to risk perjuring themselves by stating to a court what could be contradicted by what they had said outside it, either in communication with each other or with the Queen.

Further proof, if proof were needed, that ministers were not primarily motivated by a desire for a Queen's Speech came in that second week of September. The government had tabled a motion for an early general election. It needed a two-thirds majority and was not expected to secure that. If it had, the House would soon not merely prorogue but dissolve for a general election – one which I had never had any intention of fighting. To avert any possibility that the House might cease to sit before I had said thank you and goodbye, I told the House on 9 September that if it voted that night for an election, my tenure as Speaker and MP would end when that Parliament ended. Otherwise I would step down at the close of business on 31 October.

As it happened, the election motion was not carried by the requisite majority. Ministers had sought and obtained the Queen's agreement to prorogue. The ceremony in Parliament that day, 9 September 2019, to declare the prorogation was just that: a ceremony. Prorogation of Parliament is ordinarily uncontroversial, entailing a few days from the ending of one parliamentary session, during which the House would not sit, to the opening of the next. In this case, it was the subject of a blazing row politically and it was predictable that it would be pursued legally. With extreme reluctance, I played my part in the ceremony because the prorogation would have gone ahead anyway even if I had not done so. What I was not prepared to do was to behave hypocritically by conducting myself as though this prorogation was like any other. From the Chair, I made it clear that it was not, that I recognised that many Members would wish to remain in the Chamber and that I regarded the prorogation as an act of executive fiat.

The government was visibly and audibly angry with me but I make no apology for telling the truth. The matter went to the Supreme Court and the eleven judges there who heard the case took their responsibility extremely seriously. The issue was whether the advice given by the Prime Minister to the Queen that Parliament should be prorogued was lawful, and the legal consequences if it was not.

Announcing the decision of the Supreme Court on Tuesday

24 September, Lady Hale, its president, explained the process of deliberation that she and her fellow judges had undertaken. The first question for them to consider was whether the lawfulness of the Prime Minister's advice to Her Majesty was 'justiciable'; that is, subject to a trial in a court of law. The Court held that it was, citing precedent dating back to the seventeenth century. The Court was crystal clear about the limits to the prerogative power. First, the doctrine of parliamentary sovereignty meant that Parliament must be able to make laws that everyone must obey. This notion would be undermined if the executive could, through the use of the prerogative, prevent Parliament from exercising its power to make laws for as long as it pleased. The second fundamental principle was accountability. In the words of the late Lord Bingham, senior Law Lord, 'the conduct of government by a Prime Minister and Cabinet collectively responsible and accountable to Parliament lies at the heart of Westminster democracy'. The power to prorogue, Lady Hale concluded, was limited by the constitutional principles with which it would otherwise conflict.

For the purposes of the case, Lady Hale and her fellow judges concluded, the relevant limit on the prorogation power was that a decision to prorogue, or advise the monarch to do so, would be unlawful if it had the effect of frustrating the ability of Parliament to carry out its constitutional functions. If the prorogation did have that effect, without reasonable justification, the court did not have to consider whether the Prime Minister's motive or purpose was unlawful.

Contrary to what the government had claimed all along, the Supreme Court found that 'this was not a normal prorogation in the run-up to a Queen's Speech'. It prevented Parliament from carrying out its constitutional role for five out of the possible eight weeks between the end of the summer recess and exit day on 31 October. Proroguing Parliament was quite different, Lady Hale rightly emphasised, from Parliament going into recess. While Parliament was prorogued, neither House could meet, debate or pass legislation; during a recess, on the other hand, the House did not sit but parliamentary business could otherwise continue as usual.

The Supreme Court could not have been clearer. The Prime Minister's advice to Her Majesty was unlawful, void and of no effect. It followed from that that the prorogation itself was also unlawful, void and of no effect. In its words, 'Parliament has not been prorogued. This is the unanimous judgment of all eleven Justices.' It was for Parliament, and in particular the Speaker and the Lord Speaker, to decide what to do next. Later that morning I took great pleasure in announcing to the media that the House would sit at 11.30 a.m. the following day.

* * *

The issue of prorogation of Parliament is not one of the most regularly discussed topics among journalists or political scientists, let alone members of the public. Yet in the late summer and autumn of 2019, as we have seen, it became the subject of heated controversy. Members of the public with merely a passing interest in politics could be forgiven for thinking that the act of prorogation was itself a sin or misdeed. A brief explanation of the concept will, I hope, not only put this recent row into context but also demonstrate that the government's failed attempted prorogation of 2019 was not the norm, or even commonplace, but an aberration.

Prorogation is simply the means by which (other than by dissolution of Parliament, the prelude to an immediate general election) a parliamentary session is brought to an end. It is a prerogative power exercised by the Crown on the advice of the Privy Council, the body of MPs and Peers that advises Her Majesty. In practice, this process has been a formality in the UK for more than a century. The government of the day advises the Crown to prorogue and the monarch agrees to that request. Unless specific provision is made to carry over Bills, no business of a previous parliamentary session can be carried over into the next.

A prolonged prorogation very obviously reduces the influence of Parliament over the way in which the country is governed. While Parliament is prorogued, I emphasise again, MPs and Peers cannot debate government policy and legislation, or table questions to ministers, or scrutinise government activity through parliamentary committees or introduce legislation of their own. For most of its key purposes, proroguing Parliament means shutting Parliament down. However, while Parliament may be rendered ineffective, the same is not true of government. It can continue to make what is called 'delegated' legislation (law passed not by an Act of Parliament but by a 'delegated' minister) and bring it into force and to exercise its other prerogative powers. Its capacity to make policy, take decisions and administer public business is unaffected.

The typical recent duration of a UK Parliament's prorogation has been very short. Since the 1980s, prorogation has rarely lasted longer than two weeks. Moreover, between sessions during a Parliament, it has typically lasted less than a week.

In 1997 Parliament was prorogued for almost three weeks prior to dissolution ahead of the general election. On that occasion, the Opposition parties protested that that lengthy prorogation should have been instead an 'adjournment', which would have allowed the select committees to continue their functions. They argued that prorogation would prevent, and was intended to prevent, the Standards and Privileges Committee from publishing before the election a report from the Parliamentary Standards Commissioner in relation to allegations of 'cash for questions' in the House of Commons. The proof of the pudding was in the eating. The effect of prorogation was indeed to delay the publication of the Committee's report until after the 1997 election.

In 2019 it was as plain as a pikestaff that to stymie Parliament on Brexit was the purpose of the unusually long prorogation announced by the government at the height of the summer recess, with no consultation with opposition parties or me as Speaker. Ultimately, the prorogation plot failed. It failed because Parliament legislated in the first week of September to prevent a no-deal Brexit without democratic approval. It failed too because the Supreme Court declared it unlawful. The abuse of power was foiled, but make no mistake. That is precisely what it was: an abuse of power designed to stop Parliament having its say and its way over the most important matter of UK public policy in over seventy years. For any minister now to persist with the pretence that it was not about curtailing Brexit debate but about the desperate urgency of providing for a Queen's Speech – none of the provisions of which was enacted and all of which were casually abandoned within a fortnight – is not merely wrong. It is a preposterous lie and an insult to the intelligence of MPs, the media and citizens alike.

Rancorous and brutal as it was, the prorogation row offered a kind of parallel with my tenure as Speaker. My entire approach in over a decade in the Chair was to seek to increase the relative authority and influence of the legislature, specifically the House of Commons, in its dealings with the executive, the government. It was never any part of my role to serve as a nodding donkey or quiescent lickspittle of the executive branch of our political system. As I had foreshadowed in seeking election as Speaker in June 2009, I did not want to be someone, but to do something. The something was to stand up for Parliament, encourage the House of Commons to take control of its own core functions and to assert its right fully and unsparingly to scrutinise the government of the day.

Governments want a passive Speaker who will diplomatically

stand aside and leave them to call the shots. I never had the slightest interest in playing that role. Likewise, within the House administration, there were always people for whom the status quo was very comfortable and who resisted any change that would threaten that comfort and privilege. My responsibility was not just to sit there, lazily administering the existing order. Rather, it was to keep the best and, whether alone or with others, to improve the rest. Specifically, as Speaker, I had a duty to stand up for MPs individually, to champion Parliament institutionally and to try to make Parliament look more like the country we are charged to represent. It was, perhaps, a fitting, albeit unanticipated dénouement to my tenure to end as I had begun on a note of explosive controversy. The government was pitted against a Parliament that rightly and resolutely refused to bend the knee or to shut up. It was my privilege, and I was proud, to pipe up for Parliament one last time.

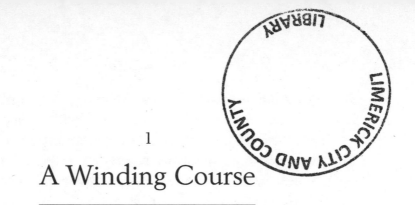

1

A Winding Course

I never knew my paternal grandparents. Jack Bercowich had come to Britain from Galatz in Romania in 1900, one of many Jews who, fearing the rampant anti-Semitism in the land of his birth, successfully applied to come to a country that offered the prospect of fairer treatment and a better life. He was about sixteen when he arrived, soon after his parents, Sam and Annie. Initially Jack made a living as a gas-fitter but he later went into the fur trade and, to the best of my knowledge, the bulk of his working life was spent as a furrier. He met and married another Romanian called Annie, Annie Rothman. She was twenty-three and Jack Bercowich twenty-seven when they married at the Wellington Road synagogue in Stoke Newington. They lived in Hackney and had four children – Bella, who for as long as I can remember lived in Switzerland and whom I never met; Reuben, more commonly known to me as Uncle Ralph, who died of cancer in his mid-fifties over half a century ago; Samson, who fell out with his siblings before I was born and whom I never met; and Charles, my father, born in July 1920.

Occasionally I would chat to Dad about his parents, and his recollections were invariably affectionate. Dad always implied that his father had been an easy-going man – no one would accuse Dad or me of that – who took life in his stride and made no more than a modest living. Dad suggested that his father was lovable but not the strong personality his mother was. She could be irritable and was inclined to complain about her burden in raising four children on a tight budget.

I knew and loved my maternal grandmother, Elsie Ellis. Grandma was short, barely more than five feet tall, and petite with blonde curly hair and strikingly blue eyes. Born in 1906, she lived in Huddersfield for most of her life. A very attractive young woman, she had a brief affair, I am told, with a local toff who, horrified that she was pregnant and fully intending to give birth, promptly scarpered, offering not a penny piece to support her in the raising of my mother, Brenda.

In the thirty years or so that I knew Grandma before she developed dementia and went into a care home in the early 1990s, she was always kind, warm and generous; one of the most tactful and pacific people I have ever met. Soft and giving though she was, she could be tough when it mattered to her. She had conceived my mother and would not be browbeaten into having an abortion. She would become a mum, and do her best. I remember Mum telling me that Grandma was a lifelong Labour voter, thought that Harold Wilson – himself a Yorkshireman, of course – was a great man and would not hear a word against him. By background and inclination, she was a Methodist. I have no memory of her ever drinking alcohol or smoking, but her one very modest indulgence – to the tune in today's money of probably no more than a pound a week – was to play bingo in a local club for senior citizens. Grandma neither advertised nor concealed the fact, but at one stage her sisters got to hear of it and formed a solemn delegation to visit her and urge her to repent of her sin. Mum and I, angry on her behalf, told her in no uncertain terms that she should do as she wished and not submit to pious and unsolicited lectures.

My father was born on 7 July 1920 and lived throughout his childhood in the East End of London. He went to Hackney Downs Secondary School and was a bright boy. As an adult, he always wrote a very good letter and was highly articulate in conversation, speaking fluently, grammatically, in paragraphs.

Mum would joke that Dad would never use one word where one hundred would do, and I have inherited that prolixity. Curiously, for someone naturally gifted in the written and spoken word alike, he had no interest whatever in reading, apart from newspapers.

As a young man, he told me, Dad had briefly aspired to become a barrister. But in the late 1930s and early 1940s the Bar, even now a profession disproportionately populated by privately educated men and women, was dominated by people with some private means. Dad had none. His parents' expectation was that he should leave school, find work, bring in a wage and thereby help to support himself and the family home. Dad accepted that situation with equanimity and for many years worked for London County Council.

Much later, in the 1950s, his elder brother, Reuben but known as Ralph, invited Dad to join his second-hand-car business as a junior partner, which he was thrilled to do. They traded in London's Warren Street for some years before eventually acquiring premises at the Homestall Parade, Colindale – proud home to Bercow Motors until ill health and declining fortunes forced Dad to sell the business in 1974. An experience a couple of years before probably hastened his decision to sell. Dad had knowingly taken on an ex-convict who had done time for a variety of offences, but who convinced Dad that he had gone straight. They seemed to work well together but one day my father was attacked, bound and gagged at gunpoint while the burglars helped themselves to the contents of the safe. The police were convinced that it was an inside job, but nothing was proven. By then, Ralph was long dead, the surge in global oil prices and resultant economic havoc hit car sales badly, and Dad knew that he was struggling to survive.

I know the second-hand-car salesman is often ridiculed, held up as a classic example of a rogue trader, a Del Boy type. But I knew my dad. He was not a great businessman, it's true. Risk-averse, quite anxious if he went a few days without making a sale and honourable to a fault, he was not at all ruthless. But he was scrupulously honest and I respected that. After he sold the business, he worked as a minicab driver before ill health forced him to stop work aged sixty-one.

Mum, Brenda Bailey, was born in Huddersfield on 18 November 1928, the first and the only child of a single mother. She left secondary school aged fourteen and took a job as a junior reporter on the *Huddersfield Examiner*. Whether she produced a piece of prose that persuaded the newspaper or simply did a good interview I don't know, but I could imagine Mum succeeding either way. She was almost certainly less academic than Dad and, like me, far less proficient than him at maths. At English, however, she excelled. She had a feel for a phrase or slogan, a talent she deployed much later as an adult in winning innumerable competitions that required the entrant to come up with a snappy phrase capturing why they liked a particular product. Less voluble than Dad or me, she was nevertheless fluent at writing and speech and I'm sure would have given a good interview.

Just as Dad had had to leave school to earn a wage, so too a few years later in Yorkshire my mother was propelled by the same pressure. Her childhood had not been unhappy as such, but she disliked being obliged to go and stay with her relatives during the week while Grandma worked, knowing that she would not see her mum for five days. Throughout life, Mum has never much liked Sundays, and it gradually became clear to me why. They reminded her of being separated, of having to part company with her mum to be raised by a strict aunt and her husband. As a child, Mum loved reading. She used the library to the full, enjoyed occasional trips to the cinema and loved the even rarer treat of watching a musical. Sadly, though, she could not do anything that cost significant money and which some of her better-off school pals did: piano lessons, dancing or tennis were all out of the question as Grandma simply could not afford them. This absence of opportunity was a formative influence on my mother and it became a key driver of her quest to ensure that my elder sister Alison and I had good opportunities to develop hobbies as children.

Even though Mum appeared to enjoy her role as a junior reporter, she found life in Huddersfield altogether too constricting. By nature mildly impulsive, she announced aged seventeen that she would go to live in London and find work there. Somehow she got work as an office assistant, took a shorthand and typing course, and went on to work as a secretary, principally for lawyers. Dad had gone to live with his elder brother, Ralph, and his wife, Betty, in north London and my parents met, I'm told, at a dance.

My father's parents were practising Reform Jews and so was my dad. Mum was a Yorkshire Methodist, albeit not a regular churchgoer. Dad's parents liked her but both thought that the idea of them getting married was unconscionable. An earnest ritual was played out in all solemnity over quite a long period. Dad's father, Jack, said to him, 'Charlie, Brenda is a lovely girl but you can't marry her. She is not Jewish. Son, it is not about me. You needn't worry on my account but you don't seem to know what you're doing to your mother, who is distraught. You will have to abandon any plan to get married.' Meanwhile Dad's mum, Annie, said to him, 'Charlie, Brenda is a lovely girl but you can't marry her. She is not Jewish. It is not about me. I don't mind, but you don't seem to know what you're doing to your father, who is terribly upset. You'll have to abandon any unrealistic plan to wed.'

Dad loved his parents, but he loved Brenda too, and wanted to marry her – preferably without alienating his parents and, better still, with their blessing. Here Ralph played a starring role. It was early 1956. He told his parents that Dad was almost thirty-six, quite old by the standards of the day to be marrying for the first time. As he put it bluntly, 'Charlie is an ugly bugger. He's very lucky to have attracted a lovely, charming young woman in Brenda. Please don't wreck his happiness by objecting. Brenda is willing to convert to Judaism.' Dad's parents were mollified. A date was set, and my parents married on 13 December 1956. I shall always be grateful to Uncle Ralph for his diplomatic prowess, without which I would not be here to tell the story.

Surprisingly, given that I have praised my parents' communication skills, they had not communicated well about their plans with regard to children. Mum wanted to have children and assumed that Dad did too, only to discover to her horror that he did not. This was less because Dad had an aversion to children and more because he feared he would not be able to provide. Mum worked to persuade him that they would be fine and she succeeded. Alison was born in August 1960 and I followed in January 1963. By then, we were living in a little bungalow in Abercorn Road, Mill Hill, of which I have no recollection. In late 1964, we moved to Woodside Park, where my parents had bought a three-bedroom semi-detached house with a garden. Number 108 Southover was to be our home for the next thirteen years.

Dad was old-fashioned. He expected and wanted to be the breadwinner. He did not want his wife to work outside the home and, to be fair, she was very happy to be a full-time mother. Alison and I got on reasonably well most of the time and when we fell out, as all siblings do, it was more often my fault. Alison was, and is, good-natured, hard-working, loyal and a wonderful sister. She started at Frith Manor primary school, Lullington Garth in Woodside Park in the autumn of 1964 and I followed in 1967. Both of us enjoyed English and History but were less adept at maths and science. We both loved sport at school, Alison excelling at netball and I enjoying though not excelling at football. I lost no opportunity to play, and as a north Londoner I was likely to be either an Arsenal or a Tottenham fan. A family friend recommended to me aged eight that Arsenal was the team to support, and I have been devoted to the club ever since.

A short, slightly built boy, with brown eyes and brown hair, I was not physically imposing or strong and I was frankly not a great athlete, though quite trim, fit and certainly able and inclined to run around for hours. I was also intensely competitive and appalled by defeat. The traditional British attitude that it wasn't winning but taking part that mattered was alien to me. I knew and played by the rules but it mattered enormously to me to win whenever possible, and I threw myself into every contest.

I was a confident speaker, however, often given to speaking out of turn in class, and was once described as 'a walking dictionary'. I played the recorder without distinction and was even less accomplished at singing, which, quite aside from the fact that I regularly and intensely irritated Mr Geaney, was quite sufficient reason for my expulsion from the school choir in 1973 – the shame of which I have borne these last four and a half decades with such stoicism and fortitude as I have been able to muster.

So I did not excel at sport or music. Moreover, I was utterly useless at art. But, for all the long list of my failures, I was keen on school drama. Encouraged by Mr Geaney, I recall that in Year 5 I played Noah in *Noah's Ark* and it was a real joy. It was not that I had no nerves at all but rather that the experience offered a terrific adrenaline rush. It was fun to learn my lines, to interact with the cast and to have my excitement fuelled by an appreciative audience. The following year my form teacher was John Stringer, who was well aware of my faults but who appeared also to appreciate my strengths. His whole approach was to try to bring out the best in his pupils, and he was without doubt the best teacher I had in primary school. We got on famously and in Year 6 our play was *David and Goliath*, fittingly played by me and by him.

It was at Frith Manor that I had my first authentic political experience. A school election was held, in 1972 – not a general election year, a factor that often prompts schools to organise their own polls. I don't recall standing on a party ticket although my school friend, Shamit Saggar, now a successful academic, did. He was the Liberal candidate and I recall him making a precociously knowledgeable and erudite speech in favour of centrist politics. His difficulty was that his prodigious knowledge and quite scholarly delivery went above the heads of some of his fellow pupils and he did not receive as many votes as he deserved.

By contrast, I stood on a platform of opposition to school meals. This will rightly be viewed as an act of rank opportunism on my part as the said meals were not outstanding. Aged nine, I had not developed an ideological thirst for competitive tendering, concentrating instead on the simple rhetorical line that the meals were awful garbage and if pupils endorsed my call for radical change, they should vote for me. I received 35 votes, took second place and won the plaudit of a local newspaper report describing my 'strong platform manner'. Nicola Crowther, who was top of the class and, from memory, brilliant at all subjects and tasks, won with 63 votes, but I was very encouraged by my effort.

It was also at primary-school age, but not through school, that I became hooked on tennis. I mentioned earlier that Mum had precious few opportunities to take up hobbies, as most would involve some financial outlay. By the end of the 1960s my parents were moderately well-off – not at all rich but with some money to spare for sports and other coaching. Astonishingly, I won a Highly Commended certificate for tap dancing, although these days I am an appalling dancer and go nowhere near a dance floor unless I have several drinks inside me. I went to Cubs and hated the map-reading. I tried Judo and did not take to it. I did not play cricket or rugby at school and Mum did not suggest either. Mum remembered that when we had lived in Abercorn Road she had walked with me in the pram past the Finchley Manor Tennis Club. She enquired about coaching there and discovered that group sessions took place on a Saturday morning: I joined the group and loved it. Mum was at first as much relieved as thrilled. I fear that she had begun to wonder if I would take to anything. Fortunately, I took to tennis.

It was not that I was particularly talented, but I seemed to have a basic ball sense and reasonable hand-eye co-ordination. We all tend to enjoy what we are good at and I was better at tennis than I had been at anything else. I went to lessons enthusiastically on Saturday mornings and then had a private lesson for an hour each week with the club pro, Dudley Georgeson. Aged ten, I reached my first Under-12 tournament final in Pinner in 1973 and the following summer, to my delight, I won my first title, the Under-12 Singles at the Coolhurst Club near Highgate. That was followed weeks later by victory in the Under-12 final of the Middlesex County Championship.

Mum had done me a fantastic favour in recommending I take up tennis as, even though I am worse now than when I was fourteen, I still love the game and have had enormous fun trying to play it and watching competitive tennis from the age of eight to the present day. Ironically, Mum never played until I taught her in her middle age, and she then did so only for a short period until an injury put an end to her playing days. But she loves the game too and, like me, hero-worships Roger Federer.

* * *

In 1974 I prepared for the transition to secondary school. I did not take the 11-plus, although the London Borough of Barnet had a number of grammar schools. Pupils had in the first instance to be recommended by the head teacher, and I was not on his list. My parents were sorry about my omission, but not angry. I went to Finchley Manorhill comprehensive, which was a lot rougher than Frith Manor – primary school had been quite a friendly place. At Finchley Manorhill there was a harder-edged attitude, boys in particular but girls too, sharper and more aggressive in talking to each other, and I soon saw evidence of physical aggression. I continued to be of slight build and was among the shortest pupils of my age. That, however, did not bother me. I progressed quite well academically and savoured modest but still uplifting success on the tennis court.

From about 1975 and for the remainder of secondary school, there were two things that threatened to spoil my general happiness. First, after years of argument and tension between them, Mum and Dad divorced in May 1975. They had first raised the prospect about four years earlier, suggesting that we might 'live separately' and I had replied, no doubt very naïvely, 'Why can't you just stop arguing and let us all live as one happy family?' To be fair, they tried. There was no third party involved. But the truth is they were just not well suited. Mum's doubts going up the aisle had been amply confirmed in the eighteen years since then. She was more of a spender, he a saver (although in no way mean). She wanted to try lots of different holiday locations, Dad preferred to go to Calafell in Spain ad infinitum. She wanted them to take more regular dancing lessons. Dad did not. She wanted to eat out more often than once a week and to sample all varieties of cuisine. Dad was naturally a more stay-at-home type, would go to a Chinese restaurant only on sufferance and, to her acute embarrassment, order English roast chicken and chips. Even our home itself became a bone of contention: Dad was house-proud and tidy – though I doubt he cooked a single meal or washed a single dish in their married life – and he thought Mum was rather untidy and slapdash.

They went to marriage guidance counselling, and Mum later told me that in one of their sessions the counsellor had suddenly said, 'You know, I think you're making progress. It's going to be fine.' Sadly, in a flash, she recoiled and thought, 'No, this is not what I want.' She felt that Charlie was a good man, but that life with him was dull. She wanted to savour new experiences, to experiment.

The die was cast by 1972 or 1973 and Mum began the then lengthier process of divorce proceedings. Dad was angry and bitter. He argued, not unreasonably, that he was the same man she had married eighteen years earlier, and to him you made your vows and kept them. He had not changed – but Mum had. He jibed that she had 'ideas above her station'; Mum admitted that her tastes had evolved, and why shouldn't they?

My sister Alison seemed stoical about the situation, outwardly much calmer than me, though in later years I came to think that she had been more affected by the break-up than either she or any of the family knew at the time. For my part, I was very upset. I loved both of my parents and, rather idealistically, wanted us to be one happy family. Some children, whatever they think, might remain neutral in a divorce situation. However unfairly, I did not. Even though I was very close to Mum, of whom I saw more, I blamed her. She was ripping the family apart and I resented her for it. That said, if I resented their falling-out, I resented at least two years of constant bickering and argument between them far more. To this day, I well recall wet Bank Holidays at home when they argued. I would hear raised voices, go into the sitting room and appeal to them to calm down. They would take heed . . . for about ten minutes before the volume rose again. Alison was fed up with it too. We both came to feel that the sooner the house was sold and they went their separate ways, the better.

As with every other subject, there is scope for difference of opinion about divorce law. Some people think it should bind couples together and, for their own benefit or that of their children, make it a harder process to divorce. I disagree. A couple usually know when they have reached the end point. Thereafter, there is no merit in the ostrich mentality and only greater pain, for the couple or their children, will result from it. In those circumstances, it is in everyone's interests to be free to start afresh. In our case, that did not happen. For two and a half years after their divorce, the family continued to live under the same roof in an atmosphere of recrimination and disharmony.

I was relieved when we moved. Mum had full custody. She, Alison and I went to live in a small two-bedroom maisonette that Mum bought in Mill Hill. Dad purchased a pleasant one-bedroom flat in a purpose-built block in Whetstone. I would go to see him on his one day off work, a Sunday, for a few hours in the evening. Occasionally, we would go out for a meal but more often I had already eaten and we simply sat down with a cup of tea to chat. From late 1977 until I went to university in 1982 we observed that enjoyable ritual and, increasingly, we discussed the subject that was my new, great interest, namely politics. Dad was strongly Conservative, a believer in hanging and flogging, initially an admirer of Margaret Thatcher but fiercely anti-American and gradually disillusioned with her premiership, not least because of her closeness to Ronald Reagan. Although he believed in nuclear deterrence, he was fundamentally an admirer of Enoch Powell – who did not – and he utterly despised Tony Benn. His objection was both to the Benn brand of unadulterated socialism and to the fact that Benn was himself a wealthy aristocrat who seemed still to enjoy a very comfortable existence.

We would talk about the economy, wealth creation, trade unions, immigration, law and order, and Rhodesia (now Zimbabwe), where Dad was, bizarrely, an admirer of Ian Smith. Life, however, in Mill Hill was not proving great fun and it took me a long time to adjust to it. After all, divorce usually makes a family poorer. We now lived in a more confined space. There was just a tiny back garden and no wall against which I could hit a tennis ball, as I had for years in Woodside

Park. This feeling of being cramped, of having no home outlet for my energy, was bad enough. My unhappiness in my new surroundings was compounded by the second blight on my adolescent life.

From the age of twelve, shortly after starting at Finchley Manorhill, I had become prone to pimples. At first, it was a modest affliction – I would apply a cream and the problem would go. But it got much worse, and before long I had severe acne. I went to my GP who was relatively relaxed about it, saying that it was very commonplace, prescribing a cream, gel or liquid solution and saying that the problem would pass. It did not. It festered. It intensified.

I have never spent a moment of my life worried or embarrassed about being short or lacking in physical strength. But I was utterly miserable about my skin and, of course, about the fact that the problem was written all over my face.

Boys at my school teased each other, naturally. A number of us mercilessly ribbed one of our mates who, asked to read in class, pronounced the name Beatrice 'Beet-rice'. He was thereafter known by that name for his remaining three years at the school. Another boy, quite intelligent and given to verbal bullying of others, was discovered to have the middle name Bartholomew, which many of us, myself included, found hysterically funny, nicknaming him Bart for the next five years. In my case, fellow pupils, especially though not only boys, dubbed me 'Crater Face' and 'Moon Base Alpha'. I tried to brush it off but it did hurt, as names can, because it pointedly highlighted the single characteristic of mine which confronted everyone I met and about which I felt so acutely self-conscious. My heart goes out to any child or young person striving to come to terms with the world who is bullied – for that is what it is – for being different. Be it physical appearance, the make-up of family, disability, faith, gender, ethnicity, sexual orientation – everyone has a right to be treated fairly and with respect. I was periodically subject to anti-Semitic abuse but it was not a recurrent phenomenon and I could always fight my corner in any war of words with a classmate or even a teacher. It was the barbs about acne that hurt.

My problem on this front persisted throughout secondary school and even through university, undermining my morale there, at tennis events and in social situations. Eventually, on advice, I had more powerful treatments and gradually, into my twenties, the problem was overcome, though I did sustain pock marks and indentations that testify that the problem was serious and caused damage. In addition to the physical damage it caused, the psychological damage, the damage to my self-confidence, was considerable and lasted for years. In truth, it was only really when I started to progress in the workplace and in politics that I judged the problem solved and my self-belief was restored.

Alongside my parents' break-up and acne, I think a third factor contributed to my own uncertainty and loss of focus. After a decent, albeit not outstanding run from the age of eleven to fourteen, my tennis first stalled and then went backwards. In the winter of 1977, all of a sudden, inexplic-ably, I became almost completely breathless one day on court. Seeing my GP, I was diagnosed with acute bronchial asthma. For several months that winter, I could barely breathe, wheezed horrendously and depended alarmingly on Ventolin and Becotide inhalers. I went weeks without hitting a ball and months playing very little, not to mention missing weeks of school. By the following summer I was largely restored, but I had definitely regressed. I played less confidently and started to lose to players I had previously beaten.

But just as I was coping with cramped post-divorce living arrangements, the effects of asthma, acne and the dawning recognition that I would never make a living as a professional tennis player, two other developments added to life's interest. First, I became fascinated by, and almost addicted to, politics. Secondly, at the suggestion of adult friends and well-wishers, I started entertaining the possibility of making a living not as a tennis player, but as a coach.

* * *

The speech I had made aged nine about the quality of school dinners had not spawned an early interest in politics. That had to wait until the so-called Winter of Discontent of 1978–9, when the country was paralysed by a wave of strikes across the public sector as the unions, feeling very hard done by at the hands of Jim Callaghan's Labour government, sought to bust his 5 per cent limit on pay rises. To me, the trade unions' actions were unreasonable and destructive. Equally, however, the Callaghan government appeared to have lost control. The country was all but ungovernable. To my mind, Callaghan and Labour were losing the authority to govern and Labour's tie to the unions meant that it would never really be free to govern for the country as a whole.

At school, I appeared to be in a tiny minority, which bothered me not a jot. Pupils expressing a view seemed to side with the unions, and my teachers appeared to be divided between supporters of the Callaghan government and Bennite critics of it. None of them was a Conservative, as far as I could tell, and they were all scathing about the Finchley MP and Leader of the Opposition, Margaret Thatcher. Dad meanwhile was utterly contemptuous both of the unions and the Labour administration, believing that the country would be immeasurably better served by a Conservative government led by Thatcher.

I started to follow Margaret Thatcher's pronouncements on the news and in, yes, the *Daily Express*. By the time the 1979 election campaign started, I was just about keeping abreast of schoolwork and preparing for my O-levels, which were but weeks away, but I was transfixed by the battle between Labour and the Conservatives. Then I happened to see in the

Hendon and Finchley Times that Margaret Thatcher would be addressing a rally at the Woodhouse School in North Finchley, almost her last such meeting before polling day on 3 May.

I arrived to listen, but not early enough, and the hall was full. A Tannoy relayed her speech to a loud crowd outside who competed to hear it against the noise of left-wing activists chanting, 'We want women's rights, not right-wing women.' Thatcher talked about the need to foster an enterprise culture, to promote innovation, reward entrepreneurship, allow people to keep more of their own hard-earned money. I was inspired both by the message and by Thatcher's passionate advocacy of it. Labour seemed stale, inept, part of the country's problem, not its solution. By contrast, the Conservative Party under her dynamic leadership struck me as bold, reforming and exciting.

I must have been very pushy because, as she left the hall, I rushed forward to congratulate her. She gave me a huge smile, doubtless pleased days before the election to be met by a young supporter, even though I was too young to vote – and that would have been obvious to her. 'Thank you,' she said. 'Are you a member of the Young Conservatives?'

'I'm afraid I'm not but I have been hugely inspired by your speech and the whole Conservative campaign,' I replied.

'Well, you most certainly should be a member,' she replied. 'Do you know Roy Langstone?' I admitted that I did not. 'He is my agent, the Conservative agent for Finchley. The office is at 221 Ballards Lane. Go and introduce yourself to Roy and he will see you right.'

Most Conservatives tended to do what they were told by Margaret Thatcher, and while I welcomed her clear advice, I did not act on it at once. I finally joined the Young Conservatives in April 1980, but someone told me that I should join the Hendon North branch as that was my home constituency. They used to meet at 8.30 p.m. on a Sunday evening in a pub near Elstree. I did not have a car and was collected and driven there and back by a young man – mid-twenties, I guess – in a

Porsche. A pleasant guy, he drove like a bat out of hell along winding roads, scaring me witless. Soon the inconvenience of getting there and the apparent absence of any regular programme of speakers caused me belatedly to follow Mrs Thatcher's advice, joining the Finchley branch in late 1980.

At this time, in one of our conversations, Dad mentioned Enoch Powell, whom he described as a 'brilliant and much-maligned man'. He explained that Powell had spoken out against mass immigration and been sacked from the Shadow Cabinet in 1968 by Ted Heath. Intrigued by my father's commendation, I became interested in Powell and read his speeches. Foolishly, and with a staggering lack of awareness that the arguments he made about New Commonwealth and Pakistani immigration could have been (and were) made about Jewish immigration to the East End of London several decades earlier, I was extraordinarily drawn to Powell. His eloquence, his intellect and the rigour of his thinking all appealed to my young and impressionable mind.

This was a very strange, unsettled and in one sense dark period for me. Around the time of my O-levels, I had opted to take English, French and German at A-level but I had come to regret my choices. Moreover, I kicked myself when I realised that I could have taken a Government and Politics A-level. If that was not bad enough, classmates doing History loved the course and I wished that I too had done it. None of this is an excuse, but it explains why I lost interest and headed towards poor results. Meanwhile, within days of my eighteenth birthday, I took and passed the Part 1 tennis coaching exam and gave private lessons at the Angela Buxton Centre in Hampstead Garden Suburb. This I much enjoyed and it earned me some modest but precious pocket money, as well as prompting me to think of a career as a tennis coach.

Also, in January 1981, I made a fateful political choice and it was the most shameful decision I have ever made. I applied to join the Monday Club, a hard-right Conservative pressure group that had been set up in the 1960s to champion traditional Conservative values and, in particular, to argue in favour of continued white minority rule in the then Rhodesia. That battle had already been lost as the Thatcher government – I later came to believe, both justly and wisely – had come to accept independence for Zimbabwe and immediate transition to black-majority rule. But at the time I was attracted by the club's support for Powell over immigration. Even more inexplicably came my appalling decision to join the club's Immigration, Repatriation and Race Relations Industry subcommittee, agreeing to act as its secretary. So here I was, a Jewish boy born and brought up in a free country thanks to the Home Office permitting my paternal grandparents to enter it and thereby escape persecution, en route to flunking my A-levels, contemplating tennis coaching as my life choice, and sidling up to racists.

Not only was it shameful and obnoxious, there was no reason or logic behind it. I had never been bullied or wronged by an immigrant or a son or daughter of an immigrant. I had long got on famously with black and Asian kids at school. True enough, there had been riots in some of our big cities in 1981 but, contrary to Enoch Powell's prediction of racial strife, of black against white, they had really been conflicts between disadvantaged youths and the police. Those conflicts were no argument for repatriation or for abolishing the Commission for Racial Equality, as the Monday Club advocated. Indeed, minority communities needed the protection of progressive race-relations legislation, as Labour, Liberal and even mainstream Conservatives accepted.

I was excessively and absurdly influenced by Enoch Powell's argument that the number of immigrants was too high. Even if that was true, and it was highly debatable, that concern in no way justified the leap to the drastic policies he espoused. I was blind to the moral arguments against him, blind to the contradiction of someone of my heritage supporting such an

objectionable prospectus and blind to the horror and outrage my behaviour provoked among my fellow pupils. How
Shamit Saggar and others could bring themselves to speak to
me at all, I will never know. Apart from being mesmerised
by Powell's prose and oratory, I have sometimes wondered
whether my own physical inadequacies led me to embrace
such an aggressive, macho, control-orientated politics. I might
be over-rationalising the past but it is the best explanation I
can offer. Dad thought that my political choice was fine, and
strange though it may seem, Mum at the time simply took no
interest in politics.

While my political interest intensified, in however misguided a direction, my commitment to my studies diminished
alarmingly, and I flunked my exams. At the time, I was unfazed
as I was giving an ever-greater number of private tennis lessons
and zealously pursuing my ugly brand of hard-right politics.

The Monday Club Immigration Committee was chaired
by the outspoken and controversial MP for Basildon, Billericay and Wickford, Harvey Proctor. I got to know him and
in November 1981 at the House of Commons we had what
for me proved a life-changing conversation. He knew that I
was coaching tennis for a living and asked whether that was
the long-term plan, or if I had another in mind. I revealed
that, fun though it was, I didn't really see tennis as my career
path. Rather, I loved politics and would one day like to be a
Conservative MP. I had been studying some parliamentary reference books and had noticed that most MPs, certainly on the
Conservative benches, had been to university. Did he think I
would be disadvantaged if I didn't have a degree? In short, he
did. Proctor suggested I retake my A-levels and try to go the
following year.

Going back home to Mill Hill that night, I resolved that
I would try to do just that. I made enquiries and gained the
clear impression that if I obtained another A-level of a much
better grade there was every prospect that I would get a place

at one university or another. For all that I fairly soon came to repent of my Monday Club dalliance, and for decades now have subscribed to a much more mainstream and progressive view of multiracial Britain, I am happy to acknowledge that Harvey Proctor gave me excellent advice. He helped to crystallise my thoughts, and even though we are today poles apart politically and I have seen him only at a distance and but once in the last thirty-five years, I shall always be grateful to him for that.

My school friend, Shamit, had gone to Essex University in 1981 to study Government. He was immersed in the course and loved university life. I decided to apply to Essex too, and he generously suggested that I visit for the day to get a feel for the place. I did so, warming to the library, the lecture theatres and the grounds, returning to London eagerly hoping that I would be able to go there in October 1982.

My delight at being invited for an interview was dimmed somewhat when I entered the office of my interviewer, Dr Ernesto Laclau. He had a poster of Karl Marx on his wall whereas my application had described my interest in the works of the classical economists Milton Friedman and Friedrich August von Hayek, to whom I had become increasingly drawn over the previous year. The omens were inauspicious. In fact, Laclau was personable and the interview must have gone well because I subsequently got an offer of a C in the new A-level on top of the three rather poor results I already had. I took up my studies again with renewed vigour and was ecstatic to pass with a top grade that June.

* * *

From the moment I arrived, I loved Essex University. First and foremost, I loved my course, a BA Honours in Government, the component parts of it, from political theory to political analysis, from Western European politics to American politics, from the British political system to international relations, and the lecturers and class tutors who taught me. In particular, I was inspired by what I call the Magnificent Seven – Dr Emile Kirchner, Professor Ivor Crewe, Professor Anthony King, Dr Michael Freeman, Professor David Sanders, Dr Dave McKay and Tony Barker. Each was steeped in knowledge, learning and, crucially, passion for his subject, and as they were all fine communicators that passion was infectious. Learning to live independently, joining and becoming president of the University Tennis Club and playing for the team, savouring the freedom to work the hours I chose – all this was new and stimulating.

From Hobbes to Locke, from Burke to de Tocqueville, from Marx to J. S. Mill, to name but a few of the thinkers covered during the course, I was hooked on study of the great minds that had shaped nations around the world. Added to them were Nietzsche, Hegel, Popper, Isaiah Berlin, Hannah Arendt, Herbert Marcuse, Ralph Miliband, Michael Oakeshott and, among politicians, Tony Benn, Keith Joseph and Ian Gilmour, all of whom prompted me to consider and evaluate where I stood. I was decidedly Conservative, though within a few months had begun to move away from the extreme Monday Club viewpoint to which I had fairly fleetingly subscribed. I attended my last meeting of that loathsome organisation in February 1983. A year later, when my subscription came up for renewal, I wrote to the chairman saying that the club contained elements whose views I now found unpalatable and I tendered my resignation as a member. To readers understandably shocked and disgusted that I ever joined the Monday Club in the first place, I offer only one plea in mitigation. I was a naïve, misguided, insecure and perhaps angry young man. I left the organisation at the age of twenty-one, and if you believe in the Rehabilitation of Offenders Act I hope that thirty-five years later I have redeemed myself.

Love the academic and social side though I did, I quickly

became immersed in student politics. This led me to do a number of interviews on university radio and on one such occasion I met my first girlfriend, Fiona. Though she was politically left of centre she told me that she enjoyed hearing me talk and we went out together for about six months. Joining the university Conservative Association, I became its chairman and launched a drive to attract visiting speakers. Teddy Taylor, the then Tory MP for Southend East, was the first I secured. He was pelted with eggs by left-wing activists, but spoke and generated interest, leading to an increase in Conservative Association membership. Next, I invited Cecil Parkinson, who had only months before resigned from the government following the disclosure of his long extramarital affair with Sara Keays, with whom he had a baby girl. In retrospect, I was wrong to have made it a private meeting, which enraged the left, though either way they were determined to wreck it. The Socialist Workers Students Society objected to his visit on the grounds that he had been a key figure in a government that had created mass unemployment, hit living standards and oppressed the working class. Others, notably the University Women's Group, objected vociferously on the grounds of his behaviour towards women, deploying placards with the slogan, 'Don't let Cecil make it at Essex'. A huge picket was organised, Parkinson could not get into the lecture theatre to speak, and the meeting had to be abandoned.

When I became chairman, the university Conservative Association had sixty members. Twelve months later it had two hundred. We were players in political debate on campus. There was interest. People attended. We held social events and I wrote articles for the student newspaper, *Vulture*, including a sincere, ideological and provocative piece in the middle of the Miners' Strike arguing for the privatisation of the coal industry.

In parallel with Association activity, I started to take part in the Students' Union. A lot of Conservatives, certainly at universities where there is known to be a strong left-wing activist presence, tend not to speak up for their Conservative views. There are a number of perfectly understandable reasons for this. Politics may not be a driving interest. As the late *Daily Telegraph* journalist T. E. Utley used to put it, 'Conservatives are not accustomed to defending their beliefs. They just believe them.' For others, a desire to avoid controversy or arguments with friends may be at work. Not only did they usually prefer not to speak, but they were less inclined to attend a Union General Meeting than a left-wing student clamouring for change. Yet when I, supported by others, started to make mainstream Conservative arguments, attendance by our members did begin to increase and, even though they were in a minority, they were far from being in a tiny minority.

Perhaps the Union meeting I remember best came when I tabled a motion condemning CND and supporting the continued British possession of nuclear weapons pending progress on multilateral disarmament. I had a basic familiarity with the issue but I was, and am, no defence expert. The national officers of the Federation of Conservative Students (FCS) advised me to contact Dr Julian Lewis, a defence specialist who was then Director of the Coalition for Peace Through Security, a pro-NATO, pro-nuclear weapons, pro-multilateral disarmament pressure group. Julian, I was told, would be able to advise me as I prepared my speech, and he did not disappoint. We spoke for forty-five minutes on the phone – or, more accurately, he addressed me with barely a pause for breath, stopping only to check that I was taking notes, which I was – and, at the end, I felt fully briefed and enjoyed a surge of self-confidence about the task ahead in delivering my four-minute speech.

Unsurprisingly, I was heckled by the left but I was a self-confident speaker with a strong platform manner and some catcalling was never going to throw me off my stride. My motion was heavily and predictably defeated but we had fought the good fight and did so on several other occasions too. When the elections for Student Union sabbatical posts came up in March 1984, I stood for president and did well in the first ballot, but it was a Single Transferable Vote system so transfers from other left-wing candidates helped the Labour candidate to beat me. Nevertheless, I had had a go, gained further campaign experience and practised public speaking in a highly charged, relatively hostile environment. Later in the year, I attended the Conservative Party Conference in Brighton when, notoriously, the IRA bombed the Grand Hotel in a determined bid to murder the Cabinet. Earlier in the week I had made my first conference speech from the rostrum, a fluent Thatcherite rant that was generously received by the 5,000-strong audience. It was great experience for me and I felt that my political skills were being nurtured.

My work chairing the Essex University Conservative Association, attendance at Federation of Conservative Students conferences and occasional speeches were noticed by the national leaders of the Conservative student movement. Mark Macgregor, an elected member of the FCS's National Committee, asked me to stand on his slate of candidates for election to the committee. I was by then quite well known to Conservative student activists and Mark was very confident that I would be elected. Speaking from the conference floor, I had pinned a vast number of badges to the inside of one side of my jacket and a much smaller number to the inside of the other side of the jacket. I then proceeded to make a demonstrative and exhibitionist speech to conference about the campaigning prowess and activity level under the right-wing leadership over the last twelve months by comparison with the allegedly feeble, lethargic, complacent approach under the 'wetter' administration that had been in charge in 1983 and 1984. Seeing the tape now, I came across as a man possessed, swivel-eyed, and somewhat alarming, but the delegates lapped it up and I was elected as a National Committee member at the top of the poll. My little success was overshadowed by a huge controversy over alleged vandalism, defecation in showers and other antisocial behaviour at a late-night party during the conference, which caused the Party Chairman, John Gummer, in his speech to our conference the next day, to condemn unreservedly the behaviour and to announce an immediate inquiry. It may be disappointingly boring for readers to be told this but I did not participate in any such outrageous behaviour and nor did I witness any of it.

After the FCS conference, I returned to university to revise for my final exams. My results put me on the borderline between a 2:1 degree and a First. Dad was very excited about the possibility of me securing the latter, encouraging me to strive for it. I told him it really did not matter, there was no evidence known to me that it bolstered career chances and I played down the prospect. In truth, however, I wanted it. As was to prove a pattern with me, I did not start university with any thought about the level of degree I might get, but once I saw the prize of a First in view I earnestly sought it, working harder in my final year and hoping that I would make it. Thankfully, I did and I was thrilled. If my parents had come from more affluent homes, they could both have gone to university. As it was, neither did as neither could contemplate it. My elder sister could have gone to university but did not want to do so and has never regretted it. I was the first in my immediate family to go to university and I was delighted to achieve the best degree available to me.

By the summer of 1985, when I graduated, my parents had been divorced for ten years. Fortunately, Dad's bitterness had all but gone and as ill health had forced him into retirement he and Mum were on quite friendly terms. So the decision of both to accompany me to the graduation ceremony was quite natural and they had no need to dance on eggshells as we spent the day together. I felt very lucky, harboured undying gratitude to my brilliant lecturers and tutors and the sense that I had achieved something worthwhile. A fish supper at one of our favourite restaurants on the way home was the culmination of one of the happiest days of my young life. But what next? If a degree was a necessary step in my long-term goal of becoming an MP, I could now tick that box. Even I was not so naïve as to think I could parachute into a safe seat straight away – but what should I do as a career for the next decade or longer?

2

A Seat Before the Chair

As a kid, I was headstrong, stubborn and uncomfortable with authority. In diplomatic language, I must have been 'challenging' for my parents and sister. In undiplomatic language, I was no doubt a right pain in the arse. I don't want to overstate the case: I didn't get in trouble with the police, or do illegal drugs or father a child. My rebellious behaviour was no doubt at the milder end of the spectrum, but I had been unfocused, wayward, dysfunctional and for a time an insecure, sad, lost soul. That was behind me now and, indeed, in common with everyone finishing their education I had thought about what I might do.

After the first year of Essex, I was so enraptured by the university experience that I thought about becoming an academic. But that was a short-lived flirtation, soon replaced by my favoured option of studying for the Bar. I was attracted to the idea of being a barrister, specifically to the challenge of advocacy, and thought I might be well suited. I had not studied law but that was no obstacle. There were then as now conversion courses for graduates in other subjects aspiring to a career in the law. While still at Essex, I applied for and was given a place at City University to study for a one-year Diploma in Law. If I was successful I would then need to take the Bar finals. If I met that challenge I would have to obtain a pupillage – then unpaid – before having the chance to practise. It was quite a long and expensive process, but I felt that the

Bar would potentially lead to a rewarding career and offer a launchpad to Parliament.

In the summer of 1985, before I started the law course, another interesting opportunity came my way. The Conservative MP for Billericay, Teresa Gorman, whom I had met at a couple of student conferences, tipped me off that the Streatham Conservatives would later in the year be selecting candidates for the following year's elections to Lambeth Borough Council. If any Conservative students who lived or worked in the borough wanted to apply, then she would ask the local Association to consider them. I promptly became her tenant in a home she owned in the borough, went for interview and to my delight was chosen to stand as a candidate in the three-member St Leonard's ward, which was one of the two most Conservative wards in Streatham. Even if the May 1986 council elections were not looking great for the party, the overwhelming likelihood was that I would be elected, gaining invaluable experience of urban politics in a Labour borough.

I was not short of commitments: undertaking a stimulating postgraduate course, serving on the FCS National Committee and campaigning to be elected as a borough councillor. The FCS chairman, Mark Macgregor, had welcomed my election to the committee and hinted heavily to me that he regarded me as his likely successor as chairman. Mark was an immensely able student politician and, even though he faced pressure from some right-wing activists to adopt more hard-line policy positions, I did not think that his leadership was under serious threat. However, Mark decided that he would not run as the Thatcherite candidate for a second year in office. Rather, he looked to me instead to stand. This was a surprise, but I was flattered that he thought I was equipped already to fill his shoes. He did, but there then followed the mother and father of all battles for the right-wing candidature for FCS chair, which I eventually won by one vote. The caucus selection meeting that decided it was undoubtedly the most unpleasant political gathering that either Mark Macgregor or I had attended, and the supporters of my right-wing rival, David Hoile, cried foul and threatened to ignore the result.

Nevertheless as I geared up for the FCS conference in Scarborough in April 1986, I was cautiously optimistic that I would win the chairmanship. Student delegations tended to be homogenous: they either agreed to back me or my opponent, a Bristol University student called Mark Francois, now the Conservative MP for Rayleigh and Wickford. It was a tradition that the libertarian faction would produce a conference magazine and that the candidate for chair would be asked to contribute to it – but enjoy no editorial control over, or even sight of, the wider content in advance. I dutifully wrote an article entitled portentously 'The Future of Thatcherism', which the editor rebranded 'Blue Wedge'. It was a reprise of themes I had long rehearsed but contained nothing revolutionary or liable to alarm the Conservative Party hierarchy.

Unbeknown to me, however, and in a desire to make me look a more macho and risqué figure than I was – or ever had been – the editor had chosen to place in the magazine an article entitled 'The John Bercow Guide to Women', a vulgar, sexist and tasteless tilt in the direction of male chauvinism. When I saw it, I squirmed. Anyone who knew how I wrote could tell that it wasn't written by me, but the fact was it had been done in my name and I was very annoyed. Mark Macgregor thought I was too uptight, said the magazine was already being distributed, nothing could be done and I should relax. But I was right not to be relaxed: soon afterwards, it was used against me by political opponents in Lambeth.

At the Scarborough conference, I defeated Mark Francois comfortably and started to contemplate the year ahead. As the national chair of the Federation I was due to take up the post full-time, with a salary of a little over £4,000 when Mark Macgregor concluded his tenure in March 1986. This suited me as I was more than halfway through my law conversion course and was due to complete it in June. In truth, I was a little worried about the views of some of the more extreme libertarians, which struck me as verging on anarcho-capitalism. That said, I hoped – over-optimistically as it transpired – to be able to hold them in check. I had struck up a good relationship with the Deputy Chairman of the party, Jeffrey Archer, who had told me that Norman Tebbit, the Party Chairman, liked the cut of my jib and wanted me to take up the FCS post at once. Mark was unbothered, and fully prepared to leave straight away, but I pointed out to Archer that I was doing a law course at the time. He waved this consideration aside, saying that I could always do it again after my year as FCS chairman. No doubt unwisely, I agreed, dropped the course – sadly never to return to it – and got my feet under the table in my little office in Conservative Headquarters at 32 Smith Square.

In my first few weeks as chair, the mood in the FCS seemed positive. I accepted many invitations to speak at FCS branches, alongside my increasingly intensive campaigning to ensure my election to Lambeth Borough Council, which was successful, and I had a healthy majority as a new councillor. As we reached June, however, a minor controversy developed behind the scenes about my refusal to submit to the Party Conference a motion critical of the Anglo-Irish Agreement. This irritated several of my FCS colleagues and it may well have been the trigger for the bigger public row to follow.

Harry Phibbs, an eccentric, hard-line libertarian with a thirst for publicity, had been elected to the National Committee in April when I had accepted the role of Chair. The idea had been mooted that he should be given a particular role that would absorb his energies. I agreed that there should be a new, regular publication from the FCS, called *New Agenda*, and that Phibbs would be its editor. As it would be the official FCS magazine, with implications for the reputation of the organisation, he would keep me informed of his plans. In particular, if any article were likely to provoke a significant controversy, he would consult me.

One day I was told that the summer issue of the magazine contained a stick of dynamite. Phibbs had conducted an interview with a Russian historian, Nikolai Tolstoy, who had recently published a book entitled *The Minister and the Massacres* in which he alleged that Harold Macmillan, as a minister in Churchill's post-war Conservative government, had sent 40,000 White Russian Cossacks based in Italy back to the Soviet Union, where they faced almost certain death. Bluntly, Tolstoy declared that Macmillan was a war criminal. Even more bluntly and provocatively, Phibbs had pictured Macmillan on the front cover of our magazine and emblazoned the photograph with the word 'GUILTY'.

Harold Macmillan was by then ninety-three years old, a former Prime Minister who had left office over twenty years earlier. He was a stern critic of the Thatcher government, arguing that its policy of privatising key industries was akin to 'selling off the family silver' to pay the household debts. A 'patrician wet', Macmillan was deeply perturbed by, and frankly antagonistic towards, Margaret Thatcher and would almost certainly have been as hostile to Norman Tebbit. In turn, Thatcher and Tebbit were as far as anyone could be from being unalloyed admirers of Macmillan.

Yet, for all that, Tebbit was angry. He felt, quite reasonably, that he had to intercede. Here was the editor of the magazine of the party's student wing launching a searing attack on a former Conservative Prime Minister, a man in his nineties, still widely revered by many people in public life, in relation to a historical event which had been all but forgotten. I asked Phibbs to explain himself and in particular I challenged him as to why he had not consulted me before going ahead with a feature that was probably intended to generate a public furore. His response was that he thought that I was very cautious in my outlook (true, by his standards), that I would almost certainly have objected to the piece (also true), and that he would therefore go ahead on his own initiative. Not surprisingly, I was unimpressed with this argument and felt no obligation whatsoever to protect Phibbs or excuse him in any way. He was forced to resign as editor of *New Agenda* but still commanded considerable support, especially among members of the Thatcherite faction of the FCS. On the National Committee – partly because Phibbs, a fogeyish, self-confident and exhibitionist character was popular, and partly because I was regarded as too close to Tebbit and Archer – opinion moved against me. At the half-yearly FCS conference, an emergency meeting was called and I was censured for my handling of the matter.

By then, I had come to the conclusion that most of the FCS so-called 'sound' faction leaders had completely lost the plot. My role model for leadership of the organisation had been Michael Forsyth, chairman in the early 1970s, when the Federation backed radical policies but had not become a playground for extremists with no real allegiance to the party. The hardliners now were in a different mould. Some might have been motivated by the age-old instinct of youth to cock a snook at authority and show that they could gain attention by making a noise. Others were pure ideologues. They were determined to pursue a hard-line anarcho-capitalist credo, which was not, never had been and never would be the stance of the Conservative Party. I approached Tebbit in September 1986 and offered to resign as chairman in light of the embarrassment caused to the party. He immediately declined my offer, said that he had every confidence in me and urged me to work to rebuild the FCS.

At the time of the row over the Tolstoy attack on Macmillan, the Conservative leadership had plenty of other challenges to contend with. The Conservatives were behind in the polls and many Tory MPs were sniping at Margaret Thatcher. Moreover, as the Party Chairman can be, and Normal Tebbit certainly was, a lightning conductor for his leader, a good many Tories rounded on him in order to get at her. I felt at the time that it was spectacularly inept and maladroit of some of my FCS colleagues to alienate Tebbit, a man we admired and the most instinctively sympathetic Party Chairman we had ever had. For my part, I had not changed from the person who, only six months earlier, had been elected chairman on a platform of support for the Thatcher government.

At the Party Conference in October 1986, I saw that on the final day there was to be a debate on party policy and public relations. I applied to speak, was called and made a speech that combined radical intent – including an aspiration for income tax at 15p in the pound – with a passionate declaration of support for Margaret Thatcher as Prime Minister and Norman Tebbit as Party Chairman. The significance of what might otherwise be thought entirely unremarkable was that some Conservatives were questioning whether Thatcher could lead the party to victory again, and others were suggesting that she could do so only if made somehow less toxic by the replacement of Tebbit with a more moderate Chairman. My message was that we could win, and win only with both of them at the helm.

In retrospect, that may have been an overstatement. At the time, it was what I sincerely believed and, given the events of the previous weeks involving the FCS, I felt that the most unequivocal and ringing endorsement of Thatcher and Tebbit was the least I owed my party. It also occurred to me, as an ambitious would-be future MP, that it would do me no harm with the leadership or the grass-roots constituency activists. That calculation, which was not rocket science, proved correct. Activists in the conference hall responded to my speech very positively and I was amused to be told that the *Morning Star*, newspaper of the British Communist Party, had described me the next day as a 'rising, rabid rightist'.

That final day of the conference was the culmination of a

good week for me. A few days before the speech I had been approached by a senior voluntary party bigwig and encouraged to apply to join the party's candidates' list. Fraught and difficult though recent times had been within the FCS, I felt that my own personal standing with the party hierarchy was high.

* * *

When I returned from Conference, my parents were chuffed that I had made a positive impact. Dad had been unwell for five years, living with an artificial artery system that had resulted from half a century of smoking twenty cigarettes per day. On 31 October 1986, I received a telephone call from a hospital in Cardiff – unbeknown to Alison or me, Dad had been visiting a friend in the city – to inform me that he had passed away overnight. It appeared that he had suffered a heart attack. He was only sixty-six. Alison and I were devastated.

Dad had his flaws, including, however bizarrely, racial prejudice. I wish that I had ignored his advice and never supped from the cup of Powellism, but I did and it was my own stupid fault. That aside, for twenty-three years he had been a wonderful father to me. Engaging, often humorous, principled, decent, conscientious and unfailingly supportive. I just wish that he had enjoyed greater personal happiness in his life. I still think of him a lot and of his oft-repeated advice, reinforced by Mum who has Yorkshire grit in her DNA: 'Be a fighter. Don't let anyone tell you that you can't fulfil your goals.'

The following month, with the conference out of the way, I was told that Tebbit wanted me to be the student head of a new Conservative Collegiate Forum, the panel of whose officers would be appointed by the party leadership. It was not an ideal outcome. When you remove the autonomy of an organisation and prevent it from conducting elections, you inevitably deter participation. I said as much. That said, the exhibitionist FCS hardliners had no grounds to complain – though complain, and vociferously, was naturally what they did. Norman Tebbit and his team were striving to ready the party for an election and needed to be sure that avoidable accidents were avoided. For my part, I continued to visit groups of Conservative students at universities and to promote our message among young voters.

After applying to join the Conservative candidates' list in the autumn of 1986, I was invited to a so-called Candidates' Weekend, in early 1987 at a hotel in Maidenhead. There my political knowledge and communication skills, both oral and written, were put to the test as I faced challenges to solve thorny political problems and organise effective campaigns. A few days later I heard that my application had been successful and that I was now on the official Conservative candidates' list for England and Wales. The only difficulty was that by then, February 1987, most Conservative Associations, including in strong Labour seats, had selected candidates already and, therefore it seemed improbable that I would contest the 1987 general election. In anticipation of this I had offered to help John Moore, one of Margaret Thatcher's favourite Cabinet ministers, on a voluntary basis in his Croydon Central constituency.

Just as I was gearing up to help in Croydon, a Conservative friend, Gary Mond, called to tell me excitedly that he had been selected to fight the Hamilton constituency in Scotland. Gary told me that the party had apparently struggled to find enough candidates of sufficient quality in the Scottish seats and was therefore soliciting interest from Conservatives on the English and Welsh list. He thought that there was still a handful of vacancies and urged me to have a go.

I promptly telephoned Bill Henderson, the director of the party in Scotland and a man I had come to know well through my FCS role. When I said that I would be interested in fighting a seat for the experience but that, of course, I was not on the separate Scottish Conservative candidates' list, he replied tellingly that the latter fact didn't matter a jot but the former fact – my interest – did. In no time, he had arranged for me to be interviewed for the Cumbernauld and Kilsyth constituency. If they chose me, great. If not, he recommended that I stay over and be interviewed for the Motherwell South seat the following day. I agreed to this plan at a stroke.

I had visited Scotland several times but, overwhelmingly, it had been to attend a conference, make a speech or take part in a debate. However, I spoke with an English accent, knew little of specifically Scottish issues and lived hundreds of miles away in London. In Cumbernauld, I made a robust speech and fielded many questions but was later told that I had been narrowly beaten by another candidate, a Scot who was well known and exceptionally close to the constituency chairman. The following day I was driven to Motherwell. A strongly working-class constituency marked by heavy industry, it was home to the Ravenscraig Steelworks. They were struggling in a competitive international marketplace and there was widespread anxiety that a Conservative government could close the works. Ministers insisted that they did not wish to do so, and I defended both the government's position and the case for steel manufacture at Ravenscraig, on which almost 12,000 local jobs depended.

I was advised that the Motherwell South Conservative Association consisted of only fifty members, most of whom were merely paper members. The activists were nearer to half a dozen. As for the selection committee, it was made up of five people, and my interview took place in the living room of one of the members. I made a tub-thumping, 'go get them, we are proud Conservatives' speech and they appeared to warm to my enthusiastic style. Dr Jeremy Bray, the Labour MP for the constituency, had a majority of over 12,000, the Association had only enough money to finance one election leaflet and I was a twenty-four-year-old Englishman who didn't know one

Motherwell street from another. The omens were not auspicious but I was raring to go.

The Association chairman, Murdo Morrison, was a fluent Gaelic speaker and the party had asked him to contest the Western Isles as the Conservative candidate. As a result, he would be away for some weeks but he and his wife, Hazel, a local teacher, had very generously offered to host me for the duration of the campaign. Day after day I trudged the streets, supported by an agent, but often alone or, in the evenings, in a small group. Yet there was no pressure as no one thought I could win and I knew that my task was simply to display maximum commitment, bonhomie and passion. The SNP pushed me into third place and I had to settle for 5,702 votes and 14.5 per cent of the total vote, down from 20 per cent four years earlier. That result reflected the wider trend across Scotland, where the Conservatives were now horrendously unpopular and Margaret Thatcher especially so. The introduction of the community charge or poll tax in Scotland had made a bad situation worse. There was anger about industry closing down, jobs being lost, the Conservatives resisting currency devaluation and, to cap it all, many Scots viewed Thatcher with distaste as a very bossy, haughty English lady who knew little about Scotland and cared less. This may have been an unfair caricature but it was the prevalent image of her north of the border.

I had no truck with any of it. I noticed how in evidently prosperous areas people looked at me with uncomprehending disbelief in a way that rarely happened in England at the suggestion that they might consider voting Conservative. Yet I was unmoved by this hostility to her and to my party. Indeed, after the election, believing there to be some evidence that the government had soft-pedalled on Thatcherite reforms being implemented in England and Wales, Bernard Jenkin, Anne Strutt (later Jenkin), Eleanor Laing (now Deputy Speaker) and I argued that the implementation of Thatcherite policies should be accelerated.

In retrospect, my attitude is different. Labour was on the march in Scotland and I doubt that any alternative approach would have revolutionised Conservative prospects for the better. The Scottish public-sector middle class was large and strong. Scotland had become a socialist country. The Conservatives would have been better advised not to treat Scotland as a test bed for the introduction of the hated poll tax. We should not have rigidly resisted devolution. Some far-sighted Tories, including Malcolm Rifkind, had earlier argued for it. Moreover, led by someone other than Mrs Thatcher, the party might have attracted less undiluted hatred. Ultimately, however, I doubt that we would have done much better in Scotland under someone else and we might well have done much worse elsewhere in the United Kingdom.

Returning from the exhilaration of a losing battle in Scotland, I had to contemplate my career path. My sabbatical year as the paid leader of the Conservative student movement had come to an end. In theory, I could try to go back to law study but in practice it was not an option. I had no place on a course and I felt that that ship had sailed. I needed to begin a career. The Deputy Chairman of the party, Peter Morrison, had been staunchly supportive of my efforts as FCS chair and then as vice-chair of the successor body. When I suggested public relations or political lobbying, he baulked. He thought that neither was a good idea, recommending instead that I pursue a more mainstream and lucrative career in stockbroking or banking. But I had never thought of banking as a career for me and, instinctively, did not feel any excitement about it. Nevertheless, Peter helped to secure me an interview at Hambros Bank. I prepared for my interview and gave the best account of myself. Within days, I was offered a job at the then very decent starting salary of £13,500.

The first few months were spent working as a trainee on the gilt market desk. My boss was delightful and so were the team around him. I liked the people there immensely and they were very good at what they did. I was not. I had no feel for the City. I derived no buzz from it. I felt that I was in the wrong business. As part of my induction, I did a spell training as a credit analyst, looking at the viability of companies seeking support. If anything, I was even worse at that and did not enjoy the experience at all. Just under a year after I had started, and in the friendliest of conversations, it was suggested to me that I was in the wrong place and Hambros, with scrupulous fairness, offered me a termination payment, which I promptly accepted. I had been probably the least gifted and most unsuitable graduate trainee they had ever suffered.

Alongside my ill-fated leap into merchant banking, the second half of 1987 was marked by turbulence and controversy in the Conservative Group on Lambeth Council, including a leadership coup in which I was involved, to my later regret. Apart from becoming embroiled in internal Conservative battles, what did I achieve as a councillor? The short first answer is far less than we might have done if we had run the council rather than being the opposition. I worked hard for the residents of St Leonard's ward, gained real experience in staging surgeries, advocating on behalf of constituents and challenging the council to deliver better services for local people. My forte, however, then as later, was the debating chamber and the committees. I asked endless questions, harried the key players in the Labour administration and spoke forcefully at virtually every council meeting. I was enormously energetic in publicising council failures and had a high profile in the local press.

There is one element of my service in Lambeth that might seem a little odd. Considering that I was not a Conservative councillor in a leafy shire county or even in a prosperous place like Kensington or Chelsea, why was I not more moved by the sight of poverty, disadvantage or racial prejudice in the police? There are really two explanations. First, in my own ward, I did not see much poverty. Mine was a still-affluent ward in Streatham whereas the main concentrations of poor citizens were to be found in Norwood and Vauxhall. Secondly, in common with Conservatives everywhere, I felt that it was Labour councils that were trapping people in poverty – they encouraged dependency and scorned the enterprise culture that could promote prosperity. Despite that I could and should have seen that the Conservative government was neglecting the inner cities, leaving a resentful underclass of people who shared little or not at all in the general increase in living standards for much of the 1980s and 1990s. Looking back, though I can see huge merit in the policy of council house sales, the Thatcher government's blank refusal to allow councils to use the capital receipts from sales to build new social housing was a terrible mistake. Any civilised society must provide low-cost housing to people who cannot afford to buy or to rent in the private sector.

Despite Peter Morrison's sincere advice to the contrary, I gravitated to the world of political consultancy. Sallingbury Casey in 1988 was a prominent lobbying firm run by a former senior civil servant called Michael Casey. Blessed with an extremely agile mind, Michael could grasp the thrust of any issue more quickly than anyone I had met. He was also a fantastic communicator. Politically, it was hard to say where he stood. He had worked tirelessly for Labour governments but he was ruthless in pursuing business for his company and, as befits an ex-civil servant, was at home among people of all backgrounds and political stripes. Fairly soon after he gave me a job as an account executive in September 1988, and following the sudden death of his long-time associate, Zaki Douek, Michael appointed Leighton Andrews as managing director.

In six and a half years at the company, I worked on a wide variety of client accounts, gradually rising within the ranks and becoming a board director after five years. I learned to digest material quickly, to marshal an argument effectively, to write well under time pressure, to exercise cost control in the budget of my account teams, to manage different groups of colleagues, to interact effectively with a wide variety of different clients and to communicate strongly in front of audiences small and large alike.

* * *

I knew that roughly halfway through a possible five-year Parliament, Conservative Associations around the country would start to select candidates for the next general election. Funnily enough, though I was widely regarded then as ravenously ambitious, I was by no means hell-bent on being selected for a Conservative-held seat. I was willing to apply for such seats and was not at all intimidated by the prospect but, rightly or wrongly, my antennae told me that I was unlikely to be chosen for a safe Conservative seat. Sure, I had fought my 'hopeless' seat in Scotland, but I had been just twenty-four years old. By 1989 I was still only twenty-six, a mere two years into full-time employment and in a traditional, small 'c' as well as large 'C' Conservative Party, I was single. In our times, now thankfully less judgemental than before, readers might think that marital status should not matter a fig. I agree. But it did then.

In the first half of 1989, Colchester North advertised for a new Conservative candidate. I applied, but was not invited to interview. I was no more than mildly disappointed. The Association went on to select Bernard Jenkin and he continues to represent the constituency with distinction more than twenty-five years after he was first elected to Parliament.

Shortly afterwards, I saw that Bristol South was seeking a candidate. It had been a Labour seat since 1935 but the majority was small. The long-serving MP, Michael Cocks, who had served as Chief Whip under three Labour leaders, had been deselected by his local party, which contained an increasingly powerful left-wing contingent. Dawn Primarolo was selected to replace him. There had apparently been a big split in the local Labour Party – many activists did not campaign for Dawn and it appeared that some did not even vote for her in 1987 as she entered Parliament with a majority 3,000 lower than Cocks had done in 1983, which had been the most catastrophic for Labour since 1918. Her majority was just 1,404.

I was contacted by a party activist in the South-West who remembered me from my Conservative student days. He told me that the Bristol South Conservative Association had a strong youth branch and that those people were keen to select a young, robustly Thatcherite candidate. He thought I would be in with a good chance. I was very attracted by the idea of fighting Bristol South and quickly decided to apply. If I won the seat for the Tories, I would be regarded as a hero. If I didn't but had worked hard and made a favourable impression, I would be better placed at the following general election to land a safe seat third time round.

In the short time available before my interview, I did some research, scouring the local newspapers, gaining a feel for some of the local issues and ensuring that I was familiar with each of the wards making up the constituency. Highlighting my experience in student politics, my track record in campaigning against opponents, current role as a councillor fighting the hard left in south London and devotion to the leadership of Margaret Thatcher, it was a tub-thumping, passionate speech delivered to the small selection committee without a note. My sense was that it had gone very well, particularly with the younger element. I left feeling upbeat and was later told that I had reached a final shortlist of three candidates. In that final round, in front of a little over thirty people, I was up against a Wiltshire councillor, Robert Syms, and a young ex-soldier named Crispin Blunt. Asked to address the topic of 'Priorities for the Next Conservative Government' – in the middle of the current administration, they wanted us to look ahead – this time I had the very generous time limit of fifteen minutes to try to wow the party faithful. I was later told that I had won by a very large majority.

I was twenty-six and had been selected for a seat where the Labour MP, Dawn Primarolo, then a strong Bennite and a member of the left-wing Campaign Group of Labour MPs, had a wafer-thin majority. I felt, and certainly the younger Conservative activists believed, that I could win the seat. It would be tough. Inevitably the national political situation would be the dominant factor in determining my chances, but I wanted to get stuck in. But there were numerous hurdles to overcome. Dawn Primarolo was the incumbent and would naturally work hard to regain votes lost to Labour in 1987. By responding effectively to correspondence, being visible in the constituency, staging regular surgeries and speaking to core Labour themes in a seat long held by Labour, she would be hard to dislodge. I could only ever be a part-time candidate as I had a day job. My home was over a hundred miles away in London. I did not drive at the time, and I certainly could not afford to buy or rent a home in the constituency.

I went to Bristol most weekends and, occasionally, for week-day evening meetings. At the weekends, I was driven around by the chairman of the Association, Iris Gillard, a shrewd and worldly-wise woman who looked kindly on me, or by the deputy chairman who succeeded her, Richard Eddy. Finally in September 1990 I passed my driving test and acquired a company car. On one visit to the constituency I promptly drove into the back of Richard's car, and had to contend for several weeks with much ribbing about my reckless behaviour in crashing into the back of my own constituency chairman.

* * *

Soon after I was selected I spoke at a Conservative Students conference in Nottingham, accompanied by Julian Lewis. In the evening, there was a large dinner: Julian and I were seated on the top table and he remarked on a glamorous and striking young woman sitting at a nearby table, who was looking more than a little bored. Although I feared she was way out of my league, I made a beeline for this woman – Sally Illman – at the party after the dinner. We became immersed in conversation for hours and got on brilliantly. She was studying at Oxford and at the time was active in the Oxford University Conservative Association (although she later confessed that she mainly joined because she had heard that they held good parties). I asked for her phone number and the minute I returned from Nottingham the next day I rang her. Her mum answered the landline (mobile phones were a rarity in 1989) and, clearly tickled that I was evidently keen to contact her daughter, explained that Sally was still on her way back from the conference.

Sally and I started seeing each other, but after a few months I ended the relationship because I had reluctantly come to the conclusion that she was just too wild and unpredictable for me. We remained friends though, regularly meeting up for drinks and dinner in London and, before long, we got together again. Once more, however, after several months, we parted – although this time it was she who gave me the heave-ho: we relished each other's company but, as a nineteen-year-old student who wanted to dance the night away, she thought I was far too staid ('a young fogey' was how she put it). Still, throughout the years that followed, we continued meeting regularly as platonic friends, even when we were happily attached to other partners. If truth be told, I always carried a torch for her and occasionally lobbied her to give 'us' another go – which she found flattering, but laughingly brushed aside. To Sally's great credit, even though we were not together at the time of the 1992 election, she came to Bristol to trudge the streets with me. Her friendship and loyalty meant a lot to me then as they do now, more than a quarter of a century later.

Quite early on in my candidature, a public meeting was organised to discuss the poll tax and the organisers, who had invited Dawn Primarolo to speak, asked me to contribute too. We spoke separately as she did not want it to be a formal debate between the two of us, for the perfectly understandable reason that she was the MP and saw no reason to accord me equal status. Naturally we took polar opposite stances, although with the benefit of hindsight, I was completely wrong and she was right to denounce it. It was never reasonable to expect people to accept a flat-rate charge when the whole basis of the wider taxation system is progressive – we expect people with larger incomes to pay a higher share.

That meeting apart, I had no real interaction with Dawn until the 1992 campaign itself when she and I both took part in a number of hustings organised by local churches. She was courteous but cool, as was I.

Just over a year into my candidature, Margaret Thatcher, who had beaten off a 'stalking horse' leadership challenge in November 1989, was challenged again when Geoffrey Howe resigned as Leader of the House and Deputy Prime Minister. The immediate cause of his departure was a fundamental disagreement about European policy, he sympathetic to the idea that the UK might in due course enter the Eurozone and she steadfastly opposed. More widely, they had come to differ on many subjects and he felt ill treated and disrespected. There was also enormous controversy over the poll tax and the Conservatives were way behind in the polls. I was unmoved by the arguments against her. My support for Margaret Thatcher was passionate and unequivocal. I agreed with her then both about Europe and about the poll tax. I was not convinced that the Conservatives were doomed to lose an election that could still be eighteen months away. Above all, I certainly did not want Michael Heseltine or anyone else to replace her.

With Nick Gibb, the Conservative candidate for Stoke on Trent Central, I organised a survey of Conservative candidates that showed that the vast majority of them supported the continued leadership of Margaret Thatcher. We publicised the findings in order to demonstrate that the next generation of potential Conservative MPs stood full-square behind her. For all our efforts, though, large numbers of Tory MPs deserted her. She felt that once the Cabinet had turned against her she had to resign, and within days John Major had succeeded her as leader of the Conservative Party and Prime Minister.

Although I had backed Margaret Thatcher to the hilt, the arrival of a new Prime Minister unsurprisingly produced a poll bounce as voters were keen that the new incumbent should be given a chance. He struck a more conciliatory tone on Europe, as well as with Cabinet colleagues, and he invited Michael Heseltine to join the Cabinet as Environment Secretary with a brief to review the poll tax – which Heseltine had opposed – and find a suitable replacement for it. The relevance of all this to me in Bristol was that we started to plan for what seemed a likely early election. February or March 1991 was floated in the media as a probable date. Following the Gulf War in 1991, newspapers speculated that Major might hold a 'khaki' election, reaping political benefit from the success of the US and UK military operation against Saddam Hussein.

Ultimately, however, John Major resisted the temptation to go early. Perhaps inevitably his honeymoon ratings fell, and some commentators felt that he would rue the missed opportunity. As we entered the winter of 1991–2, the polls were very tight.

That election came only in April 1992. I had been in place as a candidate since July 1989 and in that four-week campaign I threw myself into the fight, wearing out shoe leather, delivering tens of thousands of leaflets by hand as well as through the post, participating in hustings, conducting countless conversations on the doorsteps and, by polling day, all but losing my voice. It had been a nerve-racking and fraught national campaign and, towards the end, it looked as though Labour had the edge. The BBC exit poll thought so. Yet John Major led the Conservatives to victory with a majority of twenty-one seats and racked up a record 14 million votes for the party.

Such a victory, though immensely gratifying for any Conservative, would be nowhere near enough on a uniform national swing to deliver Bristol South for the Conservatives. As I went to the count, I was under no illusion that I had won but I was sorry to be quite heavily beaten. My share of the vote fell to 32.4 per cent from my predecessor's 38.1 per cent in 1987, and the Labour majority soared from 1,404 to 8,919. I was philosophical about it. I had always known that the seat was made artificially marginal in 1987 by the circumstances in which Dawn Primarolo became Labour's candidate, and that she was well placed to strengthen her hold on the constituency, unless there was either a big swing to the Conservatives or major demographic change favouring my party. There was neither, and so she achieved a sharply better result. Little was I then to know that eighteen years later, Dawn would be elected a Deputy Speaker, serving the House with distinction and me with unswerving loyalty from 2010 to 2015.

* * *

I focused on client work with Sallingbury Casey and was promoted to the board by 1994. Yet the experience of working as a public affairs consultant began to pall for me. We had lost a number of excellent people who had left to take up in-house roles elsewhere and I no longer had a great appetite for new business as I had once done. I offered to take voluntary redundancy and the company agreed. I had gained some experience of the private sector, and earned a bit of money, but politics was still where my passion lay. If I still had to wait to become an actual MP, maybe I should at least get as close to the Commons as I could.

I was tipped off by a friendly Conservative MP, Sir George

Gardiner, that the Chief Secretary to the Treasury, Jonathan Aitken, was looking for a special adviser. Ordinarily this was a person from the minister's political party appointed to provide an additional source of information to that provided by civil servants. The 'spad', as such an appointee has come to be known, will usually have political antennae, often some knowledge of the media, an ability to spot potential hazards before they arise and the capacity to draft speeches, articles or replies to awkward questions in a way that would fall outside the skillset or the responsibility of a career civil servant.

Arriving for my interview, I was given a warm welcome by Jonathan. I felt confident, not only because of the welcome, but because I felt that I would come over well. At one level, I might not be thought likely to prove a good interviewee. I am not good-looking, but rather rat-like and somewhat intense. On the other hand I had done my homework and can communicate fluently. I do not panic, get tongue-tied or descend into umm-ing and ah-ing in responding to questions. Jonathan was very engaging and suggested that my 'rumbustious Essex man approach' could be useful. I heard later that of the candidates he had interviewed, I was his preferred choice, but that his boss, the Chancellor of the Exchequer, Ken Clarke, wished to interview me too.

My heart sank. Jonathan Aitken was a strong Eurosceptic. Although we had not discussed individual political issues I was sure that Jonathan knew that I was sympathetic to his brand of Conservatism. By contrast, although I admired Ken Clarke as a formidable politician, I did not hail from his pro-European wing of the party. I was nervous that on straightforward ideological grounds he would veto my appointment. I could not have been more wrong to judge Ken by my own factional standards. He was engaging, courteous, apparently content with my acceptance – freely and honestly offered – that discussions with ministers must remain confidential. He mentioned that he had once had a special adviser who leaked and briefed the media on the basis of his own view and that this had made teamwork very difficult. I assured him that, if appointed, I would work supportively to Jonathan and himself alike and be discreet. Against my expectations, Ken signalled in the interview that he would be pleased to appoint me, subject only to the caveat that I should not apply for parliamentary seats without permission. His reasoning was that he thought he would have to let his established spad, David Ruffley, seek selection as a candidate. If successful David would then have to resign as spad because it was a sufficiently senior post within the civil service to be incompatible with party activity. He did not want to lose two advisers in that way before the election. This was not ideal as I very much wanted to contest the next election, but I accepted the condition and resolved not to apply for upcoming candidate selections.

I started work at the Treasury in late March 1995 and loved it. My usual course was to attend all meetings conducted by the Chief Secretary, to keep a note of what was suggested to him and offer a view where there were different options. At meetings for Treasury questions, I often offered input that, alongside some of the arid factual material supplied to Jonathan, would enable him to develop a political narrative to policy. I had a role in speechwriting, including for a variety of fixtures outside Parliament.

Soon after I arrived, Jonathan was the subject of a hostile television documentary that suggested that he had in the past procured prostitutes for Saudi princes. This was allegedly done when he had worked commercially in the Arab states. The claims were false and Jonathan sued both the broadcaster and the *Guardian* newspaper for libel. Eventually he concluded in the run-up to the court case that he could not credibly prepare for it while also putting in the gruelling eighteen-hour days required to serve effectively as Chief Secretary to the Treasury. He decided to resign from the Cabinet though he told me that he hoped that I would be able to stay, as Ken Clarke had warmed to me.

Initially, the signs were positive. I was called in by Ken after Jonathan's resignation; he had a filthy cold but could not have been friendlier or more encouraging. He told me that as well as valuing my input at meetings, he had read and appreciated my various written submissions for his ministerial box. 'You have made an excellent start,' he told me, 'and although like me you are sorry that Jonathan has left, I very much hope that you will want to continue.' I assured him that I would love to do so. But the following day I was called in to see Ken again. Looking a bit sheepish, he immediately and fulsomely apologised, explaining that William Waldegrave, Aitken's successor as Chief Secretary, wanted to bring his own spad into the Treasury, and with three other spads already in the department there was no room for a fourth. Ken was totally straight then as he is today. I respected him telling me directly and said I understood completely. It had been a privilege to serve and I wished him all the best. Four months after arriving at the Treasury, I had to leave.

Just as I was enjoying a quiet day at home a couple of weeks later, I received a phone call from Peter Ainsworth, the then Conservative MP for Surrey East who had been Jonathan's Parliamentary Private Secretary (PPS) and had now been taken on in a similar role by the Secretary of State for National Heritage, Virginia Bottomley. Peter told me that her special adviser had left and she was looking to appoint a successor. Would I like to apply? I would and I did. Gratified to be called to interview by the Secretary of State, I had nevertheless decided that I would resist any suggestion that I should not seek to fight the next general election. I told Virginia that I was on the candidates' list, had no particular expectation of being a candidate this time round but intended to apply for constituency vacancies. 'That's fine,' she replied. I was appointed in August 1995 and got to work at once.

Like all of us, Virginia had her strengths and weaknesses.

She was passionate about the merits of the National Lottery, cared about the arts and wanted to preserve a decent budget for the heritage sector. Utterly loyal to the Prime Minister, she worked extremely hard and, for the most part, she was an engaging, friendly and encouraging boss. But she also had one of the shortest attention spans of anyone I have met in my professional life. She seemed either unable or disinclined to focus on any issue for more than a few moments before wandering off into diversion on a wholly unrelated subject. Far more so than Jonathan, she was surprisingly needy for someone who had already served in Cabinet for over three years.

One day I was working on a bigger issue – the BBC Charter review or her Royal Television Society speech – when she suddenly appeared, gravely concerned that she was due to address a constituency supper club in one of the small Commons dining rooms that evening and had no speech. What a disaster. I gently pointed out that ten to fifteen minutes of what we know in politics as a 'stump speech' was all that would be expected. I did not say, but frankly assumed, that she would have such a speech in her head. The notion that she needed a written text was almost laughable. In rather more diplomatic terms, I hinted as much, whereupon she pointed out that if I made a speech and made a minor error it would not matter but if she, a Cabinet minister, did so it could cause serious embarrassment. I promptly penned a few points for her and asked the following day how it had all gone. 'Oh, it was absolutely fine. No problem at all. Thank you so much.'

Life with Virginia could be frenetic but she was public-spirited. Soon, however, a difficulty arose. I started receiving interviews in Conservative-held seats and Peter, her husband, whose Eltham seat was disappearing in boundary changes, was similarly seeking selection in some of the same seats. That problem was short-lived because, though we were both interviewed in West Worthing, Peter was selected and she was rightly delighted for him.

Thereafter I received a flurry of selection interview requests. I reached the final three in a constituency in Hampshire but was unsuccessful. In the office the following day, she asked how I had done and I told her that I had lost, to which she replied, 'I'm so pleased.' When I was eventually selected in Buckingham and had to resign as her spad, she reacted with poor grace, saying it was 'so inconvenient'. I could see that, but I had been upfront all along and she had no grounds for complaint. A formidable worker, Virginia was a hugely dedicated public servant, but not outstanding.

The special adviser role that I discharged for Jonathan at the Treasury and Virginia at the National Heritage department was fun, rewarding and a different experience to my consultancy career. That said, it was also precarious and rarely entered into by someone looking to do it for more than a Parliament. I had fought two elections unsuccessfully and was determined to be elected at my third attempt. This required very careful thought for one simple reason. After John Major's 1992 election triumph, events conspired against him and the government with alarming speed. By September 1992, on Black Wednesday, the United Kingdom was forced out of the Exchange Rate Mechanism of the European Monetary System against its will and the Chancellor, Norman Lamont, had to devalue sterling after his oft-repeated insistence that he would do no such thing. I make this point not to criticise Norman Lamont, who did what he had to do. Ultimately, free of that European straitjacket, the British economy recovered and the country enjoyed several years of growth. The problem was that people felt that the recovery was in spite and not because of the government, the result of abandoning its intended policy rather than the consequence of that policy. The government's credibility was shot, Labour went ahead in the polls, greatly extended its lead when Tony Blair became Labour leader in July 1994 and never looked back. For me, therefore, the question was how badly would the Tory Party do at a 1996 or 1997 election and what seats could we be confident of holding?

I was extremely bearish about Conservative prospects. In her diaries, the former Labour Cabinet minister Barbara Castle disclosed that Jim Callaghan had told her that every so often in politics the tide turned decisively against a party and there was nothing that party could realistically do about it. Such a turning of the tide meant, he thought, that his own government was doomed to lose to Margaret Thatcher in 1979. I felt the same, if not immediately after our ERM ejection, then certainly once Blair took charge of his party. From the summer of 1994 onwards I thought that the Conservatives would lose the next election by at least a 100-seat majority, possibly as much as 140. Many people I respect disagreed, arguing that the poll gap would narrow once people had to choose.

Convinced of my own prognosis, I decided that I would apply only for Conservative seats where the retiring MP had at least 50 per cent of the vote and a lead of at least 20 per cent over his or her nearest rival. I made only one exception: Wansdyke in Somerset had a slightly smaller Conservative majority but a number of West Country sources told me that the opposition vote was split between Labour and the Liberal Democrats – I could see that that was true – and that the Conservatives would be sure to hold the seat. I was interviewed in Wansdyke and reached the next round. The polls were horrendous at the time and I confess to doing something I never did before or afterwards. I tanked deliberately in the final round. It was thought very bad form to withdraw from a selection process unless you were badly ill – and I wasn't. I went, made a solid but low-key speech and, by my standards, was lethargic. The agent for the constituency telephoned me late that night and said, 'John, I'm very sorry but you didn't get through tonight. It's difficult to say quite why. You were perfectly competent but your speech was a bit lacking in the passion I have often seen you show.' Down the other end of the line, a wave of relief swept through my stomach and I said

I understood, it didn't matter at all, and I wished all the best to the successful candidate. I meant 'all the best' but I feared the worst for that person, and so it proved. Mark Prisk, the Conservative candidate, was defeated at the general election, though fortunately for him he secured a safe berth in Hertford and Stortford four years later.

Following a few other near-misses I was interviewed in Witney, Oxfordshire. I thought I had made a powerful and fluent speech but found that questions were delivered rather stiffly and I did not feel that I resonated. I was right. The Central Office agent, David Simpson, a very experienced hand, said to me, 'John, those were very comfortable, relaxed, middle- and upper-middle-class people you were addressing. You were too intense, staring round at each of them. They like their politics a little quieter. Try to relax.' It was a fair point and I tried to heed his advice. I am naturally intense and, by background, something of a street fighter. The problem for me was that these people didn't need to fight, and in their constituencies neither did the Tory Party. They wanted a nice chap, a good egg to socialise with and stand up for the area in Parliament, preferably supported by a jolly charming wife.

In January 1996 I was invited to interview in two plum Conservative seats, Surrey Heath and Buckingham. After successful early interviews, David Simpson phoned to say that he had good news and bad news. The good news was that I had reached the final round in Buckingham and was also through to the semi-final round in Surrey Heath.

'What's the bad news?' I asked.

'Well, I'm afraid the Buckingham final and the Surrey Heath semi-final will be on the same night, so you will have to drop out of one of them.'

I was gobsmacked by his nonchalant disclosure. Both constituencies fell within the party's southern region. Surely the processes could have been organised not to clash?

'Oh no,' Simpson replied. 'They are autonomous. Jolly bad

luck, I understand, but you'll have to choose.'

'No,' I replied. 'I have been voted through in both and I have a right to take my chances in both.'

'John, the interviews are on the same night. That fact won't change. I repeat – you can't go to both.'

'Well, if Surrey Heath will let me go first and Buckingham will let me go last, I reckon I can get from one to the other in time.' Simpson doubted this, pointing out that it was likely to be snowing, traffic conditions would be poor and the idea that I could get from one to the other in an hour, as I would need to do, was unrealistic. I had an idea in mind but did not share it with him. I simply asked if he would be willing to ask the two Associations if they would schedule me at 7.30 p.m. and 9 p.m. respectively. He did and they agreed.

My idea was that I would go by car to Surrey Heath and have a helicopter take me to Buckingham. Julian Lewis generously agreed to investigate how this could be organised and at what cost. The answer was that a helicopter could pick me up at Blackbushe airfield and take me to a field in Finmere just outside Buckingham, where a waiting car would take me to the Royal Latin School where the selection was taking place. It would cost just shy of £1,000.

So, on 7 February 1996, I was driven to Surrey, spoke, answered questions and left. I was accompanied by my then girlfriend, Louise, Julian and a friend of his, Nina. We drove to Blackbushe airport. The weather was not great but the pilot judged it safe to fly. We arrived at the field in Finmere at 8.45 p.m. and the driver got us to the Royal Latin School by nine. I just had time for a loo break and then I was on stage. I had a ten-minute speech in my head – no script or notes – and sought to impress upon the 215-strong audience how keen I was. The Association president, Miles Buckinghamshire, had explained to the meeting that I had been at another selection and that it had been a rush for me to get there in time. Louise had reminded me that I should give short, sharp answers to questions. She was right. People are invariably more interested in putting their own question and, possibly, in one's answer to it than in hearing a question from someone else. In the fifteen minutes allocated for questions, I took eleven. Possibly the most significant, and certainly helpful, came from a woman of about seventy near the front who had been beaming enthusiastically at me throughout my speech.

'Mr Bercow, thank you. I much enjoyed your speech,' she began. 'But as you have been interviewed tonight in Surrey as well, how can we know that if we choose you tonight, you will accept us? Surely you could be chosen by Surrey too and opt to go there.'

This beautiful question gave me a perfect opportunity to make my commitment crystal-clear. I explained that Surrey Heath's meeting had been a semi-final, featuring six candidates who were to be reduced that night to three, and assured her that if I were selected in Buckingham I would definitely accept. 'Oh, I am delighted to hear that,' she replied, looking as though Christmas had come ten months early.

When my interview was over, I was ushered to a back room where, with my rivals Howard Flight and David Rutley, I waited while the Buckingham Conservatives cast their ballots. After about half an hour the constituency agent, Gordon Bell, came in and told us that the first ballot had not produced an overall winner. David Rutley had come third and the members would now be asked to choose between Howard and me. David Rutley said a friendly goodnight.

Howard and I were understandably tense. Rather stupidly, I mentioned that I had made a little ice-breaking crack in my speech about arriving 'by flight', to which he disapprovingly replied, 'That was a low blow.' About fifteen minutes later the Association chairman, Charles Strickland, came in, turned to me, and said, 'Mr Bercow, I am pleased to tell you that the Buckingham Conservative Association has chosen you to be their candidate in this constituency.' I thanked him warmly, hugged Louise and shook hands with Howard, Julian and Nina. Howard looked mildly disappointed but Christabel, his wife, looked utterly devastated.

Charles Strickland asked me to rejoin the meeting to say a few words. It was now well after 10 p.m. and I knew that people would be keen to get home so I thanked them warmly, dedicated myself to serving them and the wider community to the best of my ability and said I looked forward to meeting them as soon as possible in the weeks and months ahead.

As we celebrated in a nearby Indian restaurant and then travelled back to London, I was exhilarated beyond description. People sometimes say when they achieve a personal triumph that it has not 'sunk in yet' but, for me, it had. Since the age of sixteen, seventeen years or more than half of my lifetime earlier, I had aspired one day to become a Conservative MP. I had been on the Conservative Central Office candidates' list since the age of twenty-four. I had relished fighting two constituencies, one for a period of six weeks and the other for nearly three years. Now, third time round, after applying for twenty-seven seats, being interviewed in eighteen and shortlisted in four, I was on the threshold of a parliamentary career. There had to be an election by May 1997 and, therefore, barring accidents, I should be the Conservative MP for Buckingham within fifteen months. Readers not immersed in politics might wonder how I could be so confident. The answer is that, very pessimistic though I was privately about the likely general election result, there are rock-solid seats held by each of the two main parties that, realistically, will not change hands. Buckingham had had a Conservative majority in 1992 of 20,644, the sitting Tory MP, George Walden garnering 62.3 per cent of the vote, 41.4 per cent ahead of his second-placed Liberal Democrat opponent.

Unbridled excitement though I felt at my selection, I now had no income and needed to find some, not only to pay my mortgage in Westminster but also to rent a home in Buckingham. Fortunately, this happened much more quickly than I had expected, and within a couple of weeks I had a portfolio of consultancy work. This was a huge boon as I was then able to rent an attractive cottage in a picturesque village called Adstock, halfway between Winslow and Buckingham. I buckled down to getting to know the people in my local party, wider influencers in local churches, schools and voluntary groups across the constituency and, of course, the local media. I went back and forth to the constituency every week, attending party functions, learning about the area and knocking on doors to introduce myself to voters. I built up a profile in the local press and I worked hard to raise money for the local party and to establish my rapport with the voluntary workers with whom I hoped and expected to be co-operating for years to come.

But the background to the election was scarcely propitious. John Major had been behind in the polls since Britain's forced ejection from the ERM. Once Tony Blair became Labour leader, the gap widened and the Conservatives consistently trailed Labour by 15 or 20 percentage points in the opinion polls, sometimes more. The government had fallen foul of electors, hit by a wave of sleaze stories and seriously damaged by the evidence that 'New' Labour, aiming firmly at the centre ground, was regarded as a safe option for the votes of disillusioned Conservatives.

This was the tenor of the campaign in Buckingham. Fortunately, the majority was enormous and Conservative voters in Buckingham were in large numbers both long-standing and solid. Even if they were upset about one government policy or another, they were still minded to stick with the Conservatives. Yet there was slippage and it was unmistakable. One day we encountered several people who said that they had lived in the area for two, three or four decades and always voted Conservative, but would not do so this time. Over a welcome dinner with Gordon Bell at the Seven Stars in Twyford, feeling rather deflated, I suddenly said to him, 'You don't think there is any danger I might lose, do you?'

'No, John,' he replied, with a smile. 'Most of your vote is holding up and just remember this. Buckingham is the eighth safest Tory seat in the country. So on a uniform swing – there is no particular factor here that will produce a larger anti-Conservative swing – the party would have to be down to seven seats to lose Buckingham. That will not happen.'

Fortunately, as deep down I had always expected, Gordon, whose faith was shared by my fantastic chairman, Charles Strickland, was correct. He proved a very savvy agent, not merely organising an excellent canvassing schedule and making wise suggestions for my election leaflets, but also drafting supportive letters to the local papers rehearsing my merits as a candidate for the area.

In general, I had never much relished election campaigns. They invade privacy, are inefficient, ineffective, and tedious to the point of being soul-destroying; I had always eagerly count-ed down the days to go before they concluded. Towards the end of 1996, my girlfriend Louise and I had split up so I went back and forth to the constituency alone. During the cam-paign itself, however, a good many friends came to canvass for me, including Sally, who stayed in a local B&B for a number of days through to polling day itself. Sally had quit the Tory Party several years before as, like a lot of people, she was greatly impressed by Tony Blair and, though not politically active at the time, now firmly aligned herself with the Labour Party.

As she arrived with my mother and me at the count in Stoke Mandeville, Sally's mood was a little different from that of my Conservative activists. They were anticipating a very comfortable win for me but were tense and nervous about the projected national result. Many had convinced themselves that the polls showing a big Labour majority were wrong, but they must have known it would be a tough night for the Con-servatives. They went from tension to horror to black humour as the scale of the Labour slaughter became apparent. Seat after seat held by the Conservatives fell to Labour and they started to joke that, at this rate, I might be a member of the Shadow Cabinet before the night was over.

For her part, Sally was thrilled to bits that Labour was storming it, though she was just about tactful enough not to lord it over my shaken party supporters. There was, of course, one exception to Sally's insatiable thirst for Labour gains. She wanted me to romp home in Buckingham. The count took an unconscionably long time as it was also a county council election day and the ballot papers had to be separated. Finally, at 5.50 a.m. on Friday 2 May the Returning Officer, Brendan Hurley, read out the results, concluding: 'And I hereby declare that the said John Simon Bercow is duly elected to represent the Buckingham constituency.' I made an enthusiastic acceptance speech, and Sally and I had a couple of glasses of champagne when we returned to my constituency home.

The following day, I resumed my ongoing efforts to persuade her to be my partner once again. Some may say that was foolish. If you have been out with someone several times and it hasn't worked, there must be a fundamental incompatibility and you should move on. I took the contrary view: the fact that Sally and I, when not partners, still kept in touch and kept gravitating back towards each other felt significant. We had remained firm friends for years and we adored each other's company. I found her stimulating, clever and hugely attractive. Our relationship had never been characterised by arguments: more by different lifestyles and priorities. I felt that we had both matured in our different ways and I couldn't see myself wanting to be with anyone else. I think Sally felt the same, as she promised to think about it. She did say that, delighted as she was for me, she would be quite happy if I'd chosen to become a lawyer or a carpenter rather than an MP ('and a Tory one at that!').

Days later I had dinner with Mum in London. Now that I was elected, she told me how relieved as well as thrilled she and Alison were. 'Why do you say relieved?' I asked.

'Well,' she said, 'it's a relief that you've finally been successful.' She went on to say that Alison had been worried on my behalf about the time and money I had been spending when trying to find a 'safe' seat. She feared that if I failed I would be inconsolable. I told her that the thought of failing had, literally, never occurred to me. I always felt that I would find a fit with a constituency and get to Parliament in the end. I was fortified in that belief by Fred Silvester, a former MP who, over lunch, had once said to me, 'John, you only have to be lucky once.'

3

Commons Apprentice

My journey as a Member of Parliament before my election as Speaker was unconventional, unpredictable and, to some – friend and foe alike – unbelievable. For the moment, as I entered Parliament on Monday 5 May 1997, I was just hugely excited. Naturally I intended to work hard both in Westminster and Buckingham: I was conscious of wanting to do a good job, to be an assiduous MP and to be well regarded by my constituents. In that limited sense, I had the right outlook.

Yet I am ashamed to confess that I did not at that stage think of championing causes to make Britain a better place. Many people stand for Parliament for precisely that reason but equally – and regrettably – a goodly number do not (although they are rarely rash enough ever to admit it). In all honesty, at that time I was a party hack and I was primarily thinking of myself – of wanting to be noticed, of how to make my mark and 'get on'. What's more – and this is again telling – I had no one great cause, no specialism. I was interested in education and, as a Buckinghamshire MP, keen to champion its grammar schools, but even there I was no expert. I was a generalist, at ease arguing the toss across the field of policy at a basic level of principle and straightforward knowledge. If I had any vaguely formed ambition for my political career, it was one day to become Conservative Party Chairman – an ambition Sally scoffed at when I later confided in her: 'You're nuts – what the hell have you devoted all these years to politics for if all you want to do is to work the rubber chicken circuit and hang out with elderly activists!'

The immediate challenge, however, was not to attain a political office but to find a physical one. Here I was glad that I had thought a little before polling day about how I would get started. My predecessor, George Walden, had a Commons secretary, Helyn Dudley, and she was willing to work for me. Rather than search for another secretary, I thought it best to settle in with an established staffer who came highly recommended. We soon secured a berth, a small office in Little College Street, just a few hundred yards from the main entrance to the Commons.

Shortly after I was elected, I was cock-a-hoop when Sally agreed to give our relationship another try and move in to my flat in Marsham Street, Westminster. During the week, I woke early and began to acquire the rather eccentric habit of rushing into the office by about 8 a.m. as I was inordinately keen to see my mailbag which, more often than not, did not arrive until a little later. I was genuinely impatient to see what letters I had received. What type of help were constituents seeking and what opinions were they volunteering? I started scribbling possible replies until, patiently but firmly, Helyn explained that that was her job. I should review and amend her drafts as I thought fit, but she was a bit taken aback that I seemed hell-bent on taking a first stab at a reply before she had had the chance to do so herself. In terms of efficiency, Helyn was right. MPs receive a large volume of letters and emails requesting a reply – hundreds a week and often thousands, and far more now than in 1997 – and the secretary or caseworker should take the lead in preparing responses.

I had yearned to be elected to the Commons and expected to get stuck into debates in the Chamber quickly. Two factors prevented this. First, my initial attempt to make my maiden speech was unsuccessful because the debate in question – on Europe – was heavily oversubscribed, including other would-be maiden speakers, and I was not among those called that day. The Deputy Speaker in the Chair, Michael Martin, indicated that I would not be able to speak on Europe but could open my account in a debate later that evening on firearms. This did not appeal so I decided to try another day. I had been sitting next to Ted Heath, who had made desultory conversation with me, asking, 'What are your views on Europe?' When I told him that I totally opposed any idea of Britain joining the single currency and that I was against the Maastricht Treaty, he glowered and grunted before leaving. The next day I bumped into him and he asked, 'Did you make your maiden yesterday?' I replied that time had prevented me, to which he replied, 'Given your views, that is just as well.'

The second reason I did not immerse myself in debate at once was that there was another attraction centre-stage at the time: the Conservative leadership contest following the resignation of John Major, and the question of whom to support.

Initially, there were six candidates vying to succeed Major. Many people, myself included, had expected Michael Portillo to stand if a heavy Conservative defeat forced Major to quit but, in that respect, the electorate overdid it. The defeat was so heavy that it included Michael's Enfield Southgate seat. So he was out of it.

Ken Clarke, the ex-Chancellor of the Exchequer, was the best known to the public. Almost certainly the candidate most feared by Labour, Ken was nevertheless divisive. The staunchest pro-European in the party, he was furiously resisted by the right. Though he had been good to me at the Treasury, I was not minded to pick him as I thought he would take the party in the wrong direction.

William Hague, who had served as Welsh Secretary for the last two years of John Major's government, had pulled out of an agreement to back Michael Howard after pressure from many colleagues to run himself. Intelligent and an effective debater, many thought that as a young leader he would challenge Tony

Blair and help to rebrand and reposition our party. He was certainly competent, but he just did not resonate with me. There was something rather mechanical and formulaic about his approach. A product of the Oxford Union, he gave me the impression that he thought that politics was a game and that he was there to play that game. To me it was off-putting, as was his lack of political passion. I found him a rather buttoned-up character, geeky, frankly a bit weird.

Michael Howard was clearly bright and very competent, a highly intelligent lawyer with a considerable grasp of his brief and an ability to fight his corner in any debate. Yet he was also a decidedly cold fish. Ann Widdecombe inflicted huge damage on his reputation with a coruscating speech in the Chamber denouncing in forensic detail Michael's treatment of the Director General of the Prison Service, Derek Lewis. I had not planned to vote for Michael anyway but he was now holed below the waterline.

Peter Lilley, previously Trade and Industry Secretary and then, for five years, Secretary of State for Social Security, was the candidate best known to me. He had once invited me to be a special adviser to him and recommended my appointment, only to be blocked by Number 10 in 1993 on the grounds that he already had his full complement of spads. My only significant concern was that he was not a natural public speaker and I knew that he might struggle against Tony Blair at the despatch box.

Stephen Dorrell, a centre-left candidate, soon withdrew from the race. He knew that he was fishing for votes in the same pond as Ken Clarke and would do less well. That left John Redwood. He had briefly served in Cabinet as Welsh Secretary but resigned to stand against John Major for the leadership two years earlier. Although comfortably beaten by Major, and ridiculed as The Vulcan, he had impressed many Tories with his courage in putting up in 1995 and with the clarity of his populist message. John was and is extremely intelligent and mentally quick but, like Hague and Howard, he struck many people, including me, as a rather cold personality.

I decided to go with Lilley. Sadly, at the hustings, he performed poorly. To my discredit, I hadn't the heart to tell him so. Redwood, by contrast, was superb and in the first ballot I therefore voted for him. Michael Howard was eliminated as he came bottom, with 23 votes. Peter Lilley, on 24, was three behind Redwood and withdrew, endorsing Hague. Unattracted by the rather shallow careerism of Hague, I continued to back Redwood. He was eliminated in the next round of voting. Then came decision time. Should I back Clarke, with whom I profoundly disagreed on Europe but whom I otherwise regarded as easily the more impressive character? Or should I back Hague, either out of ideological hostility to Clarke or because a lot of people thought he would win?

Redwood formed an unlikely pact with Clarke, ensuring that members of the Shadow Cabinet would be free to speak up against Britain joining the Euro. Hague's pitch was a simple appeal to mainstream Tories of a sceptical mind. I went to see Hague but came away deeply underwhelmed – he was robotic, cold and uninspiring. So, fortified by Redwood's decision, I voted for Ken Clarke. But the parliamentary party did not like Ken's link with Redwood. It felt wrong, cynical, unsustainable. There is no doubt that it damaged Ken. So Hague won the final ballot 92 votes to 70, but I was proud to back Ken and have never regretted it even though it was the first of a number of contests in which I picked 'losing' candidates.

The excitement of the leadership election over, I started to look for opportunities to make my maiden speech. I opted to try for part of a debate on Gordon Brown's Budget. Advised by my whip, David Madel, I rubbed Churchill's foot on his bronze statue in the Members' Lobby before I entered the Chamber that morning. The old superstition was that this would afford a new Member good luck in his or her first outing – so many people practised this superstition over so many years that the foot became discoloured and had to be restored. These days there is a sign next to the foot exhorting people not to touch it.

There is a long-standing convention that maiden speakers are congratulated on their debut performances. However, there is no requirement or expectation that one 'newbie' congratulates another. My decision to do so was unobjectionable, but mildly presumptuous, and quite unnecessary. Typical of me, I did it in spades, praising Julie Kirkbride, then Labour's Ben Bradshaw, then Nick Gibb, Barry Gardiner, and Eleanor Laing.

After praising my brilliant and bookish predecessor for Buckingham, George Walden, I launched into a panegyric about my heroine, Margaret Thatcher, describing her as 'the world's greatest living statesman'. After lauding the Conservative economic record, I offered a cheer to Labour for cutting corporation tax before denouncing the introduction of seventeen new taxes in the Budget. Always happy in my comfort zone attacking Labour on tax, I quoted Roy Hattersley, who had written in the *Guardian* two years earlier that Labour could either be the party of higher taxation and proud of it, or the party of higher taxation which it was ashamed to describe, afraid to admit and incapable of calculating with any accuracy.

The speech won praise from Conservative colleagues and was treated generously by the Labour minister Geoffrey Robinson. It was a typical Bercow speech of the time. Hardline, rhetorical and fluent – as well as long – and offering no evidence of expertise as I had none. As a first outing for an ambitious party hack comfortable on his feet, it was a respectable effort but not outstanding.

Emboldened by my maiden contribution, I contributed again with a speech on pensions a mere five days later. A passable effort powerfully delivered, I allowed my penchant for blunt – even harsh – description of an opponent to land me in hot water. Referring to Gordon Brown as a Chancellor 'masquerading' as a 'long-term visionary' and scolding him as a 'manipulative short-term opportunist' almost certainly raised the eyebrows of the Chair and of less acerbic colleagues, but that was of no concern to me. When I said that Brown had been 'exposed as a fraud', the then Deputy Speaker, Michael Martin, rightly stopped me in my tracks for a disorderly description that impugned the integrity of a colleague. I apologised unreservedly and blissfully continued my speech, no harm done. I only mention this as an example of my early approach, which was best summarised as crude and unrestrained attacks on the other side at all times.

Shortly before my first summer recess I was immersing myself in debates and becoming ever more focused on Parliament. Indeed, such was that single-minded focus on Parliament on weekdays and the constituency at weekends that my personal life suffered. Ironically, I had spent years hankering after Sally, but now that she was living with me I barely saw her. I was obsessed with work and, although she understood my enthusiasm and had a career herself, working in an advertising agency, she rightly felt that life required some balance and that mine had none whatsoever. I was far too wrapped up in myself, she complained. Fed up, she packed her bags at the end of the summer and moved out. Typical of me, I was upset but too stubborn and ambitious to reflect and change my outlook. We parted and didn't speak for about six months and, if anything, I threw myself into politics even more.

In the autumn, I delivered a speech attacking Labour on student finance. Previously they had pledged not to introduce tuition fees. Now, the election safely won, David Blunkett, the Education Secretary, had 'the brass neck' to come to the House to announce such a policy. I could not be accused of understatement in response to these developments. Ministers had been 'cack-handed', 'incompetent', 'guilty of deception', their behaviour the source of 'the most stupefying embarrassment for them'. It was uncompromising, attack-dog stuff, useful to one's own side in debate but, unless I balanced it with more nuanced, dispassionate or open-minded interventions, liable to cause me to be branded a one-trick pony.

Not content with attacking Labour, I could not resist taking swipes at the Liberal Democrats as well. Accusing the party of 'cynicism' and of seeking to wage 'a campaign of disinformation', I argued that the Liberal Democrats had taken different positions at different times within the previous two years on whether to raise income tax to bolster education or whether simply to devote 1 per cent of the existing income tax take for that purpose. Continuing a stream of only partly light-hearted invective, I denounced the Liberal Democrats as being 'steeped in the orthodoxy of the 1960s', declaring that 'they are fanatics for egalitarianism but know nothing of excellence'.

After these early jousts in set-piece Commons debates, I turned my mind to questioning the Prime Minister. There was a row running at the time about political donations and the disclosure regime governing them. Simply hunting as part of the opposition pack, I asked Tony Blair why, if he had decided two weeks earlier that he definitely did not want to take further donations, he asked for permission from Sir Patrick Neill, chair of the Committee on Standards in Public Life, to do so. Taunting the Prime Minister a mere six months after my arrival in the House, I asked, 'Is not the truth of the matter that the Prime Minister was begging Sir Patrick to give him the green light to take more money?' Blair swatted me easily enough, albeit without even beginning to answer the question, saying that he was intrigued that I should ask such a question as he understood that my last employment was as special adviser to Jonathan Aitken. Although Jonathan had at that stage not gone to jail for perjury, he was a hugely controversial figure widely thought to be involved in 'dodgy dealing'. In fact, my last job had not been with him, but that was immaterial. Blair brushed me aside, to howls of laughter from his benches and, in all likelihood, many Tories were doubtless happy to see this bumptious newbie knocked to the ground.

The second exchange between us came a couple of months later. The Prime Minister had been on a well-publicised foreign holiday and there was a fuss about a minister whose partner had travelled at public expense. The right-wing press were fomenting a controversy about 'partners', rather than 'spouses', being able to travel in this way. It is all incredibly dated now but it was very live then, and I was fully signed up to the Tory attack line. Even so, my tone with the Prime Minister would be characterised by a supporter as 'fearless' and by critics as borderline offensive. I had noted a number of Tony Blair's stock-in-trade lines when answering questions and lobbed this missile at him. 'May I say how delighted I am to see the Prime Minister here? Since the general election, he has spent more time in the Seychelles than in the House of Commons. Will the Prime Minister publish the rules on travel at public expense by ministers' partners as the Ministerial Code refers only to spouses? No waffle, no "I have to say", no "What is important is" – a simple Yes or No will do.' Blair said that the code of practice was unchanged from that which applied when the previous government was in office. Then, however, he added that he had reflected on me as he knew that I would be asking a question.

'The person of whom he reminds me most,' Blair said, 'is a Mr David Shaw. His hallmark, which the Honourable Gentleman shares, was to be "nasty and ineffectual in equal quantities".' Admittedly, most new Labour MPs did not know or remember David Shaw, the former right-wing Tory MP for Dover, but others did and the Prime Minister's put-down played superbly on the government backbenches, where I was fast becoming heartily disliked. But as with my first exchange, I enjoyed it and felt that I had got under the Prime Minister's skin. There were comments by journalists the next day that the PM had rather demeaned himself by personally attacking a lowly new boy when he could have risen above such an approach. I wasn't complaining then and won't now: for me, the joust was fun, although there was one person who disagreed. When I got home that evening there was a telephone message from my mother, sounding very shaken and asking if I was all right, but offering no context or elaboration. When I called her to say I was fine and why wouldn't I be, she said that she had watched PMQs and thought that Tony Blair had been vicious. Once a mum, always a mum – to her I had always been and remained her little boy.

* * *

In Westminster, I and thirty-two other new Conservative MPs were all eager to make our mark. Theresa May was the most impressive of the new female Conservatives. She was not charismatic, and expressed no strikingly original views. Rather, she was incredibly solid – well informed, carefully prepared for debates and quietly clinical in argument. She appeared to carry no ideological baggage and I have no recollection of her taking any prominent part in the post-election leadership contest. She simply kept her head down and performed competently as part of the much-depleted Tory team in Westminster. It was obvious that she would quickly and deservedly be promoted. She was never warm or friendly but always courteous and, above all, conscientious.

Philip Hammond was a colder male version of Theresa. He drew effectively on his business experience in debates on the national minimum wage and competition policy, veered neither to the right nor to the left, and struck me at once as a man whose principal concern was to be promoted. Andrew Lansley was a similar case. He had no strong commercial footprint but a good brain, the former civil servant's capacity to grasp the essence of any issue and the ability to grind opponents down with his detailed knowledge and readiness to convey it competently, with zero passion or inspiration and, ordinarily, at length. Like May and Hammond, Lansley eschewed factions within the party. Said to lean to the right, I thought of him as a solid machine politician who had undergone a charisma-bypass operation at birth.

The most intellectually brilliant, erudite and polite of the new intake was Oliver Letwin, former Cambridge philosophy tutor, Downing Street Policy Unit wonk and one-time merchant banker. On 19 January 1998, my thirty-fifth birthday, perhaps eccentrically, I stayed all afternoon and evening in the Chamber to debate the Bill that would give effect to the Treaty of Amsterdam, the latest in a succession of European treaties. I spoke for half an hour on the subject of the 'subsidiarity' provisions of the Treaty. You could be forgiven for thinking that either the subject or my lengthy disquisition on it was a cure for insomnia. That said, it was a decent effort, but it was nothing compared with the forensic speech Oliver Letwin made. In barely ten minutes, he ripped the Treaty provision to shreds and showed all of us just what an incisive mind he had. More than two decades later, I remember that speech well and my instant belief that I would encounter no sharper brain than Oliver's on either side of the House.

On the government side, the new intake was inevitably far bigger because Labour had won a landslide and numerous colleagues were elected in marginal seats – against their expectations in many cases.

Yvette Cooper, the new Labour MP for Pontefract and Castleford, struck me at once as formidable – intelligent, articulate, down to earth and relentless in debate. She and I appeared on the BBC's *Any Questions* in November 1997 and I remember feeling certain that she would rise to, or near, the top of her party. Her ascent may have been slowed by the fact that she was a known Brownite, but her progress was inevitable.

Patricia Hewitt, who had previously worked for the National Council for Civil Liberties and as press secretary to Neil

Kinnock, was clearly a heavyweight in Labour's ranks. Arriving relatively late in the Commons after many years in those intensely political roles outside the House, she seemed, and proved, a safe bet for fast-track promotion to ministerial rank.

The same was true of Charles Clarke, her fellow ex-Kinnock aide. Charles, like Patricia, was bright, and possessed gravitas and ambition. Charles could be personable but, at heart, he was a pugilist, occasionally even a thug, content if necessary with a points victory over an opponent but obviously relishing any chance to score a knockout instead. Initially I did not warm to Charles, though we came to enjoy cordial relations in later years, but I respected him as I respected Patricia Hewitt.

Alan Johnson, ex-postman and trade unionist, impressed with his sharpness and wit in debate. Like Norman Tebbit, Alan was educated at the University of Life and brought decades of workplace experience, common sense, quickness of mind and deeply ingrained values to his parliamentary activity. Very quickly he became PPS to Treasury Minister Dawn Primarolo, and it was clear that he would progress quickly. Unlike Charles, from whom casual unpleasantness was part of the *table d'hôte*, Alan was immensely likeable and that characteristic has served him well throughout his career in the House.

Claire Ward, the MP for Watford, and Chris Leslie, the MP for Shipley, had both been elected aged twenty-four in marginal seats. Neither seemed destined to hold on indefinitely but both impressed as strong performers, as did Oona King, the passionate and charismatic Labour newcomer in Bethnal Green. I recall an early exchange in the Members' Tea Room with Oona. Chatting about upcoming surgeries that weekend, Oona asked me how many people I expected to come and see me.

'Eight,' I replied.

'That's very precise,' she said. I pointed out that I ran an appointments system, fifteen minutes per person. 'How many will you see?' I enquired.

'Probably about seventy,' she told me. Her surgery was the following day, a Saturday, and she expected it to last all day. I looked aghast and said she surely needed to operate an appointments system to manage the load and avoid being detained all day. Looking amused and slightly pityingly, she offered the conclusive rejoinder, 'John, I couldn't operate an appointments system in Bethnal Green. There would be a riot. People come to see me and see me they will. That's the end of it.' Our constituencies were worlds apart and the conversation between us was an eye-opener.

Angela Smith, the new Labour MP for Basildon, was thoroughly personable from day one. I think she regarded me as a distinct oddity, something of a wild animal to be observed with interest, though probably most safely kept in a cage or stuffed and viewed as a museum exhibit. Stephen Pound, the Labour MP for Ealing North, was the House joker, wisecracking, humorous, and an irreverent cavalier who did not take himself or anyone else too seriously. Kelvin Hopkins was a 55-year-old former college lecturer of traditional, left-wing socialist, anti-EU stock and it was a pleasure to debate with him because he always played the ball, not the person. I liked him at once.

* * *

In that first year in Parliament, I was hyperactive in the Chamber. As a new backbencher I thought it was the right way to learn my craft and that it would probably enhance my prospects of promotion. On Europe, education, the national minimum wage, the cost of government, the future of Stoke Mandeville hospital, housing development, the Human Rights Bill, planning, prisons, Zimbabwe, police, Kosovo, fisheries, the Uniform Business Rate, Sierra Leone, Northern Ireland, legal aid, to name but a few examples, I questioned and, more often than not, criticised the government. In oral exchanges, I was sharp, fluent and relentlessly on the attack, striving to be a formidable prosecutor of the government for the Opposition.

In June 1998 William Hague reshuffled his front-bench team and appointed several members of the 1997 intake to it. In truth, I was mildly disappointed not to be one of them. Sally and I were once again on friendly terms by then and she was disappointed on my behalf too. Sure, I had not supported Hague for leader, but promotion should be on merit and I felt I had been a more visible and effective Opposition contributor than some of those newly promoted. The simple fact was, as I later discovered, that Hague did not like me, observing to Norman Lamont, 'When is he going to join the human race?'

I resolved to redouble my efforts from the backbenches. In November 1998, I was thrilled to be told that I had won the *Spectator* magazine's award for 'Backbencher to Watch', and in June the following year, Hague told me I had made a real impact and said he would like me to join the front bench as a junior Education and Employment spokesman in the Shadow team that would now be led by Theresa May. In making the offer, he said that I had demonstrated strong attacking qualities but would need to broaden my approach and show that I could deploy a variety of techniques beyond that of relentless Rottweiler. He was right about that, and I indicated that I would strive to build my political skills. However, there was one nagging concern I had, and I chose to put it to him. I said I should appreciate it if he would confirm that, subject to my front-bench commitments, I would still be allowed to take part in debates from the backbenches as long as I adhered to party policy.

William was not and is not an expressive character. A rather cool, distant figure, he did not emote. On this occasion, however, to say that he looked surprised by my enquiry would be an understatement. 'Astonished' would just about capture his facial expression. 'Well,' he replied, 'you will be rather busy with your new responsibilities.' I responded that I accepted that, but if I had any spare time, could I participate from the backbenches? He replied that I would have to agree that with Theresa May, my new boss. Our exchange was brief and courteous, but it was obvious that he didn't take to me and, frankly, the feeling was mutual. My responsibility now was to do all I could to help the team effort, but dislodging a popular new government in one go under the leadership of a man whose approval ratings were low would be a Herculean task.

My new boss, Theresa May, explained to me that my core responsibilities in the Shadow team were twofold. First, I would be expected to champion the retention of the 164 remaining grammar schools in England and Wales whose future we thought was now at risk from new Labour legislation. Theresa naturally knew that my own county of Buckinghamshire had a selective system and appreciated that Buckingham itself had a successful grammar school. She judged correctly that I would be instinctively enthusiastic about arguing for the continuation of such schools. At that time there was no suggestion from William Hague, Theresa May or me that the party would advocate an extension of such provision. Rather, ours was to be a defensive campaign to ensure that where grammar schools existed, I would take the lead in making the case for their preservation.

Labour had launched its New Deal for Young People, a training programme for the young jobless to equip them to enter the workplace. Our sense at the time was that the scheme was expensive and did not offer value for money in tackling youth unemployment. Theresa May explained that my second core responsibility, therefore, was to study it and start to put together a Conservative training and employment programme for the young jobless in readiness for the next general election. I took to both tasks with gusto.

As my boss, Theresa was courteous, businesslike in the

running of team meetings, fair and encouraging. Very properly, she was keen to maintain tight control of our 'messaging' – what we said and with what emphasis. The most striking fact then and now, particularly in view of Theresa's short-lived but enthusiastic embrace in 2016 of the idea of increasing grammar school provision, was that she showed remarkably little interest in the grammar school campaign that she asked me to run. She did not discourage me in any way, but I could tell that it did not much interest her. On one occasion, for an Opposition Day debate, I suggested that she focus on grammar schools, but she rejected the idea on the grounds that she had to present a much wider Conservative education perspective. I felt that Theresa was a little inclined to look over her shoulder: she wanted to be centre-stage, and to assure herself that she was the lead figure in the team and, accordingly, no one else's star could be allowed to shine too brightly. For all this, relations seemed fundamentally strong and, though Theresa was never warm or even cordial, she was fair, reasonable and approachable. I respected her competence and her commitment alike.

* * *

While I was a member of her team, the Labour government made its third and ultimately successful attempt to equalise the age of consent for gay sex. On two previous occasions, ministers had sought to amend existing statutes to deliver equality but they had been thwarted by opponents in the House of Lords. So now they came forward with a Sexual Offences Amendment Bill and the Second Reading of it was scheduled for 10 February 2000. When the subject came before the Commons in 1998 I had listened with great interest and respect to my Conservative colleagues Shaun Woodward and Eleanor Laing as they argued for equalisation. They made a strong case but the vast majority of Conservatives opposed change, and I was uncertain about it. When uncertain, it is natural, and easier, to play safe, and that is what I had done in voting for the status quo. In doing so, however, I resolved to study the question carefully, not least by talking and listening to Church leaders and head teachers in my constituency. Unanimity was, I thought, unlikely, and so it proved. However, the consensus was that the existing law – sixteen for heterosexuals and eighteen for gay men – was arbitrary, discriminatory and ineffective.

I decided that when the issue next came up I would vote for change, and the equalisation of the age of consent. This would not be a breach of party discipline as the matter had always been regarded as a conscience issue and, therefore, the subject of a free vote for Conservative MPs. Days before the debate, Tim Boswell, a socially liberal Tory who had long supported equalisation, asked me how I had decided to vote. I told him that I had resolved to support change. Very sensibly, he advised me to speak in the debate – I had changed my mind and the best course of action was to explain that fact in the House of Commons, applying in the usual way to the Speaker, Betty Boothroyd.

It is commonplace though by no means essential for a Member to give an indication why he or she wants to speak, and I sensed that the Chair – knowing I wanted to declare a change of heart – would probably call me fairly early in the debate. Sure enough, that was the case. I made three points. First, I had come to the conclusion that the statutory discrimination did not deter gay men from having sex if they wanted to and brought no other benefit as far as I could see. It was, literally, pointless discrimination. Secondly, it was worse than that. It discouraged young men from being open about their sexuality and able to take advice about safe sex. Equalising the age of consent would put gay men on a par with straight people, so that whatever people's sexuality they could have sex safely and discuss problems or anxieties equally. Thirdly, it was surely reasonable to ask what other European countries were doing, and, for the most part, our fellow EU member states had an equal age of consent. So, I said, should we.

More striking to my colleagues than these arguments was the fact that I was holding up my hands and saying, in effect, 'I was wrong. I have changed my mind. This is what I now believe and why.' Such a *mea culpa* and public conversion would be significant from any colleague and perhaps particularly from someone of my make-up – young, decidedly right-wing, opinionated and, sometimes, self-assured to the point of arrogance.

Inevitably, my speech attracted comment. In the Chamber I was praised by Dr Evan Harris, the equality-supporting Liberal Democrat MP who nevertheless was quick to point out that my arguments in support of an equal age of consent should also apply to Section 28. I had specifically denied that, arguing for an equal age of consent but for keeping Section 28. Sally had come to watch the debate and, in talking it through beforehand, had made precisely the same point to me, urging me to go the whole hog. She and Evan were right. I was wrong. The following year I spoke out against Section 28 even though it remained Tory policy. I was sometimes slow to make linkages, preferring to look at each issue in isolation.

However, this early display of liberal conscience definitely upset a number of friendly colleagues on the right of the party. One reaction was telling. Patrick Nicholls, the Conservative MP for Teignbridge, came up to me in the division lobby, asking in hushed tones if he could have a word with me. 'Why did you do it? You might not want to give the real reason in public, but you can tell me. People are saying you did it to get in with Portillo. Is that so?' No. I told him that I simply believed it and thought it right to say so. He looked taken aback but appeared to accept that there was no ulterior motive. There wasn't. I had undergone a straightforward conversion on the matter and that was all there was to it.

* * *

Around this time, out of the blue, I received a call from the Chief Whip, James Arbuthnot. I had no idea what to expect. I was not conscious that I had committed any particular misdemeanour. Equally, I had never regarded Arbuthnot as friendly to me, so I was intrigued. He wanted me to move from Theresa May's Shadow Education team to Ann Widdecombe's Shadow Home Office team. Telling me that I had done good work with Theresa, he said that Ann's team could usefully be beefed up and joining it would broaden my experience. Theresa accepted the idea – I wondered but did not ask whether she had initiated it – and Ann was enthusiastic. Though I was surprised, as no general reshuffle was under way, I was more than happy.

Ann was a great boss and fun to serve. In later years, when I told her that, probably for the umpteenth time, she replied, 'Ah. You say that, John, only because most of the time I was very tolerant and let you do your own thing.' She was and she did. Team meetings took place at 8.30 a.m. twice a week and then we were free to get on with our duties. Those meetings were chaired by Ann efficiently; the tone was businesslike; she was ready to delegate and encourage and showed herself to be a good leader.

Two issues from that happy twelve months linger in the memory. The first relates to a small but significant piece of legislation, the House of Commons (Removal of Clergy Disqualification) Bill, which repealed an ancient law preventing former Catholic priests serving as Members of the House of Commons. The ancient discrimination remained on the statute book because no one could remember any previous case of someone being affected by it. Now, David Cairns had been selected as the Labour candidate for Greenock and Port Glasgow. A safe Labour seat at the time, he was sure to win but would not be able to take up his seat unless the law was changed. Ann was very small 'c' conservative on the subject, arguing that it was hazardous to tinker with or repeal an historic piece of legislation, but she particularly objected to the fact that Labour was proposing to do so now only out of self-interest, driven by its desire to help a particular candidate. That said, she had decided that it should not be party policy to oppose the Bill. There should be a 'free vote' on the Conservative benches, and the Shadow team should operate in accordance with that spirit. She opposed the Bill. I supported it. In a wonderfully small 'l' liberal gesture – I doubt anyone has called Ann liberal before or since, and she would probably be tempted to sue anyone who did – she said that I could open from our side and she, my superior, would wind up for the Opposition. The whole debate was enormously stimulating, we disagreed courteously but fundamentally and the Bill was passed.

Another memorable experience of my tenure in Ann Widdecombe's team related to the Vehicles Crime (Reduction) Bill. Ann had again generously asked me to lead from the front bench for the Opposition, even though the Home Secretary, the formidable Jack Straw, was opening for the government and she might have been expected to do so for us.

The Chief Whip, James Arbuthnot, decided that he wanted to run the debate 'long', to minimise or, better still, remove any possibility of the debate finishing early – what is known in Parliament as 'the business collapsing' as though we had to justify ourselves by speaking up to the deadline for the debate. I was instructed to make an exceptionally long speech. Ordinarily, an opening speech from the front bench would be expected to last about half an hour, three-quarters at the most. No, I was told, take longer. Inexcusably, I did. Naturally comfortable with the mellifluous sound of my own voice, I spoke, and spoke, and spoke, to the visible, rising and understandable irritation of Jack Straw. Eventually, after one hour and twenty-two minutes, I concluded and sat down.

Later, in the division lobby, Richard Shepherd, the quirky but respected and commendably candid MP for Aldridge Brownhills, came up to me to remonstrate. I should never have spoken for so long on a relatively uncontroversial Bill. What possessed me? As I told him that I was following orders, I felt unclean. I knew that I had been foolish. I should just have told the whips that I would do no such thing. I tell this story against myself – Ann Widdecombe did not mention it, or appear to hold a view about it – not least for its irony. Later, I was to be rebellious in the face of whip instructions on much bigger matters than the length of a speech. Indeed, I went on to develop a relationship with the Conservative whips characterised by trust and understanding: I did not trust them and they did not understand me. Yet on that occasion I meekly acceded to the whips' request. It wasn't a conscious attempt to secure advantage from them but a misguided boasting – look at me, I can do it and I will. Later, I regretted my minor sin.

* * *

The 2001 election campaign was not a success. For me, it started with a minor controversy. The Conservative Party's position on the single European currency was that, if elected, we would not join the Euro for at least two Parliaments. This was widely interpreted and reported as 'Tories say no to Euro for ten years'. However, many Conservatives objected in principle to any idea of abolishing the pound and joining the Euro. I was one of them, and I drafted my election literature accordingly, declaring that I was opposed to joining per se, constitutionally, for ever.

The Deputy Chief Whip, Patrick McLoughlin, got to hear of this and contacted me to say that I had gone beyond party policy. Well, I had, but I had not criticised the party or its leader. I was stating for Buckingham electors the position of the sitting Buckingham MP seeking re-election. I told Patrick that I did not think my paragraph on the Euro would undermine the party's election campaign and, as it transpired, I was right. It did not. William Hague was more than capable of repelling the voters on his own, and did so successfully. Patrick, however, a typical whip, wanted me to pulp my leaflets and do them again. To his horror, I told him that that was out of the question. The leaflets were already being delivered. Suddenly withdrawing them, or disavowing them, would cause far more trouble. Even McLoughlin, a rather unimaginative and slow-moving control freak, understood that.

The national campaign went nowhere. I happily trudged the streets of Buckingham and was relieved not to be part of the wider effort. We had nothing of great interest to say on schools, hospitals, the economy or the quality of life generally – and the public were firmly against us. By and large, they were better off, and felt that Labour, having made a reasonable start after eighteen years out of office, should be given the chance to continue.

Even though I had never warmed to Hague, I was surprised by the scale of the rejection of him. For four years Hague had been fluent, witty and combative in the House, often devastatingly effective in attacking and ridiculing Blair, but it counted for little. Where it mattered, in the ballot box, this youthful, geeky weirdo had achieved virtually nothing. We had increased our number of seats from 165 to 166. At that rate of progress, William would have become Prime Minister at the age of 840.

Hague himself knew at once that the result was not merely a shattering rejection of the Tories but also a shattering personal rejection. He resigned immediately and for the second time in four years the party squared up to the reality of a leadership contest.

Michael Portillo, the former Conservative Cabinet minister who had been spectacularly defeated in his Enfield Southgate constituency in 1997, had returned to Parliament in November 1999 as the MP for Kensington and Chelsea. He had undergone a good deal of public soul-searching and concluded that the Conservative Party had come to be viewed as unsympathetic to public services, to inequality, to the problem of urban poverty and to the rights of women, ethnic and sexual minorities. Still fundamentally Eurosceptic, Portillo had nevertheless reinvented himself as a more caring, compassionate Conservative rooted more in the centre ground of politics than in the radical right. Many on the right had deserted Portillo, not least because they felt he had sold out. I had not. I admired him, and when I received a call from Francis Maude asking if I would support Michael for the leadership I confirmed without hesitation that I would. I did not know then who else would stand but I did not need to. I believed Portillo was a courageous change-maker, the best person to lead us, and I wanted to support him.

The day after my conversation with Maude, I was phoned by Iain Duncan Smith, who asked me to support him. He planned to run as a Eurosceptic but as someone who also believed that the party had to change, and to attach a far greater priority to social cohesion and the quality of public services. I explained to him that I had already decided to back Michael. However, I then made a foolish mistake in telling Iain that in the unlikely event of Michael being defeated, I would support Iain if he remained in the contest. In other words, I told him that he was my second choice. That was foolish – and reckless – because the campaign was not yet under way and I was closing down my options when I did not need to do so.

Of course, against my expectations and those of many of his supporters, Michael Portillo's campaign failed. We underestimated the almost visceral hostility felt by many on the right who now viewed him as a touchy-feely, socially liberal, backsliding traitor. I cannot prove it but, following his 'admission' in his 1999 by-election of gay relationships in the past, I reckoned that there was also some homophobia directed at him. Iain Duncan Smith was now receiving the support of a lot of right-wing MPs. Moreover, Ken Clarke was the standard-bearer of the left and centre of the party and of some who simply believed, as they had in 1997, that Clarke was the best person to take on Tony Blair and New Labour. David Davis and Michael Ancram were candidates too, but it always seemed likely to come down to Portillo, Duncan Smith and Clarke.

Part of the problem with Portillo was that he did not appear to want to win. Hostile MPs questioned him about Section 28 and he hinted that he favoured its repeal. I had come round to that view myself and would express it at Party Conference four months later, but it was still toxic in the Tory Party. It is to Michael's credit that he did not duck it and that he also gave a measured answer to an enquiry about decriminalisation of cannabis, but his reasonableness on both subjects reinforced colleagues' suspicions of him. More widely, his performances on the campaign trail lacked sparkle and passion.

My sense was that he wanted the leadership but only on his terms. He was not prepared to duck and weave, to placate critics, to win the prize by making concessions on policy that would constrain him in seeking a fundamental transformation of his party. His implicit message was, 'This is who I am and what I believe. Take me or leave me.' It was an honourable stance and much to his credit. Unfortunately for him, and in particular for supporters like me, too few of his parliamentary colleagues wanted him. In the second ballot of MPs, Ken Clarke received 59 votes, Iain Duncan Smith 54 and Michael 53, so he was eliminated and the mass membership of the party in the country would have to choose between Ken and Iain. After Michael was eliminated, I bumped into him and said how terribly sorry I was. I was emotional, genuinely upset, and didn't hide it. Michael, utterly calm and composed, thanked me and said words to the effect that I should not be upset. It did not matter. He seemed almost relieved that the strain of being the favourite, the heir apparent, had been lifted and he was free now to do as he wished.

Many people who backed Portillo then took no further part in the leadership contest, an honourable and even sensible choice. For me it was different. Soon afterwards, John Hayes, a prominent supporter of IDS, approached me in the lobby and reminded me of my pledge to Iain, of which he had been informed. I agreed to support Iain. I had made a promise and did not want to break it. Also, though I knew in my heart that Ken was much the more able of the two, I feared that his insistence on his own strong pro-European views would institutionalise a split between the leader and the party, which was overwhelmingly Eurosceptic. I rationalised this belief by arguing that however much Ken wanted to turn the party's attention to domestic issues of health and education, he would be permanently bogged down by disputes over Europe. The party would have been divided, and divided parties lose elections.

David Cameron, then the newly elected Conservative MP for Witney, asked me to speak in favour of Iain Duncan Smith at a meeting in his constituency, where Sir George Young was to speak for Ken. Cleverly, and properly, Cameron did not take sides. He had supported Portillo, albeit not very vigorously, and thereafter remained neutral. He chaired the meeting and kindly invited me to join him for lunch at his home in the hamlet of Dean, near Chipping Norton. David and Sam Cameron were joined by Ed Vaizey, later to become Conservative MP for Wantage, and Rachel Whetstone, a well-known special adviser and friend of the Camerons. Rachel took the lead in cooking a delicious lunch. As it was a delightful summer's day, we ate in the garden. Unfortunately, wasps aplenty hovered over the food and, to my great embarrassment, I could not hide my discomfort and, yes, phobia of the wasp plague (I am terrified of wasps to this day). Cameron, and all of the others, might well have thought that I was paranoid, feeble or both, but they were all far too polite to say so. Cameron to his credit eventually suggested that we eat indoors, a generous decision that was a relief to me.

When Iain won the leadership, he invited me to join the Shadow Cabinet as Shadow Chief Secretary to the Treasury under the newly appointed Shadow Chancellor, Michael Howard. I was thrilled to be asked to join Iain's team and accepted without hesitation. It was a big promotion for me and I wanted to take up the challenge. When told that I would be working for Michael Howard, I momentarily thought of his famous fallout with Ann Widdecombe. He had a reputation for being a very difficult person and I could certainly think of others for whom I would have preferred to work. That said, Michael was regarded as a heavyweight and I could see why Iain wanted him back in the Shadow Cabinet. I resolved that I would do my utmost to support Michael and thereby to support Iain. Within weeks, I was invited to speak at the Cambridge Union alongside Ann Widdecombe. We travelled there together and she promptly offered her commiserations to me on my new role working for Howard. On the contrary, I said, I was looking forward to it. 'Yes,' she said, 'but you're working for a bad man.'

In fact, my working relationship with Michael started well enough. He had a sharp mind, immense experience of government and, at least in terms of how to oppose Labour, a sense of purpose. He chaired team meetings briskly and authoritatively but welcomed input. We decided upon initiatives – opposing wasteful expenditure, for example – and we all knew what we had to do. In the Chamber, Howard was a competent opponent to Gordon Brown, demonstrably better suited to the role than his predecessors had been. Of course, these were very early days after the 2001 election and it was far too soon for us as an Opposition to articulate a distinctive alternative to New Labour's economic policy. Rather, we were at the stage of mounting a general critique of Labour for spending, borrowing, and taxing too much.

As Shadow Chief Secretary, my task was to scrutinise public expenditure with a view to identifying inefficient or inappropriate uses of public funds. But our approach at this point was too often tactical rather than strategic. We were also totally outmanoeuvred by the Labour government's decision in 2002 to raise National Insurance by 1 per cent specifically to fund greater spending on the NHS. We denounced it as a tax hike that would hit working people and be spent by Labour inefficiently. Yet our attack – which I joined Michael in making as forcefully as I could – was utterly ineffective for the simple reason that the public as a whole bought Labour's argument. They were fully prepared to pay more in tax if the proceeds were to be used specifically to boost the NHS. Even though we didn't realise it at the time, Labour and the public were right and we were wrong. Whether Michael would accept that today, I have no idea, but that is the reality.

As Shadow Chancellor, Michael Howard sometimes had an unusual interpretation of wider policy commitments or IDS's leadership initiatives. IDS developed a theme known as Help the Vulnerable. That must be the Tory mission, he said, and he instructed each Shadow team to consider how it could protect or improve the position of vulnerable people through its emerging policies. Howard came up with the idea that we should champion (highly skilled and highly paid) oil-rig workers who, he judged, needed to be protected by a Conservative commitment to reverse planned changes in oil taxation. I am quite sure that Michael was sincere in this position but it struck me as cynical and not quite what Iain had had in mind.

Despite these minor differences, I applied myself diligently and Michael Howard and I worked well together. That is not to say that I ever liked him. Frankly, I didn't. Some people are cold. Others are oily. Michael's peculiar distinction was to combine coldness and oiliness in equal measure. Nevertheless, I got used to him and he to me. We had regular contact and, though his public image was poor, he was highly professional and a very accomplished performer at the despatch box. Those performances might not have resonated with the public but he lifted the morale of Conservative MPs with his efforts. Most importantly, whereas his predecessors almost visibly shrank when up against Gordon Brown, Michael was not at all intimidated by him.

* * *

Politics aside, my personal life had looked up too and I had managed to get back together with Sally. She acknowledged that I had mellowed in my style and views and was less obsessive and more relaxed. She had done a lot of soul-searching too and had quit partying and become teetotal. We agreed to give it one last go and, determined as we both were to make it work, Sally moved in with me again in December 2001.

This time round, living together was wonderful and we were both loved up. In late June 2002 I asked Sally to marry me. After a day at Wimbledon I returned to take Sally to the Cinnamon Club, a modern Indian restaurant on the site of the old Westminster Library. She readily accepted my proposal and we had an unforgettable dinner. Although Sally had been a Conservative activist at Oxford University, she had now been a Labour supporter for several years (and remains a committed member to this day). She was adamant that she would not play the conventional role of 'political wife', shuttling back and forth to Buckingham and hobnobbing with my Tory activists. Rather than have this 'revealed' by some journalist as though he or she were a veritable Sherlock Holmes uncovering a crime, we decided that in announcing our engagement we would be upfront about our political differences as they did not bother either of us and, therefore, should not matter to anyone else. I had to endure some gentle ribbing from colleagues about how I was punching above my weight.

* * *

While we were planning our wedding, and shortly before the Shadow Cabinet reshuffle in the summer of 2002, Michael Howard tipped me off that it was soon to take place and reassured me that he didn't expect either of us to feature in it. I was glad to hear it, but despite Michael's attempted reassurance I was called in to see Iain. He asked me to move to Shadow Minister for Work and Pensions. I was unenthusiastic but, probably unwisely, I agreed. I told Michael Howard, assuming that he would have known, saying that I knew that I would have stayed in his team if he had wanted me to do so and not if he didn't. With an air of injured innocence, Michael said that it was a great surprise to him. He later sent me a long letter assuring me of his innocence of any involvement. I didn't buy it. He was a very senior member of the Shadow Cabinet who would almost certainly have been consulted about his own team's make-up. However, I had little choice but to accept that he had not argued for my removal and to move on to the new role. Sure enough, it was reported as a demotion because, though still a member of the Shadow Cabinet, I had no Cabinet minister directly to shadow. That was done by David Willetts.

David was a very capable Shadow Secretary of State for Work and Pensions and an upbeat, personable boss. But I was not particularly interested in pensions policy, which although important is also dry and uninspiring. I was much less interested in it than in surveying public expenditure as I had done in the role of Shadow Chief Secretary. I was also irritated to be demoted and irritated with myself for having accepted the demotion. This would probably have been true whoever had been leader, but it was all the more galling given that Iain

Duncan Smith had had a calamitous first ten months as leader, with poll ratings in the toilet and my party looking to be light years away from a return to government. Over the summer recess, these considerations preyed on my mind and I began to think that I might not want to stay in the Shadow Cabinet much longer.

In the autumn, Iain made the bizarre decision, never debated in Shadow Cabinet but simply an edict from on high, that the party would oppose the government's move to allow unmarried and same-sex couples jointly to adopt children. There had been an earlier vote on the matter when the front bench had been told to abstain. Although in favour of gay adoption myself, I had reluctantly gone along with abstention. Now to be told that 'the line' was outright opposition was intolerable. I spoke both to Iain and to the Chief Whip, David Maclean, pleading with them not to adopt this reactionary stance. I thought they were wrong on the issue and that they risked opening an unnecessary fissure between the party's traditionalists and social liberals on what many people would regard as a conscience issue. For whatever reason, whether ideological conviction or rank stubbornness, more likely both, Iain was immovable. He said that I could stay away, abstaining quietly, but I must not vote for unmarried couples' right jointly to adopt. I thought about it, and called David Maclean the day before the vote to tell him that I wanted to vote for the change the government was proposing and would resign from the Shadow Cabinet in order to do so.

The following day, 4 November, I announced my resignation. I did not seek the publicity that ensued but it was bound to follow as resignations are judged newsworthy, all the more so if the leader from whose team you are resigning is already thought to be on the ropes. I went to the House for the Report Stage of the Adoption and Children Bill and spoke in support of the rights of unmarried heterosexual and gay couples and voted accordingly. I was joined by a sprinkling of Conservative colleagues, including Ken Clarke, David Curry, Julie Kirkbride, Andrew Lansley, Andrew MacKay, Francis Maude and Michael Portillo. The Conservative backbench rebellion was small but significant, as it heightened tensions within the party and greatly intensified the pressure on Iain Duncan Smith.

There were two effects of this saga. First, my stock was damaged with Conservatives but enhanced with Labour, and I received a lovely, gracious letter from the Leader of the House, Robin Cook. Secondly, the atmosphere of crisis around IDS was exacerbated by his decision to stage a press conference declaring that people were out to get him. He would have been wiser to play the issue down and simply focus on his agenda.

With the benefit of hindsight, I would do the same again. Iain was wrong on the issue – and the Conservatives have never subsequently sought to remove the right of unmarried heterosexual and gay couples jointly to adopt children. He was supremely unwise to make it a matter of party policy and a whipped vote, when he knew that there were principled differences of opinion on the Conservative benches. The more serious charge against me was about loyalty: I had been elevated to the Shadow Cabinet by Iain only fourteen months earlier, and my resignation was bound to add to his difficulties. I could see that argument but, frankly, though I was party to no plot against him, I had by then concluded that Iain's leadership was doomed. Either the party in Parliament would vote him out before a 2005 or 2006 election or he would lead us to heavy defeat at the polls. Therefore, even if resigning deepened his problems, it was only bringing forward the inevitable.

Many readers will conclude that I am not a team player. They would be right. I might have been a more 'successful' career politician if I were. We all have to make some compromises – at work, in our families, with friends. If Michael Portillo or Ken Clarke had been leader, neither would have taken Iain's stance on the issue, so I would have faced no such dilemma. However, there might have been some other issue on which I disagreed with them. Out of loyalty to and wider belief in them, perhaps I would have swallowed hard and remained in their front-bench team. I don't know. What I do know is that the public always say they want – and I think the country should have – honest politicians who don't simply toe the line and take the easy course, but who do what they think is right. I did and I have never regretted it.

* * *

Now on the backbenches, my thoughts and time were focused on my upcoming wedding.

On 7 December 2002 Sally and I were married in the Chapel of St Mary Undercroft in the House of Commons. Julian Lewis was my best man. With the kind permission of Michael Martin, our reception kicked off with drinks in Speaker's House and we were struck by its splendour – never imagining that, seven years later, we would end up living there ourselves. Sally and I then enjoyed an idyllic honeymoon in Cobblers' Cove, Barbados and the Grenadines. With fabulous weather, beautiful surroundings, amazing service and the minimum of human company, we savoured a kind of paradise. Completely relaxed, diverted from politics, looking at not a single newspaper or news broadcast, we ate, swam, sunbathed, read books to our hearts' content and unwound together. I had first met Sally thirteen years earlier. Our relationship had been up and down and we had been apart longer than we had been together, although we had remained firm friends throughout. Yet we wanted to be with each other and, for me, our wedding was the fulfilment of a thirteen-year quest.

* * *

In March 2003 the Labour government brought forward a proposal to repeal Section 28 of the 1988 Local Government Act. This was the provision inserted when Michael Howard had been Minister for Local Government that prohibited the 'promotion' of homosexuality in schools. I had concluded in 2001 what, to be fair, Labour and the Liberal Democrats had said back in 1988 – the idea that anyone can 'promote' homosexuality, persuading or lulling a young man or woman into being gay when he or she would not otherwise have been is frankly preposterous. If Michael Howard cannot now see that, he is not as clever as some people say he is and he thinks he is. If he can see how wrong he was, he ought to be ashamed of himself because Section 28 was one of the nastiest pieces of legislation in living memory. It achieved no positive benefit. It stigmatised. It humiliated. It needed to be repealed and Tony Blair's government was 100 per cent right to do so. When the House debated the matter in March 2003, I intervened briefly to make the case for repeal and voted accordingly.

Shortly after the Section 28 vote my constituency AGM took place. The atmosphere was frosty as many local activists were upset that I had resigned over gay adoption and, in particular, uncomfortable with my public criticism of Iain Duncan Smith. I had given a television interview to David Frost in which I had lamented the party's poor poll ratings, blamed Iain's leadership and declared that on present trends the Conservatives' chances of winning the next election were about as great as those of finding an Eskimo in the desert.

Speaking the truth is often unpopular. It was certainly unpopular with my activists. They had predominantly voted for IDS, with my encouragement, only eighteen months earlier and they didn't like being told that they and I had got it wrong. Yet that was the simple reality.

Iain's leadership of the party continued to be weak. His performances in the Chamber were poor and, increasingly, colleagues felt that he had shrunk rather than grown into the office of leader. Having been a rebel under John Major, albeit a few years back, this was neither forgotten nor forgiven by many mainstream colleagues. It was hard for him credibly to demand loyalty from backbenchers – a problem later suffered by Jeremy Corbyn in his leadership of the Labour Party – and some colleagues were aghast at the fulsome support he gave Tony Blair over the Iraq War. Here, as it happened, I did not dissent and criticise him, and I would not do so now. I thought Blair was right about Iraq and, indeed, I think so to this day. On 18 March 2003 I voted for military intervention. Standing next to Tony Blair in the division lobby that evening, I congratulated him to his evident stupefaction. 'Well, I'm very grateful, John, but you have never previously supported me on anything.' This was not entirely accurate, as my votes on the age of consent and gay adoption testify, but I could understand his surprise.

A few months later Francis Maude approached me to say that IDS was flailing and liable to sink. In his view there were only two people who might be able to take over the party leadership without a bloody contest: Oliver Letwin and Michael Howard. I said that of the two, I favoured Oliver. He replied that Oliver would almost certainly not run for the leadership but, if pressed, Michael Howard would. That was no surprise. I expressed a lack of enthusiasm for Howard – in particular a real concern that he would not appeal to the public – though I accepted that he might, not least in Parliament, be more competent than Iain.

Before long, the requisite number of letters from Conservative MPs to the chairman of the 1922 Committee, the backbenchers' convener, Michael Spicer, had been received. A vote on IDS was thereby triggered and he was defeated by 90 votes to 75. I had eventually written to Michael Spicer requesting a vote and I then voted against Iain. I felt no personal malice towards Iain. I simply felt that he was doomed to fail. He had been in post for fourteen months, suffered dreadful ratings and showed no sign that he could lead effectively. Typically, Iain accepted his defeat with good grace and the way was cleared for a leadership contest if the parliamentary party wanted it. However, it didn't. As Francis Maude had correctly surmised, the party wanted not a contest, but a coronation. Michael Howard, capable but profoundly unattractive, wanted to lead the party. Neither Michael Portillo nor Ken Clarke, who would have enjoyed broader appeal, was interested and so Michael Howard was elected leader uncontested. It was the only way he could win – with no opponents.

In his public pronouncements, Michael worked hard to portray himself as a One Nation Conservative – moderate, a healer, committed to bringing not merely the party but the country together. I was agreeably surprised by his pitch, which he reinforced in a telephone conversation with me, insisting that it was his genuine view and his commitment as would-be leader.

By December Sally and I were expecting our first child and staying with my mother-in-law in Surrey while our London flat was being renovated. It was one of the few occasions in our marriage when Sally and I just did not realise what the other thought. She remembered that I had not warmed to Howard when I served as his deputy and, more particularly, she thought that he had no chance whatsoever of leading the Conservative Party to victory in an election. She was therefore surprised when I told her that I did not expect to be asked to serve on his front bench but that, if I were offered a meaningful role, I would take it. Sure enough, Michael offered me the post of Shadow Secretary of State for International Development. In one sense, it was a mistake for me to accept. I should just have stayed on the backbenches, and spent more time with Sally and our about-to-arrive son. In another sense it was positive, as I started to get to grips with a new brief and developed a real passion for the agenda of tackling global poverty.

I was shadowing Hilary Benn, who was fast establishing himself as an effective and popular Secretary of State for International Development. My task was difficult for two reasons: Hilary was extremely good, and Michael Howard showed little knowledge of and less interest in development policy. Instead he was obsessed with the EU aid budget, which he wanted to repatriate to the UK. This was not legally possible without the agreement of all the other EU member states, and gave the aid community the impression that the Tories were simply obsessing about Europe again. However, it played well with right-wing backbenchers and I made frankly half-hearted efforts on this score to appease the barking dog.

One of the challenges of being an Opposition spokesperson on international development is that, unlike the government, you do not have access to a budget that enables you to travel widely to see some of the most wretched living conditions on the planet. But through an organisation called Christian Solidarity Worldwide I came to know one of their advocacy officers, Ben Rogers, and he asked to meet me to discuss Myanmar. What did I know of the country? That it was run by a brutal military dictatorship with contempt for human rights. Beyond that, I was ignorant. Ben, who struck me at our first meeting in Westminster in early 2004 as principled, wise and determined, confirmed this and asked if I would join him and others from CSW on a trip to the Thailand–Myanmar border to observe the plight of the refugees there. I agreed. CSW organised and funded the trip. It was an eye-opener. On that fateful trip – fateful because it imbued me with a fascination for Myanmar and its people that endures to this day – I heard shocking accounts of the most egregious violations of human rights. Rape as a weapon of war, extra-judicial killings, forced labour, compulsory relocation, deployment of human minesweepers, the use of child labour on a scale proportionately greater than anywhere in the world, the destruction of churches, the incarceration of political opponents in the most bestial conditions – all these were part of the cocktail of sav-agery served up by the ruling regime's army, the Tatmadaw. I heard eyewitness accounts of children who had seen their parents shot dead in front of them and, even more shocking still, accounts of parents who had been forced to observe their children shot dead in front of them.

I met people of different faiths and backgrounds, but one extraordinary experience remains indelibly imprinted on my mind fifteen years later. I was introduced to a Karen – native of Karen state – Christian, an opponent of the military junta, who had been seized by the Tatmadaw and subjected to ex-cruciating water torture by a soldier. Through an interpreter, I asked him what he thought of his torturer, expecting a flow of furious denunciation. To my utter astonishment, he looked me in the eye and replied, 'I love him, for he is my broth-er.' Almost mesmerised by this man's stoicism and spirit of forgiveness, I knew from that moment that the people of My-anmar occupied a special place in my heart and would always do so. Time and again, on that trip and in subsequent visits, I was struck by the formidable combination of dignity, love and resolve in the hearts of the people – religious or irreligious, ethnic Myanmarans or from minority national groups – which impelled me and others to reflect on the plight of the country.

I became ever more immersed in the development role and convinced that my party should commit, as Labour had done, to spend 0.7 per cent of GDP on overseas aid. As I saw it there was plenty of scope for the UK, a relatively rich country, to do more to help the world's most destitute people. Of course, there was and no doubt always will be a right-wing lobby in the Conservative Party and parts of the media who argued that aid spending was a waste of money or preached that 'charity begins at home'. The answer to the first point is to ensure that we constantly seek value for money and the assurance that money goes where it is needed most. The answer to the second is that the UK can and should do both – help the poor at home *and* abroad. It is a false dichotomy to say that we have to choose between the two. Also, upgrading our commitment to the fight against global poverty was also vital politically to the Conservative Party if it was to overcome its 'nasty' image and prove that it had changed.

* * *

As has been well documented elsewhere, in the aftermath of the Iraq War, controversy raged about the government's claim that Saddam Hussein had possessed 'weapons of mass destruction' and that he was capable of unleashing an attack on us in forty-five minutes. There was a widespread belief that Tony Blair had led the country to war on flawed intelligence, thereby inadvertently misleading Parliament or, worse still, under false pretences by deliberately misleading Parliament. I have never believed that he wilfully misled anyone, but many did and still do. Inquiries by Lord Hutton and the former Cabinet Secretary, Robin Butler, examined the issues. The Hutton Report exonerated Blair. The Butler inquiry was more nuanced, containing much criticism, but it stopped short of any fatal allegation. When that report came to be debated in Parliament, Michael Howard, who had voted for the war and given no previous indication that he regretted it, delivered an extraordinary, embarrassing and excruciating speech in July 2004. When I say embarrassing, I was frankly less embarrassed by Michael, more embarrassed for him. It was a pitiful, risible speech in which he attempted to turn up the heat on Blair by suggesting that if he (Howard) had known at the time of the vote what he knew now, he would have voted differently. It came across so badly, making Michael look shifty and opportunistic. The speech was judged to be that of a contortionist, trying to shift his stance for personal and party advantage. Blair brushed the attack aside with ease. Far from damaging Blair, Michael's attack damaged only Michael.

Writing to Tony Blair shortly afterwards about the situation in Darfur, I began by congratulating him on his speech in the Butler inquiry debate and, rashly, leaked it to the media. I should not have done so but it was my honest view that Blair had made a compelling case. Of course, feeling strongly that Michael was wrong, I should have told him so directly or kept my mouth shut. I didn't because I knew that it would make no difference, that I didn't have much of a rapport with him anyway and telling him a hard truth would exacerbate relations. Moreover, I readily acknowledge that at that point I was still enjoying the Shadow International Development role and preferred to retain it.

Understandably, however, that was not to be. In September 2004 Michael Howard reshuffled his front bench. I received a message to go to his office. There he told me that he did not think that I had shown myself to be a team player, and intended to remove me from that post. However, he would like me to remain on the Opposition front bench as Shadow Secretary of State for Constitutional Affairs. Unfortunately there was no Secretary of State for Constitutional Affairs to shadow. Michael also started talking about the Labour Party having packed quangos with Labour appointees – the idea was that I would study the record and expose the great 'jobs for chums' scandal. It sounded neither an inspiring task nor much of a scandal. All in all, I found the offer unattractive but Michael claimed that he would be pleased if I would take it. I asked if I could think about it and get back to him within the hour. I did so, spoke to Sally, who thought it an absurd offer, and returned to decline it.

Knowing that I was leaving the Conservative front bench and feeling some relief, I told Michael that I did have some thoughts about him and the state of the party but, of course, he was entitled to tell me to leave. To his credit, he said that he was happy to hear them. I said that when he had stood for the leadership he had presented himself as a One Nation, moderate Tory – a departure from his established image as a right-winger – but I did not think that he had effectively developed that 'brand'. More widely, he had achieved no cut-through with voters. He had not even begun to establish himself in the public mind as a credible alternative Prime Minister to Tony Blair, and his attack on the Prime Minister over Iraq had been painfully ineffective.

At this point, Howard, who had listened patiently, said that he recognised that the speech had not been well received but that he stood by it. Warming to his theme, he said he intended in the approach to the election to expose Tony Blair as a liar over his handling of the run-up to the Iraq War. I replied that I thought that would be a terrible mistake.

'Why?' he enquired. 'It's true. He is.'

I replied that I did not subscribe to that view. Voters do not like hearing one politician attack another for lying. They regard it as cheap, childish and sordid. It would be ineffective, and would just make him and us look nasty. Given that the party had had this image problem for years, we should be seeking to counter, not reinforce it. He added that I had spoken to him in very blunt terms. Indeed I had. I indicated that I had come to the conclusion that Ann Widdecombe was right about him, and that I was now very happy to return to the backbenches.

When I had entered Parliament, I had been excited to be a parliamentarian, spending time in the Chamber, debating great issues, speaking up for my constituents. Unlike many on both sides of the House who have a clear vision of how they wish to progress and what portfolio they might like to hold, I had had no such vision. If anything, I had for a time flirted with the idea that it would be fun to be Party Chairman, rallying the troops. But as I saw more clearly from 2001 onwards just how reactionary, out of touch and dwindling a bunch the grass-roots activists across the country had become, I recoiled from any such idea.

I could now face the truth that I was unsuited to service

on the front bench. I had not rated Hague, Duncan Smith or Howard as leaders, and was not interested in signing up to a collective line when I dissented from important parts of it. For now, I was happy to serve on the backbenches and to represent my Buckingham constituents.

4

From Backbench to Chair

In September 2004 Labour were still ahead in the polls and there seemed every prospect of an election the following spring. Relieved of front-bench duties, I wanted to spend a little more time with Sally and our son, Oliver, now nine months old. I also wanted to persuade the Conservative whips to allow me to join the International Development Select Committee, so that I could pursue my interest in scrutinising the Labour government's work on tackling global poverty. I intended to speak in the Chamber on issues important to me and, of course, had to prepare for the expected election ahead.

Fortunately, the Chief Whip seemed happy enough to put me on the select committee and I made an early visit to Malawi, Mozambique and Botswana in January 2005. Just before leaving I was surprised to receive a call from Michael Howard, who wanted to tell me that he was about to make a major speech on immigration. It would attack the Labour government and call for tighter controls. I was uneasy about it as I had strongly supported the attempt first made in 2001 by Iain Duncan Smith to change the Tory narrative: I was nervous that we would simply retreat into a right-wing laager and license more extreme Tories to fulminate about immigrants, rendering us unpleasant and unelectable. Already, as I had told Michael in our meeting when I left the front bench, he had retreated from his One Nation pledge and I feared a further descent, this time into dog-whistle politics. Michael assured me that his approach would be measured, though when I told him that I would be abroad for twelve days on a select committee trip, he sounded very relieved indeed. Sure enough, he made his speech and it was followed by a continued focus on the subject up to and through the general election.

Three issues stood out for me in the run-up to the 2005 general election. In October 2004 I spoke and voted for the Second Reading of the Civil Partnerships Bill. Labour wanted to give legal recognition for the first time to same-sex partners keen to enter a formal union with each other, though it stopped short of calling such unions marriages. In retrospect, it is possible to argue that the government should have been bolder, and simply legislated for same-sex marriage. Yet at the time Stonewall, the leading LGBT campaigning group, was not arguing for marriage and ministers were anxious not to ride too far ahead of public opinion. In 2004 the government's proposal was viewed as bold and progressive, generally welcomed by the LGBT community and objected to by traditionalists who saw it – in a way correctly – as marriage in all but name.

Some of those traditionalists voiced their opposition explicitly and uncompromisingly, but Michael Howard sprang a welcome surprise not only by announcing that Conservative MPs would have a free vote on the Bill but also declaring that he himself would vote for it. Obviously I would have voted for this Bill, whip or no whip, but there is no doubt that Howard's decision led to lots of Conservative MPs voting for progressive change who would not otherwise have done so. He led and they followed, and having had a woeful record on LGBT matters his change of tack was welcome.

When I spoke on the issue I reminded the House that my own party had much to prove on LGBT equality, as none of the current Shadow Cabinet had voted for an equal age of consent in February 2000 and only one had voted in March 2003 for the repeal of Section 28. I urged my Conservative colleagues to support the Bill – there could be no better signal that my party had changed than for them to do so. It is impossible to say how many of them backed the Bill in its original, progressive form, before an unwelcome and unnecessary amendment by the Conservative Peer Baroness O'Cathain. Yet the fact that sixty-six Conservative MPs voted to allow the Bill to progress into committee was heartening.

Shortly before Christmas 2004, I spoke again, in opposition to Labour's Identity Cards Bill, motivated once more by small 'l' liberal principles. This put me at odds with both government and Opposition front benches, but that did not bother me or the handful of other Conservatives who objected to what we saw as an unnecessary and draconian measure.

Just before the House dissolved for the 2005 general election, the government introduced a new Equality Bill, which provided for the creation of a new Equality and Human Rights Commission, a one-stop shop for alleged victims of discrimination. The law would prohibit discrimination on grounds of religion or belief and it would impose a new duty to promote gender equality. Parliament would need to return to the issue but the government was on the right track and, fortunately, my party did not oppose it.

From that happy moment of cross-party unity, we departed for our constituencies. As always, I took the campaign seriously just as I always worked hard in between elections. Every MP should treat his or her constituents with respect – serving people effectively and earning, not assuming, their support. I knew that my seat was likely to be safe and that the biggest factors in determining the size of one's majority are the national standings of the parties and how one's opponents' votes divide. In other words, the content of a candidate's literature probably makes very little difference, though 'very little' does not mean none. In any case, I wanted to put my own Conservative message across and, now holding no front-bench role, I was free to write my own leaflets without signing up to screeds of text recommended by campaign headquarters. With an eye to the tiny band of Conservative activists who deplored my support for gay equality, I deliberately highlighted it in my literature. Generally, though, the campaign in Buckingham was quiet. I took part in a few hustings with the other candidates. Good-natured in tone, they will have shifted few votes, but I thought it right to show my face, defend my record and answer questions.

The national context was again inauspicious for the Conservatives. Blair had been damaged by the finding that Saddam Hussein had had no weapons of mass destruction, and his standing was not what it had been at the election four years earlier, still less that of 1997. Nevertheless, the economy was strong, public services better than the Conservatives had left them and Blair still came across as a competent leader who understood and shared voters' priorities. Michael Howard was competent and efficient but he was very much a throwback to the past: he looked and sounded passé, out of touch, a relic from a bygone age to which people had no wish to return.

Labour's vote share fell to a mere 35.2 per cent, but those peeled off from Labour mostly went to the Liberal Democrats, who saw an historic sixty-two MPs elected under their banner. The Conservative vote share rose by a paltry 0.7 per cent, but the Party was rewarded with thirty-three extra MPs. My own majority in Buckingham rose significantly from 13,325 to 18,129, and I notched up over 57 per cent of the vote. Personally, I was content in my patch but nationally the result was poor. I offered a post-mortem in the *Independent* the Monday after polling, arguing that the campaign had been limited in scope, disciplined in execution and as successful as could be expected – i.e., not very. The daunting fact was that we still had fewer than 200 seats in the Commons and we would need very big gains next time to form a majority government. I was critical on several fronts. Calling Tony Blair a liar had been unwise. It made us look nasty and played straight into the hands of the Liberal Democrat leader, Charles Kennedy, whose party was a more natural repository for anti-Iraq War votes anyway. Our manifesto had been embarrassingly thin, offering neither a vision for Britain nor a programme for government.

I argued that we needed new priorities, beginning with a Tory vision of economic efficiency and social justice. On top of that, we had to acknowledge that people expect governments to offer quality public services. Simply offering an escape route to the private sector was a counsel of despair that left people concluding that the Conservatives had given up on them. The party itself needed to change, as we were woefully short of women, black, Asian and minority ethnic (BAME) candidates and people from less affluent backgrounds. A wholesale modernisation of the party from top to bottom was required.

Yet of all the criticisms by which I stand to this day, the charge that stung Michael Howard above all was that we had focused far too much on immigration, even though it was nowhere near the top of voters' priorities. 'Repeatedly highlighting the issue seemed at best obsessive and at worst repellent,' I said. The leader was furious. A meeting of the parliamentary party had been called shortly after the election but, because I had a family commitment that morning, I did not attend. I was amused when my colleague Andrew Mitchell phoned later to say that Howard had singled me out for particular criticism. Poor old Michael, a failed leader impersonating a fire-breathing dragon. I stood by my critique – if he didn't like it, he could lump it, and soon would when the party replaced him as leader a few months after his justified resignation.

The leadership contest that followed Howard's announcement of his plan to depart was a lengthy saga. The party was rudderless for months, but it did mean that pretenders to the Tory crown had time to decide whether to run and, having done so, to make their case. This favoured David Cameron. On the day after the election, David Davis was best placed, the obvious right-of-centre candidate, while Ken Clarke, a two-time loser of Conservative leadership contests, was the clear alternative. Still with a high profile and widely admired in the country, Clarke had added another distinctive selling point to his unique claim to be the only pro-European candidate on offer. He had opposed the Iraq War from the start, and would therefore have great credibility in criticising Tony Blair for his handling of it, whereas all of the other candidates had sided with Blair on the issue and could not risk displaying the slippery opportunism that had made Michael Howard look so ridiculous.

Straight away I decided to back Ken Clarke. I did not agree with him on Europe or on Iraq, so why on earth was I backing him? I did so because I thought that in political weight and potential appeal to voters he was streets ahead of anyone else. I didn't need to see a full field to make this decision. David Davis I knew and regarded as sharp, but with limited judgement and the weakness of being a poor public speaker. Liam Fox was a hard-line Thatcherite. Politically, I had long parted company with him and, while I did not dislike him personally and we had continued to enjoy civil relations, I felt that he would be more of the same. Liam was not a moderniser. However, David Cameron did present himself as a moderniser and many people thought he was. Why did I not consider backing him, especially given that Ken Clarke had lost twice, was already sixty-five years old and had little interest in themes that mattered to modernisers?

Put bluntly, I didn't like Cameron and, wrongly, I thought that the country would not either. I had known him – albeit not well – since the end of the 1980s. He had been a very capable researcher at Conservative Central Office and later a special adviser to Michael Howard and Norman Lamont. He was fluent and superficially charming but I simply did not accept that he was a believer in modernisation as I had become, or frankly a believer in anything much in particular. I would always defend him against the charge from the right that he was not a Conservative at all. That is wrong. He was, and is, fundamentally Conservative, a supporter of tradition, the status quo and the idea that people like him, of his background and class, were born to rule. He travelled light in terms of firm policy ideas – he had very few – and whereas some thought that a political advantage, I felt that he was insubstantial, lightweight, someone who saw politics as a game that it was his inherited duty, and right, to play and win. He always strode the corridors with an air of superiority – sniffy, supercilious and deeply snobbish.

Secondly, I made the perennial mistake not merely of politicians but of most people much of the time. If we dislike something, we often think that others will too. I genuinely believed that David Cameron, blue-blooded, born with a silver trolley service in his mouth, a stranger to any material disadvantage, would just not cut through to millions of ordinary voters who had to struggle. Of course, Tony Blair, a product of Fettes, often known as the Scottish Eton, had also been posh but I thought he was different – less obviously posh, not superior in manner and, above all, the leader of the workers' party. It struck me that it was easier for him to get away with his poshness as he led a party that was not made up of, or in existence to protect, the affluent.

The Conservatives, I reasoned, had not been led by a proper toff since Douglas-Home (unsuccessfully) or, just before that, by Macmillan. Instinctively, I felt that for all his fluency, easy charm and apparent blokeishness – 'call me Dave' – he would not resonate with the mass of voters. I mention his easy charm but, like most politicians, Ken Clarke and myself included, there has always been an 'edge' to Cameron, who knows what he wants and is gritty in pursuit of it. When things don't go his way, he can be irascible, even petulant.

It has almost been lost in the mists of time, but during that 2005 leadership campaign Cameron started slowly and lagged well behind other candidates in the polls. Indeed, it was even briefly suggested in some quarters that he might drop out, though I doubt he ever intended to do so. At one stage, he launched an attack on Ken Clarke for his pro-European views. It struck me as at best intemperate, at worst plain nasty. That weekend, I was on media duty for the Clarke campaign. Interviewed by Steve Richards, I was scathing about Cameron, noting that he was struggling, inexperienced and suggesting that he needed to calm down. I also had a few digs at his privileged background. It was a personal attack and reported as such. Yet, as the record shows, Cameron turned the contest around with an accomplished conference speech delivered without notes but based on having committed tracts of material to memory. By contrast, David Davis, never a strong platform speaker, delivered an unremarkable speech badly and it was written up in damning terms. Ken Clarke delivered an excellent conference speech but I feared that when Conservative MPs voted, he would struggle, and so it proved. To his credit, Ken would not compromise his pro-European stance but it was that stance, together with his age and two previous failed leadership bids, which worked against him. Of the fifty-one new Conservative MPs elected in 2005, only one, John Penrose, declared for Ken. It looked bleak for my preferred candidate and when MPs voted in October 2005, Ken came fourth behind Davis, Cameron and Fox, and was eliminated.

Shortly afterwards, George Osborne called me and asked if I would come in to see Cameron. Of course, the contest was about to go to the mass membership so my vote was no longer of much significance, but Cameron naturally wanted to be able to claim the maximum support among MPs. I had denounced him in my support for Clarke, but when it came down to a choice between him and David Davis, I told him at that meeting that I would vote for him, and did. At that same, one-to-one meeting he asked me what I wanted to do. I said that I looked forward to continuing on the backbenches and acting as an outrider for modernisation. He mentioned that there were no hard feelings on his part about what I had said about him, rushing to explain that he knew that he probably should have resigned from the all-male White's Club but had not done so because his father had been a long-standing member and because the club served 'a jolly good lunch'.

Frankly, I did not buy his profession of 'no hard feelings', thinking that it was his attempt at magnanimity when he knew he now had my vote, was likely to become leader and would thereafter certainly not need me. It was an amiable enough exchange and I genuinely looked forward to continuing on the backbenches and biding my time before standing for Speaker when there was a vacancy. More important than any of the above, I looked forward to being a dad again as Sally gave birth to our second child, Frederick (Freddie) James on 8 November 2005.

* * *

The idea of one day standing for election as Speaker myself had first been planted in my mind a few years earlier, in 2003. One summer's evening, Sally and I had gone for a drink with the former Conservative Cabinet minister Jonathan Aitken and his wife, Elizabeth, at their home in Chelsea. As we have seen, I had first come to know Jonathan in 1995 when, as Chief Secretary to the Treasury in John Major's government, he appointed me as his special adviser. Throughout his subsequent travails, we had remained on friendly terms and are to this day.

By this time I had enjoyed the freedom of the backbenches for several months, but Jonathan told me that night that he hoped I would return to the Conservative front bench. After telling him that I was not at all sure that I wanted to do so, his ears pricked up.

'Of course,' he said, 'there are other routes to fulfilment in politics than simply becoming a government minister. You may recall that my godfather, Selwyn Lloyd, was sacked as

Chancellor in 1962. He stayed in Parliament as a backbench MP and, nine years later, he was elected Speaker.' He added, with a grin, 'Just a thought, John.'

As Sally and I went home that night, we discussed the idea and it appealed. I loved Parliament, delighted in debating but also in hearing others debate, and was none too keen on the idea of singing from a collective hymn sheet as ministers and Shadow ministers inevitably have to do. One way to bolster my credentials for the Speakership when it arose would be learning to chair debates. From the moment I had returned to the backbenches in September 2004, I had intended to apply to join the Speaker's Panel of Chairs, responsible for chairing debates in Westminster Hall and Bill committees in the so-called Committee Corridor. Once the new Parliament was under way I sidled up to the senior Deputy Speaker, Sir Alan Haselhurst, who had day-to-day responsibility for appointing Members to the Panel of Chairs and expressed interest in joining. He was friendly, noted my interest but made no commitment. However, within days, I had a letter from him, confirming my appointment as from 7 June 2005.

Soon afterwards, Eric Forth, Conservative MP for Bromley and Chislehurst and himself a member of the panel, congratulated me and volunteered two immediate thoughts. First, he told me that new members of the panel tended to be inducted gently – it might be at least six months and probably twelve before I was asked to chair a Bill, which ordinarily would be shared with a panel member from the other side of the House. I felt slightly deflated at the thought of such a wait as, typically, I was bursting with enthusiasm and self-confidence, wanting to get stuck in. Nevertheless, for once in my life, I made no fuss, simply indicating to the House officer whose task it was to find a chair for each Bill that I was ready to help whenever he wanted.

Eric's second point was that if I had to rebuke a Labour Member for being 'out of order' – going on too long, off the subject, or using unparliamentary language – it was helpful to my credibility as an impartial chair to be able to rebuke someone from the Conservative side on the same day if possible. It was sound advice and I sought at once to follow it.

When I joined the panel, I told my good friend Julian Lewis of my longer-term plan to become Speaker. His immediate reaction was that I would be bored stiff listening to others speak when in most cases I could do so as well or better myself. I assured him, as Sally had long been convinced, that I would enjoy it, and that in the run-up to any Speakership contest I would set out a credo for necessary reform that would enhance Parliament. Fairly soon afterwards, Julian accepted that I was enjoying my panel-chairing and that there was scope for positive change in terms of scrutiny and backbench opportunity. He could see what many did not: that I would have a decent chance of becoming Speaker and then of trying to bring about reform.

I sat on the panel for just over four years. In that time, I chaired eight Bills, thirty-nine delegated legislation committees and eight European committees, as well as dozens of debates in Westminster Hall. In total, I took the chair in those proceedings for an estimated two hundred hours. What may be said of the experience?

First, the transition from being a participant in debates to chairing them was real enough. It caused friends to ask me if that transition was difficult, either in the sense that I would lapse inadvertently into making my own points or in that I simply had to hold myself back while privately wanting to hold forth. In truth, neither was a problem for me. I was obliged to remain impartial, and anyway any hint of partisanship would have been obvious and my membership of the Speaker's Panel of Chairs would have been lucky to last four weeks rather than four years. Also, I was by then working cross-party on issues close to my heart and had largely lost interest in the wider party battle.

Serving on the Panel of Chairs led colleagues to see me in a different role and, perhaps, to start to see me in a different light. Alun Michael, for example, the then Minister for Industry and the Regions, noted when he saw me in the chair for a Westminster Hall debate on enterprise that he would not be able to 'enjoy [my] usual vigorous interventions'. He went on to say that 'putting you in the chair is probably the only way to keep you in order. Nonetheless, a poacher turned gamekeeper can demonstrate characteristics that have not previously been seen, and I am sure that you will be strict.'

I could suggest to readers that chairing Bill committees, delegated legislation committees or Westminster Hall debates is very difficult but I won't because, frankly, it isn't. When I first joined the panel, I was surprised by the number of colleagues who said that they would not feel at all comfortable with the task. Puzzled, I asked why. They gave one or other of two reasons, sometimes both. First, colleagues cited the difficulty of remembering the names of their fellow MPs. Bill committees are rarely attended by more than twenty people at a time and there is a list of all the Members on the chair's desk, so it really isn't difficult. In any case, if you do momentarily forget a name or constituency, a clerk of the Public Bill Committee is seated next to the chair and can invariably fill the gap.

Others baulked at the procedural complexity. True, the chair had to keep track of the order in which new clauses and amendments are debated and then voted on, and deciding what amendment in a group should or should not be subject to another vote can be awkward. You cannot afford to lose concentration, be answering emails or doing a crossword. Otherwise, the techniques are easy enough to learn and the chair improves with practice, growing with confidence in the process. Throughout, as a chair, I valued the presence, administrative help and, when necessary, the procedural expertise of the Clerks.

Some of the debates I chaired were more interesting than

others – Israel and the Occupied Palestinian Territories, Child Poverty and Air Ambulances were more stimulating than debates on double taxation relief, but I can honestly say that I invariably found a point of interest in what a colleague said or how he or she said it. I remember bumping into a fellow panel member, a down-to-earth, likeable colleague from the North-East, and asking him what he had done that day.

'Chairing in Westminster Hall,' he replied.

'This morning or this afternoon?' I asked.

'Both,' he complained. 'Bored out of me fookin' skull.'

I admired his honesty but that was not my experience. I enjoyed it, and the sense that someone had to chair these meetings, and I could do it as least as well as the next person and, perhaps, better than most, was inspiring to me. In some debates, I might need to interrupt frequently if it became rowdy or discourteous. More often, I would need to do so very rarely but, like driving on a motorway, a committee chair cannot switch off. I had to be alert at all times as I could not be sure if or when I might need to intervene, to respond to a Point of Order or to deal with an unseemly spat that would suddenly break out between colleagues. For the most part, I tried, like a good football referee, to intervene very little. Good chairing is about commanding respect for your knowledge, concentration, fairness and capacity to facilitate a free-flowing though orderly debate. It is much less about imposing discipline.

* * *

As I moved to the centre politically from 2001 onwards, it was perhaps inevitable that I would be informally approached in Westminster corridors by Labour and Liberal Democrat MPs urging me to ditch the Conservatives and join them. It was not a very frequent occurrence, but it would happen from time to time. The tenor of the appeal would be, 'John, you deserve better than to be ignored by your party. You would be more comfortable with us and our leadership would recognise your talents.' These blandishments were often sincere but I rebuffed them in every case.

However, after the 2005 election, two newly elected Labour MPs with whom I began to establish some cross-party rapport were Ed Miliband and Ed Balls. The former had seen my Buckingham election literature, commented favourably upon it and suggested that it contained nothing Labour would oppose, and much that it would embrace. Miliband and I did not mix socially but we got on well in Parliament. I respected his intellect and commitment to social justice. When Gordon Brown became Prime Minister in June 2007 both Eds were deservedly promoted to the Cabinet. An early priority for Gordon was to try to reach out to disaffected Conservatives and, more widely, to develop a so-called 'GOAT' (Government of All the Talents), drawing in people from outside the Labour Party who were either willing to join his government or to advise it in some way. On day one of his administration, Gordon Brown was delighted to secure the defection from the Conservatives to Labour of the MP for Grantham and Stamford, Quentin Davies, an intelligent pro-European ex-banker who had represented his Conservative seat for twenty years and served in Iain Duncan Smith's Shadow Cabinet.

I was friendly with Quentin from our work together on the International Development Select Committee but had no inkling he had been in discussion with Labour about the possibility of crossing the floor. After all, defection is analogous to a government decision to devalue the currency. It has to be decided in a very tightly knit group and kept secret, even denied, until the last minute. About half an hour before Quentin was due to go public, he had popped in to see me to tip me off but I was not in the office at the time. Shortly afterwards, he made a minor attempt to persuade me to join him but I indicated that I preferred to make the case for Conservative modernisation and to proceed with my own, probably long-term, bid to become Speaker of the House.

No sooner had Quentin lobbied me than Ed Miliband called and asked if I would meet for a chat. It was no surprise when we met that he appealed to me to reconsider my allegiance to the Conservatives. I was far too progressive for them, he felt. There was no way that they would change fundamentally, as most Conservative MPs and activists had no desire to do so and David Cameron wanted a superficial respray rather than a wholly new direction. By contrast, he said, Gordon Brown would want me at the heart of his Labour project. I told him I felt a basic commitment to Conservative values and to my Buckingham constituency. Although my party was flawed, I preferred to be an independent-minded member of it than to jump ship. Ed accepted this with good grace but said that Gordon Brown was interested in looking afresh at a number of areas of policy. He hoped that I would consider working with Ed Balls on special educational needs. I agreed to meet Balls and at that meeting he asked that I lead a review of services for children and young people with speech, language and communication needs. I would be able to put together an advisory group, to take evidence and to issue recommendations to him and the Health Secretary, Alan Johnson. I agreed, believing that there was a chance to deliver improvement in services to vulnerable young people.

The reaction to my acceptance of this role was instructive. David Cameron, who had in earlier years professed great interest in special educational needs and had the most understandable and powerful personal motivation for doing so, showed no interest whatsoever. The Conservative Chief Whip, Patrick McLoughlin, was characteristically surly, grudgingly acknowledging that I had every right to do the work but moaning that my appointment was a propaganda coup for Gordon Brown. However, I told McLoughlin that any PR gain for Labour was tiny and short-term. If the Labour government implemented the advisory group's recommendations, the winners would be the young people who would benefit.

In my constituency, among voters, I received warm encouragement. However, in my local party I was warned by my agent that a few activists were grumbling about my decision and half a dozen members of the Conservative executive went so far as to vote against my reselection. None of them has ever said a word to my face before or since in criticism of my conduct.

Naturally the speech and language community was delighted that there was to be a renewed focus on the sector. I appointed an advisory group comprising many able and committed people, who eventually formulated five themes: communication is crucial; early identification and intervention are essential; a continuum of services designed around the family is needed; joint working is critical; and the current system is characterised by high variability and a lack of equity. To address those five themes, we devised forty detailed recommendations to government as to how to improve the situation. To my, and the review group's delight, Ed Balls and Alan Johnson accepted all of the recommendations and announced a package of £52 million to implement them.

Improving speech, language and communication requires a relentless drive to place the subject centre-stage in a raft of domestic policies. The ability to communicate is a vital piece of equipment for citizenship, fundamental to our humanity and central to the quest to improve life chances in the twenty-first century. Between September 2007 and July 2008 the review absorbed the largest single share of my professional time, and leading it was the most stimulating policy endeavour of my parliamentary life. It was worth every minute of it. In the midst of it, Sally gave birth to our third child, Jemima Clemency Rose, on 1 April 2008.

* * *

Another important part of my life as a backbencher from the autumn of 2004 to the early summer of 2009 was spent as a member of the International Development Select Committee. Our role was to scrutinise the policies, expenditure and administration of the Department for International Development (DfID). My first impression, looking at our government's humanitarian aid and development programmes, was that the creation of DfID itself in 1997 was a great breakthrough. Before then, overseas aid and development had been a subset of the Foreign and Commonwealth Office. In other words, it was viewed almost as a function of, and invariably secondary to, foreign policy. That was wrong. It prevented the UK from viewing aid and development in their own right and denied the subject an independent political champion within the Cabinet. Tony Blair's decision to establish a new department changed that. Clare Short, the first Secretary of State, was certainly a controversial figure but she was highly effective in levering resources for her department and passionate about its drive for poverty reduction. DfID sent a message far and wide that the UK was serious about its commitment to fight poverty around the world.

As I have touched on before, there is a narrative in some right-wing circles that foreign aid is a chronic waste of money, that it simply fosters a culture of dependence and that it involves poor people in rich countries giving money to rich people in poor countries. In other words, our funds are corruptly siphoned off by kleptocratic leaders who binge on champagne and caviar while their people starve.

This critique is vastly overstated. Sure, there is sometimes waste. There can be duplication of efforts between different aid agencies or the policies of different donor governments. And it is true that recipient governments sometimes misuse aid – it has happened in Ethiopia, for example – and we are right to insist on change when that happens. Yet overwhelmingly I saw the evidence of our aid helping very poor people to live, get an education, bear children safely and enjoy the opportunity to earn a living. Aid policy is far from perfect but, married to trade reform and debt relief, it can and does make a positive difference to millions of people in some of the poorest countries in the world.

One of my overseas trips in this role was to the Occupied Palestinian Territories (OPT), where we saw for ourselves the dehumanising conditions in which people were forced to live. As we travelled there, we met a group from Conservative Friends of Israel. The leader of that delegation asked where we were staying. The answer was on the Palestinian side close to the West Bank. He immediately suggested that we would be 'biased' against Israel in our report. I have supported the right of Israel to exist as a free state ever since I first visited with my father as a bar mitzvah present more than forty years ago. Other members of our committee did too. Yet we also supported the right of Palestinians to live in their own autonomous and secure state. We were not naïve. We knew the wider context of the Israel-Palestine conflict, and recognised that Israel had to defend itself against rocket attacks and other terrorist outrages. We also knew that our duty as a committee was to look at the plight of very poor people in the West Bank and Gaza, to state what caused or exacerbated that plight and to recommend what the UK government should do.

The simple fact was that the Israel government's policy was deliberately making life as difficult as possible. Sadly, that remains so today. DfID does what it can to mitigate that plight and should be supported in doing so. Of course, people can and do argue that the humanitarian situation in the OPT will improve sharply, and the prospect of meaningful development with it, only when there is a durable peace. I agree. Yet it would be a counsel of despair there and in many other conflict-ridden parts of the globe to say that nothing can be done until political differences are sorted. That would be morally indefensible too.

Even with the rising budget that it has rightly enjoyed in recent times, DfID cannot help everyone everywhere. There is a real debate to be had about whether the UK should provide development assistance to large, powerful countries that have aid budgets of their own, notably India and China. Neither is a poor country by globally recognised standards, but both contain very large numbers of extremely poor people who lack essentials of health, safety and education that we take for granted. Given that India is home to an estimated 300 million such people and the international community is decades behind schedule in striving to meet the Millennium Development Goals, those goals will be even more elusive if the Indian government does not support its poor and DfID and other donor nations walk away.

Finally, what may be said for relations with other members of the committee? Answering that question enables me to respond to those who throughout my career have asked me if MPs mix with members of other parties at work or socially. Of course, the answer is yes. For much of my parliamentary life before becoming Speaker, I probably mixed with Conservatives more, partly because the Members' Tea Room and the Members' Dining Room are organised along party lines. However, I always mixed with Labour, Liberal Democrat and other MPs as well, because we were members of all-party groups together on various issues. And in fact, probably the more lasting and significant relationships I formed with other members of the International Development Committee were with members of other parties.

The senior Liberal Democrat MP for Gordon, Malcolm Bruce, for example, proved an excellent committee chair – competent, hard-working, fair, good company and keen to include everyone. He was fond of recalling that he had once publicly described me years earlier as 'a silly man' before proceeding to say how he had come to like and respect me. The feeling was mutual. One night, over a late drink together,

I confided in Malcolm that I was minded to seek election as Speaker. He was quick to say that he thought I would be a credible candidate, though I might have to settle for serving first as a Deputy Speaker. He did not promise at that stage to vote for me, though when the contest came in 2009 he nominated me in preference to his long-time party colleague, Sir Alan Beith. I have always been grateful to him.

I got on well with all of the Labour members of the committee. Two relationships were particularly enjoyable for their own sake and later politically significant. First, I struck up an excellent rapport with Joan Ruddock, Labour MP for Lewisham Deptford. Fiercely intelligent, Joan always impressed me as accomplished in debate – possessed of a well-organised brain, she was articulate, measured and unruffled. We got on well and talked naturally about our backgrounds, experiences, likes and dislikes.

Strange though it may seem, I have no recollection of discussing my Speakership ambitions with Joan while we served on the committee together. But I noted her brilliant and successful campaigning for Harriet Harman to succeed John Prescott as Labour's deputy leader when Tony Blair resigned as Prime Minister, and broached the issue with her. Even though she was a busy minister, she found time to lobby her colleagues on my behalf, especially several female Members. I can say with complete confidence that she increased my vote and bolstered my morale.

The second member of the committee I came to know well was the Labour MP for Birmingham Northfield, Richard Burden. A Member of Parliament since 1992, Richard is a serious-minded, thoughtful, collegiate parliamentarian who hailed from the soft left of his party. He and I shared a belief in House of Lords reform and an admiration for Robin Cook. Richard shared a similar political outlook to Robin; I simply respected Robin's intellect, razor-sharp debating skills and principle in opposing the Iraq War at the cost of his membership of the Cabinet. Gradually, Richard and I got to know each other, and although he was aware of my interest in becoming Speaker I don't think we discussed it at any length. I was advised that, once the campaign was under way, I should have a team of geographically spread parliamentary lieutenants, each taking responsibility for whipping up support for me in a particular region of the country. I suggested Richard for the West Midlands, and he was outstanding – diligent, informative in reporting back and politely persistent in pursuing waverers. Like Joan, Richard made a difference, and I will always be grateful to him.

I had no patronage to dispense. I could not offer Joan or Richard anything beyond their right to fair treatment, which I have sought to afford every colleague whether he or she voted for me or not. Like Joan, Richard favoured a reformer, someone who came from the backbenches and would champion Parliament. The fact that I was a Tory MP did not bother him. I was not a figure of the Tory establishment. Indeed, that brigade couldn't abide me, which Richard regarded as a plus factor for me. So, unlike in a leadership election in which key members of the winning candidate's team can expect a prize, Joan, Richard and others could not. I asked for their support and it had to be unconditional. It was and that meant a lot to me.

* * *

By the summer of 2009, Westminster was in an unusally febrile state. For years, there had been growing media interest in the issue of politicians' expenses. These fell into a number of different categories but the most controversial was the so-called Additional Costs Allowance, more colloquially known as the second homes allowance, which enabled the vast majority of MPs to buy or rent a second home either in London or in their constituency. Under the Freedom of Information Act

2003, Parliament had for the previous five years published the totals of each MP's expenses since 2001, but many journalists and others had long complained that simply releasing bald totals – with no detailed breakdown of expenditure on individual items – was inadequate. More information should be provided, they insisted. All of a sudden, it was.

A computer disk containing details of what each MP had claimed for, including under the second homes allowance, was leaked to the *Daily Telegraph*. Its publication of those details, day after day for several weeks in April and May 2009, caused a political earthquake. The media and general public alike were horrified by the nature and scale of public subsidy that allowed my colleagues (and me) to purchase a second home, to decorate and furnish it and to equip it with fridges, washing machines and other items. A few MPs were later imprisoned for fraud; several suffered career-ending damage from the disclosures, which forced them to retire from Parliament at the 2010 election; and a much larger number, myself included, experienced embarrassment. The vast majority had not behaved corruptly, but we had all profited from a generous and loosely administered system which we had designed for ourselves and of which the public, when they became aware of it, furiously disapproved.

As Speaker since October 2000, Michael Martin was chairman of the House of Commons Commission, the strategic governing body of the House. The Commission had been in the lead in deciding what information to publish about the expenses scheme and in taking some early but modest measures to tighten it, pending possible reform. By May 2009, the media were in full cry about the scandal and wanted blood. Someone had to be held responsible. That person was the Speaker.

Michael had been in post for just over eight and a half years. He had been elected with massive Labour support and little from other parties. A modest and decent man, who could show great humour, Michael had often struggled to command respect. He had not managed to gain anything more than sullen acquiescence from most Tories – I myself had voted against him in 2000 – and some were deeply hostile. At least as damaging was that some senior Labour MPs had become impatient with him and the Liberal Democrat leader, Nick Clegg, had publicly called on him to resign. Another MP, the Conservative Douglas Carswell, had tabled a motion of no confidence in Michael. The media became convinced that he was the shameful defender of the discredited expenses system and called for his head.

Although he did not respond quickly to public anger, the Speaker was a convenient scapegoat. The Prime Minister, Gordon Brown, told Michael that he did not enjoy the confidence of colleagues and, in a short but dignified statement to the House on 19 May 2009, Speaker Martin announced that he intended to resign.

Parliament was at the nadir of its fortunes. Individual MPs were mired in controversy, the House had suffered reputational carnage and Michael Martin had become the first Speaker in 300 years to be forced out of office. This was the somewhat inauspicious backdrop to the election of a new Speaker.

Inevitably, the period of campaigning for the election would be dominated by arguments about how to replace the now utterly discredited expenses system. But it could also provide the opportunity for debate between candidates, other MPs and the media on the wider question of how to recover and assert the strength of Parliament, and restore public faith.

* * *

Three colleagues in particular had encouraged me to seek the Speakership: Dr Julian Lewis, the Conservative MP for New Forest East; Charles Walker, a kind, passionate, warm-hearted Tory colleague from Broxbourne, and Martin Salter, Labour

MP for Reading West. Martin had entered the House in 1997
with me and at first had been no fan of mine. Over the years,
we had got to know each other better and he was impressed
that I had mellowed from the shrill right-winger of 1997 to
the moderate, centre-ground humanitarian Tory of 2009. He
also felt, and told me that many Labour MPs felt, that as there
had been two Labour Speakers in succession, the next Speaker should be a Conservative. He offered to be my campaign
manager and I enthusiastically accepted.

In standing for election, I decided my pitch would be
threefold: the Speaker should strive to enhance scrutiny by
Parliament of government through more rigorous questioning of ministers; the administration of the House should be
modernised (it was absurd, for example, that Parliament had
a pistol shooting gallery but no nursery where MPs and staff
could pay to put their children during working hours), and, finally, the Speaker should be an ambassador for Parliament and
a robust advocate for democratic politics. Instead of remaining
almost incarcerated within the Palace of Westminster, dressed
up in a fancy uniform, I thought the Speaker should get out
more – visiting schools, universities, faith groups, charitable
organisations, public bodies of one sort or another, talking to
people about democracy, Parliament, and how to get involved
in the political process.

Ironically, given my commitment to modernising, I was
myself distinctly old-fashioned. I had and still have a rather
formal speaking style, characterised by a preference for long
sentences, subordinate clauses and rhetorical flourishes. Not
only that, I am an appalling technophobe. At the time I did
not even possess a mobile phone. Just as my campaign was
about to start, Julian Lewis started one of his 'I hope you don't
mind me saying what I am about to say, but . . .' conversations.
I didn't mind. It needed to be said. 'Over the next few weeks
many colleagues and friends will be trying to get you elected.
It will be maddening if we're trying to contact you and your

PA has no idea where you are or how to reach you. Go out and get yourself – or, better still, ask Sally to get you – a bog-standard, idiot-proof mobile.' Sally did so, acquiring for me a simple Nokia.

From the moment that Michael Martin announced his resignation in May, the campaign to succeed him was effectively up and running. I announced my candidature within days and was first out of the starting blocks. I issued a short manifesto, a moderniser's charter for reform and attempted renewal of Parliament. Within days, other candidates followed, of whom Sir George Young, former Conservative Secretary of State for Transport and chair of the Standards and Privileges Committee, struck me as the most formidable. He had sought election as Speaker in 2000, coming second to Michael Martin. A moderate Tory, a traditionalist, George was both able and decent. His main handicaps were that, among the 350-plus Labour MPs, the largest contingent in the House, he was an old Etonian toff who had privatised the railways. These facts did not endear him but he had a strong support base in the Conservative Party, from David Cameron downwards, and potentially a great many voters in other parties.

Margaret Beckett, the Labour MP for Derby South, was a late entrant to the contest, having declared her candidature a mere twelve days before the election and within days of leaving her position as Housing Minister in Gordon Brown's government. A Member of Parliament for over thirty years, she enjoyed considerable respect on both sides of the House. I could well imagine her attracting the votes of Labour MPs and that would be potentially fatal to my chances. As with George Young, however, there were debits on her balance sheet. Many colleagues took the view that ministers should not have all the prizes and that a real backbencher with long experience of the challenges should be Speaker, as he or she will better understand and cater to the needs of the majority of MPs. Some were aghast that she should leave government one day as part of a reshuffle and with scarcely a pause for breath announce her candidature for Speaker the next. Finally, the mood music of the Speakership election was that the House must reform, empower itself, scrutinise far better the government of the day. Fairly or unfairly, Margaret was widely viewed as a no-change candidate backed by the top brass in the government whips' office.

Sir Alan Haselhurst was the fourth contender judged to be in with a shout. A Tory MP for over thirty-five years, Alan had been chairman of Ways and Means, the most senior of the three Deputy Speakers, and the person who for the last twelve years had by convention chaired the Chancellor's Budget speech. An enormously efficient and authoritative figure in the Chair, albeit occasionally a little abrasive, Alan was widely respected and, when Michael Martin had taken leave in 2006 to undergo heart surgery, Alan had taken the Chair each day for six weeks and was generally thought to have acquitted himself well. But he too had drawbacks: he was over seventy, was fishing in the same pool for support as George Young, and it was hard to visualise a long-serving occupant of the Chair as the most credible cheerleader for change. Alan had also been castigated by the *Daily Telegraph* for his gardening expenses. They had been 'within the rules' but the media coverage had been both hostile and prominent. My sense was that he had been damaged.

There were six other candidates, but none struck me as a likely winner. They included Sir Alan Beith, the former Liberal Democrat deputy leader; Ann Widdecombe, Conservative MP for Maidstone and the Weald; Parmjit Dhanda, the 37-year-old Labour MP for Gloucester, and Richard Shepherd, Conservative MP for Aldridge Brownhills since 1979. Judged to be quite an old-fashioned candidate, Richard was thought to be a romantic and, in truth, too emotional. He often became so worked up in delivering a speech as to convey the impression that at any moment he would burst into tears. He was by no means disliked but he was too maverick and 'off-piste' to have any real chance of winning.

If Richard was an improbable choice, Sir Patrick Cormack was inconceivable. Another candidate who had stood against Michael Martin nine years earlier, Patrick had served as a Staffordshire MP for thirty-nine years, almost exclusively as a backbencher. An excellent speaker, deeply versed in parliamentary procedure, Patrick wanted greater scrutiny of the government, more scope for backbenchers and an enhanced role for select committees. He would have been no stooge of the government. His problem was not merely that he was seen as 'old hat'. Rather, for all his parliamentary ability, diligence and sense of fair play, Patrick had acquired a reputation for medal-winning pomposity. I was certain that Patrick would receive few votes.

Finally, Sir Michael Lord, yet another candidate who stood in 2000, was intent on having a second go. Michael had been a very solid Deputy Speaker, although perhaps without the force of personality of Alan Haselhurst. His appeal was broadly similar to that of George Young and Alan, and my antennae told me that he would come off worst.

* * *

At the start of the campaign, I had bumped into the Leader of the House, Labour's Harriet Harman. She had just hosted a meeting for some of her party colleagues and asked them, *en passant*, how they intended to vote in the Speaker election. Most of them apparently expressed support for me. 'You're going to do very well,' Harriet concluded. I was also buoyed by support from David Blunkett, Ed Balls, Yvette Cooper and Alan Johnson. Nevertheless, the weekend before the ballot on the Monday, Margaret Beckett overtook me as the bookies' favourite. I heard that government whips were lobbying hard for her, although the revelation that they were doing so might backfire. The front page of *The Times* on 22 June, the day of the election, carried the headline, 'Whips turn the screws for Beckett.' That might well irritate a lot of MPs on both sides of the House.

Crucially, it would be a secret ballot. Each candidate had to be proposed by a minimum of twelve and a maximum of fifteen fellow MPs. At least three had to be from another party to that of the candidate. That was no problem for me. Fortunately, there was no minimum requirement for nominations from one's *own* party, probably as no one had thought that would be a problem. In fact, it would have been for me, as most of my Tory supporters, knowing that I was not popular on my side as a whole and was in fact heartily detested by Cameron and his Notting Hill cronies, preferred to support me privately. Worse, Cameron had banned frontbenchers from nominating candidates so Julian Lewis, a Shadow minister, could no longer nominate me unless he resigned his post, which I would never have dreamed of asking him to do. I was nominated by fifteen colleagues: MPs from six political parties and an independent.

Why was I finding favour in parties other than my own? I had pledges of support from Liberal Democrat MPs as well as Labour (there were 62 MPs in the Liberal Democrat parliamentary party then), Scottish and Welsh Nationalist MPs, and MPs from the Social Democratic and Labour Party in Northern Ireland. There were several reasons why these MPs rallied behind my campaign. First, Labour MPs in particular knew that David Cameron and the Tory hierarchy wanted anyone but me, so they decided to elect me and kick the Tories in the teeth. Secondly, in my capacity as a member of Speaker Martin's Panel of Chairs for the last four years I had built up a reputation as a fair and competent chair of legislation committees and debates. Thirdly, they knew that as I had spent many years as a backbencher – and a mildly rebellious one at that – I would be sympathetic to the rights of backbenchers, including

My father, Charles (left), with his two brothers, Ralph (centre) and Sam (right).

Me in the late 1960s, and with my sister Alison.

Aged 10. I reached
my first under-12
tournament final at
Pinner, Middlesex
in 1973.

I graduated from Essex
University with First Class
Honours in Government in
July 1985.

Addressing the Federation
of Conservative
Students' Conference in
Scarborough in April 1986
when elected Chair.

Margaret Thatcher, who was a formative influence on me when I was young.

The sitting of the United Kingdom Youth Parliament which I chaired every year throughout my tenure as Speaker.

Norman Tebbit addressing the 1986 Conservative Party Conference. He was a big influence on me for more than a decade.

Michael Howard, whose 2005 General Election campaign focus on immigration I blasted as 'obsessive' and 'repellent'.

Ken Clarke, the post-war Conservative whom I most admire.

Harriet Harman, Parliament's greatest gender-equality campaigner in the post-war period and a strong supporter of mine when I was Speaker.

Theresa May, elected to Parliament in 1997, the same year as me.

Michael Portillo, whose unsuccessful
leadership campaign I supported in 2001.

Iain Duncan Smith, from whose
Shadow Cabinet I resigned in
November 2002.

Prime Minister Gordon Brown,
for whom I produced a report
in 2008 with recommendations
for improving speech, language
and communication services for
children and young people.

David Cameron, with whom I formed a doubles partnership in the Parliamentary tennis team. Relations between us in later years were poor.

Andrea Leadsom, the Leader of the House, with whom I repeatedly clashed as I championed the rights of Parliament in holding the Government to account.

Michael Martin, whose resignation as Speaker paved the way for my election to the Chair in June 2009.

With my wife-to-be Sally Illman, announcing our engagement in June 2002.

independent-minded, contrary and heretical backbenchers wanting to stand up to the government. Fourthly – and this is human nature – centrist and left-of-centre MPs were comfortable voting for a (by now) left-of-centre Tory. Finally, I am a state-school product, and Labour MPs far preferred me to the alternatives of a Tory toff or yet another privately educated establishment figure.

There were 196 Tory MPs but I reckon I gained the votes of maybe twenty or thirty of them. Why did most Tories not want me? I expect I was resented by some for my political journey – a sincere but apparently infuriating journey from right-wing Thatcherite to left-of-centre, one-nation, socially liberal, equality-supporting backbencher who was widely – though wrongly – suspected of having contemplated defecting to Labour. The Tory leadership knew that they could not control me if I became Speaker and were therefore hell-bent on stopping me. Cameron was personally hostile as I had attacked him during the 2005 leadership campaign. I accept that I had made enemies by the sharpness of my tongue, and a tendency too readily and undiplomatically to let a colleague know if I thought he or she was wrong, dim-witted – or both.

I also summoned up all the worst prejudices of some of my Tory critics. I am pro-gay rights (as one blinkered Tory put it to me, 'I'll never forgive you for supporting the poofters' – yes, really). I am short, and the bigots among my opponents thought that a prominent office-holder had to be tall. I am from a lower-middle-class background – an 'oik', not a gentleman, as one observed. So snobs were against me too. And – yes – I am Jewish. Nonsense, people might say – the Tory Party has been led by Disraeli and Michael Howard and many others from Keith Joseph to Nigel Lawson, from Malcolm Rifkind to Oliver Letwin, have served in its highest counsels. That is true: the Conservative Party has always been ready to embrace Jews and other minorities if they conform and can be useful. To them, however, I could not be relied upon to do either. I was not merely an outsider by background but, in a sense, by inclination. In short, therefore, since I could not be captured for others' uses, I must be stopped at all costs. Anti-Semitism was for some part of the very personal attack – 'pushy little Jew', as one said of me behind my back. In recent years, the Labour Party has been lambasted both for anti-Semitism and for its tardiness in tackling the scourge. As it happens, I never experienced anti-Semitism from a member of the Labour Party. However, I certainly experienced it in the Tory Party throughout my career.

One conversation in the Chamber before I had officially declared my candidature was both amusing and revealing. A middle-of-the-road but quite trad Tory MP, Richard Ottaway, was sitting next to me. He had heard rumours that I might stand. I did not confirm or deny it but acknowledged that I was thinking of doing so. He rushed to advise me against, saying that I was too new to the House. Anyone would have thought that I had been in the House twelve months whereas I had by then been a Member of Parliament for twelve years, a point I gently made. Completely failing – or just refusing – to grasp the point, he replied, 'Well, yes, as I say, you are rather new.' Sensing correctly that his less than weighty objection had failed to sway me, he opted for a different tack.

'How old are you?' he enquired. 'Forty-five or forty-six?'

'Forty-six,' I replied.

'Yes, and you would aim to serve for eight or nine years as per the most recent holders of the office?'

'If I stand, that would be my intention,' I replied.

'So, wait a minute, you would finish in the Chair by fifty-five or so. How are you going to make a living after that?'

'Richard,' I responded, 'how many unemployed ex-Speakers do you know? As of now, I have no idea. I would go off and do something else, and I daresay I would manage to keep body and soul together somehow.' He looked at me open-mouthed, gaping like a goldfish. It was no surprise when a few days later

I heard he was beavering away on behalf of one of my rivals, Sir George Young.

There was time for one more opportunity to ruffle feathers before MPs chose their new Speaker. It was a speech in support of the government's Equality Bill, which was given its Second Reading in the House of Commons in May 2009. Introducing the Bill, the Minister for Women and Equality, Harriet Harman, argued that equality of opportunity before the law was right in principle and necessary in practice. It included a raft of measures to counter discrimination and promote equality, but two were most significant and controversial. One was to create a public-sector equality duty, requiring public bodies actively to promote equality. The other was to allow employers to practise positive action. For example, where two candidates were of equal merit, but one was male and the other female, or one white and the other BAME, the employer would be allowed to choose the woman or BAME candidate in order to address under-representation.

These two provisions appeared to horrify and enrage parts of the Conservative press and the Conservative Party. The Shadow Minister for Women and Equality was Theresa May. She did not want to support the Bill, not least because of those provisions, but nor did she want simply to vote against it, leaving her and the party wide open to the charge that they opposed action to fight discrimination and promote equality. So they resorted to the device – to be fair a commonly used and procedurally proper device – of a Reasoned Amendment, declining to support the progress of the Bill because of its various defects, while emphasising support for equality.

I thought the party's position was feeble, wanting to have it both ways, though leaning more to opposition than support. By then, my track record of support for LGBT, gender and wider equality was long-standing and well known. It was hardly a surprise to my party that I supported the Bill.

However, on the morning of the day of the debate, I saw the Opposition Chief Whip, the curmudgeonly Patrick McLoughlin, in the Members' Tea Room. As a courtesy, I tipped him off that I intended to support the Bill. He briefly ran through the argument against it – bureaucratic, costly, unnecessary – and I explained that I did not buy any of that. He started to ponder aloud whether the debate would finish early or run until 10 p.m. I said that that didn't matter to me either way, as I would be there from the start because I wished to speak.

'Oh no,' he replied, 'why do you need to do that?'

'Because I am a Member of Parliament, Patrick. I have views, and I wish to express them.' He looked at me openmouthed. To say that there was no meeting of minds would be an understatement.

In concluding my speech later that day, frustrated that the Conservative Party would not support the Bill, did not want to oppose it and opted for the halfway house of declining to give it a Second Reading, I took aim at my colleagues on the front bench who were led by Theresa May. In reflecting on my party's stance, I said that it reminded me of Churchill's verdict on Stanley Baldwin in the face of German rearmament – that he was 'decided only to be undecided, resolved to be irresolute, adamant for drift, solid for fluidity, all powerful to be impotent'.

I doubt that my colleagues on the Conservative benches thanked me for that verdict, but it was honest. The Conservatives had the chance to show that the party had changed. From David Cameron and Theresa May downwards, they flunked it.

That was a shame, but so be it. Having pursued the goal of becoming Speaker of the House of Commons for some years now, the prize was in my grasp, and I had other things to worry about than my own party's shortcomings. Chief among them was trying to restore not just the reputation of Parliament in the light of the expenses scandal, but its ability to hold the government to account. A great revival of the Commons was not just desirable, but vital.

* * *

After a month of campaigning, decision day arrived. By the middle of the evening of 22 June I would in all likelihood know my fate. In the previous four weeks, I had consciously chosen to focus where it mattered: on colleagues – and not Conservative ones. That this strategy might be vindicated was suggested on the day of the election by a chance exchange in the loo between Sadiq Khan, then the Labour MP for Tooting, and David Cameron. Duly amused by it at the time, Sadiq had tipped me off about it minutes afterwards.

'Who are you voting for today, Sadiq?' Cameron asked.

'I'm voting Tory for the first time in my life,' Sadiq replied. 'I'm voting for John Bercow.'

Cameron's response spoke volumes about the hostility I faced from most of my Conservative colleagues: 'Bercow? He doesn't count.'

Nor did I give media interviews as they could easily be distorted and do more harm than good. If they were hostile, I could not change that. They would largely appeal to people who had made up their minds against me anyway. Similarly, if, as with the *Independent* and the *Guardian*, they were mildly well disposed or neutral, they would make little difference. So I felt comfortable that I had spent the campaign period as productively as I could. All I could do now was make the best possible speech on the day and hope that colleagues would come my way.

Overwhelmingly, throughout my parliamentary career, I opted to speak without notes, ordinarily drawing on my basic knowledge of a subject and a mental list of points to make. Yet every rule has its exceptions. On a big occasion, with a large audience or a tight time limit, there can be real advantage in having a text to read or committing it to memory. I opted for the latter so that I would be able to make eye contact with colleagues as I spoke.

At around 8.30 a.m., our friend Nicola took the boys – Oliver, five, and Freddie, three – to school while Sally, baby Jemima and I walked from our Westminster flat to the House of Commons. En route, we bumped into Margaret Beckett who responded tersely to my 'Good morning, Margaret,' and, looking at Jemima, said, 'She can't vote, you know.'

Around lunchtime I received a message that I had been drawn to speak fifth. Margaret Beckett was up first. She made a cautious, somewhat defensive, rather wooden speech, looking and sounding more nervous than usual. By her high standards, she was below par. George Young, making a moderate moderniser's pitch, was witty, urbane and impressive. Ann Widdecombe was competent, mildly humorous, and a touch sanctimonious. Alan Beith made a reasonable fist of it and, as ever, came across as unfailingly decent and irredeemably dull.

I started my speech by telling the story of the colleague (Sir Peter Tapsell) who told me that I was far too young (at forty-six) as the Speaker ought to be 'virtually senile'. I recounted my conversation with Sir Peter without naming him but by impersonating him. Encouraged by the amused reaction I continued by explaining that, by eighteenth-century standards, I was not particularly young, Speakers Grenville and Addington having been elected at twenty-nine and thirty-two respectively, and both having gone on to become Prime Minister. This was a cue for further good-natured laughter – I knew there was no danger of that in my case.

I then made the argument for an independently determined expenses system, a strengthened Parliament to check the executive and a Speaker who acted as an ambassador for the House. I had committed the speech to my head and delivered it fluently. It went down well, especially with Labour and Liberal Democrat MPs, who were my main sources of support.

What can be said of the remaining speeches? Richard Shepherd was eloquent in support of an assertive Parliament but there had been two new intakes of MPs since he last stood for the Speakership and I felt that those MPs were looking elsewhere. Sir Michael Lord, after twelve years as a Deputy Speaker, had not spoken from the backbenches in that time and, sadly, it showed. He did not look comfortable, spoke for too long and lost the House. Sir Patrick Cormack was eloquent but pompous. Sir Alan Haselhurst was very competent but I sensed that the House was tiring and wanted to get on with the vote. The last candidate to speak, Parmjit Dhanda, the most radical of us all, made an excellent speech but I thought that he would probably lack the votes to make any progress.

Just under one and a half hours after the speeches had concluded, Alan Williams gave us the result of the first ballot. For me, and probably for her, the big shock was that Margaret Beckett, the bookies' favourite over the weekend, got only 74 votes to my 179, with 112 for Sir George. These two rivals, plus Sir Alan Haselhurst (66), Sir Alan Beith (55) and Ann Widdecombe (44), joined me in the second ballot. Andrew Dismore, Labour MP for Hendon and a key campaign ally, was cock-a-hoop, convinced that transfers from other candidates would produce a run-off between George and me, which I would win. He was right. At 8.30 p.m., six hours after proceedings began, Alan Williams announced the results of the third and final ballot. 'John Bercow, 322, Sir George Young, 271.' He went on to declare that I was duly elected to serve as Speaker and congratulated me. As I let out a huge sigh of relief, I was also congratulated by Julian Lewis on my left and Charles Walker on my right. Glancing up at the gallery opposite, I saw a beaming Sally sitting with my slightly surprised-looking mother.

The convention dictates that the new Speaker is then dragged to the Chair, a tradition dating from before the English Civil War when not merely the tenure but the life of the Speaker was extremely precarious, a truth supported by the fact that no fewer than seven of my predecessors met their ends on the executioner's block. That evening, Sandra Gidley, the Liberal Democrat MP for Romsey, and Charles Walker dragged me to the Chair though my resistance was somewhere between minimal and nil. I made a short speech, thanking colleagues for the honour they had done me and promising to serve the House impartially and competently. Gordon Brown led the congratulations, making a good joke at my expense. Referring to my statement earlier in the day that, if elected, I would cast aside all my previous views, he observed, 'Some of us thought that you had done that some time ago.' David Cameron and Nick Clegg followed the Prime Minister in offering congratulations to 'Mr Speaker-Elect' as I still awaited the Queen's approval. This I then received at a brief ceremony in the House of Lords, stylishly overseen by the Lord Chancellor, Jack Straw.

I returned to the Commons, announced that the Queen had approved my election, and called the Leader of the House, Harriet Harman, to move a motion effectively recommending my predecessor, Michael Martin, for a peerage. After that, the House adjourned. I then had a celebratory drink in my new office in Speaker's House with my superb campaign chief, Martin Salter, a few colleagues, Sally, Mum, Commons secretary Jemima Warren, former Commons secretary Rosie Daniels and my old friends Michael and Gillian Keegan, who had sat with Sally and Mum all afternoon.

As we started to think about going home, Sally and I suddenly remembered that very soon, if we wished, we would have the right to move into the Speaker's residence, which is above the office in Speaker's House. We were both intrigued to know what it was like. I had never been there – only to the office and State Rooms downstairs, where the Speaker held official functions – and in standing for election I obviously could not ask Michael Martin, 'Is it OK if I have a nose around your gaff?'

As it was then empty – Michael Martin having left in the last few days – I asked Angus Sinclair, Speaker's Secretary, if it would be all right for us to have a very quick look there and then. 'Of course,' he said, so Sally and I wandered up there. It was a sizeable apartment of four, potentially five bedrooms, with an en suite bathroom for us, two other bathrooms, a kitchen, a dining room, a sitting room, a utility room, a study and a room that could conveniently be made into a playroom for our three children. It was a little like a horseshoe-shaped hotel corridor with several rooms. It had red carpets, a number of old, somewhat gloomy portraits and a smattering of framed prints of politicians from previous centuries on the wall by the front entrance. The dining room, with State silver, was beautiful, although we would not eat there as a family day to day – it was far too grand and a bit of a trek from the kitchen. After all, Speakers don't have servants to fetch and carry for them nowadays. The flat offered wonderful views of the River Thames. I went away hoping that we could soon move in and Sally seemed to be up for it too.

I took up my new post at once, arriving early the next morning for a series of internal meetings, to be followed by preparations for my first day in the Chair. Mid-morning I was surprised by a visit from Gordon Brown. I did not expect the Prime Minister to visit me. Rather, ordinarily, it would be the other way round, on the rare occasions that I had ever asked for such a meeting over the years. Brown, who was much better one-to-one than his public image would suggest, was warm, congratulatory and encouraging. He told me that the last time he came to Speaker's House it was to tell Michael Martin that he had lost the confidence of the House and should step down. That morning Brown told me that he thought we should try to hasten the Legg Review of MPs' expenses. He knew that the government was taking a bigger hit than the Opposition, and he wanted to move on from the issue as quickly as possible.

In the Chamber that afternoon, we had Health Questions.

Determined that I should start as I meant to go on, I stressed that I wanted brief questions and brief answers so that we could make progress and more MPs could take part. Harriet Harman later made a statement designed to show that the government had recognised public anger over expenses and was pressing ahead with reform. In particular, she flagged up the Parliamentary Standards Bill that would establish a new independent body to regulate MPs' expenses. She hoped that that proposal, together with greater transparency on claims and the work of Thomas Legg investigating claims from the last five years, would reassure the public.

I hoped that Harriet was right and that the public would see that we were putting our House in order. Frankly, we had all been to blame for 'the system'. It had been designed decades earlier when successive Prime Ministers had decreed that it would be politically unacceptable to increase MPs' pay significantly when their governments were strictly limiting pay rises in the public sector. The generous expenses system had been dreamed up as a kind of income substitution. That, however, is an explanation, not an excuse – and still less any form of justification. It was wrong. The system had been excessively secretive, overly generous, loosely administered and patently indefensible. My colleagues and I should not blame the staff who ran the scheme. We devised it and we had now to abolish it and provide for an independent body to devise an alternative, which should be characterised by equity, transparency and accountability.

I was determined to support such a system as that would be right in itself. But it was also essential for any eventual revival in the standing of Parliament. I wanted to lead and work with colleagues to deliver sustainable parliamentary reform in the interest of achieving a healthier, more vibrant and inclusive democracy. We would have a fighting chance of achieving that transformation for Parliament if, but only if, Parliament was clean and seen to be clean.

5

Mr Speaker

Although I was by now highly experienced in chairing legislation committees and Westminster Hall debates, nothing
could fully prepare me for serving as Mr Speaker. On day
one, 23 June, at the lunchtime briefing where senior Clerks
ran through with me the day's business in the Chamber, I
was tickled by the nonchalant speed with which the Clerk
of the House, Dr Malcolm Jack, dealt with the agenda.
In his words, 'After the main debate, there are a couple of
deferrables—'

'Sorry Malcolm, deferrables?'

'Yes, Mr Speaker, motions subject to deferred division' (in
other words, a vote at a later date). 'You simply put the question, collect the voices—'

'The voices?'

'The "ayes" and the "noes". If the motion is not opposed,
you declare it carried. If it is opposed by a shout of "No", you
announce that the division, i.e. the vote, is deferred until the
day specified in your dossier for the division.'

I had probably observed my predecessors, Betty Boothroyd
and Michael Martin, handling such motions countless times,
but I had not given any thought to them. Malcolm, evidently content to have taught a new pupil, continued blissfully,
'Thereafter, Mr Speaker, there is a "nod or nothing" . . .'

'What's that?' I had never heard the expression 'nod or
nothing' – and would almost certainly have that inexperience

in common with every other member except the three Deputy Speakers now serving under me.

'Forgive me, Mr Speaker,' Malcolm explained, 'I have so long been immersed in the Commons lingo that I use it without a moment's thought. A "nod or nothing" is a procedural motion taken after the "moment of interruption" – the scheduled end of the debate.

'Either it is agreed to without a division of the House,' he continued, 'or, if even one Member shouts "Object", nothing happens.' In other words, the motion could not proceed. The government would have to try again another day. If it was being objected to a third time, the government whips would conclude it was controversial and if they still wanted the motion to pass, they would have to allocate time for it to be debated and voted on.

After the 'nod or nothing' was disposed of, Malcolm explained that we would come to the adjournment debate. 'Very straightforward, Mr Speaker: whip to move.' This meant that I would turn to the government whip on duty and say, 'We come now to the adjournment, the whip to move,' meaning that the whip should now move the motion that the House adjourn.

Once the whip has proposed that motion, a thirty-minute debate would then follow as the last business of the day, after which I would simply declare, 'The ayes have it, the ayes have it. Order, order,' and leave the Chair. Why did I repeat the words 'aye' and 'order'? It was ordained by history and precedent. Unnecessary you might think, but harmless.

The House always starts sitting on the half-hour: 2.30 p.m. on Monday, 11.30 a.m. on Tuesday and Wednesday, and 9.30 a.m. on Thursday and on the thirteen Fridays we sit each year. It is said that we Brits often enjoy ceremony and a little pomp and circumstance doesn't go amiss. So I didn't just beetle along to the Chamber on my tod. Oh no, I processed from my office in Speaker's House behind a parliamentary doorkeeper and the Serjeant-at-Arms carrying the mace. Behind me followed the trainbearer, though as I wore the State Robe only on the day of the State Opening of Parliament his presence was largely ceremonial. I say largely because he carried a sword and was also there to protect me in the unlikely event that somebody raced forward in Central Lobby to attack me. Behind him, there were the Speaker's Chaplain and the Speaker's Secretary.

The procession would depart Speaker's House at twenty-six and a half minutes past the hour precisely, go along the library corridor, through the Lower Waiting Hall, into the Central Lobby before turning right to walk through the Commons corridor and the Members' Lobby into the House of Commons Chamber itself. The Serjeant-at-Arms and I would stop at the bar of the House – the red line that marks entry to the Chamber – and, absurd as it sounds, nod to my empty Chair at the opposite end. This extraordinary spectacle is repeated six paces later by the Serjeant and me before he then installs the mace at the table. As he does so, the Chaplain and I walk forward past the Clerks' table and nod – for the third time – to the Chair before the Chaplain leads prayers from the table, which are attended by Members only. When they conclude three minutes later, we both stand and bow to each other before I ascend the Chair – a very comfortable cushioned seat reminiscent of a throne. Fortunately, the Chair also has a stool on which to rest my feet since they would not otherwise touch the ground. The Chaplain then departs the Chamber – backwards – bowing to me at intervals. Even though the then Speaker's Chaplain, Robert Wright, kindly talked me through all of this palaver on my first morning, it still felt rather quaint and over-elaborate. So much so that I struggled to keep a straight face that first day.

I would then start the proceedings of the House by uttering the words 'Order, order'. This basically means 'Pay attention, we now begin our work,' as the departmental Question Times got under way. As I will explain later, there is a ballot in the

House from Monday to Thursday so MPs can apply to put a question. Anyone whose name is drawn in the ballot – conducted electronically with no involvement whatsoever by me – will get to ask his or her question. Other Members who have not been lucky in the ballot will stand to signal to me their wish to join the debate. Those Members, by standing, are trying to catch the Speaker's eye.

So, my first task is to know the name, party and, preferably, the constituency of every Member because I am trying to secure a balance between the parties, geographical areas, intakes (new as well as longer-serving Members) and different points of view (pro- or anti-Brexit, for example). How do I recognise my 649 colleagues? Well, I could pretend it is fiendishly difficult and I manage it on account of my cleverness, but I won't because it isn't and I'm not. At least 400 will already be known to me as colleagues for a number of years. True enough, after a general election there is turnover as some MPs retire and others are defeated. House officials take pride in quickly producing a booklet featuring photographs, names, party affiliations and constituencies of the 'newbies' – some 227 of them after the election of 2010. I memorise about thirty a day for just over a week, tested by Sally. During Question Time I am supported by my Secretary in the Chamber who, if I forget a name, can prompt me – but that is rarely necessary. I know some very clever colleagues who have poor memories for names and might not cope but, for all my many faults, I have reasonable capacity to recall who's who.

My first priority as Speaker on taking over was to make the business of the House of Commons livelier and more interesting both to MPs and observers. That made quickening the pace at the daily Question Times a priority. Despite being on the receiving end of a torrent of media abuse and snobbery, my predecessor, Michael Martin, cared deeply for the House, its Members and staff alike. He was almost invariably a tolerant Speaker, frankly more tolerant and less impatient than I was.

Yet the flip side of his patience was that at Question Times MPs were often long-winded – myself included – sometimes to the point of self-indulgence.

The effect of this very relaxed regime was that we got through fewer questions than we should. Parliamentary colleagues came to realise that if they had a question lower down in the balloted list – say number thirteen or fourteen – they would probably not get to ask their question. They would either spend an hour waiting in vain to be called or they would give up and go and do something else instead.

This struck me as demoralising for them and bad for the House. I wanted to attract MPs to the Chamber, not repel them from it. From the outset, I acted to quicken the pace, insisting on shorter questions and shorter answers. That way, I enabled more MPs to speak up for constituents, conscience and country, and ensured that ministers could not avoid awkward later questions by a calculated 'go-slow' on earlier enquiries. Instead, they were held to account for their policies, administration, expenditure and conduct over as wide a terrain as possible.

At first, in my relentless pursuit of faster progress, I erred on the side of being abrupt, occasionally even perhaps harsh, in cutting off a Member who was boring the House and stopping another colleague taking part. With time, I got better at the use of humour and gentle exhortation. 'I am *extremely* grateful to the minister' was correctly interpreted by the late *Guardian* sketch-writer, Simon Hoggart, as meaning 'Shut it, sunshine'. Sometimes I would just say, 'We have got the gist', 'I think a question-mark is coming now', or 'The abridged rather than the *War and Peace* version would be appreciated'.

In dealing with heckling, barracking or very loud noise, I varied my approach. If a single colleague made a very noisy exhibition of him- or herself, I would intervene and urge them to contain themselves and stop yelling or 'chuntering from a sedentary position'. Those words were my preferred rebuke because Members are supposed to speak only when on their feet, not from their seats. If a large number of Members were making a racket, I would urge them to calm down and remember how much the public disliked orchestrated barracking – I received a regular trickle of letters complaining about such behaviour. Other improvisations came later in my tenure. I would urge a Member to lie down in a dark room, take a soothing medicament or take up yoga. 'Calm, restraint, zen', were my oft-repeated watchwords. Most Members then heeded the advice and were altogether more restrained.

Whether I was a good Speaker is not for me to say. But on this marker at least, I felt I did achieve what I set out to do: I promised to speed up Question Time and I did. From 2004 to 2009 at Foreign Office Questions, for example, we got through an average of 39 questions in the allotted hour. Between 2012 and 2017, by contrast, while I was in the Chair, an average of 52 questions were heard in the allotted hour, an increase of 33 per cent. Similar rises were seen across different departments, and we got through considerably more questions than before in many sessions.

That does not prove that the exchanges were of better quality, though most ministers would acknowledge that a short, sharp question is often more challenging than a long one, especially if the latter is unfocused: responding to such an enquiry, it is a piece of cake for any competent minister to duck the parts he or she doesn't like and to deal with the easier bit. When the question is blunt and to the point, there is no escape – the minister has to produce a relevant response or admit that he or she does not know the answer. There is no disgrace in the latter course, though obviously if a minister has repeatedly to take that approach, the House (and probably his or her own whips keeping a note of ministers' performances) will conclude that he or she is not in command of their brief.

Another point is worth addressing, which has often been put to me by members of the public. 'Mr Speaker, I watched

Question Time yesterday. The minister simply didn't answer the question asked. Why don't you insist that the minister does so?' It is a fair question. My answer is that if I were to do so, I would cease to be a referee and become instead a player of the game, which the House does not want. The Speaker is not responsible for the content of answers by ministers. If it is obvious to you that a minister is dodging the question, it will be obvious to others too, and those others – whether MPs, journalists, or members of the public – will make their own judgement. It is not for me to interfere on those grounds.

There are, however, two reasons why I might interrupt a minister, including the Prime Minister. One is that the minister was simply going on too long. Dozens if not hundreds of times over the years I cut a minister off, as I did backbenchers, for that reason. The other is that the minister went off-piste, talking about something quite unrelated to what he or she had been asked. For example, a minister might start to bang on about the Opposition's policy – but ministers are not responsible for the Opposition's policy, only for their own. On several occasions, I cut off ministers for that reason, including Gordon Brown, David Cameron and George Osborne.

In addition to delivering on my pledge to quicken the pace, I was keen to grant decent applications from MPs to put Urgent Questions to ministers. Standing Orders of the House had long permitted such questions, but few applications appeared to have been made in recent years and, in the twelve months before my election to the Chair, only two had been granted by the Speaker. The urgency, the relevance, the topicality of our proceedings were gravely undermined by the absence of such questions. MPs who had such matters to raise were blogging, writing for newspapers or giving radio or TV interviews instead, sucking the life out of the Chamber. Meanwhile, ministers were getting off scot-free. Instead of being questioned and held to account by the people's elected representatives, they were free either to say nothing at times of controversy or to take to the airwaves. Whichever they did, they were not answering to the House of Commons.

I was determined to restore the basic and inviolable principle that government ministers – members of what we call the executive branch of our political system – must be accountable to the legislative branch, namely Parliament. By granting an Urgent Question, I was not saying that the government was wrong on an issue, though in some cases there was an implicit criticism of them for not volunteering to account to the House by offering an oral statement. It is not for the Speaker to pronounce whether the government or Opposition is right or wrong on a policy issue. Rather, I was simply ruling that the issue warranted the presence of a minister and the attention of the House that day.

In July 2009, not long after my election as Speaker, the Liberal Democrat MP for Oxford West and Abingdon, Dr Evan Harris, submitted an Urgent Question to ask the Home Secretary if he would make a statement on the actions of the authorities in respect of the use by newspapers of illegal surveillance methods. Serious allegations had appeared in the media that morning that newspapers had paid the police for information and that in a number of cases – well beyond those previously known to Parliament or the public – newspapers had used illegal surveillance methods, notably phone-hacking, to obtain information about the private lives of public personalities. My instinctive view was that the issue should be aired in Parliament as a matter of urgency. It concerned the behaviour of public authorities and powerful professional interests. Potentially, there could be illegality involved and invasions of privacy. While the details were for criminal investigation rather than trial by Parliament, my sense was that the House would want to flag up its concern and to hear something from a government minister in response.

The Home Secretary, Alan Johnson, was speaking at a conference in Manchester and so the Minister for Policing, Crime and Counter-Terrorism, David Hanson, responded to the question. His statement was brief and to the point, choosing not to pre-empt a formal statement from the Metropolitan Police due later that day (which refused to reopen the inquiry, insisting no new information had come to light). In response, Dr Harris warned that neither the House nor the public would be in any way relaxed about 'fears not only of surveillance by the government, but of surveillance by newspapers and their agents', adding that 'it would be extremely toxic for our democracy if vested interests were seen to be able to in some way buy their way out of the criminal justice system'.

David Hanson responded further, and there were contributions from Chris Grayling, then the Shadow Home Secretary, Chris Huhne for the Lib Dems, David Davis and others. This Urgent Question was significant not for what the minister had to say. His was, perhaps of necessity, a holding operation, along the lines of 'I understand the concern and I'll get back to colleagues when I have more information'. The significance of the occasion was that it was the first time that a Member, operating on the back of a press story, raised the possibility that phone-hacking by the *News of the World* had taken place on a substantial, perhaps even systematic, scale. If true, this would demolish the notion that there had simply been an isolated case involving one rogue reporter, Clive Goodman, who had already been convicted of phone-hacking and subject to discussion in the House. In the next Parliament, the issue was to rear its head again very soon and Parliament would have a key role to play in highlighting and uncovering what was, without doubt, a major public scandal.

A few months later Michael Gove applied for permission to put an Urgent Question to his opposite number, the Secretary of State for Children, Schools and Families, Ed Balls. The question simply asked the Secretary of State to make a statement explaining his policy on the appointment of the next Children's Commissioner. The background to the question was a brewing political controversy. Following what Ed Balls described as a rigorous process, the independent selection panel had recommended Dr Maggie Atkinson as the next Children's Commissioner, and Balls had accepted the recommendation.

However, the relevant select committee had promptly held a pre-appointment hearing with Dr Atkinson and, while acknowledging that she demonstrated 'a high degree of professional competence', raised some concerns about her appointment. Ed Balls had to assess these concerns before deciding whether to proceed, and concluded that there were no new facts that should cause him to overturn the decision to appoint her. Michael Gove, however, asked me to allow him to air the issue in the House.

To my surprise, before the daily meeting at which I made such decisions, I received a telephone call from Ed Balls, who was at pains to emphasise that Gove's application should not be granted. It was not an urgent issue, he argued. He had made his decision and he had also written to the select committee about it. I heard him out, told him I would think about it and decide at our daily briefing meeting at midday. His department would then be informed. In response, he sounded disappointed not to have closure but accepted what I said without complaint.

I decided that Gove's UQ should be heard. Of course, there was an element of politics to it. Gove was stirring the pot, but that is part of our profession. Perfectly properly, he was looking for an argument with Ed Balls. Even though there had been an independent appointment process, the Secretary of State had appointed the panel and approved the outcome, before a select committee with a Labour chair and a Labour majority had effectively thrown a spanner in the works by casting doubt on the suitability of the appointee. Understandably, Michael Gove saw the potential for making a row about it. Yet, objectively, was there not good ground for asking the Secretary of State to account to the House? There was. The appointment was important. It had caused some controversy. Some MPs had discussed the matter and aired their views, but the rest of the House had had no such opportunity. I thought the House should now be afforded the chance to hear from and question the Secretary of State.

Ed Balls duly came to the Chamber at the appointed time and explained himself, concluding that Dr Atkinson would be 'a strong defender of children's rights in England against all comers'. Gove objected to the decision on a number of grounds, and complained that the Secretary of State was overruling the unanimous view of a 'Labour committee'. Balls emphasised that his responsibility was to consider whether any new information should cause him to overturn the independent panel's recommendation. He concluded that there was no such information.

Ultimately, and perhaps not surprisingly, the government stood by its position. However, Parliament had the chance to hear the Secretary of State's account, and Members had the chance to question and challenge him. In the name of transparency, and of respect for the role of Parliament to hear about and question ministers on urgent matters of public policy, it was the right course of action. To his credit, although Ed Balls had put to me his reasons why it should not be heard in the Chamber, he accepted my ruling and never mentioned it to me again. Indeed, it was the only occasion in the period up to the 2010 election when a minister approached me to try to fend off a decision to grant an Urgent Question.

Sometimes an Urgent Question resulted in specific action, but not always. Sometimes it was enough for the debate to be seen to have taken place. Later in 2009 the Conservative MP for Enfield Southgate, David Burrowes, submitted an Urgent Question to ask the Home Secretary if he would make a statement on his decision not to intervene to stop the extradition of one of his constituents to the United States. The constituent in question was Gary McKinnon, who was accused in 2002 of having repeatedly hacked into US government computer networks and then copied encrypted information onto his own computer, shutting down one of the US Army's district computer networks for twenty-four hours. Under the terms of the Extradition Act 2003, the US government sought his extradition to face trial in the United States. In August 2008, McKinnon was diagnosed with Asperger's Syndrome and made fresh representations to the Home Secretary claiming that, because of his medical condition, his extradition would breach the European Convention on Human Rights. This had been denied.

David Burrowes argued that a more recent medical report raised new and material evidence, namely that McKinnon was suffering from a serious depressive disorder and was a suicide risk. Putting it more bluntly, he said, how ill and vulnerable did Gary McKinnon need to be not to be extradited to the United States? After Burrowes, no fewer than twenty-one MPs questioned Alan Johnson and, overwhelmingly, they argued that he had made the wrong decision and urged him to reverse it. He did not and the argument was played out for a number of years in the courts before his successor as Home Secretary, Theresa May, announced that extradition would not take place. The significance of the 2009 exchange was that David Burrowes, representing his constituent, but also raising effectively a wider issue of policy, successfully sought the presence of the responsible Cabinet minister. The Home Secretary set out his position, other colleagues expressed theirs, and a matter of intense public interest and media coverage was aired in the House of Commons in prime time thanks to the mechanism of the Urgent Question. Far from Parliament being sidelined from an important and urgent national conversation, the legislature was at the heart of it.

Similarly in May 2010, an Urgent Question to the Chancellor of the Exchequer interrogated the measures that would be implemented across government to deliver £6 billion of spending cuts that had been announced earlier that week. I granted the Question as the announcement of the figure, through press briefings days before, had been news to me and, I suspected, to most MPs. As Speaker, I was taking no view as to whether the government's chosen figure for savings was right or wrong. Rather, it struck me as a new and significant development that should therefore be announced in the House and subjected to scrutiny by its Members.

The new Chancellor, George Osborne, did not appear. It is the government's prerogative to decide which minister to field and, instead, the Chief Secretary, David Laws, came to the House. Interestingly, in the exchanges that followed, the first backbench Conservative contributor, Michael Fallon, was quick to say that 'it is always best if these announcements can be made to Parliament first'. Thirty-one Members questioned the Chief Secretary. It was the first real debate on the savings and as well as being worthwhile and procedurally proper, I had sent out a signal that oral statements to Parliament in such circumstances should be the norm. However, if they were not volunteered, a minister would not escape scrutiny. Almost inevitably, he or she would be subject to a UQ request, which I would invariably grant. In other words, ministers would always have to appear at the first opportunity in Parliament. Whether under a Labour, Conservative or coalition government, that is how it should be and must be in a system of parliamentary democracy. As Gladstone famously put it in his speech at Sebastopol, 'The business of the House of Commons is not to govern the country but to hold to account those who do.' I was determined that Parliament be enabled to do its duty.

* * *

As noted above, some questions can extract a golden bullet, achieving a dramatic impact. Others simply ramp up pressure and ensure that the spotlight is not switched off but continues to shine. Labour MP Tom Watson returned to the subject of phone-hacking by the *News of the World*, raised in the summer of 2009 by Evan Harris, when he asked the Home Secretary, Theresa May, if she would make a statement on the Metropolitan Police investigation into the alleged hacking. In total, the Home Secretary was questioned by twenty-two Members, but did not shift a millimetre from her stance that it was an operational matter for the police and she proposed no action. In one sense, it might be thought an ineffective set of exchanges. In another sense, it was far from it: many Members and the wider media could see that much remained unanswered and those, including Tom Watson, who suspected wrongdoing were motivated to continue to highlight the issue and seek a resolution.

A similar chain of events leading to a positive outcome began with an Urgent Question put to the Department of Health by the Labour MP for Kingston upon Hull North, Diana Johnson. This related to the publication of the Penrose Report into the contaminated blood scandal, which Diana Johnson described as the biggest disaster in the history of the NHS. It set the context for future campaigning for a further inquiry, and left both front benches in no doubt that the drive for proper closure on the subject would not be forgotten.

Other questions revealed strong opinions from surprising quarters. The Labour MP for Rotherham and former journalist, Denis MacShane, applied to me for permission to put an Urgent Question to the Foreign Secretary about proposed cuts to the BBC World Service. Press reports had appeared on the subject but the government had made no announcement about it in the Chamber. My sense was that colleagues on both sides of the House would want to air their concerns. Much of the time when I granted Urgent Questions, the senior Clerks who advised me on procedural issues tended to advise against, suggesting that I wait for another day, see what happens, or urge the Member concerned to apply for an end-of-day debate instead. Clerks tend to be cautious, and most of the senior ones rose through the ranks in an era when colleagues were not seeking Urgent Questions, Speakers were not granting them, or both. Yet to my amusement, all three senior Clerks piped up in unison that this request absolutely warranted the urgent attention of the House. All were devotees of the BBC World Service and shocked by this looming threat to it.

And sometimes questions had unexpected outcomes. In September 2012 John Baron, the Conservative MP for Basildon and Billericay, requested an Urgent Question to the Defence Secretary, Philip Hammond, about the alleged change in NATO's strategy in Afghanistan. Hammond was questioned by twenty colleagues but nothing especially new emerged. One of them, Paul Flynn, the Labour MP for Newport West and a long-standing critic of UK policy in Afghanistan, said that the country was 'arming and training our future enemy'. He went on to say, 'Is this not similar to the end of the First World War, when it was said that politicians lied and soldiers died, and the reality was, as it is now, that our brave soldier lions were being led by ministerial donkeys?'

At this point I intervened, asking him to clarify that he was not claiming that ministers had been lying to the House of Commons. Flynn said that that was precisely what he *was* saying and, although I gave him a further opportunity to withdraw what was a disorderly allegation in Parliament – allegations by one Member against another of dishonesty are out of order other than on a substantive motion alleging misconduct – he refused to do so. I therefore named him and asked the Deputy Leader of the House, Tom Brake, to move the motion under Standing Order 44 that 'Paul Flynn be suspended from the Service of the House'. The motion was agreed without a division and Mr Flynn withdrew from the House without complaint. He had indicated that he was prepared to accept the consequences of what he was saying, so he knew that he would be suspended.

I will mention one final example for its interesting array of issues and the firmness of its conclusion. On 8 January 2018, the first sitting day in the House of Commons after the Christmas recess, the Shadow Minister for Women and Equalities, Dawn Butler, submitted an Urgent Question seeking a statement on the appointment of Toby Young to the board of the Office for Students. The appointment had caused controversy since its announcement a few days earlier. Toby Young, a journalist by background, was founder of the West London Free School and Director of the New Schools Network, a champion of schools enjoying the autonomy to operate outside local authority control. A Conservative himself, Young had long been admired by other Conservatives and by some parents dissatisfied with the quality of local state schools. To them, Young was a welcome force for good. To the bulk of the Labour Party, however, Young was an elitist heretic whose work they regarded as damaging to mainstream state education. But the catalyst for the row that erupted after his appointment was the discovery of thousands of tweets by Young – some a decade or more old, but others more recent – which suggested that Young was a misogynist who also held deplorable views about gays, the disabled and the poor.

The question was fielded by the Universities Minister, Jo Johnson. He began by praising Young's record in promoting choice for consumers and encouraging competition in education. Regarding the controversial tweets, Johnson said that they were 'foolish and wrong', that he had made clear he regretted them and that Young had since done 'exceedingly good work' in education. For Labour, Dawn Butler said that she was 'flabbergasted' by the decision to appoint Young, which she believed left 'the credibility of the Office for Students in tatters'. She wondered if it was a case of 'jobs for the boys'. The minister's brother, Foreign Secretary Boris Johnson, had declared that Toby Young had 'caustic wit', making him the ideal man for the job. However, Butler concluded that 'if boasting of masturbating over pictures of dying and starving children is caustic wit, I most definitely have lost my sense of humour'.

Forcefully though Dawn Butler challenged Johnson, a further twenty-eight Members followed her and the real damage to the appointment was inflicted, unusually in such a situation, by the government's own backbenchers. Robert Halfon, Maria Miller and Sarah Wollaston all spoke powerfully against the appointment.

The minister had a very sticky and turbulent time at the despatch box that afternoon. The following day, Toby Young resigned from the board of the Office for Students. The general feeling that I detected in the Commons was that due diligence had not been done. Someone had badly wanted Young appointed but the appointment had spectacularly backfired. A week after the man was appointed, he had quit. There can be no doubt whatsoever that the Urgent Question played an important part in his downfall.

* * *

Another development was to champion the case for establishing a Backbench Business Committee (BBCom), which would choose the subject for debate when government Bills or other policies were not on the agenda. Thankfully, my efforts and those of many others came to fruition when the House, shortly before the 2010 election, debated and approved the establishment of such a committee, which duly happened at the start of the 2010 Parliament.

One of the most significant BBCom debates of that Parliament took place on 17 October 2011. As many readers will know, the Hillsborough Disaster was a fatal crush of football fans at Hillsborough stadium in Sheffield on 15 April 1989, when the FA Cup semi-final between Liverpool and Nottingham Forest was due to be played. Ninety-six people died in the crush and 766 were injured, making it the worst disaster in British sporting history. Shortly before kick-off, in an effort to ease overcrowding outside, the police match commander ordered an exit gate in the Leppings Lane stand to be opened, which led to even more supporters flooding in to standing-only pens that were already overcrowded. It was later established that the police planted false stories in the media indicating that Liverpool fans themselves were to blame for the disaster, despite the Taylor Report of 1990 concluding that the main cause was a failure of control by South Yorkshire Police.

The first coroner's inquest into the disaster, completed in 1991, ruled that all deaths that occurred that day were accidental, a verdict rejected by families of the victims, who sought a fuller inquiry. In 1997 Lord Justice Stuart-Smith ruled there was no justification for a new inquiry, and later private prosecutions brought against the police match commander, David Duckenfield, and his deputy also failed.

In 2009 a Hillsborough Independent Panel was formed to review all evidence. It was the work of this panel, and what many saw as an attempt to frustrate that work, which led to the debate in October 2011. In response to a Freedom of Information request by a BBC reporter, the Cabinet Office decided not to disclose papers relating to the disaster. This decision provoked huge resentment and anger. Some 140,000 people signed an online petition calling for the government to release all the Hillsborough documents in its possession. On the back of that grass-roots public protest, Steve Rotherham, the Labour MP for Liverpool Walton, applied to the Backbench Business Committee for a debate. He was supported in his application by an unprecedented 100 MPs from nine political parties. The House proceeded on 17 October 2011 to debate the following motion:

That this House calls for the full disclosure of all
Government-related documents, including Cabinet Minutes, relating to the 1989 Hillsborough Disaster; requires
that such documentation be uncensored and without
redaction; and further calls for the families of the 96 and
the Hillsborough Independent Panel to have unrestricted
access to that information.

Opening the debate, Steve Rotherham delivered a stunningly
powerful speech unforgettable for its combination of information and passion. Rotherham set out to debunk three
myths that had been levelled at Liverpool fans on the day
and perpetuated for decades thereafter: that thousands had
turned up late and ticketless; were drunk and aggressive; and
broke down a gate, causing a catastrophic crush. Rotherham
accused David Duckenfield of 'cowardice and deceit of the
highest order'. Before concluding his speech by reading into
the official record of Parliament the names of the 96 victims –
a rare, symbolic and powerful statement in itself – Rotherham
declared:

A botched inquest, a flawed inquiry, a farcical review of
evidence and a system that worked against, instead of for,
the families, have left a bitter taste. An unsympathetic
government, an unsatisfactory judicial process and an
unforgiving press have led observers to believe that an
organised conspiracy was acting against the best interests
of natural justice. We need the Government to act, and
we need this House to support the motion, to ensure that
there is no further backsliding on this issue.

If he lives to be a hundred, I doubt that Steve Rotherham will
speak better or feel prouder to stand up for victims and other
innocent folk than he did that day.

The Home Secretary, Theresa May, spoke immediately

after Rotherham. In her brief but dignified speech she made two crucial points. First, that she would do everything in her power to ensure that the families and the public got the truth. Secondly, she addressed head-on the reason for the debate. She said that the government's position had 'absolutely nothing' to do with the Cabinet Office's decision not to disclose papers relating to the disaster following the Freedom of Information request. She said that she was sorry that the way in which the government responded to the FOI request caused anxiety among the families and concern on Merseyside and beyond. The default position of governments is ordinarily to resist disclosure of documents but she had no desire to cover up, and she shared families' determination to establish the truth.

May's speech was very well received across the House and it set the tone for a consensual but passionate debate lasting just over four hours. In that time, twenty-nine speeches were delivered and several were quite outstanding, including those of Andy Burnham, Derek Twigg and Maria Eagle. For me, that of Alison McGovern was the most emotionally charged of all. Steve Rotherham called it 'brilliantly moving', and it was, delivered with an intensity, a humanity, a passion and an unbreakable insistence on the achievement of justice that made it for me both unforgettable and great.

The most significant fact of all was that the House rose to the occasion. No petty point-scoring took place. Speeches were delivered and heard in an atmosphere of dignity, respect and constructive endeavour. The motion was passed without a division of the House. Colleagues were unanimous.

Following the debate, and with sight of all relevant papers as the House had insisted, the Hillsborough Independent Panel reported in 2012. It confirmed the criticisms expressed in the 1990 Taylor Report, while also revealing new details about the extent of police efforts to shift blame on to fans, the role of other emergency services and the errors of the first coroner's inquest. The panel's report resulted in the previous findings of accidental death being quashed, and the creation of a new coroner's inquest. It also produced two criminal investigations led by police in 2012: Operation Resolve to look into the causes of the disaster, and that of the Independent Police Complaints Commission (IPCC) to examine actions by police in the aftermath. In June 2017 six people were charged with various offences including manslaughter by gross negligence, misconduct in public office and perverting the course of justice for their actions during and after the disaster.

* * *

Another of the most significant BBCom debates of that Parliament took place a week later, on 24 October 2011. It was secured and opened by the backbench Conservative Member of Parliament for Bury North, David Nuttall, who proposed the motion:

> That this House calls upon the Government to introduce a Bill in the next session of Parliament to provide for the holding of a national referendum on whether the United Kingdom should (a) remain a member of the European Union on the current terms; or (b) leave the European Union; or (c) renegotiate the terms of its membership in order to create a new relationship based on trade and co-operation.

I did not select any amendments to the motion because it struck me as clear and worthy of a vote.

Nuttall put a number of arguments to the House in support of a referendum. He claimed first of all that petitions and opinion polls showed that the vast majority of the British people wanted a vote on EU membership. Furthermore he contended that the EU intruded into ever more areas of our national life, that we had increasingly become run by Europe, and that millions of people wanted a self-governing Britain. Thirdly, he pointed out that more than thirty-six years had passed since the public had had their say in a referendum, that in that time not a single EU power had been repatriated to the UK and that 84 per cent of the current voting-age population had never voted in favour of Britain's continued membership of what was then the European Economic Community.

Speaking for the government, the Foreign Secretary, William Hague, began by recognising that disillusionment with the European Union in this country was 'at an unprecedented level' but gave a number of reasons why he believed the referendum proposition was wrong. Hague was joined in his opposition to David Nuttall's motion by the Shadow Foreign Secretary, Douglas Alexander, and by the Liberal Democrats.

In total, fifty-three MPs spoke in the debate, including the government and official Opposition front benches. Thirty-two speakers backed the motion for a referendum, twenty opposed it and one declared that he would abstain. So the debate was not monopolised by referendum supporters, but they did dominate it – at least numerically. Perhaps unsurprisingly, given that it was a whipped vote – that is, a matter of party policy for the three major parties to oppose it – that motion was duly defeated overwhelmingly, by 483 to 111. Yet, ironically, that was not the real significance of the vote. The most striking fact was that eighty-one Conservative MPs rebelled against a three-line whip to back the motion. To the horror and arguably the terror of the government whips, over fifty of those rebels were new Conservative MPs, first elected less than eighteen months earlier. Ordinarily, new MPs tend to be less rebellious as they have been elected on the back of their party leadership, are learning the ropes and tend to be loyal, even eager to please. Yet here they were – feeling no compunction in voting against instructions but in line with their consciences, constituents or constituency party or any combination of the three. Whether you agree with their vote or not, it was a striking assertion of backbench independence and should be respected as such.

There is little doubt that the Conservative leadership was not merely angry about the rebellion but shaken by it. In my view, it was the first major straw in the wind that would ultimately lead to Prime Minister David Cameron reversing his opposition to an EU referendum and signalling fifteen months later an intention ultimately to hold an in/out vote, which eventually took place in 2016.

Consistent with an important theme of the 2010–15 Parliament, that it was marked by very pronounced displays of backbench freedom, the second such straw came in May 2013. The Brexit-supporting MP for Basildon and Billericay, John Baron, tabled an amendment to the Queen's Speech calling for a referendum on Britain's EU membership in that session of Parliament. His amendment attracted 92 signatures and I selected it for a separate vote. His amendment was defeated but it garnered 133 votes (116 of which were those of Conservative MPs) – demonstrating once again that there was strong support among Conservative MPs for a referendum. The issue simply would not go away and, a year later, the Prime Minister bowed to the pressure from his Eurosceptic MPs for such a referendum. Whether you believe that that was a good move or a bad move, the move resulted from parliamentary pressure from Cameron's backbench colleagues. The BBCom debate, and the vote on the Baron amendment, made a real difference to government policy and to our EU destiny.

* * *

On 14 June 2012, the Conservative MP for Loughborough, Nicky Morgan, opened a debate on the apparently bland motion – what we call in the House of Commons a 'take note' motion – that 'This House has considered the matter of mental

health'. She had secured cross-party support for the debate
and had been granted time for it by the Backbench Business
Committee. Her rationale was straightforward and twofold.
First, she said that she and her colleagues had wanted a full
debate on the floor of the House because it had been at least
four years since the general topic of mental health had been
debated in the Chamber. As Morgan stressed, that was a long
time given that one in four of the population would experience
a mental health problem at some point in their lives. Secondly,
mental health challenges came at an economic and social cost
to the UK economy of £105 *billion* per annum, yet mental
health had been a 'Cinderella' service – poorly funded compared with other conditions and insufficiently talked about
inside or outside the House. It was, she said, the largest single
cause of disability, with 23 per cent of the disease burden of
the NHS. Yet the NHS spent only 11 per cent of its budget on
mental health problems.

Nicky Morgan made a thoughtful, well-informed, compassionate speech. It was a fine start to the debate but it was for
the two speeches that followed that it will be remembered.
Elected as the Labour MP for North Durham in 2001, Kevan
Jones had served as a junior Defence Minister from 2008 to
2010. A blunt-speaking, moderate Labour MP with a reputation as a tough cookie, Jones began by talking about his local
work as president of the MIND group in his constituency. He
set out what he regarded as a key distinction between different
types of mental health issues: life crises triggering short-term
problems on the one hand and the situation of those managing long-term conditions throughout their lives on the other.
He went on to discuss the effect of the health and social care
funding squeeze on mental health services and the impact of
welfare reform. These issues, knowledgeably and sensitively
addressed, absorbed the first twenty minutes of his speech. Yet
that was not what set it apart.

What made the speech memorable, and the atmosphere in

the Chamber one of spellbound respect, was the shift from the general to the personal. In his words:

> Now I am going to throw my notes away – I thought long and hard last night about whether to do this – and talk about my own mental health problems. In 1996, I suffered quite a deep depression related to work and other things going on in my life. This is the first time I have spoken about this. Indeed, some people in my family do not know about what I am going to talk about today. Like a lot of men, I tried to deal with it myself – you do not talk to people. I hope you realise, Mr Speaker, that what I am saying is very difficult for me.

Jones went on to say that depression 'creeps up very slowly' and added that 'we in politics tend to think that if we admit fault or failure we will be looked on disparagingly by the electorate and our peers'. Yet, that said, Jones emphasised that 'learning to admit that you need help sometimes is not a sign of weakness'.

Jones concluded his compelling speech with a heartfelt, perhaps plaintive, appeal for recognition of the pressure of being a Member of Parliament:

> Although being an MP is a great privilege – I have always thought that; it is a great thing that I love – it also has its stresses. Unless someone has done it, they do not know what those stresses can be personally, in terms of family, and in terms of what is expected of us in the modern technological age. A little more understanding from some parts of the media and some constituents about the pressures on the modern day MP would be very valuable.

The next Member I called to speak was Charles Walker, the Conservative MP for Broxbourne. In ten minutes, he delivered as powerful and moving a speech as anyone could wish to make. As if to unburden himself at the outset, he broached his own situation with the politically incorrect observation: 'I am delighted to say that I have been a practising fruitcake for thirty-one years.' One day, aged thirteen, at St John's Wood Tube station, he was 'visited by obsessive compulsive disorder'. Since then, it had played a 'fairly significant part' in his life, on occasions manageable and on other occasions 'quite difficult'. The condition had taken him to 'some quite dark places'. He told colleagues that he operated to the rule of four, so he had to do everything in even numbers. He had to wash his hands four times and he had to go in or out of a room four times. Woe betide him, he said, if he switched off a light five times because he would then have to do it another three times. He told the House that he had been 'pretty healthy for five years' but just when he let his guard down his condition, which he described as 'this aggressive friend', came and smacked him 'right in the face'. The example he gave was indeed arresting, inviting listeners to appreciate just how miserable and soul-destroying, as well as irrational, a mental health condition can be:

> I was on holiday recently and I took a beautiful photograph of my son carrying a fishing rod . . . I was glowing with pride and then the voice started, 'If you don't get rid of that photograph, your child will die.' You fight those voices for a couple or three hours and you know that you really should not give in to them because they should not be there and it ain't going to happen, but in the end, you ain't going to risk your child, so one gives in to the voices and then feels pretty miserable about life.

What has happened since those remarkable speeches were delivered seven years ago? Very quickly, at my suggestion, the House of Commons Commission approved funding of £25,000 per annum to allow us to direct MPs or House staff to access mental health treatment under contract with a Westminster-based provider. That sum, of course, would be nowhere near enough to help significant numbers of people with intensive or long-term requirements, but it was a start. I know of a number of colleagues who were distraught about their situations and have derived real help and comfort from the service that, perhaps belatedly, we have put in place.

Since that debate, at the time of writing there have been three Urgent Questions on mental health services as well as seventy-six debates. The government is now spending £11.9 billion on mental health services. The Opposition insists that services face spending cuts and the issue is a matter of real contention between the parties. That said, all of the major parties are now committed to parity of esteem between patients with physical health problems and patients with mental health problems. Again, at my request and that of others, the government repealed Section 144 of the 1983 Mental Health Act, under which anyone who had to be sectioned for six months would be disqualified from service as a Member of Parliament. Now people with acute difficulties can get help and return to the workplace.

Those are worthwhile markers of progress. Yet surely the biggest impact of that backbench debate and, in particular, of Kevan Jones's and Charles Walker's speeches, was to help to destigmatise the issue of mental ill health and to demonstrate why it was not merely desirable but imperative to discuss mental health constructively and sensitively, with a view to maximising understanding, improving services and enabling people with issues to be included fully, fairly and without discrimination in our society.

* * *

I have always been an early riser, usually leaping out of bed at 6 a.m. Ever since I entered the House of Commons in 1997,

I opted to start the day with a swim four times a week at a local health club. I am not a good swimmer. Mine is a pretty mediocre breast-stroke but I keep going for forty-five minutes at the very least and do not pause until I have finished.

When the kids were all at primary school, I would do the school run before beginning work. Often the day would begin with meeting parliamentary colleagues who had asked to see me. Their request could be for any number of reasons – they might be interested in using the State Rooms for a charitable function, for example. More often than not, I said yes as I was always keen to celebrate good causes and if I could help a colleague in the process, all the better. It was the right approach in principle and an easy way to keep or regain the support of one of my 'electors' in practice. I never forgot that my bosses were my fellow MPs: they elected me and they could sack me.

Sometimes a Member would come in to complain about the conduct of a parliamentary neighbour. Almost invariably I declined to get involved, emphasising that colleagues should try to resolve these differences themselves. I was the Speaker, not a personnel officer. Occasionally, a Member would come to tell me of his or her poor health and the length of an expected absence from the House. There was no requirement to tell me, as I was not an attendance monitor, but it was done as a courtesy. Also, although not as often as you might think, Members would come to tell me about amendments or new clauses that they planned to table, in some cases seeking advice on what would be 'in order' and seeking comfort that such amendments would be selected for debate and vote. I was always happy to guide them on the former and to steer them to seek advice from the Clerks, but I never made any promises on the latter. I had to consider all of the issues together at the relevant time, objectively and fairly. That meant I could not be in the business of giving advance promises to colleagues.

As well as MPs, there was a regular flow of meetings with senior leaders on the staff side of the House, and two regular daily meetings in Speaker's House. The first was with my Secretary, Peter Barratt, his deputy, Ian Davis, the diary secretary and my media adviser. Typically, it would last about twenty minutes, covering my schedule in the Chair for that day, speaking and media invitations and charitable requests. From day one until my final day in post, my instinct was to chair more rather than less – doing my allotted three hours in the Chair but, very frequently, four, five, six or more. This was obviously not my only role as I had to chair several internal House bodies, but it was the best-known, most visible, public-facing part of the role. It was also the part of my job that I relished the most.

Soon after being elected, I recall telling one of my senior staff that I fancied chairing more of the debate that day, and hoped that the Deputy Speakers would not mind. His response was typical.

'Mind, Mr Speaker? The question of minding does not come into it. The clue is in the title. It is called the Speaker's Chair. The sole purpose of the three Deputy Speakers is to take the Chair when the Speaker does not wish to do so.' In short, I would much rather be accused of hogging the Chair than of being an absentee landlord. In later years, in particular, I tended to do more and more.

The second of the daily meetings was the so-called 'briefing meeting'. That meeting was purely about the business of the House that day. In attendance were my Private Secretary and his deputy, the Clerk of the House, his deputy and one other senior Clerk, the three Deputy Speakers and the Serjeant-at-Arms. We would go through the House agenda for the day. Two main issues arose. First, whether to select an amendment to a motion and, if there were several, which to choose. I consulted the Clerks and then made my choice. Secondly, I had to decide whether to grant a Member's application for an Urgent Question to be put to a minister. Ultimately, it was down to me. I am told that my predecessor did not seek the views of

his Deputies at all, deciding on his own, and overwhelmingly against such applications. As well as seeking the views of
the Clerk and his colleagues – who were usually against – I
would ask the Deputies for their views. If I was undecided in
a particular case, I was happy to be influenced by them. If I
knew that I was minded to grant a UQ application, however, I
frequently just announced my decision in order to save time.

I had simple criteria. Was the question not merely important but *urgent* for that day? Decisions on such questions
were rarely matters of objective fact; they involved subjective
judgements. Many such questions failed to meet the test of
urgency – often they were what I dubbed UIMOM – Urgent
In Mind Of Member – and I rejected them. Yet I did grant 685
during my Speakership.

In the Chamber itself, I had to decide whom to call to ask
supplementary questions – the initial questioners having been
determined by random ballot – and whom to call to speak in
debates. With questions, there were several factors: how often
a Member asked questions, the need to hear different points
of view, the importance of accommodating select committee
chairs and others with known expertise, gender balance and
geographical spread were all to the fore in my reckoning. Similar considerations applied to debates. The Deputy Speakers
drew up a draft list of speakers and I would amend that list if
I judged it necessary. I usually did, though not dramatically.

Most Members took the rough with the smooth uncom-
plainingly. Some days they were called to question or make
speeches, other days not. A minority of colleagues could be exceptionally self-focused, viewing the occasion purely in terms
of the importance of them speaking and not taking account
of others. I well remember a senior Labour Member coming
up to the Chair to remonstrate with me: why had I not called
him in the third Question Time session that morning, thereby
censoring him and his opinions? Completely taken aback, I
pointed out that I had called him in each of the first two.

'Oh yes,' he replied, 'but I wasn't bothered about the first two, it was the third that mattered.' I said that I was not psychic. As he stood on the first two occasions, I rather assumed that he wished to put a question or to give the House the benefit of his views. I could hardly be expected to know that it was all merely net practice in readiness for the third session. He then astonished me further by enquiring again why I had not called him the third time.

'Others,' I replied.

'I don't follow you,' he said.

'The existence of other Honourable and Right Honourable Members who also wish to take part.'

To that, he offered the rejoinder, 'Yes, but I feel very strongly about the subject.' As I explained to him, the same could be said of and by every other Member.

All that I have described above concerns my work as Speaker. Yet I was still a constituency MP, and I would also see the staff in my constituency office every day. I took a very close interest in my correspondence, seeing every letter or email sent to me, signing off straightforward replies and proposing an approach to tackle some of the more difficult issues – major planning enquiries, responses to local controversies and the like. There was no unchanging routine but I tended to deal with Buckingham correspondence either at the start of the day, or when I came out of the Chair at night, or both. It absorbed a couple of hours per day, sometimes more if I had arranged to meet a minister in Speaker's House with constituents to discuss an issue of local concern – HS2, school funding, the local NHS, for example.

I mention my enjoyable and rewarding work as MP for Buckingham. However, many constituents argued that as the Speaker of the House I could no longer represent them as a local MP. I could not speak in debates, table questions or vote unless there was a tie and I had to exercise a casting vote. That scenario arose only once during my tenure, in April 2019.

People often said that they were 'disenfranchised' by my role as Speaker. My answer was and remains that I represented constituents in a fashion analogous to the way in which a government minister represented his or hers. My parliamentary neighbour in Aylesbury, David Lidington, a minister from 2010, spoke in the Chamber only from the front bench as a minister. He could not speak as a local MP but he represented constituents in correspondence with ministers, local authorities, public bodies and other organisations. If necessary, for example on a big issue, he would ask for a meeting with a minister, which a number of his constituents could attend alongside him.

That is exactly what I did – correspond and meet. Very early in my Speakership, I was struck by the greater speed and comprehensiveness of replies I received and by the fact that the replies started coming from Cabinet ministers, rather than their junior underlings. Jack Straw, the then Secretary of State for Justice, was the best example. I remarked favourably on this point to the then Speaker's secretary, Angus Sinclair, who said that it was a great mark of shame on a minister if he or she so hacked off the Speaker that the latter complained about slow or inadequate replies from their department.

'Oh I see,' I replied. 'So if I were annoyed with Jack on this score I would go to see him at the Ministry of Justice to remonstrate, would I?'

'No, Mr Speaker,' Angus replied. 'You would not go to see Mr Secretary Straw. He would come here to see you in Speaker's House for a meeting without coffee!'

Happily such a situation never arose. Ministers in successive governments sent me timely and full replies in recognition of the office of Speaker and of the fact that I could not raise constituency matters in the Chamber. Similarly, dozens of ministers came to see me in Speaker's House with constituents to discuss significant local issues. None ever refused or failed to do so. As a result, I enjoyed excellent access to the powers that be – far better than I had had as a regular MP – and was able to offer a speedier and better service to my constituents.

True enough, I could not ordinarily vote, whereas ministers do. Yet a minister can vote only with the government. If David Lidington had wanted to vote against the government on a local issue, for example HS2 (which most people in his constituency and mine opposed), he would have had to resign as a minister. Not surprisingly, David did not do so as, rightly or wrongly, there was a large pro-HS2 lobby in the House and his resignation would not have changed that. Instead, understandably and sensibly, he stayed as a minister and tried to influence government policy behind the scenes. That is how I worked too – making representations privately.

Nevertheless, some constituents still complained that because as I stood at election time in Buckingham as 'the Speaker seeking re-election' and, in keeping with convention, no Conservative, Labour or Liberal Democrat candidate stood against me, they were disenfranchised as they could not vote for a major political party. I totally get that point: if someone is committed to a party, they want to be able to show their support and vote for it, not to find that they can't because the local MP happens to be the Speaker. Yet the fact was that the House wanted the Speaker to be a local MP, representing constituents, dealing with a postbag and hearing public opinion, but the House did not want the Speaker to be dragged into controversy by having to wage an election campaign on a party political manifesto. Some people suggested that there should be a 'Speaker's seat', effectively a rotten borough with no constituents, meaning that I would become an ex-officio Member of the House and Buckingham could hold a normal party election. However, the Procedure Committee in the House rejected the idea repeatedly.

It is only fair to recall that, alongside the complainants, many constituents professed themselves perfectly happy. Thousands of people of all political hues told me that they voted for me because they reckoned me to be a good local MP, a good Speaker, or both. In 2010, amidst expenses controversy and local confusion about the fact that I was now the Speaker, I was elected with a reduced majority of 12,529. That rose to 22,942 in 2015 and to a record 25,725 in 2017. Of course, to err is human. I could not please everyone but I must have been doing something right.

* * *

The work of the House has been transformed for the better over the last decade. On top of rapid progress at Question Time, the award of hundreds of Urgent Questions and the important contribution of Backbench Business Committee debates, there are two other changes that have helped to tip the balance in favour of backbenchers and the House, rather than allowing the government to reign supreme.

First, I have reminded colleagues of the scope to seek urgent debates of up to three hours under something called Standing Order No. 24. Such debates are on 'take note' motions and therefore do not direct or bind the government. That is a weakness and should be changed. Nevertheless, they do allow colleagues to debate fully important, indeed urgent, matters for which the government has refused or failed to provide time. It is for the Speaker to grant a Member permission to speak for up to three minutes to justify up to three hours the following day being provided for such an emergency debate. If I am satisfied that the debate is proper to be held under the Standing Order, but there is evidence of opposition to such a debate, the Member applying must then rise with the support of forty colleagues or more. Assuming that he or she has that support, the Speaker then grants the debate, announcing the date and time for it.

During my Speakership ninety such applications were made to me and I ruled in favour of thirty-five of them. The House has then, on each occasion, shown its support for the decision. They have covered a very wide range of issues: from Chris Bryant's unsuccessful call for a public inquiry into the *News of the World* phone-hacking scandal to the then Prime Minister's backing for a debate on a Royal Charter for regulation of the press (from which he later backtracked); from Yvette Cooper's passionate debate to highlight the enormity of the Syrian refugee crisis to the Liberal Democrat Tom Brake's debate on breaches of electoral law by the Leave campaign in the EU referendum, the House has been enabled to air its concerns, anger and demands when the government and sometimes the official opposition have not opted to allocate time for the issues. My task has been to facilitate colleagues to speak on urgent matters whether their party wants them to or not. That is a crucial part of the role of the Speaker, in my view – not to be an agent of the government or the Opposition, but a dependable champion of backbenchers.

As we saw in the Prorogue, in 2019 the 'SO24' procedure was used for the first time to secure for non-government parties the control of the House's agenda. That control was used to introduce the so-called Benn Act, which provided for statutory protection against a no-deal Brexit on 31 October 2019 unless Parliament authorised such a departure.

The other change worthy of note is the election of the Deputy Speakers. The three Deputy Speakers when I became Speaker had all been nominated by their parties and nodded through the House without a debate or a vote. All were excellent. Yet the fact that the House now elects all three Deputies by secret ballot means that the House feels an involvement in, an ownership of, and empathy with the occupants of the Chair whom it has chosen. Similarly, the Deputies are ever-conscious that they owe their office not to a government or Opposition whip but to all Members, whom they must attempt to understand and serve. That is healthy democracy for you.

Reform is a process, not an event. Any institution should challenge itself. Keeping the best and improving the rest should be our guides. Of all the possible reforms that could have been made during my tenure but weren't, I would highlight three to which Parliament should return.

It is high time that the House of Commons took control of the organisation of government business, so that it is no longer determined exclusively by the whim or will of the Prime Minister and the Government Chief Whip. If they have the votes, they have a right to get their business through Parliament, but they should not have monopoly control of what is scheduled for debate. There is one very good reason for that. If they enjoy exclusive control of what is debated, it follows that they enjoy exclusive control of what is *not* debated and can keep kicking cans down the road. That is wrong in a democracy. The Conservative-Lib Dem coalition government pledged to introduce a House Business Committee to satisfy the democratic appetite of MPs and to do so by 2013. This would have meant that opposition parties and backbenchers could have had a say in the management of parliamentary business. Sadly, David Cameron chose to bin his promise but the argument for such a committee is as strong as ever, if not more so, and I earnestly hope that parliamentary colleagues will revive the idea.

The way in which the House of Commons deals with Private Members' Bills attracts scorn and often provokes fury when a popular measure is blocked by being 'talked out'. My own view is that there is a role for Private Members' Bills but it is a mistake to debate them on Fridays when the vast majority of Members are undertaking constituency duties. It would be much better to schedule a middle-of-the-week slot when a single Bill could be debated for, say, three hours before the House voted either to give it a Second Reading and send it into Committee or to reject it altogether. The status quo is a very poor advertisement for Parliament.

Finally, under our Standing Orders, Parliament can be re-called from recess but only if a member of the government, ordinarily the Prime Minister, asks the Speaker to agree to do so. Vesting the power solely in the government in this way is quite wrong. In recent times, David Cameron did recall Parliament in circumstances of crisis – notably the inner-city riots and when contemplating military action in Syria – but it is easy to envisage a situation in which MPs would like the House to be recalled, or indeed to sit longer, but a weak or embarrassed government would much prefer to shut up shop and keep MPs scattered in their constituencies, where they could mount no challenge to public policy. The Speaker does not have the power to recall Parliament on his own initiative and I am not suggesting that he or she should. A modest amendment to Standing Orders would create a trigger mechanism – for example, if 200 MPs from across the House requested a recall – that allowed the Speaker to recall the House.

None of the measures advocated above is revolutionary. All of them are eminently practicable. They would make Parliament more democratic, more relevant and more sensitive to the national mood.

6

Moderniser

Early on in the five-week campaign for the Speakership in 2009, I was having lunch in the Members' Dining Room when the Conservative MP for Gravesham, Adam Holloway, who had been elected in 2005 just shy of forty, told me that he would vote for me if I promised to wear the traditional Speaker's wig in the Chair each day. At first, I thought he was joking – but no, he was deadly serious. He felt that the wig conveyed the dignity of the office of Speaker and he rued its demise over the previous seventeen years.

Traditionally, for centuries, the Speaker would wear a white shirt, with a wing collar, a black waistcoat, a court coat and a black robe with a train, together with tights, knee breeches, buckled shoes and, crucially, a wig, typically of long grey/white hair in the manner of the eighteenth century. On the occasion of the State Opening of Parliament, and when other ceremonial events took place, the Speaker would wear a lace jabot (a kind of ornamental frill) around the neck and a State robe of black and gold. Up to 1992, all Speakers wore what became known in the jargon as 'the full regalia'. When my predecessor but one, Betty Boothroyd, was elected in 1992, she chose not to wear the wig and her successor, Michael Martin, followed suit eight years later, but in every other respect they were conventional, wearing the historic and 'approved' attire.

I had not given a moment's thought to 'the uniform' but when Michael Martin resigned in May 2009 I realised I was likely to be asked about it. I decided I would not wear the traditional outfit on a day-to-day basis for two reasons. First, I genuinely did not think it looked right on me, a short fellow who would look preposterous in such grand garments. In particular, I would never wear a wig, which struck me as absurd and pretentious. Secondly, I felt that the very elaborate and fussy uniform did not resonate with millions of people, especially young people. Instead of such outdated dress, on normal working days I would wear a business suit with a plain black gown, to denote that I held a particular role in the House that was different from that of my colleagues. Throughout the election campaign I was clear about my plans.

There were some mutterings of disapproval from Conservative MPs but I had done as I had intended. In any case, there was no rule on the subject. However, within days, Betty Boothroyd came in for a chat in Speaker's House. She told me how disappointed she was that I did not wear 'the uniform' and said that in recent days she had been stopped by people in the street who told her how horrified they were to see me on television wearing an ordinary suit. I explained that practices change over time and pointed out that she herself had 'abolished the wig'. Looking taken aback, she replied that she certainly had *not* abolished it but had merely decided 'not to wear it'. This struck me as splitting hairs and, albeit politely, I said words to that effect. It was, I suggested, 'a distinction without a difference'.

'Not at all,' she replied. 'I decided that I would prefer not to wear the wig and I asked the House for its agreement, which it gave. By contrast, you decided without consulting anyone not to wear it or any of the established uniform. It is most regrettable.'

I felt then and feel now that the traditional regalia is anachronistic and unnecessary. She thought, and a handful of people who wrote to me in protest at my choice agreed, that the uniform somehow reinforced the authority of the Chair. I don't think it does in modern Britain. The Speakership is not defined by the dress of the office-holder. It is defined by the role of the Speaker – championing parliamentary democracy, standing up for the rights of the House and facilitating its will.

In the first few months of my tenure, my refusal to wear court dress was used as a stick to beat me with, but it didn't bother me at all and in the years that followed the protest petered out altogether.

When I took office, I also thought that it was outdated that the senior Clerks in front of me in the Chamber wore court dress and wigs. However, my impression was that the Clerk, Dr Malcolm Jack, was comfortable with the arrangement and wanted it to continue. One can fight only so many battles at once. I had plans for other, more important, changes and I decided not to make an issue of it.

David Natzler became Clerk of the House, the most senior procedural officer in the place, in 2015. He had said to me that he would be happy to stop wearing a wig and for others to do so but the matter receded from our minds and, for two years, he and others continued to wear their court dress and wigs. In 2016 the question cropped up again and he suggested that wigs be scrapped. I encouraged him to put a paper on the subject to the House of Commons Commission, which supported the change. The only dissenter was the Leader of the House, David Lidington, who had a traditionalist's attachment to the wig, but he knew he was in a minority. I announced the change in the House in February 2017. A few Conservative MPs expressed their unhappiness but, as David Natzler and I had predicted to each other, there was no weight in the protest in terms of numbers or strength of feeling.

There was a similar non-controversy over neckwear. Shortly after we had discussed wigs, Tom Brake MP asked me whether it was a rule of the House or a condition of being called to speak that a Member should wear a tie. I told him that it was not a rule. The 'Conventions and Courtesies' note circulated by me at the start of each Parliament stipulated that members should wear business attire, which was generally interpreted by men to mean a suit and tie. However, things change. Millions of people in offices around the country do not wear ties or formal dresses, though they may be perfectly smart and businesslike. While I enjoyed wearing ties and would go on doing so, I had no intention of refusing to call a Member to speak if he was tieless. Most male colleagues continued to wear ties. A few did not and were free to make their choice. Eventually, on 29 June, months after the change had been implemented without fanfare, Peter Bone, the backbench Conservative MP for Wellingborough, said that he had noticed that a Member was allowed to ask a question in the Chamber without wearing a tie. Had there been a change in the rules? I told him that businesslike attire was necessary but that such attire did not demand a tie. Nothing further was said that day and, as with wigs, the matter has ceased to agitate anyone on any scale.

* * *

Some other changes, though, were more significant, and were commensurately harder to bring about. In seeking election as Speaker, I was very aware that there was a pistol shooting gallery on the Parliamentary Estate – situated at basement level in the House of Lords – but no nursery where MPs or staff in the House could pay to place their young children during the working day. I had no particular objection to the shooting gallery, though it did seem quaint and something of a throwback to a bygone age. But the asymmetry was appalling: a sporting facility for a tiny minority, predominantly men, but no nursery which could facilitate a better work-life balance.

I thought the main issue was the provision of an emergency facility – most colleagues already had some childcare arrangements in place, and it was only when these broke down that there was a problem. In those circumstances, Members often had to resort to depositing their children in their party's whips' office during votes. At best, this was plainly unsatisfactory and at worst it could be thought to be an act of wanton cruelty to subject a young child to the care of a whips' office with, to put it mildly, no skill or experience in the sensitive handling of young children. Opinion about the capacity of whips to deal sensitively with strong-willed adults would itself be divided.

I asked to see the relevant official in the House with responsibility for allocation of rooms and offices. After explaining what I had in mind, he agreed that it was a good idea in principle but feared it was undeliverable in practice as there was 'no suitable site, Mr Speaker'. I professed astonishment at the idea that there was 'no suitable site' throughout the entire Palace of Westminster. He suggested that he prepare a paper, listing and assessing any options and giving his advice, but I was uneasy about that as he had sounded so downbeat. I suggested that we look at possible sites together, and among those we visited was the shooting gallery. In terms of space, it would have been adequate but the House of Lords might well have objected and it was in their part of the estate. More importantly, it was underground and had no windows, and did not seem a healthy or feasible proposition to try to accommodate up to forty children there. We eventually concluded that there were two credible locations – North Curtain Corridor, which is on the ground floor adjacent to Speaker's House, and Number 1 Parliament Street, barely 100 yards from the Commons, a site which consisted of a set of offices, a café and Bellamy's Bar, used predominantly by MPs' researchers.

Throughout these deliberations, it was known that I was planning a nursery. As often happens, sympathetic MPs said nothing because they did not object. My reading of the situation was that the objectors were a minority, but a vociferous minority. Sure enough they began asking questions in the House about the plans. Some were openly hostile on grounds of alleged unsuitability or cost; others claimed not to be averse *in principle* but to know that the sites being suggested were inappropriate. In a number of cases it was blindingly obvious that some knew nothing and cared less about the need for a nursery: it was my first big project as Speaker, and they simply wanted to undermine me by blocking it.

The House of Commons Commission discussed the matter several times from July 2009 onwards. In November that year it became obvious to me that in the debate about the nursery I had an advantage and a disadvantage. My advantage was that I had strong support from the Leader of the House, Harriet Harman, and, slightly to my surprise, from the Conservative backbencher on the Commission, David Maclean. He backed me partly because he genuinely believed that there was a compelling case for a nursery but also on the grounds that, within reason, what the Speaker wanted the Speaker should have.

The disadvantage I had was that Stuart Bell, the Labour chair of the Finance and Services Committee, whom I suspected all along was against the idea, finally broke cover and blurted out his opposition. Previously he had suggested that any proposal would have to come before his committee. I had resisted that, as it was obvious to me that he would promptly kick the whole idea into touch. Now he helpfully confirmed my suspicions by revealing that he had informally discussed the proposal with members of his committee and they had been opposed to it.

The stance of the Shadow Leader of the House, Sir George Young, was more nuanced but less than supportive. He loftily declared that he was 'not philosophically opposed' to the idea of a nursery but he wanted to wait until after the dissolution of Parliament before making a final decision, based on projected costings and anticipated demand, as to whether to go ahead. The cat was out of the bag. He and Stuart Bell hoped to scupper the project. There and then I resolved that I would happily allow further work to be done, costings undertaken and so on, but that I would ensure that the Commission – by consensus if possible, but by majority vote if necessary – would decide the matter before the general election in 2010 and sign contracts accordingly.

In December we considered a paper from officials which invited us to choose between the North Curtain Corridor site and Bellamy's Bar in 1 Parliament Street. Previously, my impression had been that the Commission was mildly veering towards the former but, on grounds of cost, space, and both the speed and risk of delivery, the paper recommended 1 Parliament Street. Either way, the cost of refurbishment and conversion for use as a nursery would be approximately £400,000, later rising to a little over £500,000. One downside of North Curtain Corridor was that it would involve the requisition of half a dozen MPs' offices, including those of senior Labour MPs Margaret Beckett and Denis MacShane, which was likely to be stiffly resisted. The closure of Bellamy's Bar would lose some revenue and would be vigorously resisted by researchers who enjoyed it, not to mention their bosses who might (and did) complain on their behalf.

Harriet Harman and David Maclean backed me in arguing that we should go for the Bellamy's site and ride out the clamour of protest. As Labour MP Tom Watson later put it so pithily, 'The objection to the nursery site, that it involves closing a bar, is feeble. There is no shortage of places where you can get a beer on the Parliamentary Estate but there is nowhere you can put a baby.'

As previously noted, Sir George Young had earlier informed the Commission that he was not 'philosophically opposed' to the idea – itself most welcome – but, despite my gentle exhortation to him to advance to a statement of practical support, this *éminence grise* of the Conservative Party could not bring himself to make so bold a move. Nick Harvey seemed unhappy about the bar's closure, fearing that it could cause 'adverse comment'. Well, it might among a small minority of people, but not among most colleagues or the public. Sir Stuart Bell insisted that the cost would have to be met by new resources as no other budget could be cut. Harriet argued that we should find savings elsewhere so that the House's financial plan was undisturbed.

I was relaxed either way. It was a one-off capital cost for an invaluable project that would endure long into the future, and the money was justified. But if colleagues preferred it to be met from within existing budgets, I was fine with that. Savings could be and would be found, and this was finally agreed: a nursery would be established in 1 Parliament Street to be operational in September 2010, on the basis that it would seek to recover the full running cost from users. I wanted to cheer from the rafters. Instead, Harriet and I exchanged approving glances.

After five months, the Commission had made a decision that would make Parliament more convenient, more human and more in keeping with the modern world. In doing so, moreover, we had faced 'no philosophical objection' from the Rt Hon. Sir George Samuel Knatchbull Young Bt. How very good of the fellow, and I am sure we counted ourselves lucky not to be more vigorously opposed by such a senior parliamentarian.

Today the nursery is a thriving concern and for that I shall always be grateful for the support in particular of Harriet Harman and David Maclean. They share the credit for a project that continues to be a godsend for individual staff, members and children and an emblem of progress for the House.

* * *

Another skirmish in pursuit of a more modern Parliament came at the beginning of 2013, when my attention turned to the pay levels of the lowest-earning staff on the Parliamentary

Estate. It was actually Sally who asked me whether the House paid the London Living Wage and used zero-hours contracts. She encouraged me to look into it and make it my mission to get it sorted – and I am extremely glad she did.

I asked the then Clerk and Chief Executive, Robert Rogers, whether everyone employed by or contracted to work for the House was paid at least the London Living Wage. 'Oh, I should certainly imagine so, Mr Speaker. The House is a very good employer,' was Robert's immediate reply.

I had come to know Robert well over the previous few years. His natural disposition was one of breezy self-confidence and great satisfaction with everything for which he could be held responsible. Accordingly, I was not reassured. I told him that what he *imagined* was not what I asked. Within a couple of weeks, Robert told me that he understood that everyone was paid above the LLW, though there was some uncertainty over whether we could insist on external contractors paying that wage as a condition of their contracts. Months later, however, Robert told me that it had become apparent to him that a very small number of contractors might not be being paid the LLW after all.

Myfanwy Barrett, our excellent Director of Finance, and her team ploughed through all the contractors' agreements, satisfying themselves that the overwhelming majority entailed payment of the LLW. Where they didn't, she sought and obtained assurances. Once we had put our House fully in order, we received accreditation as a Living Wage Employer by the Living Wage Foundation.

I have always appreciated the support of Commission colleagues on this matter and the great work done by Myfanwy. Not only would the change make life just a little easier for a small minority of low-paid workers, I felt that it said something important about the DNA of Parliament as an institution that we treated people fairly. Goodness knows why no one had thought of it before 2013.

There was similar reform over the matter of casual staff, after I was disturbed to find that around 150 people were on the House's books on zero-hour contracts. House management had apparently decreed that it was acceptable, not least in catering, to use people on that basis. But there was no mutuality of obligation – in other words, contracts of this type imposed an obligation on staff to be available to work but carried no obligation on the part of the House to guarantee them work. We had very lengthy discussions on the subject at two Commission meetings before agreeing to end zero-hours contracts for all directly employed staff of the House. The Shadow Leader, Angela Eagle, and Frank Doran, the backbench Labour representative on the Commission, were stalwart allies on the issue.

* * *

Another early and continuing priority for me was to try to make the senior staff of the House more diverse and representative of modern Britain. In senior positions, the norm was very much 'male, pale and stale': there were – and still are – a great many white, middle-aged, middle-class men.

When I was elected to the Chair, the Speaker's Chaplain was Canon Robert Wright. The role had existed for centuries and Robert himself had been in the post since 1998. A shy and diffident, but also learned and kind man, his duties were to conduct daily prayers in the Chamber of the House, to conduct a weekly Eucharistic service in the Chapel, to conduct weddings, marriage blessings and baptisms of Members, and to be responsible for the pastoral care of both Members and staff of the Palace of Westminster. I had known and got on well with Robert, but it was not a great surprise when he told me that he would look to retire just after the 2010 election.

When his decision became more widely known, a couple of Members suggested that I should not look for a successor but decide instead that the role was an anachronism which should be discontinued. I respected that view but did not agree with it. I am proud of my Jewish origin but would not claim to be a person of faith, let alone an Anglican. However, I sensed that the daily prayers before the start of each sitting day were popular and that a great many colleagues – of faith and of no religious faith – would miss them, so I had no hesitation in agreeing that we should begin the search for a successor.

For as long as anyone could remember, the Speaker's Chaplain had also served as the Rector of St Margaret's Church, Westminster, and as a minor Canon of Westminster Abbey. I was told that the Abbey and Church would, as usual, establish an interview panel, and I made it known that, since the successful applicant would be working closely with me, I wanted to see all shortlisted candidates myself, and wanted the trawl of potential chaplains to include a determined drive to attract female and BAME candidates. This was readily agreed.

The post was duly advertised and a few weeks later a shortlist of six emerged, with four male candidates and two female. One of the latter was BAME. Would I like to see each of them? Indeed I would. The four men seemed competent and solid. All were unexceptionable; none was to me outstanding. In fact, after the hour of interviews, two of the four men had morphed in my mind and frankly I could not remember one from another.

Of the two women, however, a vicar from Hackney called Rose Hudson-Wilkin, struck me as hugely charismatic, insightful and engaging. Instinctively, I felt that she would be a deeply empathetic Chaplain, building and nurturing strong relationships across the House and serving as a fine ambassador for Parliament as an institution. The other female candidate also made an uplifting impression, but I was bowled over by Rose and determined that she would be the next Speaker's Chaplain.

To my amazement, though, I was told that neither woman

had found favour with the Church interview panel. They had not felt that Rose would 'fit well with the congregation' and I was told that her taste in Church music would jar with the known preferences of parishioners. The panel had apparently been united in support of one of the male candidates and did not want to appoint Rose.

I was asked if I wanted to meet the intended appointee.

'Certainly not,' I replied. 'First of all, I have already met him when I saw all six candidates. Secondly, it would be quite wrong of me to meet him now, for that would imply a willingness on my part to appoint him as Speaker's Chaplain which I have no intention of doing.'

Shortly afterwards, the Dean of Westminster, John Hall, renowned for his impeccable courtesy and emollient manner, came in for a chat. We had a very civilised exchange in which we agreed honourably to disagree about whom to appoint. I felt I had no right to seek to impose a Rector he did not want but, equally, he had no right to impose on me a Speaker's Chaplain I did not want. We realised the only solution was to split the role: he would ask his preferred candidate to serve as Rector of St Margaret's Church and minor Canon of the Abbey and I would ask Rose if she would accept the role of Speaker's Chaplain only. Happily for me, and the House, Rose agreed. Initially, she would work for us for thirteen hours per week, though later her hours tripled.

Initially, as with any candidate, Rose had to work to prove herself. In particular, there were people who, totally wrongly, thought that I had wanted her only because she was female and black. I wanted Rose because she was the outstanding candidate. More than nine years later, Rose was hugely liked in the House. Gracious, compassionate, humane, imaginative and eloquent, she proved an outstanding ambassador for Parliament. As I left the Commons, she became Bishop of Dover. Her appointment was immensely popular and richly deserved. I was thrilled to give a reading at her consecration service in

November 2019 and could not be happier that her talents have been belatedly recognised by the Church.

The Serjeant-at-Arms was another senior position in the House. As the name suggests, traditionally the Serjeant concerned himself with the security of the Chamber, although in recent years (with the appointment of a separate security director) the focus had shifted, and become a more MP- and public-facing role: arranging access, solving problems and organising ceremonies. When the Queen visited the House of Commons, for example, or we received visits from distinguished foreign leaders, the Serjeant-at-Arms was in the lead in formulating arrangements in concert with Black Rod in the House of Lords.

This function had been carried out by a woman, Jill Pay, since 2008 – she had been the first female Serjeant-at-Arms. When Jill retired in 2012 I expected that her deputy, and the number three in the Serjeant's team, would both apply. Among senior officials, one rushed to say to me, 'What you need in the post, Mr Speaker, is a good ex-military man.' Actually, I was not so sure about that – we might recruit another woman, and again I wanted to ensure a diverse supply of candidates.

I was delighted when the Assistant Serjeant, Lawrence Ward, put his name forward. A state-educated guy, who left school at sixteen and later obtained an Open University diploma, he had had a number of roles in the House and shown great dedication, attention to detail and striking interpersonal skills in getting the most out of his staff. He would face stiff competition but I was glad that he applied. The very senior staffer who had favoured 'an ex-military man' observed to me sniffily, 'I think you can do better than Lawrence Ward, Mr Speaker.' It was rank snobbery of a kind which I so often encountered among those public-school types who were socially grand, thought that they were socially grand, or aspired to be socially grand. I have never had much time in life for people who look as though they have a smell under their nose and think that it's a frightful cheek for the 'lower orders' to try to rise above their station.

Lawrence interviewed superbly and we appointed him. Without fuss or controversy, he created the most diverse team of doorkeepers Parliament had ever known and served us effectively, proudly and cheerfully for three years until he was headhunted to be Head of Global Security for PA Consulting. Lawrence was completely dependable and a great appointment. Our loss was that company's gain and I took vicarious pride in the fact that someone we valued in Parliament was valued beyond it.

After Lawrence's departure, we had to find a new Serjeant, and we appointed Mohammad (Kamal) El-Haji, who had previously served as Head of Security at the Ministry of Justice. A black belt in karate, Kamal is not only physically impressive but has excellent interpersonal skills and came with glowing references. He also happened to be the first BAME Serjeant in the history of the House.

These and other appointments – Saira Salimi, for example, became the first female and BAME Speaker's Counsel – are all to senior roles. They have been made on merit and have therefore been right in themselves. Yet they also possess the merit of making the House look a little more like the country it is supposed to represent. However, I am under no illusions: one-off appointments are no substitute for cultural change, and there needs to be a strategic approach to recruitment, retention and promotion that will enable every department in the House to be more diverse and representative. We now have a series of Workplace Equality Networks seeking to support and encourage staff from historically and still under-represented groups – ParliAgender for female staff, ParliOUT for LGBT+ staff, ParliAble for disabled staff, ParliReach for BAME staff and ParliON for people from lower socio-economic groups. I have done what I can to support them and to support the drive to change the look of the House. I set up a BAME Advisory

Panel which researched some of the reasons why the House of Commons has failed to attract BAME applicants to more senior roles. With the new and dynamic Head of Diversity and Inclusion, Jennifer Crook, a systematic approach is now under way, supported by specialist recruitment consultants, to make the House a sharply more diverse place over the next five years.

* * *

As long ago as 2006, the Administration Committee in the House of Commons and the Information Committee in the House of Lords had produced a proposal for the creation of an Education Centre, with a capacity to accommodate up to 100,000 school children every year and teach them something of the workings of Parliament. There was a huge demand for school visits, and this proposal had been endorsed by both Houses in 2007, but soon ran into the sand. The proposal would have entailed a cost in the tens of millions which, in the light of the financial crisis of 2008 and beyond, was widely thought to be unpalatable and unrealistic.

Having been in post for nearly four years, I decided to try to resurrect the idea. Discussions were undertaken and a paper produced, which identified a possible site in Victoria Tower Gardens, adjacent to the House of Lords. I sensed there would be resistance from our colleagues in the Upper House, and went as far as enquiring whether it would be possible to proceed without the say-so of the Lords. John Pullinger, Director General of Information Services, indicated that it would, but he didn't think it would be necessary. He assured me and the Commission that the points being made by Peers were 'points of detail, rather than concerns about the project as a whole'.

My political nose told me that John was wrong about that. My sense was that the Lords were identifying multiple points of detail on which they would remain dissatisfied, allowing them to object to the particular proposal while claiming to support the 'principle' of an Education Centre to be built somewhere, somehow, some time – just as long as it was not here and now.

We also needed planning permission, but after one further discussion at the Commission in July 2013, there was unanimous, cross-party agreement to deliver an Education Centre in Victoria Tower Gardens. I told the Commission that 'should the Lords not want to back the scheme, the Commons should proceed on its own'.

Predictably, the Lords objected on a number of grounds: they disliked the Centre's proposed design, thought it cost too much, and weren't keen on the idea of hundreds of school kids trooping through their patch. They appeared implacably opposed.

But I was just as immovable. In one of my one-to-one meetings with the Clerk, he neatly encapsulated the two issues involved – financial propriety and political prudence. On the former, I welcomed his confirmation that it was legitimate to go ahead with the project. He asked if I wanted to proceed in the face of Lords resistance and hope that Peers would come round in the long run, or play for time in the hope of garnering support in the other House. Instinctively, and without hesitation, I told him that I wanted to press ahead. It was always the easy option to put the issue on the back-burner and avoid a row. The result would be a decade or more of delay and a denial of opportunity for the young people I wanted us to serve and engage. We should go ahead on our own. If the Lords came round in due course, fine. If they didn't, so be it.

Construction work began in earnest in late summer 2014 and the Centre was opened by the television scientist Professor Brian Cox in July 2015. It contains a series of learning spaces which are housed within individual rooms. Each of the learning spaces has a theme: Commons, Lords, Monarchy and My Parliament. The rooms each contain augmented reality experiences: in the Commons, Sir Winston Churchill introduces young people to the Chamber; in the Lords, students can explore a 3D model of the Chamber and follow the Yeoman Usher as he puts the mace in place at each session; and in the Monarchy room, portraits of Queen Victoria and King Charles I come to life and talk about their relationship with Parliament. Demand to visit the Centre heavily outstrips supply and there is, as a result, a long waiting list of school groups wanting to visit. It was gracious of the then Lord Speaker, Frances D'Souza, to turn to me on the day of the official opening and say, 'Well done, John. You were right to pursue this. It will be great.' It is now no longer a matter of any controversy. Sadly, and perhaps inevitably, because it is a great success story, it is of no interest to the media whatsoever.

* * *

I am proud too of other progressive changes, which may seem minor but which help remind those who work in Parliament that we do so in the twenty-first century. In March 2010, after I had successfully applied for a licence to hold civil partnership services on the Parliamentary Estate, Chris Bryant made history by marrying his partner, Jared, in the Members' Dining Room. Other same-sex couples have followed in their footsteps although, regrettably, the privilege of Members being able to marry in the Chapel of St Mary Undercroft in Westminster Hall cannot be extended to them since, to my continued frustration, the Church of England is exempted from the equal marriage legislation. Another change is that I accepted the argument that Members with children should be able to bring them through the division lobby rather than having to deposit them in their whips' office or some other unsatisfactory location. A Lib Dem couple, Jo Swinson and Duncan Hames, were the first to do this with their young son Andrew, but other parents of young children have followed suit. Some objected, of course, but many colleagues, myself included, think that far from offending any democratic norm, it humanises the House of Commons when children are present on the Parliamentary Estate. Sometimes, during a division, a Member now brings his or her baby into the Chamber itself while the votes are being counted and before debate resumes. At first, this prompted tut-tutting from traditionalists, but even they have now piped down. Such a scene is regarded as entirely normal and, indeed, rather lovely.

* * *

Towards the end of the 2010–15 Parliament, I was approached by a number of Members who believed strongly that there should be a Women and Equalities Select Committee. After all, they reasoned, we had a Minister for Women and Equalities, which, despite being a part-time position, was an executive role in an increasingly high-profile area of public policy. It was only right that a light should be shone on the minister's work by a select committee. David Natzler told me he was not averse to the idea – though each committee costs money and I sensed that he was mildly anxious about that, whereas I was not – but he advised that there was no way the government would agree to it in the last few months of the Parliament. He suggested instead that I press for it at the start of the next Parliament before all the select committees were re-established – something that, perhaps unsurprisingly, the government of the day was never in a tearing hurry to do.

Days after the 2015 election, I saw the new Chief Whip, Mark Harper, and made the argument for such a committee. He was open to the idea but had reservations about the cost: the staffing costs of a typical select committee are around half a million pounds a year. Harper made no firm commitment but undertook to consider the idea. Meanwhile I tipped off the Labour Chief Whip, Rosie Winterton, and urged her to fight for it, emphasising that many of her own colleagues were extremely keen. Harriet Harman did the same and Rosie was a faithful ally as usual. Ultimately, Mark Harper told me that he was willing to endorse such a committee as long as a Conservative MP could be its first chair. I agreed, the Opposition agreed, the House agreed and it has now been operational for four years.

A further welcome and modernising touch came about in 2019. Knowing that several Members were pregnant, I was strongly taken by the case for MPs on parental leave to be able to vote by proxy. The rationale was simple and compelling. Members who had had a baby and were on leave could not vote in person without interrupting those crucial early months of motherhood. Yet by not voting for months, they were viciously attacked in the media and on the internet. For example, Lucy Powell, the hugely assiduous Labour MP for Manchester Central, was denounced as the laziest MP in Britain. All the bigots, chauvinists and misogynists clamoured to condemn MPs who were legitimately on leave. However, if MPs on baby leave could nominate a colleague to act as their proxy, they could vote, and this particularly nasty attack would fall away at a stroke.

I raised the issue with the Leader of the House, Andrea Leadsom, and the Chief Whip, Julian Smith. Leadsom told me that she was sympathetic to the idea. However, the government whips were not, arguing that MPs absent on parental leave could be 'paired' with a Member from the other side of the House, each agreeing simply not to vote. That way, the result would be unaffected and the House would not need to invent a new system.

The trouble with that approach was that it still left a Member on baby leave open to the charge of being lazy by not voting. The House debated the issue and supported change a number of times in 2018 but the votes were non-binding and the government refused to act. Then came a catalyst for change. In the summer of 2018, a furious row broke out when it emerged that Julian Smith, the Government Chief Whip, had asked Brandon Lewis, the Conservative Party Chairman, to break a pairing agreement and to take part in a crucial Brexit vote. The pair in question was Jo Swinson, the Liberal Democrat deputy leader, who was on maternity leave. Smith claimed that it was an innocent error on his part but Opposition MPs did not buy that for an instant. The pairing system was now irretrievably broken. After a further six months' delay and obstructionism by the evidently frazzled and exhausted Smith, during which time I repeatedly made clear in the Chamber my own impatience for change, that change finally came. Andrea Leadsom tabled the motion in January 2019 and it was passed by the House without a division. Several Members have now benefited from this modest, necessary and long overdue reform.

Other changes were perhaps less visible to outsiders but no less important for the effective running of the House. When I became Speaker, the Clerk of the House, our most senior procedural adviser, was also its Chief Executive. That had been the case since the early 1990s and a review of House management in 2007 had endorsed this twin-hatted role. New in post, I was not bothered by the arrangement, and had other priorities, but over time I came to the view that the two roles should be separated after the retirement of Robert Rogers, Malcolm Jack's successor. In theory, it was possible that the person best equipped to be our most senior constitutional adviser, the Clerk, would also top the class at the Harvard Business School or excel as a management consultant at McKinsey. In practice, it was very unlikely. However, it became clear that proper separation would require new legislation and that there were probably enough people inclined to the status quo for that to be difficult. So the next best option, it seemed to me, was to choose someone with managerial expertise who could also perform the role of Clerk, rather than the other

way round, and in July 2014 we appointed Carole Mills, the
Chief Executive of the Australian Parliament, in preference to
our Clerk Assistant, David Natzler.

The decision was leaked within a few days. We were in recess.
The newspapers had little to report. It was an unconventional
appointment to which the outgoing Clerk and a number of
traditionalists on both sides of the House strenuously objected. The press delighted in reporting the controversy and I was
advised that the appointment would simply not be acceptable
to the House. To this day, I am not sure that many colleagues
felt especially strongly – indeed, I know a large number of
members who told me that they had no idea who the Clerk
of the House was – but the political reality was that several
people on the government benches were adamantly opposed.
Also, there were plenty of people who had previously shown
no interest in the subject but who, for ideological or personal
reasons, were hostile to me and determined to prolong the
row.

In September 2014 the House resolved unanimously to
establish a select committee on the governance of the House
under the chairmanship of Jack Straw. Perhaps to the surprise,
and certainly to the dismay, of the senior Clerks and other
supporters of 'no change', the committee heard from multiple
witnesses who favoured change in the way the House was run.
To me, most importantly, it recommended that the joint role
of Clerk and Chief Executive should be discontinued. There
should be a Clerk who would be Head of the House Service
– a nod to the important work of the Clerk – and there should
be a 'Director General' (the traditionalists on the committee
absolutely resisted the title Chief Executive) who would be in
charge of day-to-day management of the Parliamentary Estate,
reporting to the Clerk and the House of Commons Commission, chaired by the Speaker.

So it was a compromise, but a compromise that achieved
the split that I wanted. The committee knew that the change

required primary legislation and recommended that the government find time in the New Year to introduce the very modest Bill required for the purpose. The government agreed, and the Bill was introduced, going through all of its stages in one day without a division. The House was subsequently able to appoint David Natzler as Clerk and a person with real commercial experience, Ian Ailles, as Director General.

I should have made the argument for change earlier, though the Conservative government was not receptive and it may well have made no difference. I could have handled the matter better, and the process was messy. Several of my opponents were not interested in the merits of the arguments but simply wanted to pick a fight. As usual, most of the media had no understanding of or interest in the merits of the arguments either, viewing it purely in personality terms. Ultimately, however, common sense prevailed.

* * *

Common sense was not always in abundant supply, however, and what came to be known as 'Clerkgate' rumbled on in various forms. On 8 March 2018 the BBC's *Newsnight* programme broadcast allegations that MPs had bullied House of Commons Clerks over a period of years, perhaps even decades, and had escaped unpunished. It was suggested that allegations had been 'hushed up' and, in a number of cases, victims had been shifted to other jobs without their tormentors having to take responsibility for their behaviour.

Not a single named witness was quoted. One historic case involving a Member and a Clerk was highlighted from 2012/2013, since when our internal Respect policy had been changed and improved. One of my parliamentary colleagues was named as a bully with no named accuser and not a scrap of evidence produced against him.

In addition, and obviously very importantly to me, I myself

was named. *Newsnight* had written to me nine days earlier alleging that I had bullied my Private Secretary, Kate Emms, who had worked for me in the Speaker's Office from July 2010 until March 2011. The *Newsnight* journalist who wrote to me alleged that such had been my behaviour that Ms Emms had left and been signed off with post-traumatic stress disorder. He claimed in addition that she had originally been featured in a portrait of me at work in the Chamber but had been removed from the painting, implying that I had effectively airbrushed her from the record.

At the time, I confined myself to an explicit and unequivocal denial of the charge of bullying. I was in no position, and it would have anyway been quite wrong, to comment on the point about PTSD – I have no way of knowing about an employee's medical circumstances unless I am told by that employee, which I certainly was not. Foolishly, I ignored the point about the portrait, considering it too ridiculous to warrant comment. However, I underestimated the *Newsnight* team's sense of theatre and desire to hype up a story for which, when broadcast, they produced not a single on-the-record witness.

The truth about the picture was prosaic. I had decided on a different type of portrait to those of my predecessors, featuring me at work in the Chair accompanied by my then Private Secretary, namely Kate Emms. However, Kate left in March 2011. The portrait was completed in the autumn and unveiled in late November 2011. It had previously been a work in progress. When completed, it naturally featured the incumbent Private Secretary, Peter Barratt, not his predecessor. That has nothing to do with airbrushing and everything to do with accuracy.

On the main issue, namely the charge of bullying, I confess that I was astonished that *Newsnight* apparently thought it proper to run a feature containing an allegation against me without any named witness to support it. I would have been happy to offer a full account of what happened between July

2010 and March 2011 but I was advised by Speaker's Counsel, Saira Salimi, not to talk about the employment relationship as I owed Kate Emms a duty of confidentiality. Instead, I stuck to my truthful denial of bullying, but news outlets happily reported the charge – even though Kate herself did not publicly make any such charge. At no time during our work together did she complain to me. Neither did her line manager indicate that she wished to complain, and I have since been advised by the then Clerk of the House, David Natzler, that no such complaint was made. All of this may leave you confused and, perhaps, still thinking, 'Well, there's no smoke without fire.' What, then, is the truth?

When I became Speaker, I inherited a Private Secretary, Angus Sinclair, from my predecessor, Michael Martin. We worked together for a year but we were very different. Angus was a professional but our approaches were incompatible and we parted company. The senior Clerks in the House had asked that Kate be allowed to join my office to do some work and in the knowledge that Angus and I were not finding it easy to work together. In retrospect, I should never have agreed to such an arrangement, which was informal. However, when Angus left, there was a vacancy and it had to be filled. Then came my second mistake. Crazily, I agreed that I would not sit in on, let alone chair, the interviews for the appointment of Angus's successor. Instead, again on the advice of senior Clerks, I allowed one of them to do so. From the shortlist, Kate Emms was appointed.

Only weeks before then, the Clerk of the House, Dr Malcolm Jack, had suggested to me that the departure of Angus represented a fine opportunity to reorganise my office. It was time, in his view, to clear out people who had worked a very long time in the office and to replace them with fresh blood. Malcolm, ordinarily the most courteous of people, but every inch the ex-public schoolboy, said he advised that 'Barratt and Davis should go, Mr Speaker'. This was a reference to my then

Assistant Private Secretary, Peter Barratt, and his deputy, Ian Davis. Former state-school boys and neither of them university educated, Peter had worked in the Speaker's Office since 2000 and Ian since 2001. Both were excellent – competent, efficient, reliable, dedicated and, crucially, loyal to the Speaker.

I was taken aback by Malcolm's suggestion and said so. Shortly after that conversation, Malcolm's deputy, Robert Rogers – who soon after was appointed Clerk after Malcolm retired – invited me out to lunch at his club. During an otherwise pleasant meal, Robert too brought up the issue of my office and made an eloquent and forceful pitch along the lines that Malcolm had set out weeks earlier. Robert is a highly articulate and persuasive man and, without committing myself, I said that I would reflect on his advice.

In retrospect, I wish that I had known that this pitch by the Clerks effectively to run the Speaker's Office was not the first such attempt. It was an old ploy, and had been rejected by my predecessors. The Clerks wanted both to exert greater influence and to add to the career opportunities for Clerks. I should have realised this and rejected it.

When Kate Emms – a Clerk – became Secretary in July 2010, she did not flag up this agenda on day one, though I was quickly told that she went back and forth to the Clerk of the House's office much more frequently than previous Private Secretaries, including Angus Sinclair, had done. A few months in post in the autumn of 2010, Kate told me that she had been thinking about the running of the office and would like to recommend changes. She produced a diagram of a restructured office in which she would have a new deputy, and Peter Barratt would leave. It was also her wish that Ian Davis should be moved out, but Peter would be the first to go.

At this point my wife, Sally, who had rung Peter Barratt about a diary clash and learned of the plan for him to be moved, told me bluntly that she thought I would be completely bonkers to lose Peter unless there was some weakness in his performance that I had never disclosed to her. No, there was not, I told her. She said that it was blindingly obvious what was afoot.

'The bloody Clerks are trying to take control of your office. Peter and Ian are fab, fucking loyal and they've never let you down – don't throw them under the bus just because the Clerks want to pack your office with their Oxbridge-educated clones, for God's sake.'

I realised Sally was absolutely right. I went in to see Kate and said that I had some news that she would not like, but on which I was decided. I did not want Peter or Ian to leave – the existing set-up worked perfectly well and, though I was a change-maker, I did not believe in change for the sake of it. She took a deep breath and said, 'Right. OK, Mr Speaker. It's your decision.' I was told that minutes later Kate went off to see the Clerk.

After that decisive moment, Kate continued in her job, though I sensed a change in her. I had never completely warmed to her as a person but now found her a little abrupt, even occasionally curt or peremptory. But we continued to work together, and went to the Isle of Man in January 2011 for a Commonwealth Speakers Conference and then to Slovenia in early February, where I had been invited to celebrate that country's independence anniversary. We got on perfectly well on both visits and I had no complaints.

On Monday 7 March 2011, however, Kate did not come to work. I received no letter, phone call or text. I simply popped into her office to be greeted by the Clerk, Malcolm Jack, who said that she was off sick and had decided that she would not return.

From that day until the BBC wrote to me on 27 February 2018 – seven years later – not a single soul suggested that I had bullied her or that she thought I had. I repeat: no complaint was ever communicated to me by Kate Emms, by her line manager, by the Clerk of the House or by anyone else. Moreover, on *Newsnight* on 8 March when the 'charge' against me was first broadcast, not one on-the-record or named witness was quoted. Kate Emms herself made no such claim then or afterwards.

Being accused on national television in this way is unpleasant and traumatic, and it is only fair that I should now be able to put the facts on the record. I did not bully Kate in any way: I disagreed honourably with her about the running of my office. I make no apology whatsoever for safeguarding the jobs of two outstanding servants of the Speaker's Office in Peter Barratt and Ian Davis, and in resisting the takeover that the Clerk and his deputy appeared to favour.

* * *

Almost eight weeks later, on 1 May, *Newsnight* had another go. A representative of the programme wrote to me to allege that I had bullied Angus Sinclair, my first Private Secretary, and that he had been paid £85,000 to leave the House after signing a Non-Disclosure Agreement. I knew nothing whatsoever of the NDA or of the size of his 'pay-off' but, once again, I honestly refuted the charge of bullying. Sure enough, *Newsnight* went ahead with its programme, this time with an interview with Angus Sinclair himself.

He had left back in July 2010, and had made no complaint in almost eight years. But now he was claiming that I had bullied him, an allegation I can only conclude stems from an admittedly heated argument we had behind closed doors in early 2010, in which I expressed my disappointment and displeasure over a matter in which I felt he had let me down (it concerned my wife and children's living arrangements during that year's election – a topic on which I felt strongly, perfectly naturally). In the *Newsnight* interview, he confessed that he felt he was failing to deliver for me, but said that my reaction had been disproportionate. These are matters of perspective, of course: for my part I felt my reaction was entirely proportionate, and certainly did not constitute bullying. Sinclair went on to say that he wished he had complained at the time. He did so now in the light of what *Newsnight* claimed had happened to his successor.

There was no way he could have known the details of my working relationship with Kate Emms but, just as his own departure had been reported in 2010, together with press speculation about a pay-off, so Kate's abrupt departure had been in the *Mail on Sunday* in March 2011. It is a little odd that it was only now that he felt a moral compunction to speak out, but that was his choice. So what happened?

Before I go on, let me tell you what didn't happen. In my opinion, the disagreement between us did not constitute bullying in any way. At the time he went public, 1 May 2018, I confined myself to a simple rebuttal of the charge of bullying and said no more, for two reasons. First, it was not for me to prove my innocence. Everyone has a right in law to a presumption of innocence. Secondly, Speaker's Counsel again advised me that I should not talk about the employment relationship as I owed Angus a duty of confidentiality. However, given that he has spoken out against me and that his claims have been very widely reported, I am surely entitled to put my case.

As noted, I inherited Angus Sinclair from my predecessor, Michael Martin, whom he had served as Secretary for the previous four years. He struck me at the outset as dedicated, conscientious and loyal. But it soon became clear also that Angus was a traditionalist and I was a reformer. We were chalk and cheese. Nevertheless, I resolved to work with him and strive to build a successful partnership – as I had managed to do with the two staff immediately junior to him, Peter Barratt and Ian Davis, both of whom worked with me for over ten years.

It is true there were differences of opinion. Angus believed that on a day-to-day basis, I should wear the traditional uniform of the Speaker, including a morning coat, and had arranged for the specialist tailors, Ede & Ravenscroft, to measure me for that purpose. I explained that, as I had made clear in campaigning to be Speaker, I had no intention of wearing a morning coat each day and would wear it on ceremonial and a few other special occasions only. Angus accepted this, but when I received a letter criticising my decision he urged me to reconsider.

When a *Daily Telegraph* journalist called to ask about an aspect of my salary and my press spokesperson was away from her desk, Angus responded to the journalist, 'It is not appropriate to discuss the remuneration of Mr Speaker.' I politely explained to Angus that that approach, frankly pompous, would cut no ice with the media and that he should leave comments to the press spokesperson and me. Instead of accepting this rather basic point with good grace and moving on to the next business between us, Angus dug his heels in, saying that he was right.

When in the autumn of 2009 I visited the Welsh Assembly, Angus did not wish to accompany me, leaving his third-in-command, Ian Davis, to do so. Ian did so with his useful cheerfulness and spirit of service, but it was odd that Angus just did not want to come. During the year we worked together I undertook no fewer than thirteen visits to schools, universities and other organisations. I invited Angus to accompany me but his reply was always, 'No, Mr Speaker. I shall stay at base. Peter, Ian or someone from the House's Education or Outreach Service can join you.'

Years later, Ian Davis told me that early on he had gently suggested that Angus should join me on some of my visits but that Angus had flatly rejected the idea, indicating that it was not his style. The fact that it was mine, and that he was working for me, just did not weigh with him. Angus did not adjust to me – if anything expecting that I should adjust to him, or what he regarded as unbreakable tradition, the parliamentary equivalent of Holy Writ.

* * *

After the 2010 election Malcolm Jack asked me again – months earlier I had indicated that Angus and I had not gelled and he had said that a change could easily be made if I wanted – whether I wished to continue with Angus or not. Sadly I realised that it did not work. We were too different. I had concluded that Angus had neither the desire nor the capacity to adjust to me, a reformer. Malcolm said that it was not a problem – he would speak to Angus and tell him that the working relationship was over. I promptly insisted that I owed it to Angus to speak to him myself. Malcolm said that that was fine but that I should not discuss the terms of his departure, as that was for others to handle.

I therefore called Angus in, thanked him for his efforts but said that I did not feel our relationship was working. Instinctively, we differed too much on too many fronts too often, and I would like to make a change. To his great credit, Angus said that he quite understood. He then offered his hand and we shook hands. I suggested a leaving party but he said that he would prefer to 'slip away'. He had been offered other jobs in the House but declined them. I knew nothing of his NDA or pay-off.

Again, for the avoidance of doubt, Angus did not complain to me at the time and at no stage did the Clerk, the personnel boss or anyone else suggest that I had bullied Angus. He was a highly paid official whose job had come to an end, and who had received a termination payment (although I did not know that at the time). It would be almost eight years before he said anything about the matter, and decided he should come forward and say he had been bullied.

It seems to me that in any other field such a claim would be dismissed out of hand. In civil matters, there are statutes of limitation: people must bring cases to courts or tribunals within a specified period. I felt sure it was only because I was a public figure and the media were up for creating a storm that the story was judged significant.

Frankly, the entire episode was completely ridiculous. It was not merely that I had not maltreated anyone. The reality was that I had superb staff in my office; the team spirit was outstanding; we worked harmoniously and we treated each other with respect. As a result, turnover was low and morale high. I had about ten office staff at any one time and two of them were with me throughout my ten years in post. A further five served for an average of eight years. They supported me and I supported them. Whatever the nay-sayers think, the fact is that ours was a smooth-running ship operated by a happy crew.

* * *

From dress to childcare, from workers' pay and conditions to the promotion of staff diversity, the House had been dragged into the twenty-first century. Similarly, from the establishment of the Women and Equalities Select Committee to the introduction of proxy voting for Members on baby leave, from showcasing the House of Commons to young people to managing the Parliamentary Estate better, Parliament had become much less lazily self-satisfied.

There is still a huge amount to be done and I would like to have done more, but the fact remains that little happens unless Members are onside and there is an appetite to act. On electronic voting, for example, which to me makes perfect sense, it remains a minority taste among colleagues. I would have had no procedural right to introduce it and an attempt to harangue colleagues into it would have been doomed to fail. For all that, I feel I did achieve considerable modernisation and the evidence is there for all to see. But the process must continue, and that will now be for others to pursue.

7

Ambassador and Diplomat

The impartiality of the Speaker is fundamental to the integrity of the office. But the fact that I had to be impartial between the political parties did not mean I had to be impartial about Parliament itself – far from it. Throughout my campaign I had emphasised that I envisaged a role for the Speaker as a kind of ambassador for Parliament: engaging with people from all walks of life to explain what the role was, how Parliament worked and why it mattered.

As some of the stories from the previous chapter suggest, the House of Commons is a small 'c' conservative institution. Most members and staff value its traditions and are, to varying degrees, cautious about, even resistant to, change. That said, I was surprised by two reactions to my 'ambassador' idea. A fellow candidate for the Chair, Sir Patrick (now Lord) Cormack, expressed strong disapproval. If I 'took to the public square', as he put it, 'doubtless opining' on matters of great political controversy, his judgement, borne of his almost forty years' service as a Member of Parliament, was that the consequences for '*Parleeament*' – his inimitable pronunciation of the word always tickled me – would be 'profoundly injurious'. I begged to differ.

The second instance of opposition came when the Conservative MP for Mid-Sussex, Nicholas Soames, came up to me in the Chair. He and I had not been friends. We were very different and had often clashed. On this occasion, he was both

extremely gracious and unusually hesitant. He told me that
he had not voted for me to be Speaker – I did not need to
be Sherlock Holmes to work that out – but had voted for Sir
George Young Bt, whom he regarded as 'a bloody good egg'.
That said, he generously told me he thought I had made 'a
jolly good start' as Speaker, but asked if he may be so bold as
to make a point.

'Please do,' I replied.

'Well, Mr Speaker,' he proceeded, 'I am bound to say that
this outreach business of yours I don't understand. I don't get
it. It's a rum business.' For those readers unfamiliar with the
works of P. G. Wodehouse, 'rum' is not just an alcoholic drink
but can also mean 'rather strange'. Why, I asked, did he think
it strange? Apparently Soames thought it 'beneath the dignity
of the office', and felt I should not be 'trudging across the land,
speaking to school students, to universities or to Women's Institute branches, gathering in draughty village halls. If people
want to hear you they should bloody well come to the House
of Commons.' I replied by thanking him for his candour
but saying that I thought his view was anachronistic. In the
modern world, an age of pervasive cynicism about politics and
politicians, it was not good enough for people holding public
office simply to look important and expect to be revered. I
felt I had to make a case, to talk to, engage with and hear from
the public who paid my salary. A model of courtesy, Nicholas
nevertheless looked at me with blank incomprehension.

It is often said that young people have no interest in politics,
so it made sense to try to build relations with school students
and their teachers. Every MP worth his or her salt visits
schools in the constituency and I have always made a point of
visiting every school in mine. On top of that, I visited over 100
schools in my decade as Speaker. Of these the majority were
secondary schools, and although I did visit some fee-paying
schools my priority was the state schools that educate well
over 90 per cent of the nation's children. What I talked about

would vary but I often focused on a number of core themes: the importance of politics, the value of democracy and the part that young people could play in it, as well as the role of the Speaker. Almost invariably, I concluded by encouraging pupils to take an active part in politics to improve their lives and the lives of their fellow citizens.

Often I would ask my audience at the start how many of them were interested in politics and only a minority of hands would go up. This seemed to support the idea – usually voiced by not-so-young people imagining they knew what young people thought – that they were indeed disengaged from politics. But I would then ask a few follow-up questions. How many of you are interested in the type of educational opportunity you will have after school? How many of you care about being able to find a decent home to rent, or even buy? How many of you care about the state of our transport system, or the quality of the environment, or the effectiveness of our efforts to help the poorest people on the planet, or the nature of our relations with the EU, the US, or Russia?

In response, most students said that they certainly did care and think about these things, though in some cases they felt powerless to do much to affect the issues I highlighted. My approach was to start by deducing that they might not be interested in the formalities, the structures or the culture of politics – suits, very formal language, traditional ceremonies and rituals, the tendency of MPs to yell, heckle, bait or shout each other down – but they were interested in the substance of what politics was about: the arbitration between competing interests and claims on resources, and the pursuit of support to shape one kind of future for the country rather than another.

Another misconception among older folk was that young people thought that politics wouldn't affect them. Bluntly, I stressed to young audiences that it would, whether they were interested or not, because policies impacted on living stand-ards, public services and the options open to them in later life. Similarly I was told by older cynics that young people felt that political parties were all the same, and that it scarcely mattered which way young people voted as the outcomes for them would be unchanged. I have never subscribed to this view and suggested to my young audiences that they shouldn't buy it either. The idea that there was no difference between the Labour government of Gordon Brown and the Conservative alternative of David Cameron, or between the Conservative government first led by David Cameron and then by Theresa May and the Labour Opposition led by Jeremy Corbyn, is patently absurd. There were profound and honourable differences between those alternatives and it is lazy thinking to suggest otherwise.

On the value of democracy, I was forthright, passionate and insistent. The beauty of our democracy, however imperfect, was that people had the right to choose their representatives and, at least as importantly, they had the right to change their choice.

Questions from primary school pupils varied but there were regular favourites, including whether I had met the Queen and 'Who is the worst-behaved MP?' (I generally ducked that question, saying that several were over-excitable, but it was quite hard to identify just one.) With secondary school students, other topics came to the fore, including of course my thoughts on Brexit. I would point out that in the referendum, I voted to remain in the EU but that, as Speaker, my role was to ensure that everyone had a fair hearing and that the government was subject to scrutiny of its policy – a topic we will return to in Chapter 11.

Aside from those visits to schools, I welcomed groups of school children to Speaker's House from time to time and at the request of John Mann, the outspoken and independent-minded Labour MP for Bassetlaw, played host every year from 2009 to 2019 to the Bassetlaw Summer School, a collection of fifty or more sixteen-year-olds from local state schools visiting

Parliament to learn more about politics and democracy. There were also regular 'Skype the Speaker' sessions with schools across the country, and frequent engagements with teachers too.

Compelling evidence against the idea that youngsters had no interest in politics was the existence of the UK Youth Parliament (UKYP). On taking office I had modest experience of the UKYP, having once spoken to a conference of theirs in London several years earlier. I did not know their leaders, still less the members from around the country, but I had a positive view of the purpose and work of the Youth Parliament. When, in March 2009, the House voted to allow the UKYP to hold – in the Chamber – a series of debates on motions they had chosen following consultation with young people across the country, I intervened briefly to express support and voted accordingly.

The decision to allow delegates to sit on the green leather benches was not without controversy as previously only elected members of the UK Parliament had been afforded the privilege. Some MPs thought that the UKYP should be no exception, but the House felt that it was an exceptional case. Their 300 or so members – so-called MYPs – were aged between thirteen and eighteen and the great majority were therefore ineligible to vote. MPs, including me, concluded that in order to encourage young people and give them a precious opportunity to display and improve their communication skills, we should allow them access to the Chamber, initially on a trial basis. One of the objectors was Sir Nicholas Winterton, who was implacably opposed to the idea.

When I was elected Speaker, my staff informed me of the upcoming UKYP sitting, saying that it would take place on 30 October (a non-sitting Friday) under the chairmanship of the Senior Deputy Speaker, Sir Alan Haselhurst. With no disrespect to Sir Alan – and he felt none – I indicated to him that I would chair the UKYP proceedings myself, leaving him free to go to his constituency. Alan readily accepted this and I began to look forward to the event as I have done every year since.

Sir Nicholas Winterton became aware that I intended to chair the proceedings. He approached me with a face whose puce colour was testimony to his fury and outrage. Staring at me in horrified disbelief, and looking every inch a man possessed of some unfortunate demon, Sir Nicholas gave full, angry, bigoted, pompous and expansive expression to his displeasure.

'Mr Speaker, sir, I understand that you are to chair the proceedings of the UK Youth Parliament on the floor of this House to which, you will doubtless recall, I am profoundly and resolutely opposed?'

I indicated that I was indeed aware of his opposition – I imagined that every Member of the House and, quite possibly, innocent passers-by within a few miles' radius would be similarly conscious as he had left none in doubt as to the intensity of his displeasure.

'I am very sorry indeed that you propose to confer on the proceedings the seal of approval of your great office, as no such honour is warranted.' I replied that I disagreed, believing that it was only right that I should recognise the significance of the occasion and offer my personal encouragement to the young people present. Aghast, Sir Nicholas declared, 'Let me tell you, it will be a complete disaster.'

'Oh? Why is that?'

'With respect, Mr Speaker, sir, I know what I'm talking about and I remind you that I have been here a great deal longer than you.' I acknowledged that but repeated my question, asking what his argument was for predicting doom and gloom. Even though Sir Nicholas had a reputation for being outspoken and somewhat reactionary, I was flabbergasted by what came next.

'You mark my words, Mr Speaker. At best, chewing gum will be left all over the Chamber. At the worst, pen knives will be used and damage will be inflicted on these benches which I love.' I told him I respected his candour but did not respect his casual calumny of young people. I made three predictions: the UKYP members would be proud to come to the Chamber of the House of Commons; they would speak well; and they would behave 'a damned sight better than we do'. In tribute to the members of the UK Youth Parliament, I am proud to record that I was right on all three counts.

* * *

Another feature of my public engagement work was lectures and 'In Conversation' discussions at universities, and I also forged a link with the University of the Third Age (U3A), a nationwide network of local groups run by and for predominantly retired people and catering to a wide range of different interests. There are over a thousand branches across the UK offering thousands of different interest groups and boasting over 400,000 members. These audiences were consistently interested and engaged, and I made a point of canvassing their opinion. I would ask, in neutral terms: 'Who thinks Prime Minister's Questions are fine as currently conducted?' About a fifth of the audience's hands would generally go up. 'Who thinks it is too noisy?' By a margin of three or four to one, audiences consistently told me that they thought it too noisy.

Interestingly, though, despite the fact that the U3A audiences contained a lot of educated people, questioners frequently used the words 'government' and 'parliament' interchangeably, as if they were synonyms, whereas they are distinct branches of our political system. Unlike in the US, we do not have a separation of powers, so members of the government do sit in the two Houses of Parliament, but they are a small minority. About a hundred ministers, government whips and Parliamentary Private Secretaries sit in the Commons. But there are 650 MPs, the vast majority of whom are not members of the government but simply of the legislature. The principal role of the legislature is to debate, scrutinise, amend and vote upon legislation and policy proposed by the executive (the government). MPs also debate subjects of their own choice and individual Members can introduce Bills, though unless they enjoy government support they have little chance of being passed into law.

There is a continuing challenge for Parliament to explain its distinctive role in the political process. MPs and government tend to be viewed as an undifferentiated mass, an amorphous block of 'them up highs', but this characterisation fails to do justice to the important work that Parliament is charged to undertake.

* * *

In seeking to communicate my core messages about the need to promote a recovery of Parliament, I was lucky to be given platforms by a number of different institutions including the Hansard Society – the country's leading charity for the study of Parliament – the Centre for Parliamentary Studies, the Institute for Government and the Study of Parliament Group. Sometimes I would speak to a think-tank of left or right and I received many invitations to address the staff of government departments, trade associations and bodies like the Institute of Directors and the CBI. None of those fixtures was commented upon in the national media; quite rightly, they were regarded as unexceptionable.

However, in 2015 I received and accepted an invitation from the TUC General Secretary, Frances O'Grady, to address the plenary session of the Trades Union Congress in Brighton. The *Sun* and the *Daily Mail* pricked their ears up on learning of this and tried, rather feebly, to suggest that my decision to speak there was 'controversial' as no Speaker had done so before and it would be regarded as 'political'. So, speaking to a business organisation of the kind that the right-wing media judged sound and reasonable was OK, but speaking to the umbrella organisation embracing the representatives of organised working people across the UK was thought controversial. There you have it.

I was honoured to be asked to address the TUC, and acknowledged at the end of my speech that things had changed a lot in thirty years – not only would my younger self have baulked at the idea of addressing the TUC, it was also inconceivable they would have wanted me to do so. But some things also stayed the same: I pointed out that we were then marking the 800th anniversary of the signing of Magna Carta and the 750th anniversary of the first English Parliament, and I suggested that those historical landmarks handed down to us a number of important principles as valid and compelling today as they were then. Whether uttered in medieval Latin or in modern language, the case for the accountability of power was the same and just as strong. As the late Tony Benn was fond of observing, 'Whenever I meet anybody in power, I always ask that person five questions. What power have you got? Who gave it to you? In whose interests do you exercise it? To whom are you accountable? And how can we get rid of you?'

* * *

The other side of the public-engagement equation was welcoming people into Parliament and into Speaker's House. For want of a better term I call that 'in-reach', but it is all part of the same desire to break down the barriers between Parliament and the people.

Speaker's House was home both to my office and function rooms and, upstairs, to me and my family. Sally and I and our three children lived in the apartment directly above the office, my study and the grand State Rooms where I held functions. I resolved that I would open up the State Rooms as often as possible, sometimes to host functions for colleagues and staff – retirement events, the unveiling of new House initiatives, book launches, wedding receptions for fellow parliamentarians and lectures for Members, staff and visitors alike – but more often for outside organisations, especially charities. Opening the State Rooms to them conveyed Parliament's thanks and allowed them to showcase their successes and future plans.

Often these visitors would thank me for my hospitality in opening up my home. This was courteous of them but I was always at pains to emphasise first that the State Rooms were paid for by their taxes; and second that these palatial function rooms were not the same as the very welcome, and spacious, but less palatial rooms above in which my family and I lived. The rather grand State dining room was not where we had our breakfast or dinner, and the State bedroom was not where I slept – unless in the unfortunate eventuality of being kicked out from upstairs by my wife. It contained a ceremonial bed that looked grand but was in fact incredibly hard and uncomfortable. Invariably visitors were tickled by this tale and were curious to see the bed.

I hosted a lecture series every year from 2011 onwards in which MPs or Peers would address fellow parliamentarians, House staff, academics, journalists, civil servants and others on subjects of special interest or knowledge. Often the focus was on great parliamentarians down the ages, or I asked contributors to discuss a particular theme. In the best traditions of Speaker impartiality, I invited figures as diverse as Ken Clarke and John Redwood, Tony Blair and Jacob Rees-Mogg to speak their minds. The late Tessa Jowell delivered a memorable lecture on Parliament and the media, Harriet Harman spoke powerfully on the battle for equality and Stella Creasy, one of the star backbenchers of the new generation, did so too.

Yet my main mission was to attract organisations from outside. My particular interests included help for those with special educational needs and disabilities; the promotion of social mobility; the fight against global poverty; care for vulnerable children and young people; action against killer disease, and the promotion of human rights, gender, LGBT and racial equality. Organisations like Afasic (the Association for All Speech-Impaired Children), ICAN (the children's communication charity), the Royal College of Speech and Language Therapists and the British Stammering Association were all welcomed to Speaker's House as they do fantastic work to help and advocate for young people who struggle to communicate their needs, interests and aspirations. Other visitors included the National Autistic Society, Christian Solidarity Worldwide, Amnesty, Variety, the Stephen Lawrence Charitable Trust, Stonewall and many others.

There was a common theme to all this outreach and in-reach. Whether I was visiting people, or welcoming people visiting Parliament, I was struck by the enormous warmth and enthusiasm I met. People genuinely appreciated the visits, and I found meeting people directly both fun and reassuring. The media were forever cynical and, being right-wing dominated, largely hostile to a Speaker thought – correctly – to be a liberal leftie, but the public were not. They were with few exceptions pleased to be visited, and welcomed the opportunity to come to Parliament and to be recognised, thanked and appreciated for what they did.

* * *

There was another category of visitor to the House of Commons, of course – foreign leaders and dignitaries. The first such senior visitor to Parliament in my time as Speaker was Pope Benedict XVI – formerly Joseph Ratzinger – who had been invited to address both Houses of Parliament in our most prestigious setting, Westminster Hall. I am of Jewish origin and proud of my heritage, but over the last forty years and more I have always been secular. Sir Patrick Cormack, a deeply committed member of the Church of England, once asked me if I was religious. I will never forget his conclusive riposte to my claim that I was 'profoundly irreligious' – 'Oh my dear chap, I am afraid that is not possible. You may be irreligious but there can be no profundity about it.' Of course, I accept that religion can be the basis of civil obligation, but it is by no means the only such basis – I try to behave ethically and with respect for people but I don't think, as some do, that it is necessary to be religious to do so.

But even a moderately sensitive politician has to be able to empathise with people with different beliefs, and I understood the significance of the Pope in the lives of over a billion Roman Catholics around the world. This would be the first visit by any Pontiff to the Palace of Westminster, so as well as being of great interest to British Catholics it was a historical occasion. Many people, though, including Sally, took a dim view of this particular Pope, citing his reluctance to come clean about his involvement in the Hitler Youth as a young German; his notably undynamic response to the child-abuse scandal that had begun to embroil the Catholic Church, and his dogmatic condemnation of abortion and homosexuality. Sally had no interest in hearing his speech and lost no time in tweeting her disapproval of him. She even urged me to boycott the visit but I demurred: he had been properly invited and, though I was not a chirpy enthusiast for his visit, I had not objected to it.

The Pope's stance – which of course reflected that of the Catholic Church – on abortion, homosexuality and embryo research was undeniably controversial, and inevitably attracted opposition and even fierce condemnation, not least among many of my fellow parliamentarians. In my address I wanted to acknowledge the fact that there were differences between MPs and Peers on the one hand and the Vatican on the other. However, one of my advisers, Tim Hames, thought that mentioning abortion and homosexuality directly would be akin to swearing in front of the Pope, and I accepted his advice to make my point more diplomatically by referring instead to the benefits of 'robust and respectful debate'. More particularly, I highlighted the difference between Parliament and the Vatican on social, scientific and sexual issues.

In his own thoughtful address, the Pope expressed concern at 'the increasing marginalisation of religion that is taking place in some quarters, even in nations which place a great emphasis on tolerance'. He suggested, but offered no example of who he had in mind, that there were those 'who would advocate that the voice of religion be silenced or, at least relegated to the purely private sphere'. He stressed that there was a need to recognise 'the legitimate role of religion in the public sphere'. As an irreligious person, I can readily accept that people should be able to invoke their religious convictions as the basis for their moral or political convictions. My sense is that difficulty arises when people argue that their religious freedom allows them, perhaps even requires them, to discriminate. For example, a Christian hotelier under our law cannot refuse to supply a room to a gay couple because he or she disapproves of homosexuality. I do not believe that that represents discrimination against Christians. It simply represents the application of equality legislation.

The Pope had a reputation as a capable, if deeply conservative, theologian. Looking back, his address reads better than it sounded. Perfectly reasonably, he spoke in English, but his delivery was uninspiring, even monotonous. He looked down at his text, spoke rather softly, and I doubt that he won any new admirers that afternoon.

The same could not be said of the state visit of President Obama in May 2011. He too was invited to speak in Westminster Hall. The night before his scheduled address, the Queen hosted a state banquet for the President and the First Lady, Michelle, at Buckingham Palace. Sally and I were fortunate to be invited and we were introduced to the couple. Both were warm and charming, but the most striking point about the President was his self-deprecation. I said how much I looked forward to welcoming him to Parliament the next day.

'And I hugely look forward to coming,' he replied, 'but I must take care not to speak for too long.' The idea that guests would be fretting about the length of his speech or tutting if he went on for forty-five rather than thirty minutes was laughable.

On 25 May the Presidential limousine drew up at the Sovereign's entrance to Parliament, what MPs tend to call 'the House of Lords end' of the Palace of Westminster. The Lord Speaker and I met him and gave him the tour of both Houses. In the Members' Lobby of the Commons, I showed the President the statue of Winston Churchill, pointing in particular – to his evident amusement – to the shiny left foot where the bronze has been worn away by repeated touching for good luck. As the Lord Speaker and I escorted Obama on his brief tour, which was private and not televised, he made a point of approaching and shaking hands with the doorkeepers on duty outside the Lords Chamber, in the Central Lobby and in Members' Lobby. It was done spontaneously, with a warm smile and a friendly hello. Cynics might say that it was a simple public relations gesture. Yes, it was good PR, no doubt, but there was no wider audience. It was a human gesture, visibly welcome to, and destined to be for ever remembered by, our staff.

In a thirty-four-minute address, delivered with humour, acknowledging our ties and focusing laser-like on the challenges facing the world, President Obama demonstrated both his skill as a communicator and his principled vision of a better future for billions of people across the globe. His oration began with a textbook display of humour, which immediately lightened the atmosphere and ensured that he had the undivided attention of his audience: 'I have known few greater honours than the opportunity to address the Mother of Parliaments

at Westminster Hall. I am told that the last three speakers
here have been the Pope, Her Majesty the Queen and Nelson
Mandela . . . which is either a very high bar or the beginning
of a very funny joke.' He ranged far and wide in a lucid, pithy
and funny speech. In terms of nuance, sophistication, the need
for flexibility, it was a speech of which his successor would be
entirely incapable unless he had rehearsed for it for a century
or so. But more of Trump later.

* * *

In early 2012, in a chance conversation at the Speaker's Chair,
the then Foreign Secretary, William Hague, had told me that he
expected the Myanmar opposition leader, Aung San Suu Kyi,
to come to the UK 'soon'. I said that if she did so she should be
invited to address both Houses of Parliament in Westminster
Hall. This was well before her appointment in 2016 as the
first 'State Counsellor' or Prime Minister of Myanmar, and the
later controversy over her government's genocide against the
Rohingya people. Back in 2012 she was widely regarded as an
inspirational figure, a Nobel Peace Prize laureate, author and
advocate of human rights: it seemed entirely suitable for her
to be afforded this honour.

Through my friend Ben Rogers, with whom I had worked
on Myanmar in my days shadowing DfID and who knew
Daw Suu well, we established that she would be delighted
to accept such an invitation, and her visit was fixed for June
2012. For me, it was even more exciting than the Obama visit,
simply because I had taken a close interest in Myanmar and
the work of Daw Suu for the previous eight years. And she
did not disappoint: she was charming, eloquent and splendidly
direct. She was clear that Britain provided a 'shining example'
of democracy and recognition of people's desire to be part of
their own legislative process. Yet, of course, as she indicated,
we in the UK might be inclined to take our rights for granted.

Elections in Myanmar, she said were 'very different'. Apathy, especially among the young, was 'not an issue'. As she put it, 'For me the most encouraging and rewarding aspect of our own elections was the participation, in such vast numbers and with such enthusiasm, of our young people . . . The passion of the electorate was a passion born of hunger for something long denied.'

My colleagues are not given to rapture. Understatement is part of our psyche. Yet the warmth, respect and enthusiasm which greeted Aung San Suu Kyi that afternoon were palpable. Tragic and shocking events have unfolded in Myanmar since but, on that day, there was no doubt how positive people felt about the prospect that Daw Suu could obtain power and lead a process of lasting, beneficial change.

To say her reputation has taken a hammering in recent years is an understatement and, inevitably, her actions – or lack of them – have changed my attitude towards her. I admire her struggle to obtain office but I am dismayed that she has not stood up for the rights of the Rohingya minority or spoken out more strongly against the wider persecution of Muslims across Myanmar. True, the army is dominant and she has no power over it, but nevertheless words are weapons. As head of government, she could – and should – have sought to use her position and her moral authority to curb the violence. Instead, her silence was deafening and support and leadership were absent. Consequently, it is nigh on impossible to envisage her ever being invited to speak in Westminster Hall again.

* * *

In 2014 the House of Commons was offered two different but overlapping perspectives on our relationship with Europe. In February it was agreed that the German Chancellor, Angela Merkel, should address both Houses of Parliament in the Royal Gallery, situated in the House of Lords. In my introduction I noted that she had been 'Europe's anchor, the essential force for stability at a time of immense turmoil and potentially catastrophic change'. Little did we know then of the further turmoil that would be unleashed just two years later.

Merkel is a hugely sophisticated and accomplished leader. She was our guest. She had words of tribute. She showed how savvy she was at the outset by highlighting the expectation that she would either 'pave the way for a fundamental reform of the European architecture which will satisfy all kinds of alleged or actual British wishes' or, alternatively, that 'the rest of Europe is not prepared to pay almost any price to keep Britain in the European Union'. People expecting either one or the other would be disappointed. Well, let's see.

Having paid her respects, Merkel lost no time in celebrating 'European integration' which, she argued, 'has brought us peace, freedom and prosperity for more than half a century now'. She said that it seemed like a miracle 'from the Franco-German friendship to the excellent co-operation among the 28 EU member states in today's European Union'. As she said this, I looked at Prime Minister David Cameron, sitting impassive in the front row. I doubt he was enjoying it very much.

She insisted that 'European integration shows that we have learned the lessons from bloody conflicts and a painful history'; change was needed if 'the success story of European integration' was to continue, but she was unequivocal that Europe's 'economic strength and social model' had provided durable prosperity. In politics, words are weapons. Her references to 'European integration' could scarcely be uttered by any contemporary British Conservative politician other than Ken Clarke. Praising the European 'social model' is a red rag to the Eurosceptic bulls who have become increasingly vocal and even dominant in the Conservative Party over the last thirty years.

Merkel was absolutely unmistakable in championing 'the four freedoms of the single market – the free movement of goods, the free movement of persons, the freedom to provide services and the free movement of payments and capital'. Sure enough, after lauding the Europe without borders as 'one of the great achievements of European integration', she noted the need to 'acknowledge adverse developments and try to correct them', but it was abundantly clear what she meant. Free movement had been a success and should continue.

The thrust of her speech was clear beyond doubt. She referred to the need for a 'united and determined' EU. She said that the Union needed 'a strong United Kingdom, with a strong voice' – but she gave no indication that she thought the EU should shift from its core commitments to accommodate the UK. It wouldn't and it shouldn't. That was her message. Moreover, it was to me striking that her references to UK leaders were references to Winston Churchill. With David Cameron, by then in government for nearly four years, sitting less than ten feet away, she made not a single positive reference to his leadership. That told its own story. She had always thought it bizarre that Cameron led the Conservative Party out of the main centre-right grouping in the European Parliament, and in all likelihood she probably wondered why he pandered to his right wing as a matter of course. In a weighty, thoughtful, twenty-minute address, there was no tribute to Cameron whatsoever. She was and is a leader. Perhaps she didn't regard him as meriting the title.

Some six weeks after Chancellor Merkel's address, we were reminded again of the dangers of meddling with our position in Europe by the President of Ireland, Michael D. Higgins, who also addressed Members of both Houses of Parliament in the Royal Gallery.

Surprisingly, this was the first state visit of an Irish President to the United Kingdom and a telling testament to the extraordinary transformation of the relationship between and within these islands, in our lifetime. Having acknowledged the achievement of the Good Friday Agreement and highlighted the trade and investment that were to the mutual benefit of Ireland and Britain, Higgins moved on to a clearly heartfelt invocation of the words of the Irish nationalist MP, Tom Kettle: 'This tragedy of Europe may be and must be the prologue to the two reconciliations of which all statesmen have dreamed, the reconciliation of Protestant Ulster with Ireland, and the reconciliation of Ireland with Great Britain.'

Of course, both were important to President Higgins, but he had a more pressing and topical concern in mind. He thought it 'significant' that Kettle referred to 'this tragedy of Europe'. Kettle, he declared, 'died as an Irish patriot, a British soldier, and a true European ... He understood that to be authentically Irish we must also embrace our European identity. It is an identification we proudly claim today, an identification we share with the United Kingdom, with whom we have sat around the negotiating table in Europe for over forty years. We recognise that it has been in that European context of mutuality and interdependence that we took the most significant step towards each other.' It requires little decoding. What he was saying was, 'You have been with us in Europe for four decades. Don't leave.'

* * *

In October 2015 the Chinese President Xi Jinping addressed both Houses of Parliament in the Royal Gallery as part of his four-day state visit. Should there have been a state visit? Yes, a case can be made that there should: China is a major global player; we have diplomatic relations and substantial trade ties. Realpolitik suggests that it made sense. However, should there have been an invitation to address both Houses of Parliament? That is much less certain given the fact and scale of China's human rights abuses. Prime Minister Cameron, supported by his Chancellor, George Osborne, clearly wanted to suck up to the Chinese, and asking the President to speak in the

Royal Gallery was his chosen method of ingratiation. I was underwhelmed by the prospect, but it was to be in the Royal Gallery, in the House of Lords, so I had less chance of objecting successfully than if the visit had been proposed for Westminster Hall, which I would have strenuously resisted. The Chinese economy had opened up but the Chinese polity had not. The country was run by a dictatorship. China is rich – in history, culture, philosophy and cuisine – but as far as democracy is concerned the leadership is not even sitting primary school SATS yet, let alone passing them. I resolved to be polite but also to underline the importance of democracy, freedom and human rights, and made a point of saying in my words of welcome that 'The world will be watching and waiting expectantly on the outcome as the emerging superpower that is China takes its new place in the world. In this century, no country can exist in isolation: in all matters, from international law to individual liberty, we should all aspire to be seen not merely as a powerful force in the world, but as a moral inspiration to it.'

As to the speech by the President himself, well, 'oh dear, oh dear, oh dear' was my initial thought. To say that it was platitudinous is a notable unkindness to the inventor of that adjective. To say it was dull would be an understatement. It was staggeringly, mind-numbingly, ball-breakingly dull. What passed for a press release from the Chinese Embassy stated that the President and his wife were 'warmly greeted' by the Lord Speaker and me. Frances d'Souza can speak for herself. I greeted him with courtesy but without warmth. My expectations were low and President Xi effortlessly fell below them.

One of his most feeble assertions was that China had started codifying laws 2,000 years ago. Quite so. This appeared to be his little effort to counter Westminster's status as an ancient Parliament. More to the point is how decisions are made now, under a government controlled by him in which the Chinese people have had no say. Unsurprisingly, the President made no mention of the fact that a copy of Magna Carta had recently been sent to China and was to be publicly exhibited at a Beijing university, only for the exhibition to be cancelled at the last minute.

President Xi went on to offer a mish-mash of observations – Britain had supported Chinese resistance to Japanese aggression in the Second World War; there was a 'proposed friendship' between our two countries, a proposition for which there is not a scrap of contemporary evidence; the UK was the first major Western country to recognise the People's Republic of China, a recognition of fact by the UK and an undergraduate debating point by the President; the UK was the largest offshore trading centre of the Chinese currency renminbi (RMB) after the Hong Kong Special Administrative Region, a nod to the City of London doubtless welcome to Mssrs Cameron and Osborne; the UK was the first major Western country applying for membership of the Asian Infrastructure Investment Bank, and our two countries were becoming 'increasingly interdependent'.

He offered no acknowledgement whatsoever of concerns in the UK and around the world about Chinese contempt for human rights. I saw afterwards that an unnamed 'senior' – oh, of course, senior – Foreign Office official said of the speech, 'It was perfect. There was absolutely no content to it whatsoever.' That is exactly the kind of 'clever, clever' cynical boast one expects of the Foreign Office. Style, not substance, was what it was all about. Meanwhile, hundreds of millions languish under a dictatorship. No public comment was made by any minister about the egregious human rights abuses practised by the Chinese government. Cameron later said to me, 'Well spoken, you said what I couldn't.' He could have done, but he didn't want to.

I was more enthusiastic about the visit in November 2015 of the Indian Prime Minister, Narendra Modi. Early in his address, Modi referred to the statue of Mahatma Gandhi outside the Houses of Parliament. He said he was once asked on a foreign tour why it was situated there. His answer was that the British were wise enough to recognise his greatness, Indians were generous enough to share him; both of our countries were fortunate to have been touched by his life and mission and we were both 'smart enough to use the strengths of our connected histories to power the future of our relationship'.

Asserting that London was 'still the standard for our times', the city that had 'embraced the world's diversity and represents the finest in human achievements', Modi was keen to stress the strength of the links and relationship between our two countries. It took, he said, an Indian icon, Tata, to run a British icon, our steel industry, and become the UK's largest private-sector employer. The UK, he acknowledged, remained a preferred destination for Indian students, and he was especially upbeat as he spoke of his population containing 800 million people under the age of thirty-five. India was boosting its manufacturing sector, making its farms more productive, ensuring its services were more innovative and efficient; and, crucially, creating a revolution in start-up enterprises as well as building the next-generation infrastructure that would leave what he called 'a light footprint on the Earth'. Time will tell if his fine words are borne out.

* * *

I have written above about visits by seven different leaders to our Parliament. Ironically, however, there was more media coverage, probably than all of those visits and speeches combined, of the non-visit to Parliament in 2017 of President Donald Trump.

Trump was elected on 8 November 2016. Within weeks, and certainly before he took office on 20 January, there was speculation about a Trump visit to the UK, including to Parliament. I received an informal communication from the government that sought my view about a possible visit by Trump to Parliament. I indicated that I was unenthusiastic to say the least. In particular, I was vehemently opposed to any invitation to President Trump to speak in Westminster Hall, the most prestigious setting for any visiting statesman. I also started to see newspaper articles which hinted that the government was keen to get in with an invitation earlier rather than later, as an augur of good intent: a keenness to forge a positive link with a President whom most of the British establishment, across the party divide, had not wanted or expected to succeed.

Just as the government and the media were contemplating a visit, fifty Opposition MPs were lining up to oppose it. The Labour MP for Cardiff South and Penarth, Stephen Doughty, tabled an Early Day Motion deploring Trump's recent Executive Order on Immigration and Refugees and calling on me and other Commons officials to deny him permission to speak at Westminster. The motion eventually achieved a total of 206 signatories, including Labour, Liberal Democrat, Scottish Nationalist, SDLP and Green MPs, though no Conservative signed it.

On 6 February 2017, a week after he had tabled the motion, Stephen Doughty raised a Point of Order with me about a possible Trump visit, asking me what approaches had been made to me about the matter and how those with deep concerns about President Trump could make their views known. Of course, he had instantly achieved his objective of airing his views and those of the EDM signatories. However, I responded by describing the procedure for such visits in some detail and leaving him and the House in no doubt whatsoever what I thought:

> I must say to the Honourable Gentleman, to all who have signed his Early Day Motion and to others with strong views about this matter on either side of the argument that before the imposition of the migrant ban, I would

myself have been strongly opposed to an address by President Trump in Westminster Hall, but after the imposition of the migrant ban by President Trump, I am even more strongly opposed to an address by President Trump in Westminster Hall ... I conclude by saying to the Honourable Gentleman that we value our relationship with the United States. If a state visit takes place, that is way beyond and above the pay grade of the Speaker. However, as far as this place is concerned, I feel very strongly that our opposition to racism and to sexism and our support for equality before the law and an independent judiciary are hugely important considerations in the House of Commons.

The reaction in the Chamber was positive, with vociferous support from the opposition side. There was a sprinkling of Conservative members present and they were subdued, possibly shocked. In the coming days, a controversy erupted with Labour, SNP and Liberal Democrat MPs supporting my stance and a number of Conservatives criticising me, either because they favoured a Trump visit or because they thought I had exceeded my authority, showing a bias, or because they disliked me anyway or for a combination of these reasons. For a couple of weeks, the media, led by the *Daily Telegraph* and the *Daily Mail*, stirred the row claiming that there would now be a major move to oust me as Speaker.

I remain unapologetic. I said what I meant and I meant what I said. I wanted to get my view out there as there was definitely serious thought being given to an invitation, and I wanted to try to snuff out that prospect, knowing that most MPs did not want a Trump visit. In some quarters it was suggested that I was giving vent to anti-Americanism, but that is unadulterated drivel. I love America and have friends there, support free enterprise, back NATO, believe in the American nuclear umbrella and recognise that whoever is President, we have to maintain a working relationship. The issue was whether President Trump had earned that honour of an invitation to address both Houses of Parliament. Manifestly he had not. He had been President for only just over a fortnight, had been guilty of shameless misogyny and racism and had not even begun to establish credibility on the global stage.

Some critics suggested that whether people were pro- or anti-Trump, I had breached my duty of impartiality as Speaker. Again, I feel the charge is wrong. I am obliged to be impartial between the political parties and on issues of known controversy between them. However, as I had explained to Stephen Doughty and the House, the Speaker is a keyholder to Westminster Hall and a signatory of any invitation to speak in the Royal Gallery. One cannot be impartial as between wanting to invite a leader to speak and not wanting that leader to speak. It was my duty to have a view, and I expressed it.

It was also said that I was guilty of double standards because the Chinese President Xi Jinping and the Emir of Kuwait, both controversial figures in their own ways, *had* spoken in Westminster. There was some force in that criticism. My answer is that two wrongs don't make a right. President Xi had been in office considerably longer – so the indecent haste to suck up to Trump was not as obvious with the Chinese – but with hindsight I wish I had opposed Xi's visit, which was a vacuous, stomach-churning and undignified attempt at ingratiation by David Cameron. As to Kuwait, I queried that idea at the time, only to be advised that Kuwait was relatively moderate among Arab states and the Emir was being invited only to speak in the Robing Room of the House of Lords. At the time, I acquiesced, but I should have said, 'No, Parliament should not be used to conduct diplomacy with countries that abuse human rights.'

You live and learn. Nevertheless, the fact that I got it wrong with Kuwait and China did not stop me getting it right with Trump. In the three years since I issued my condemnation of

Trump, nothing has happened to cause me to change my mind about the wisdom of resisting a visit by him to Parliament. By contrast, a great many things have happened to reinforce my view that the UK Parliament had a lucky escape. Trump is a bigot, a menace and a global embarrassment.

* * *

Hosting overseas visitors to Parliament is an established and accepted role of the Speaker. It also occasionally happens that the Speaker is invited to visit other countries, too. My infrequent trips overseas as a representative of Parliament were a matter of no controversy in the Commons whatsoever, but were often criticised in the media on grounds of cost to the taxpayer. But in my experience discussions with other Speakers, parliamentarians and civil society activists can be informative, reassuring or the motive force for changes at home. They were almost always worthwhile.

As Speaker, I was a member of the G8 Speakers' Group – incorporating the UK, the US, Canada, France, Germany, Italy, Japan and Russia. It later became the G7 when the Russians left the group. A three-day annual conference took place every year hosted in turn by each Speaker (we all boycotted Russia in 2014 over the invasion of the Crimea and the event did not take place). In September 2009 I went to Rome with Sally, the Clerk of the House, my Secretary and his deputy. We discussed procedural issues including conduct in the Chamber, approaches to public engagement and so on. On that first visit, the most experienced Speaker was the Canadian, Peter Milliken. He asked me if we had time limits on questions in the Commons. I said no but the Speaker was arbiter and could stop someone speaking if the Member was off the point or too long. He said that their limit was thirty-five *seconds* for questions – which is tight, though I have tried to foster brevity – with five seconds' grace left to his discretion. Milliken was avuncular, witty and great company. The most cerebral Speaker was the German, Norbert Lammert, who could speak superbly on any subject at any notice. The then American Speaker, Nancy Pelosi, was enormously welcoming to me and Sally and hugely amused by the fact that my wife and I hailed from different political parties. Nancy was great fun, shrewd and impressive. She was also a far more party-political figure in the US – in her case, a Democrat – than the Speaker in the UK, now demonstrating both her mettle and her principles as the effective leader of the opposition to President Trump. She came with a very large retinue of staff – dozens – and the UK delegation of five people was by some distance the smallest. Nevertheless, in subsequent years, I travelled only with the Clerk and my Secretary to minimise costs.

There was one minor amusement at dinner on the last night. Sally and I were introduced to the Italian Prime Minister, Silvio Berlusconi, who was charm itself to Sally. He said to me, 'Ah, Mr Speaker, I gather you are quite a naughty boy. I know that I can show you how to be a really naughty boy.' I chuckled along but had no idea what he was on about.

Over a period, I accepted invitations to visit Poland, Hungary and Romania. In one sense, it was inspiring to visit the new democracies. Yet I noticed, especially in Poland, that there was no sense as in the UK that the Speaker was an impartial umpire and someone – as I was – with no ambitions for further political office. The Marshal of the Sejm (the Speaker), Grzegorz Schetyna, evinced no interest in Parliament, ours or his. He wanted to know what was my ambition. When I told him about my plans to improve scrutiny and to modernise the parliamentary workplace, he looked disbelieving. He was sorry, he told the interpreter, that he had not been clear in his question. To repeat, 'What was my ambition after I concluded my term as Speaker?' I explained that I had no desire for any further political advancement. His expression suggested that I was mad, a saint or both. 'You?' I enquired. 'Up, up, up,' he replied. Clearly the Marshal role was a stepping stone to greater things – as, to be fair, the Speaker role had sometimes been in the UK centuries ago.

Visits to Estonia and South Korea opened my eyes to the use of electronic voting within their chambers – vastly more efficient than our long-winded approach in the UK. Moreover, the Estonians had introduced online voting in elections and a quarter of voters were safely casting their ballots in that way. I felt, and still feel, that we should develop the option in the UK but the House of Commons as yet shows little appetite for e-voting in the House, let alone in elections. I believe that both changes will come but probably not for a decade or more.

Speaker Bronwen Bishop in Australia was utterly formidable and in conversation she made Margaret Thatcher seem a left-leaning liberal. I respected Bronwen's intelligence and she was an excellent hostess. In the Chamber, she had the power to send people to a sin bin for an hour – quite a good idea – but her victims, 200 or so, had all been opposition members. I was told that she was quite popular on her own side but cordially loathed by the parties of the left. 'Hm, the opposite to me,' I mused. I could be a diplomat for Parliament, and carried out those duties to the best of my ability, but there would always be those back home resistant to my efforts, as well as those who went out of their way to help. It is to these allies and adversaries that we now turn.

8

Allies and Adversaries

Throughout my Speakership, I was lucky to be able to call upon several allies who believed in me, wanted my tenure to be successful and offered advice, support and friendship. Yet because I was a Marmite character, a controversial choice for the Chair and someone determined to shake up the House of Commons, I also had powerful adversaries who either wanted me kicked out as soon as possible or, failing that, to thwart my reform plans.

Over the years, much has been spoken and written about my wife, Sally. David Cameron, his senior colleagues and a lot of Tory MPs loathed her. Most of them were men married to conventional, Tory-supporting wives who loyally helped the party in their husbands' constituencies and kept their opinions to themselves. To them, Sally was 'jolly vulgar' and a 'poor show'. She has supported Labour devoutly since the mid-1990s and has made no secret of that, or of her loathing for the Tories. She often attacked the coalition government on social media and was thought to be a malign influence on me.

Some of the local Conservative activists in Buckingham were appalled by Sally too. When she briefly considered standing as a Labour candidate for Parliament, one woman wrote to me to protest, saying that she had always believed strongly that a husband and wife were a team who must 'face the world together'. It would, she thought, be very wrong for Sally to serve as a Member of Parliament while I was Speaker.

I told her that, in truth, what she could not abide was the notion that Sally might become a *Labour* MP. If she had been a Tory, it wouldn't have mattered.

The third category of person who loathed Sally were journalists in the right-wing media. Their reasoning was largely that of the Conservative establishment: she was a rebel, off-piste, a gobby woman who dared to say what she thought. The way she conducted herself, they suggested, was not 'in keeping' with how a Speaker's wife should behave. The snobs and chauvinists running those newspapers attacked her at every opportunity.

Sure enough, she gave them material. Denouncing Cameron and Osborne for their austerity policies provoked their ire, but Sally was unrepentant, correctly insisting that she had every right to voice her views. Wearing a bed sheet in an *Evening Standard* photoshoot, as Sally did in the run-up to Valentine's Day in 2011, was a misjudgement: Sally was bounced into it on the day and thought that it was harmless fun, although she later admitted that she had been naïve. Nevertheless, the photograph was hardly a scandal, merely the cue for prudes and stuffed-shirts to express outrage, whether genuine or feigned. Taking part in *Celebrity Big Brother* in 2011 gave those papers another excuse to lambast her. I thought it a trivial programme and advised against it, but Sally was adamant that it wasn't a big deal. What's more, she pointed out that she would secure a £100,000 donation for the charity of her choice, Ambitious About Autism, in the process. In the event, she was right and her appearance merely led to a few days of sanctimonious sermonising by people with little better to do.

Of course, the media had a field day in 2015 when Sally left me because she was having an affair with a cousin of mine. How did I feel about that? As anyone else who loved his wife would. I was disappointed, hurt and miserable, but it did not remotely reflect on me as Speaker. It was a private matter, and these things happen. It was for us, in our interests and, crucially, in the interests of our children, to try to sort it out as we saw fit. That's exactly what we did.

But the difficulties pale into insignificance by comparison with the love, support, advice and friendship I have had from Sally over the years. She was the earliest, most convinced and privately vociferous advocate of my standing for the Speakership. Rightly, she judged that Cameron had no time for me and would offer me no ministerial job of interest. She accepted, albeit reluctantly, that I was not minded to defect to the Labour Party and she felt that I had more to offer Parliament than I could as a Tory backbencher. As she put it to me, 'You would be fair, brilliant at it and popular with Labour – they will want to stuff the Tories by electing someone call-me-Dave can't stand.'

Sally, herself a free thinker and something of a radical, had zero tolerance for fusty traditionalism. She was glad that I decided not to wear the traditional outfit of the Speaker as she regarded it as laughably anachronistic. When Betty Boothroyd appeared to suggest that by declining to wear it I was somehow letting the side down, or even being scruffy, she was much more irritated than I was. The critics, she reminded me, were a minority of elderly voters who would soon get used to it, or MPs already hostile to me who would pick some other line of attack if it weren't this, and for whose opinions frankly neither of us gave a damn. 'Bubble' or 'beltway' was a term each of us used to refer to something only of concern in Westminster and not to the public. As I depended on MPs for my position, that did not mean I could automatically disregard it. But if, as Sally reminded me, criticism came just from usual suspects in the 'beltway' or 'the bubble' – in other words, long-standing and irreconcilable Tory critics – it wasn't worth taking up headspace thinking about it or them.

On almost all of the big issues for me, Sally was terrifically supportive, invariably encouraging me when I was minded to challenge the Clerks' innate caution and conservatism. When

I opted to build the parliamentary nursery – the absence of which until now she regarded as shameful – Sally wisely urged me not to pay too much heed to people obsessing about how the facility must break even financially. 'Sod that,' was her verdict. 'It's a service, demand will fluctuate, don't get boxed in by agreeing that the net cost must be zero.' The facility is now a great success but, frankly, she was right.

As to outreach activity, she was a sceptic, thinking that I was reaching relatively small numbers of people for the time involved, but she accepted that I felt it was worth it. She would tease me about my love of university audiences, characterising them as the 'easy-to-reach elite', but if the audience was 500 or more, as it sometimes was, she could see some merit in it, albeit she would have preferred me to address the Durham Miners' Gala. Outreach took me away from home, but even after long stints in the Chair Sally never complained, knowing I was doing my duty and what I loved. Instinctively, each of us usually anticipated correctly what the other would think about a subject. When the early election came in 2017, she briefly thought and, in truth, hoped that I might decide not to stand again for Parliament and another term as Speaker. She knew that I would probably not want to go on until 2022 and reckoned that it was perhaps a convenient moment to step down. I disagreed, saying that just because the PM had changed her mind didn't mean I should. I had wanted to oversee the Brexit legislative process, realistically up till 2019, and I would not be deterred from that. To her credit, she accepted that at once. I say to her credit because Sally didn't much like living in Parliament, but she felt that it was my call and she was happy to support me.

We have known each other for thirty years and been married for nearly seventeen. She is my wife, my trusted adviser, my unfailing ally and yes, my best friend. Without Sally's insight, encouragement and advice to go for the Speakership, my career in Parliament might well have panned out very differently. What other people think of her doesn't matter a damn. What we think of each other matters a lot.

* * *

Julian Lewis and I have now been friends for over thirty-five years. I am a lark, rising early to swim, read or work. Julian is an owl, beavering away at his desk late into the night or early hours, but a man to whom morning is almost a profanity. As he had said to me in 1983, 'please try not to call me before 9.30 a.m. and preferably not before ten'. He has a brilliant if unusual brain, often narrowly focused on a very small number of subjects. Yet for all that he could apply his mind to almost any topic by thinking in terms of first principles and the percentage chances of any particular course of action being successful. He takes friendship as seriously as anyone I have ever met, giving time, thought and clear advice whenever they are sought.

On two subjects, though, Julian profoundly disagreed with me. He thought I was wrong in principle and foolish in practice to speak out publicly against the idea of President Trump speaking in Parliament. He said it hugely upset lots of Conservatives. He was not convinced that my intervention thwarted any such planned visit, and reckoned that I caused myself and my allies who went out to defend me more trouble than it was worth. Julian is not a Trump supporter but he is passionately in favour of the alliance with the US and, whereas I thought my pro-Americanism did not stop me speaking out against Trump, he thought that diplomacy dictated that I shouldn't. Nevertheless, when the usual suspects started trying machinations against me, he was, as always, robustly supportive.

Julian also felt that I was wrong to reveal publicly that I had voted to remain in the EU. It was no surprise to him and, he thought, probably no surprise to most colleagues but, he

argued, I didn't need to say it. I could and should have cited
my role as umpire to justify declaring no allegiance. I felt that
I had a vote like everyone else and there was no harm in saying
how I had cast it, as I had been scrupulously fair to Brexiteers
at all times. Julian was utterly fastidious about observing the
Chinese wall between our friendship and his interests in the
Chamber. He knew that I could not and must not offer him
special treatment. Through a decade as Speaker, it was rare
for a week to pass without us getting together for a cup of
tea, a glass of whisky or dinner and I have always enjoyed
his company. I said that he didn't like to be called before 10
a.m. Equally, Julian knew never to call me during a football
match involving Arsenal or a tennis match involving Roger
Federer. In those scenarios, everything else bar family health
took second place.

Another staunch ally was Tim Hames, whom I had first met
in student politics in the 1980s. At that time he was an active
Conservative but later gravitated to academia, studying for a
doctorate and then tutoring at Oxford. From there he forged
a career in journalism, ending up as assistant editor of *The
Times* before departing that scene and working for the British
Venture Capital Association from 2009 until 2019.

Back in 2009, when Michael Martin quit, Tim contacted me
to say that he thought I could and should win the Speakership
as his contacts told him that I had very big support on the
Labour benches. He offered to help and I accepted: I liked his
style, particularly his use of humour, and embraced a number
of his campaigning suggestions. When I won, we agreed to
work together on a more formal basis. He served as my special
adviser until just before the 2010 election. For the nine years
after that, he worked for me on a consultancy basis and was
always invaluable. He had a talent for devising ice-breaking
jokes to begin formal speeches and could compose light, self-
deprecating sentences to punctuate passages of high-minded
seriousness. In nearly four decades of speaking in public, I was

happiest and best speaking without a note, let alone a text. However, perhaps half a dozen times a year I had to deliver a lecture that might later be published or put on a website. In short, a text was required and, having talked through the subject, Tim would undertake to produce a draft. Every single time – I think it was the journalist's training to work to a deadline – Tim produced a draft on time or ahead of time and it has been superb.

Because he had worked as a senior journalist, Tim knew what did matter and what didn't. So long as a 'story' didn't appear on the front cover or page two of a newspaper, he scarcely raised an eyebrow. Stories on later pages, not to mention hostile editorials or feature articles by predictable detractors, were not worth a minute of my time, in his view. Likewise outbursts by individual MPs, almost invariably Tories, were irrelevant. They would sound off. A paper would report it. The following day I would still be the Speaker and the paper would be wittering about something else. It just did not matter.

If a senior minister took a swipe at me, Tim might recommend lowering the temperature or disarming a detractor with courtesy but, again, it rarely mattered. Dozens of times over ten years in the Chair there were rumours suggesting a Tory plot to oust me, but they always came to nought. Tim's view was that unless there was a House-wide loss of confidence in the Speaker, the incumbent was pretty much impregnable. I could not be forced out just because the government was fed up with me.

Two other factors made him an even more invaluable ally. First, he thought in terms of sticking to my priorities – anything that did not impact upon those he tended to view as 'marginal', 'not core' and 'no ground for concern'. Secondly, Tim had a wonderfully equable temperament. Calm, good-humoured, upbeat, he is one of life's 'glass half-full' men. Any leader in an organisation needs some of those people.

I came to regard Gordon Brown as an ally. When I first entered Parliament, I was an uncompromising critic of his, viewing him as an implacable political enemy and, sadly, from the Conservative point of view, an effective opponent. With Tony Blair, he had helped get Labour elected and re-elected. By 2007, when I had moderated from the politics of the 1990s, he hoped that I would join Labour. I declined but I was happy to work with his ministers, Ed Balls and Alan Johnson, and there was no hostility on his part, if anything some goodwill. As Prime Minister when the election for Speaker took place, he indicated that he would not vote but leave the House to choose, and when I won, his speech of tribute was both humorous and gracious.

In late 2009, Sarah, his wife, kindly invited Sally to take Oliver, approaching six, and Freddie, four, to Downing Street for a play date with Fraser and John, the Brown boys. I was in the Commons at the time, but our sons had a great time. The Prime Minister made a point of coming out of his office to greet them.

'Hello, Freddie,' he said, 'I'm Gordon.'

To which Freddie replied, 'Like the train.'

'Yes,' said the Prime Minister, laughing. 'That's right, Thomas's friend.'

Thereafter, Gordon Brown would often encourage me to visit Scotland. When I told him that we were doing so for a few days in the summer of 2010, just months after he had lost office, he invited us to visit him at his lovely Victorian house in Kirkcaldy. We did, our three children and his two playing happily together in the garden. Gordon insisted on making an early dinner for all the kids, refused any offers of help and proceeded to cook fish fingers and chips for five.

Whatever his critics say about him, my experience was that, one to one or in a small group, Gordon Brown was extremely personable, stunningly well read, and able to range widely over different topics. Years later, when I published a book on tennis, he urged me to speak at a literary festival in Scotland about it and my work as Speaker, facilitating such a visit through a friend of his. Often, when Sally or I was under fire, he would make contact to express solidarity.

* * *

In standing for election, you find people support you for a variety of reasons – friendship, agreement with your ideas, belief in your competence. Ambition can play no part as the Speaker must not and does not grant favours. If anything, backing me was a bad career move for a Tory as I was heartily detested by Cameron and his chums.

With Charles Walker, it was most of the above. We became friendly acquaintances almost immediately after I met him when he was elected in 2005. After graduating in American politics and history from the University of Oregon, Charles had worked in industry before becoming the Conservative MP for Broxbourne. A warm, outgoing, avuncular character, we found ourselves sitting next to each other in the Chamber. Having attacked the two immediate past Tory leaders, Iain Duncan Smith and Michael Howard, I would well have understood if a young, bright, articulate new Conservative MP kept a distance from me. Charles wanted to engage, professing doubts about trying to become a minister, saying that he would much prefer to hone the craft of a dedicated, principled backbencher and, perhaps, one day to chair a select committee. He complimented me on my speaking skills and asked what I aspired to do. When I told him that I wanted to be Speaker, his face lit up: 'You'd be great in that role, standing up for backbenchers. I would be delighted to support you when the time comes.'

Importantly, as my Speakership evolved, he stood by me both when he agreed with me and when he didn't. In some respects Charles was not a natural 'moderniser', but disagreement never meant desertion. He was a true ally, wanting to calm tensions on his side of the House and to protect me from any attempted insurrection. The fact that he is fundamentally well liked on both sides helped me too.

Throughout my time in the Chair, Harriet Harman was a staunch and shrewd ally. In the 2010 Parliament, when she served as Labour's deputy leader under Ed Miliband, we enjoyed excellent relations. When I decided that a Member should be free to take a baby through the division lobby she was warmly supportive, and at the start of the 2015 Parliament she welcomed my efforts to persuade the government to establish a Women and Equalities Select Committee. In the 2017 Parliament, with several Members giving birth, Harriet and I campaigned successfully together for the right of Members on paternity or maternity leave to vote by proxy – a civilised, progressive and democratic move.

On the opening day of the 2015 Parliament, when the House met purely to elect the Speaker, Harriet was fulsome in my support. Saying that I 'may be small in stature', she added: 'In that office, he is a giant. Of all the Speakers who have sat in the Speaker's Chair since I was elected, he is the best.' During the controversy over alleged bullying, when a number of the usual suspects demanded my resignation, Harriet was as dependable as ever. Although by then she had declared her interest in succeeding me as Speaker, she strongly encouraged me, as I intended, to stay put. Her reasoning was that if innocent people were forced to quit an institution because of media pressure, the atmosphere of that institution was poisoned. In her judgement, I had not merely a right but a duty to remain in the Chair, insisting on my innocence and getting on with the job. I shall always be grateful for her powerful backing in fair and foul weather alike.

From 2010 to 2016, Rosie Winterton served as Opposition Chief Whip. Thereafter she served on the House of Commons Commission and in 2017 was elected as a Deputy Speaker and still held that post when I retired in 2019. Over nine years, therefore, I worked with Rosie in three different roles. She was the best team player and the most collaborative person I have ever worked with, in Parliament or anywhere else. Rosie is a deeply Labour person, but she was not a natural parliamentary reformer. She has been a minister and could see situations from the government's point of view. When the House set up the Straw Committee to look at the governance of the House, the Tories voted on to it some Members who were against me and keen to ensure a result that represented a defeat for me. Rosie took great care to appoint two Labour Members who, along with most of their colleagues, would support my preference for a proper split between procedure and management.

It is no secret, and this chapter will demonstrate again, that most of my allies – people who subscribed to some or all of my agenda, believed in me and put themselves out on my behalf – were from the Labour Party. Yet for much of my Speakership I had some Conservative allies, beyond Julian Lewis and Charles Walker, and rather more of them than my most hard-core foes realised. One such was Jacob Rees-Mogg, the Conservative MP for North East Somerset and often referred to more or less affectionately as the Member for the eighteenth century, a reference to his traditionalist views, manner and speaking style. Sally had been at Oxford with Jacob but when he was first elected in 2010 we did not know each other. That soon changed. I heard him speak and we chatted at the Chair, as many colleagues and I do.

Jacob is a one-off, a singular specimen of humanity. As my colleague Stephen Pound, the Labour MP for Ealing North, observed, Jacob sits sideways on to the Chamber, usually one leg over the other. In order to speak, he does not so much stand up, 'he uncoils'. Overwhelmingly, he speaks without a text or notes, and addresses the House in perfect English. He does not hesitate, um or ah, but develops and presents a logical argument on whatever subject with admirable fluency. Always ready to accept interventions in his speeches, he deals with them thoughtfully, playing the ball, not the man or woman, and exhibiting unfailingly courtesy. He has a good sense of humour and is content not only to be teased but to take the mickey out of himself.

When the Conservative leadership sought, on the last day of the 2010–15 Parliament, to change the rules on the re-election of the Speaker, Jacob was scathing. He knew underhand, dishonourable behaviour when he saw it. Not only would he not go along with such chicanery, but he voted against it, humiliating the Leader of the House, William Hague, in the process – albeit I doubt Hague had the emotional intelligence to realise that he had been humiliated.

* * *

I benefited enormously from the support of these and other allies, including people like Peter Hain, David Blunkett, Angela Eagle, Margaret Hodge, Hazel Blears, Ben Bradshaw, Alison McGovern, Seema Malhotra and Tasmina Ahmed-Sheikh, to name but a few, but I also had to contend with powerful adversaries. As I pointed out at the beginning of this book, David Cameron was vehemently opposed to my election and attempted, clumsily and ineffectively, to prevent it. When I was elected, he immediately told the House that I could depend on his party for support. It probably struck him at the time as the right response to the House's choice of Speaker. It was also the traditional approach of the Conservative Party to support the Chair, as it did when Michael Martin was Speaker, even though very large numbers of Conservative MPs disapproved of him.

However, although Cameron pledged his support publicly, the reality was that his support ranged from minimal to zilch. He was only too happy to take a swipe at me from time to time whenever he judged he needed to toss red meat to his Conservative anti-Bercow colleagues. He had wanted anybody but me, and appeared affronted that I, a maverick Tory, who had not been sanctified by his blessing, nevertheless had the nerve to stand for Speaker, the temerity to win and the determination to be the House's champion, rather than his personal plaything. It seemed to me that he bore a grudge. Part of that grudge derived from my impression that he was a 24-carat snob, who felt that people like him were born to rule. He could accept social inferiors, and even welcome them into his circle, if they were useful to him. Those who had no desire to be were a frightful nuisance, to be rubbished whenever possible.

Having said that the Conservative Party would support me, he had no real choice but to observe the convention of not putting up a party candidate against me in the general election and I was therefore comfortably re-elected in Buckingham in 2010, and even more so in 2015. In between elections he set out to be as unfriendly as he thought it safe to be.

In seeking election as Conservative leader, Cameron had gone to great lengths to portray himself as a moderniser, some-one who wanted his party to 'stop banging on about Europe', to focus on public services, to support gender equality and facilitate a better work-life balance. He wanted a policy on childcare. Yet when I successfully led the drive to establish a nursery in Parliament – which he used for a time – Cameron took not the slightest interest, extended no support, and stood idly by while some of his Neanderthal backbenchers sought to block the project. If a new idea could be presented to the greater glory of D. Cameron, he was ravenous for it. If it could not, he had no appetite for it whatsoever.

When he was under legitimate pressure over his links with News International and Rupert Murdoch, and I granted an Urgent Question to Ed Miliband to probe him, he was visibly furious. Too bad, I thought. The subject needed to be aired. It was his responsibility to step up to the plate and account for his government. Above all, what Cameron couldn't abide was when I cut him off at PMQs for going beyond his brief, talking too long, or both. No doubt the resentment welled up in him.

If Cameron was emotional, prone to fits of pique and inclined to flare up over some real or imagined slight, William Hague, former leader of the Tory Party and later Foreign Secretary and then Leader of the House in the Conservative-Liberal Democrat coalition government, was very different. As I have described earlier, I found him buttoned-up, inscrutable, a cold fish. When I entered Parliament in 1997, I could see that he was bright. Yet he struck me as impersonal, mechanical, an upmarket, efficient hack – and an ex-teenage nerd who as a schoolboy had pored over parliamentary debates – who would not resonate with disenchanted voters we needed to win back. At the time deeply Eurosceptic myself, I went to see him to ask about his personal attitude to the Maastricht Treaty. Narrow and anorakish of me, for sure, but he was standing for leader and I wanted to know whether he had supported it out of loyalty to John Major or from personal conviction. His answer might be a guide to how he would lead. Taken aback, he told me that the attitude we took as a party on European treaties depended whether we were in government or opposition.

He would not be alone in that view but I didn't respect it. He would be driven not by principle but by opportunism. Ultimately, as noted earlier, I voted for Ken Clarke in the final ballot because I thought that Ken would have made a better leader. Well, he would have done. William applied himself to the task of leadership for four years with great determination and deployed all the rhetorical devices he had learned at the Oxford Union – achieving the impressive outcome of the net gain of one Tory MP in four years.

In the two decades and more since our chat in his room about the 1997 leadership election, we have not discussed it. Clearly, however, it rankled with him. When I was embroiled in Trumpgate, and he had started writing a column for the *Daily Telegraph*, he wrote a piece calling for my resignation and harking back to 1997 and how I, then a right-winger, had chosen Ken Clarke over him. The simple fact is that Hague was always hostile. Superficially polite to me, I was unfailingly courteous to him, asking him to deliver two lectures in Speaker's House, which he did creditably. But there was no empathy between us. When he served as Leader of the House, he and I met regularly. No major issues arose and the interaction between us was professional and workmanlike. Yet as the end of the Parliament approached he was preparing to try to cook my goose.

The third major adversary was Michael Gove. Cameron and Hague's dislike of me was visceral: you could smell their hostility, particularly Cameron's, a continent away. Gove was less obvious but it seemed he disapproved of my political journey. Though he told me in 2014, probably while plotting against me, that he thought I had been a fine reforming Speaker, he used the past tense. He wanted to see the back of me, not on account of a put-down by me from the Chair – when he was Education Secretary I had publicly told him at PMQs that he should write out a thousand times 'I must behave myself at Prime Minister's Questions' – but because I was a nuisance and his boss, the Prime Minister, was irreconcilably opposed to me. A part of Gove was also personally annoyed. When Theresa May had tabled a motion on a range of security measures, it did not allow for a specific vote on the European Arrest Warrant, a vote Conservative Eurosceptics thought that they had been promised. When I had been challenged as to the meaning of the vote, I had emphasised that there was no specific EAW vote and the Tory backbench anger was then fuelled by Labour, exploiting tensions on the government benches. There was a sense that the Home Secretary's motion was too clever by half and almost certainly either written by, or produced in agreement with, the then Chief Whip, one M. Gove. He thought that I had gone beyond my duty in the Chair and unfairly, even provocatively, criticised the government. I stand by my candid conduct on the day. The salient point is that Gove wrote to me in protest and I expected that he stored his discontent to resurface in the dying days of the Parliament in March 2015.

Unbeknown to me, the Prime Minister, David Cameron, the Leader of the House of Commons, William Hague, and the Government Chief Whip, Michael Gove, planned to translate their personal vendetta into what they hoped would be a decisive move against me. As noted earlier, no sooner had I been elected in 2009 than a number of colleagues floated the idea that as a new Speaker was now elected by secret ballot, so he or she should have to be re-elected by secret ballot on the first day of a new Parliament, in other words after every general election.

Arguments can be made for and against this proposition and, from the start of the 2010 Parliament onwards, proponents of a secret ballot emphasised that the Deputy Speakers had to be re-elected that way and so did the chairs of the select committees. If that system was right for them, surely it must be right for the most important elected post of all in the House, namely that of Speaker.

The counter-argument, which I believe is compelling, rests on the fact that the Speaker is in a unique position because he or she is the only MP not to fight a general election on a party political ticket. Instead, they stand as an impartial candidate (as 'The Speaker Seeking Re-election') in the expectation that, if elected by their constituents, they will continue in office. If, on the very first day of the new Parliament, the House then decided not to re-elect the Speaker, it would immediately need to select a party candidate rather than a non-party candidate as their new Speaker. Of course, if the House wishes not to re-elect the Speaker, it can do – but it is not unreasonable that the decision be made by an open division. If people want to vote against the Speaker, let them go through the division lobby and do so transparently.

The Procedure Committee of the House of Commons had agreed a few years earlier that the House should decide whether to keep the existing re-election method or change to a secret ballot. In meetings between the Procedure Committee, led by Charles Walker, and the Leader of the House in early 2015, Charles told William Hague that they would be very happy for his Committee's report on the subject – which recommended no change – to be debated and voted upon. But they felt that if there were to be such a debate and vote, they should take place in government time on a main sitting day, when a full House would have the chance to consider the matter.

In none of the one-to-one meetings I had had with Hague in the previous eight months had he suggested to me that it was a subject he planned to put to the House, or about which he had a strong view. Yet, late one Wednesday afternoon in March 2015, Hague came to see me and dropped a bombshell. He told me that the government would table a procedural motion for the following day, debatable for just one hour, that would provide for a secret ballot for the re-election of the Speaker after the general election if anyone objected to that re-election. This would enable colleagues who wanted to vote against the Speaker to do so anonymously, so that their constituents and the wider public would not be able to identify them.

Implausibly, unbelievably, absurdly, Hague told me that although the motion would be tabled in his name as Leader of the House, it would be a free vote. That was a lie – not a little lie, but a big lie, a bare-faced lie, as I subsequently discovered. I told Hague that what he intended to do was beneath contempt. He had always been an upmarket hack and this was proof. Unmoved, he mechanically repeated his mantra that the House should decide the issue and that it would be a free vote. I asked if the Procedure Committee had been consulted and he said it was a government decision. I told him candidly that this was not the way major procedural changes in the House were handled and he knew it. Such changes were considered by a committee, brought forward by agreement with it, and put to the House with due notice so that colleagues could arrange to be present and prepare for the debate accordingly. This had been decided without consulting or even informing the committee, or the Opposition, to be determined on the last sitting day of the Parliament when no votes had been indicated and very large numbers of MPs had returned to their constituencies to begin campaigning. Frankly, it was underhand, dishonourable, indeed despicable.

The following morning Julian Lewis told me that the Tories had cancelled canvassing in a key marginal and instructed their MPs on a three-line whip – in Parliament that means that a direction from a party is compulsory, not a request but an instruction – to be present at 10.30 a.m. for a strategy meeting in Portcullis House with their Australian election guru, Lynton Crosby. Julian Lewis and hundreds of others attended that meeting. The Chief Whip, Michael Gove, opened the meeting by highlighting the motion on the re-election of the Speaker, told his colleagues that it was William Hague's birthday and that they should give him a present by voting for it. That was the conclusive proof of the lie shamefully told to me by Hague that it was a free vote. The opposite was true.

Earlier in the week, the government had tabled and passed an apparently innocent motion to prevent any emergency debates on the final day, so that if anyone applied for such I could not grant it. However, I was not precluded from selecting Urgent Questions and there were a number of candidates. Rosie Winterton advised me that many furious Labour MPs, who had returned to their constituencies to start campaigning, were now hurrying back to Westminster to vote against Hague's motion. I selected three Urgent Questions, which meant that the debate on the Hague motion did not begin until after midday.

In a speech that made me embarrassed not by, but for, him,

Hague, the party hack masquerading as Leader of the House, said that when it became clear on the Tuesday evening that there would be no Lords amendments to Bills to consider, he had decided to put this motion to the House so that the matter could be decided. He said that he favoured a secret ballot, though in twenty-six years in the House there was no record of him ever arguing for it, and he had not told me of his view, consulted the Shadow Leader, Angela Eagle, or discussed either his view or his intention with the chair of the Procedure Committee, Charles Walker.

Angela Eagle laid bare the truth that it was a spiteful attempt to get rid of a Speaker who had had the temerity to stand up to the government. Colleague after colleague lined up to denounce Hague's behaviour, led by the Father of the House, Sir Gerald Kaufman, and followed by Members on both sides. The point was repeatedly made that, giving the House only an hour to debate such an important constitutional issue, without proper notice on the last day of Parliament, was an outrage. It was sheer, dishonest trickery and Hague demeaned himself by going along with it. Undoubtedly, however, it was Charles Walker who exposed the underhand behaviour of Hague, utterly humiliating him with the concluding line, 'I have been played as a fool and when I go home tonight, I will look in the mirror and see an honourable fool looking back at me. And I would much rather be an honourable fool, in this and any other matter, than a clever man.'

Gove tried to browbeat Tory MP Jack Lopresti, an old friend of mine, into voting for the motion but he defiantly voted against it. The whips called Nadine Dorries in similar vein and she told them to get lost. Jacob Rees-Mogg was withering in denunciation of Hague. Twenty-one Tories voted with Labour. The motion was defeated. Hague seemed shrunken, diminished, ridiculous and I looked at him, I confess, with disdain. Later, astonishingly, he looked me in the eye and said that it had been a free vote and the result proved it. That is often a weakness of a clever person – to think that others are stupid. Of course, the result proved nothing of the kind. It simply proved that there were colleagues otherwise well-disposed to the government, and even to Hague himself, who could not abide such disreputable trickery.

* * *

There is one other minister I came to believe was also profoundly hostile to me. Perhaps not coincidentally, she was also Leader of the House of Commons. Andrea Leadsom, the Conservative MP for South Northamptonshire, had been elected to Parliament in 2010 after a career in the private sector. An apparently capable, articulate new Member, she became a junior Treasury minister in 2014 and then Minister of State at the Department of Energy and Climate Change in 2015. When David Cameron resigned in the wake of the EU referendum result, Leadsom, a strong supporter of Brexit, stood for the leadership and in the ballot of Conservative MPs she came second to Theresa May. Under the party's rules, there was due to be a nationwide ballot of members to choose either Theresa or Andrea as the next leader. In an unfortunate newspaper interview, Andrea – a married mother of three children – appeared to suggest that she had a greater stake in the country's future than Theresa May because she had children – the future of the country – whereas Theresa May was childless. This provoked a storm of criticism and, within days, Andrea Leadsom withdrew from the leadership contest and Theresa May was the new Prime Minister. Leadsom was brought into the Cabinet as Secretary of State for Environment, Food and Rural Affairs and held that post until just after the 2017 general election, when she agreed to serve as Leader of the House of Commons, attending Cabinet but ceasing to be a member of it.

The Leader of the House has a role, alongside the Chief

Whip, in scheduling the business of the House, especially the government's business. The Leader also sits, ex-officio, on the House of Commons Commission which I, as Speaker, chair. In her early months, Andrea struck me and a number of colleagues as uncomfortable in her new role. It was as if she had not come to terms with attending a regular meeting she did not chair. Yet that was the reality. She was an important figure in the House but, and this I fear she found incongruous, she was not the Secretary of State for the House of Commons.

Early on, she found herself in a minority of one in opposing the expenditure of over £60 million to repair Big Ben, and later found herself similarly outnumbered when she publicly argued that the chimes of Big Ben should ring on the day the UK left the EU, as it was a day of celebration. The rest of the Commission and I strongly disagreed and, once again, she failed to get her way. Meanwhile, in the Chamber, she resolutely defended the government's move to give itself a majority on each select committee – even though it no longer commanded a majority in the House, refused to commit to the requisite number of Opposition Days over a two-year session of Parliament, and insisted that the government was entitled not to give effect to motions passed with which it disagreed. At no time was the Leader in breach of any parliamentary rule but her attitude upset some Conservative Members who felt that the government was disrespecting Parliament, an institution bigger and more important than any one government. Needless to say, she also faced unanimous disapproval from the Opposition parties, save for the Democratic Unionist Party, which was propping up the government.

In the autumn of 2017, press stories emerged about alleged sexual harassment and bullying in Parliament, including allegations that the Defence Secretary, Michael Fallon, had behaved inappropriately. Specifically, it was suggested that fifteen years earlier he had put his hand on the knee of the journalist Julia Hartley-Brewer, who had brushed him off. It was hinted darkly that this was but one example of a wider pattern and Fallon resigned, admitting that in the past his behaviour had not always been of the required standard. Some media reports suggested that Andrea Leadsom had complained to the Prime Minister and had a hand in his departure.

On Monday 30 October I granted an Urgent Question to Harriet Harman on the sexual harassment and bullying issue. In response, Andrea Leadsom proposed the establishment of a cross-party inquiry into the subject and this was quickly agreed by the Commission. In December I gave evidence to the Leader's inquiry, answering questions about the House's Respect policy, the range of other services we had in place, and my openness to recommendations for further improvements. At this stage, relations between Andrea Leadsom and me were amicable and she showed no sign of personal hostility.

That all changed when the first of the BBC *Newsnight* programmes on the personal bullying allegations against me was broadcast. On Monday 12 March I granted an Urgent Question to the Green Party MP Caroline Lucas, seeking a statement from the Leader in the light of the allegations. Caroline was genuinely motivated by a concern about the issue – she did not refer to me and I have never had any reason to believe that she feels any personal hostility to me. As usual, I called every Member who wanted to put a question to the Leader, including the Conservative for Rochford and Southend East, James Duddridge, a persistent but uninfluential critic of mine. He lambasted me, provoking intense anger on the Opposition benches in particular, and rather clumsily demonstrated that he would seek to use the issue, in which he had never before shown the slightest interest, to attack me. More importantly, although she made no direct reference to me, Leadsom declared that she had always treated all of her staff with respect, and appeared to look meaningfully at me as if to suggest that I had not done so.

I am not the most sensitive of colleagues, but several friends present at the time thought that her words and manner represented a dig. In terms of substance, the Leader indicated that she would be asking the House of Commons Commission at its next meeting to initiate a new inquiry on the back of the *Newsnight* programme. The following week, she presented a paper to the Commission which envisaged that this inquiry would take evidence in confidence and attempt to determine whether there were House practices or a culture which led to bullying. It was set up in April 2018, chaired by the retired judge Dame Laura Cox.

At the beginning of May, my former Private Secretary, Angus Sinclair, gave his explosive interview on *Newsnight*, as described in Chapter 6. One of the first people to comment publicly was Andrea Leadsom, who suggested that Dame Laura may wish to extend her terms of reference to investigate me. Dame Laura soon indicated that she would not do so. She was running an inquiry – an inquiry that Andrea Leadsom had requested – and would proceed with it. By implication, it appeared that she thought that the notion that she should change its basis mid-stream because of a television broadcast was out of the question. Nevertheless, to me, the significant point was that Andrea now appeared to be gunning for me. In the ten months since we had started to work together, she had never raised any concerns with me about alleged bullying or intimidation, but her attitude and conduct towards me now were unmistakably hostile.

In May 2018 a row blew up over the government's handling of the business of the House. It was an Opposition Day when Labour chose the subjects for debate, and the first was to be on the plight of residents of Grenfell Tower. The government scheduled a Transport Statement by Chris Grayling which inevitably ate into the time for the Grenfell debate. This scheduling was not unprecedented but it was unusual, and I shared the Opposition's view that it was disrespectful to Grenfell survivors. Ordinarily, the House expects the

Leader to have a regard not merely to the convenience of the government but to that of the House. Leadsom displayed no such concern, said nothing about the matter and, sitting on the front bench, looked unperturbed. By contrast, I was angry and when the Opposition complained I made it clear that I deprecated the government's handling of the situation. Under my breath, I muttered 'stupid' in relation to that handling. I am certain that I did not say 'stupid woman' as was alleged, and there is no evidence that I did. But clearly the description 'stupid' referred to the government's conduct, for which the Leader of the House was at least in part responsible.

The response in the right-wing press was to whip up a new storm, accusing me of sexism and misogyny. Frankly, it was ridiculous and, deep down, I suspect that some of the scribblers who wrote that rubbish knew it. I received many supportive messages from colleagues, constituents and friends, but Andrea Leadsom absurdly wrote me a long letter – more than three pages – complaining about my publicly expressed criticism. Astonishingly, she suggested that my criticism was expressed in 'aggressive' and 'threatening' terms. It was not. My style is forthright but not threatening, and in the previous nine years of my Speakership, no one had suggested it was.

Outside of the Chamber, seeing Andrea Leadsom, I asked if she wanted to talk about it. To my amazement, she said that she had no desire to talk to me as I had already reduced her to tears that day. Needless to say, I had witnessed no such distress and I can have no way of knowing whether she had been tearful. I mention the matter because it seemed to me to be part of a pattern. Leadsom was personally hostile. Quite properly, she was staging a cross-party inquiry into alleged bullying and harassment in the House, but I came to believe she was seeking to weaponise 'bullying' in her arguments with me. Bullying is a serious matter and, frankly, a loathsome practice. Maltreating someone, for example, by discriminating, humiliating, insulting, overworking or excluding that person must be wrong. Often, bullying takes place where there is a power imbalance. Yet Andrea Leadsom was the Leader of the House, and an experienced parliamentarian. To me, it was and is implausible that she can be a tough, no-nonsense political leader one minute and a shrinking violet the next who, when criticised by the Speaker, can suddenly claim to be brought to tears by a ruling or pronouncement from the Chair. My behaviour to her was not bullying. We had a robust, professional disagreement. It was both feeble and sinister for her to cry bully when I said what I thought and stood up for the rights of the House of Commons.

To my mind, it is wrong in itself and a grave disservice to victims of bullying in the workplace for one senior Member to lay that charge against another, when the publicly observable exchanges between the two of us offered not a scrap of evidence to justify such a claim. Brevity is not my strong suit. However, when Andrea wrote me that long, rambling three-page letter I decided not to engage point by point as there was no need to do so. I replied politely, disagreeing with her analysis but suggesting that we resolve to work together in the interests of the House.

In handling the matter in that way, I had ringing in my ears the privately offered advice of a senior member of the government.

'Mr Speaker, may I offer you some advice in your dealings with the Leader?'

'Of course,' I replied.

'Remember this. She was not uninvolved in the departure of Michael Fallon. She is trying to provoke you. Don't give her what she wants.'

The Speaker regularly meets a great many different office-holders, including the Leader of the House. Thereafter, I took care always to be accompanied and to give her the chance to be, so that there was an independent view on what was said by whom and when.

9

PMQs and Party Leaders

The institution of Prime Minister's Questions, or PMQs, is a relatively recent creation. From 1961, a process of regular questioning of the Prime Minister by the Leader of the Opposition began to take place. As with much British political procedure, it then became part of the custom and practice of the House without any formal decision to enshrine it. Yet for more than a quarter of a century Prime Minister's Question Time went largely unnoticed outside Westminster, even though it was broadcast on radio. That changed when the televising of Parliament began in 1987. Then the clashes – first between Margaret Thatcher and Neil Kinnock, followed by those between John Major and John Smith and between Major and Tony Blair – became visible to a much wider audience.

Until 1997, Prime Minister's Question Time was a twice-weekly event taking place on a Tuesday and a Thursday for fifteen minutes a time. The Leader of the Opposition would be able to put three questions. In one sense, it was more challenging for the PM, who had to undergo two sets of preparation and briefing – undoubtedly the factor that motivated Tony Blair to shift to once-a-week inquisition – but, on the other hand, the event did not enable a relentless roasting of the Prime Minister of the day.

Since 1997, the event has taken place once a week for a scheduled thirty minutes, though over the years, when there have been frequent interruptions or excessively long exchanges between the Prime Minister and the Leader of the Opposition, I have extended the session to ensure that backbenchers have the chance to probe the PM. When Tony Blair became Prime Minister, many people were shocked that the new government summarily ended the twice-weekly tradition of PMQs. The simple fact was that there was no procedural bar to the change. The government schedules most of the business of the House and is free to determine which Question Times take place, when and for how long.

The Leader of the Opposition is allowed by the Speaker to ask six questions. They can be asked in one uninterrupted sequence of six, or in groups of three and three or four and two, or any other formulation not exceeding six. Occasionally, he or she will want to raise very different issues – perhaps one set of statesmanlike enquiries about a non-party political issue facing the country and another set of a more partisan kind. However, in most cases the Leader of the Opposition chooses to do them all at once, no doubt hoping to build momentum and score a clear victory over the Prime Minister. The leader of the second largest opposition party in Parliament – for decades the Liberal Democrats but since 2015 the Scottish National Party – is permitted to put two questions to the Prime Minister.

Aside from those protected rights, there are two factors that dictate which other MPs ask questions. First, there is a weekly ballot: Members must submit their names in the Table Office of the House – so called as that is where questions are tabled – by close of business on the Thursday before the following Wednesday's PMQs. Unlike other ministerial Question Times, where the Member putting into the ballot must table a specific enquiry, they can enter the ballot giving no indication of what their question will be. Most do that to allow flexibility to choose their subject nearer the time. A small minority will table a specific question, perhaps in the hope of receiving a specific, detailed, perhaps comprehensive answer. The top fifteen Members whose names emerge from an electronic ballot (in which the Speaker has no say at all) are then listed on the Order Paper. Subject only to the constraint of time, the Speaker must call those MPs to put their questions.

However, there is a second method to 'get called' to ask a question. That is to 'bob'. In other words, Members not selected in the ballot can and do stand, usually at the start of the session and, if necessary, throughout it in order to try to 'catch the Speaker's eye' and be called to ask their question of the Prime Minister.

The established process is for the Speaker to alternate between the two sides of the House, so if there are two Opposition Members drawn immediately after each other in the ballot, I would look to call a government backbencher in between them. This is the concept of a 'free hit' – not an allotted space or booked spot, but a spontaneous opportunity to take part. Some weeks there are several such opportunities and other weeks there is none. How did I decide to whom to give a free hit? There is an internal arrangement whereby leaders of the smaller parties, namely the Liberal Democrats, DUP, Plaid Cymru and the Greens, are given a rotating slot because it is important to ensure that minority parties get a hearing. Once every four weeks, if there is time, one of them had the chance to put a question. Beyond that, the Speaker's office has a complete record of exactly how many times someone 'bobbing' has asked a question. As Speaker, I tried to ensure that everyone who 'bobbed' regularly had an opportunity and naturally I looked to call people who had a lower score. That was a big, but not the only, factor. If I knew that a Member wished to ask a question topical only for that week, I might call her or him. Similarly, a Member in whose constituency an atrocity, a tragedy or some other unwanted event had occurred and had tipped me off might find favour. I worked to achieve gender balance. If there were half a dozen free hits, there was no way on earth that I would call half a dozen men, unless no female Members were standing; likewise I sought to achieve an ethnic balance. It was important to try to accommodate Members from different parts of the country and from different intakes.

Just as importantly, I set out to ensure that dissident or maverick voices were heard. It is completely natural that government backbenchers will normally want to ask supportive questions of the Prime Minister, partly because they do support the Prime Minister, coming as he or she does from their party, and partly because they are ambitious. However, over recent decades there has been a growing and, to me, regrettable tendency for MPs to ask 'toady' questions, often supplied by the government whips' office, known to the Prime Minister in advance, and allowing the Member to reel off a list of achievements real or imagined. Readers may or may not be shocked by this but it is a fact and lies outside the influence of the Speaker. It is not for me to prescribe types of questions other than that they must relate to the responsibilities of the Prime Minister and be delivered briefly.

Often, however, I saw backbenchers standing whom I knew to be independent-minded, fearless and certain to ask a question of their own choosing – no one else's. Often such a question was critical of the government and unhelpful to the Prime Minster. So be it, was my attitude. It was no part of my role to seek to shield the PM from challenging enquiries and, if anything, it was my duty to give free-spirited backbenchers the best opportunity to raise their concerns with the leader of our country. I could not control the answers but I could at least give the free-spirited Members their chance. That's why I was keen to call Labour MPs Dennis Skinner, Paul Flynn, Frank Field and Kelvin Hopkins and, from the Conservative ranks, Bill Cash, Sarah Wollaston, Bernard Jenkin, John Baron, Peter Bone, Philip Davies, Heidi Allen and Anna Soubry, to name but a few from the two biggest parties. They were not guaranteed to be called – that itself would give them an unfair advantage – but my instinct was to give the blunt-speaking fraternity their say because, frankly, that should be what Parliament is about.

What is the point of Prime Minister's Questions? Well, there is a point but the answer to that question differs according to your perspective. The straight, constitutional answer is that the point of it is to allow the legislature to scrutinise the head of the executive on the policies for which he or she is responsible and that, of course, means all of the policies of the government. From the standpoint of the Prime Minister, the point of it must be to demonstrate his or her knowledge, understanding and competence in answering for his or her government and, through fluency, mental agility and debating powers, his or her superiority over not just the Leader of the Opposition but, as necessary, any challenging Member of Parliament. In the process, he or she is seeking to create a narrative in and for the media that he or she is fully abreast of all that matters and demonstrably more effective than anyone who takes him or her to task. There is also credit to be gained for exhibiting the ability or sensitivity to vary tone or content from one type of question to another, showing sympathy, gravitas and humour as appropriate.

For the Leader of the Opposition the point of the exercise is to expose the failings of the government and the Prime Minister, and to plant in the media and the public mind the idea that a government led by him or her would tackle more effectively the problems facing the nation. Basically he or she is auditioning for the role of Prime Minister. The third party leader is seeking to gain recognition and to differentiate him-or herself from the other two.

In addition to the outward-facing feature of the session, the desire to impress listeners and viewers in the country at large, there is the simple but valid purpose to rally the troops. Building and sustaining the support of the leader's parliamentary party is very important to her or his credibility and, potentially, to that leader's survival in office.

To backbenchers looking to ask a question, the point of Prime Minister's Questions is often to impress constituents that they are raising an important subject at the highest level and, in the process, to show their mettle to the party leadership and whips, ordinarily in the hope of promotion. Others might be looking to gain the support of colleagues for an upcoming election and will seek to excel for that reason. So the motivations vary but the common thread is to seek to display knowledge, gumption and fluency in the best-attended and most high-profile session of the parliamentary week.

I mention attendance. For all that dozens of colleagues sought to catch my eye to ask a supplementary question, 'dozens' is the operative word. It was not hundreds. In other Question Times – to the Health, Education or Transport Secretary, for example – there might be a hundred MPs present. They will be Members either with a particular interest in that subject as a whole – that was the norm – or seeking to participate in exchanges on a particular question, in all probability for reasons of constituency relevance. Those Question Times are participation sports. By contrast, Prime Minister's Question Time is a spectator sport. At one time or another, most MPs will want to ask a question but most weeks they attend in order to cheer their leader and, very likely, to jeer her or his opponent. Moreover – and this is true of other ministerial Question Times too – no minister can ask a question. Ministers are members of the government, bound by collective responsibility for its policies and obliged to support its leader. On the Opposition side, the convention is not as strong because the Opposition is not in office. Nevertheless, by convention, members of the Shadow Cabinet do not ask questions at PMQs. Other Shadow ministers, however, are free to do so.

Superficially, one might think that the Prime Minister of the day is on the defensive or even under siege as he or she is questioned by up to thirty people and, particularly in the case of Opposition Members, he is unlikely to have been told in advance what they intend to ask. In fact, I would argue that the advantage is with the Prime Minister because he or she has greater numbers of MPs behind him or her, providing a vocal wall of noise in his or her support and against the Leader of the Opposition; he or she will have prepared meticulously on all the issues that he might be expected to raise; and finally, the Prime Minister has the last word. Measured against that, if there is a 'losing' feel to the government – a sense of drift, an economic downturn, a belief that the PM's administration is divided, has run out of steam, or both – an Opposition leader can come across as the face and voice of the future. In the early years, however, and sometimes indefinitely, the PM has the advantage.

* * *

As a Member of Parliament for twenty-two years, I had the privilege of observing party leaders at Prime Minister's Questions from two distinct positions, politically and geographically. For twelve years, I sat on the Opposition benches as a Conservative, periodically questioning the Prime Minister but predominantly observing Tony Blair up against first William Hague, then Iain Duncan Smith, Michael Howard and David Cameron. In my last two years as a Tory MP, but by then largely non-party political, the match-up I watched was between Gordon Brown and David Cameron. Elected Speaker as I was in June 2009, I then observed from the Chair the Brown–Cameron dynamic and, from October 2010 until May 2015, the weekly spar between Cameron and Ed Miliband. When Ed was succeeded by Jeremy Corbyn in the autumn of 2015, I watched Cameron and Corbyn lock horns and then, from July 2016, the battle was Theresa May pitched against Corbyn. Finally, Boris Johnson squared up against Corbyn at just two PMQs before Parliament dissolved for the 2019 election.

For a few months after the 1997 election, John Major continued as Conservative leader while his party went about the process of electing a successor. The Blair vs Major warm-up was of no great significance; the point of interest was to see how the new Conservative leader would fare against Tony Blair. William Hague was seen by a majority of Conservative MPs as a mainstream Eurosceptic of intelligence, competence and notable skill as a debater. Even though I had not voted for Hague I was sitting there as a new young pup, a right-wing, Eurosceptic Tory who couldn't stand the sight of Tony Blair and eagerly hoped that Hague would either score the parliamentary equivalent of a knockout or, at the very least, a points victory. Initially, I was not disappointed. Hague was an accomplished debater who, with a deft turn of phrase and use of humour, would often get the better of the Prime Minister. Frequently, Hague had us rolling in the aisles with his jokes. At one stage, when Labour was torn as to who should be its candidate for London Mayor, Hague cheekily suggested that Tony Blair should divide the job into two – with Frank Dobson as his day Mayor and Ken Livingstone as his nightmare. It was funny, he delivered his lines well and it rallied Conservative MPs, who were impressed – myself included – that here was our man, our chief, our leader, socking it to the Prime Minister whom we all opposed and many of us actively disliked.

However, although William Hague's debating skill and wit shaped him up as leader, the Conservatives remained way behind Labour in the polls and, importantly, Hague's poll ratings as a leader consistently and heavily trailed behind those of Tony Blair. There was a lesson for Conservative MPs there, though most of us did not see it at the time. Voters form a view of a leader very quickly – certainly within a hundred days or so. If it is positive, that is naturally encouraging and a party, of either government or opposition, can take advantage of it while it lasts because that popularity rating will usually go down, sometimes dramatically, over time. However, if a leader starts with poor public ratings, those ratings are unlikely to rise significantly for a sustained period. Unfortunately for William Hague, the public did not take to him. Constantly replayed images of him making an impassioned speech aged sixteen to the Conservative Party Conference, instead of impressing voters, made him appear nerdy and weird. When Hague then tried to cultivate a more populist image by appearing in a baseball cap and claiming that as a youngster he had been known to drink fourteen pints of lager, voters found this view of him both inauthentic and implausible.

For the first eighteen months or so of his leadership, Hague deployed his clever lines to good effect in the Chamber, delighting Tories but leaving the mass of the electorate comparatively unmoved. Thereafter, there was a major change which testified to the shrewdness of Tony Blair and his advisers. Blair developed a line that Hague had great jokes but no answers to the country's problems. In other words, he was contrasting Hague the showman with himself, the statesman. Effectively the message to the watching media and, through them, to the public was, 'If you want a comedian, Hague is great. If you want a leader, I am that person.' It was simple, he repeated it each week if necessary, and it was extremely effective. From that point on, the days of Hague's ascendancy were over for good. Even if he put in barnstorming, knockabout, witty performances – which were increasingly rare – Blair could gently tease him by saying, 'Good joke, but where's the beef?' If he was no longer so funny, it was a straightforward attack on the policy issues, and Blair, becoming more authoritative, statesmanlike and formidable by the week, frankly trounced him.

Appallingly though the Conservatives had performed in 1997, they were still by far the largest Opposition party and, therefore, the official Opposition. This meant in practical terms that Hague had a right to put six questions a week to the Prime Minister. That enabled him fully to develop a theme and a sequence of questions to make his case. By contrast, Paddy Ashdown, the leader of the next largest Opposition party, the Liberal Democrats, was entitled to two questions per week, typically taken consecutively. Ashdown, by then MP for Yeovil for fourteen years, had emerged strongly from the 1997 election, leading his party to a total of forty-six seats, more than double the tally of twenty-five years earlier and the Liberals' best performance in decades. A strong, distinctive, even charismatic figure, Ashdown was able up to a point to impose himself on the media and public consciences, not least by his interventions at Prime Minister's Questions. He would impose himself because he was a striking, physically impressive figure who had served as a Commando in the Royal Marines and he had a presence in the Chamber. An intelligent, articulate man of real gravitas, he put crisp questions to the Prime Minister and Blair treated him seriously and respectfully.

I said he could impose himself up to a point. What do I mean by that? It was scarcely a state secret that Ashdown would have been willing to form some kind of pact with Labour in a hung Parliament if electoral reform had been offered. However, once Blair had secured his landslide victory – Labour's majority was 179 – he lost interest in any deal with the Liberal Democrats. Sitting there in the Chamber, my sense was that colleagues felt that the Liberal Democrat leader had been jilted at the altar. Fairly or not, he appeared to have been damaged by bearing the reputation of a discarded suitor.

In 1999, after eleven years as leader, Ashdown resigned voluntarily as Liberal Democrat leader. He was replaced by Charles Kennedy, who hailed from that other bastion of Liberal Democrat strength, the highlands of Scotland. Elected at just twenty-four in June 1983 as the Liberal Democrat MP for Ross, Skye and Lochaber, Kennedy had a reputation as a skilful and witty debater but, cut from a very different cloth to the ex-military man Ashdown, the two had never completely

gelled. Charles Kennedy had been a student politician, enjoyed a joke and a drink and was often thought to be talented
but lazy. What's more, doing TV programmes like *Have I Got
News for You?* had played to his talent for humour and quick-
wittedness but in the formal world of Westminster it had done
nothing for his reputation as a serious politician – perhaps the
reverse. Yet he was able all right, wanted to be leader and got
the job.

Kennedy was likeable. I had always been told that he was
both bright and a good speaker. To me, in the quick-fire atmosphere of PMQs, those qualities did not always come across.
Whereas Paddy Ashdown had been sharp, to the point, a bit
clinical in posing questions and making points, Kennedy struck
me as too laid-back and often undisciplined. Yet in retrospect
I think I overestimated the importance of forcefulness and
rapier-like fluency.

A key part of effective communication is looking and
sounding appealing. To a lot of voters – notably young voters
– Kennedy's impact on them may not have been at PMQs, as
they scarcely watched it, but instead from occasional glimpses
of him on television, including perhaps at his party's annual
conference. Others will have seen and heard him questioning
the Prime Minister and liked the cut of his jib. He was blokeish
and down to earth, without an ounce of pomposity. Although I,
a political insider, was not especially impressed by his speaking
style in the bearpit of PMQs, a lot of people warmed to him.
All of that was true from 1999 to 2003 – the first four years of
his leadership. Then he struck lucky. Whereas Paddy Ashdown
had not had a defining issue of mass public interest where he
dramatically disagreed with both Labour and the Conservatives, Charles Kennedy was gifted the polarising issue – and,
in fairness, for some, the tragedy in terms of lives lost – of the
Iraq War. Tony Blair and Iain Duncan Smith almost competed
in the strength of their support for the war and UK involvement in it. Duncan Smith's successor, Michael Howard, also

supported the decision to go to war. Charles Kennedy led a united Liberal Democrat Party in opposition to what he called an illegal war. In doing so, he did what he thought was right but, crucially, he gave his party definition and distinctiveness in the process. He pressed Tony Blair on the subject and, though the Prime Minister more than held his own, Kennedy established himself as the only major party leader who was explicitly and unhesitatingly against the conflict.

There is truth in the old adage 'nothing succeeds like success'. Pumped up by the life-or-death significance of the debate, and the knowledge that he was speaking for a lot of people, Kennedy grew in self-confidence and stature as a leader. By the 2005 election, the Liberal Democrats became the repository for left-of-centre voters alienated by the Labour government's decision to go to war in Iraq and he led his party to its best result in modern times, notching up 62 seats. Eight months later, after struggling with alcoholism, Kennedy was forced out of the leadership, but there is no denying that he made a mark. Although I disagreed with him on Iraq and much else besides, I respected Charles Kennedy as a patriotic, public-spirited, conviction politician. His premature death in 2015 was a tragedy for his family and a real loss to the country.

* * *

After the 2001 election in which the Conservatives under William Hague suffered a second successive slaughter, winning only 166 seats, a gain of just one in four years, Iain Duncan Smith was elected leader as I have described earlier. IDS was principled, hard-working and set out a vision of a Conservatism much broader than that of a party preoccupied with Europe – even though he himself had been prominent in opposing the Maastricht Treaty and the whole EU integration project. Yet in PMQs, in other Commons exchanges and in the country as a whole, Duncan Smith was a calamitous failure.

He crashed and burned. Almost from day one, he shrank into office. The problems for him were manifold. First, in this tele-visual age, though the former Captain in the Scots Guards was smartly dressed – as William Hague had been – Iain looked to be a dull, grey man. Unkind references to his baldness were made. Hague was bald but spoke well. Iain was bald and didn't. Secondly, for all that Iain had some modest experience of leadership in the army and must have known that it was vital to inspire the troops, he entered the Chamber for the weekly PMQ joust looking racked with anxiety. To say that he was a rabbit in front of the headlights does not begin to convey how terrified he appeared at the prospect of taking on the super-confident, articulate, towering and telegenic Prime Minister Tony Blair. Thirdly, if Iain looked terrified, he sound-ed it. He continually cleared his throat in asking questions of Blair. Remember the misery that Theresa May endured at the 2017 Conservative Party Conference when she was suffering from a severe cough, spluttered repeatedly and all but lost her voice? Her plight was much worse and it received blanket media coverage. Yet it was a one-off and she recovered. Iain's 'frog in the throat' did not afflict him once but repeatedly, week after week, leaving many to fear or sneer that it was a psychosomatic condition. He seemed terrified, weighed down, out of his comfort zone. He was just not up to it. There is a world of difference between successfully shadowing a Secre-tary of State and leading a party. The latter requires a much wider grasp of the essentials in multiple fields of policy as well as the ability to project strength in Parliament and to the country as a whole. Unfortunately, Iain could not do it.

When he was elected leader on 13 September 2001, the world was in shock from the horrific terrorist attacks two days earlier on the United States and the UK was preparing to send troops to fight the Taliban in Afghanistan. Dreadful though 9/11 was, and as obvious as the challenge in Afghanistan appeared to be, there was a premium on national leadership.

My mother Brenda, Sally, me and Sally's mother, Eileen, on 7 December 2002.

Sally and me electioneering with our first child, Oliver, in the run-up to the 2005 general election.

Feeding our seven-week-old daughter, Jemima, in May 2008.

With Freddie, Jemima, Oliver and Sally in Speaker's House in October 2010.

Newly elected as Speaker on my first full day in office, 23 June 2009.

President Barack Obama toured Parliament in May 2011, guided by me
and my Lords counterpart, Baroness Hayman.

Applauding Angela Merkel after the German Chancellor spoke in the Royal Gallery in February 2014.

Listening to China's President Xi Jinping delivering a speech in the Royal Gallery in October 2015.

With Her Majesty the Queen, March 2012.

At the State Opening of Parliament in May 2013.

Prime Minister Boris Johnson, whose attempted five-week prorogation of Parliament I immediately denounced in August 2019.

Jacob Rees-Mogg with whom I got on well, though latterly we were sharply at odds about Parliament's role in relation to Brexit.

'Colleagues. Welcome back to our place of work.' In the Chair, 9 September 2019, after the government's plan to prorogue Parliament had been foiled.

Leaping to my feet to cheer Roger Federer in the Wimbledon final in 2019.

Interviewing Roger Federer – my hero.

With my family in Speaker's House on 30 October 2019, before I chaired Prime Minister's Questions for the last time.

Leaving the Chair for the last time on 31 October 2019.

Tony Blair, now Prime Minister for over four years, had the foreign policy experience, the confidence born also of two seismic election victories and the support of the media and public alike, in contrast to the unknown new Conservative leader. Iain rallied behind Blair on the foreign policy front and I reckoned that he was right to do so. Politically, however, he was hemmed in and found no space that he could capture. At PMQs, when he agreed with Blair on foreign policy, the PM thanked him but, by definition, the Leader of the Opposition was not thereby making a case for a change of government. When he disagreed, notably on domestic policy, Tony Blair was remorseless in juxtaposing Labour's spending on schools and hospitals with the Conservative record of allegedly starving them of funds. Even on Europe, where Iain's opposition to joining the Euro was widely shared by voters, Blair skilfully contrasted his pragmatic statesmanship in the national interest with the extreme, dogmatic Europhobia of IDS and the Conservative Party.

To this day I recall the occasion when Iain delivered a prepared question less than convincingly. Tony Blair brutally dismissed him, saying, 'He read it, he read it badly and it wasn't worth reading at all.' At the 2003 Conservative Party Conference, Iain delivered an extraordinary speech, describing himself as 'a quiet man' who was now 'turning up the volume'. He challenged his internal critics to put up or shut up. He received the Conservatives' usual, loyal standing ovation but MPs took him at his word. Within weeks, Tory MPs triggered a vote of confidence which he lost by 90 votes to 75. I was one of the 90. It was a sad end to his two-year tenure as leader.

If the dismissal of Iain Duncan Smith was swift and brutal that was because the party has a keen survival instinct. As we have seen, Michael Howard was elected unopposed as the new leader on 6 November 2003. As Employment Secretary and Home Secretary, he had been shadowed by the then up-and-coming Tony Blair and there was even a feeling among some colleagues that Howard, a QC before he entered the Commons, would floor Blair in the Chamber combat. That always struck me as optimistic because Blair, over six years by then as Premier and himself a former lawyer, had become ever more formidable. Nevertheless, Michael had done a credible job up against the Chancellor, Gordon Brown, and there were grounds for optimism.

Howard started well. His questioning of Blair was crisp. Indeed, when he said that he looked forward to holding the PM to account for his record, including over the Iraq War, he sounded confident, almost threatening, and it took a little while for Tony Blair to acclimatise himself to a more heavy-weight opponent.

Early on the two leaders clashed over tuition fees in higher education. Howard was positioning the Conservative opposition against them, a populist ploy but not a very Conservative position. Blair lectured Howard that if more people were to go into higher education, that had to be paid for and that was what Labour was doing. Seizing his chance, Howard cleverly declared that 'this grammar-school boy' would take no lectures from 'that public-school boy' on the importance of expanding access to higher education. But this was emblematic of Howard's approach as leader: a debating triumph that led nowhere. Tactical it was, but not strategic. No one seriously believed that a Conservative government would scrap tuition fees. Howard basked in the ritualistic cheers of his colleagues but it was no substitute for charting a clear alternative to New Labour. Soon enough, Tony Blair regained his poise, contrasting Labour's invest-and-reform approach to public services with the slash-and-burn policy that Howard had so zealously practised as a Cabinet minister for seven years.

Ironically, Howard's leadership took a dramatic turn for the worse as a result of a chronic unforced error not in PMQs but in a separate debate – when during a discussion on the Butler inquiry in July 2004 he claimed he would not have voted for the Iraq War in March 2003 if he had known then what he knew now. As I have explained, it may have been sincere but it sounded cynical, stunned Conservative MPs and was scorned by everyone on the government benches. Blair saw his chance and seized it with both hands. He responded by saying that people respected someone who honestly supported the war. They respected someone who was against the war. But they did not respect someone who was for and then against it.

The attack by Blair was crude but devastating. The air had gone out of Howard's tyres. He looked shifty, unscrupulous, even ridiculous. His authority as Conservative leader was dented and in the Chamber he never recovered, compounding his error by opting to brand Tony Blair a liar. It made him feel better but look nasty, and obviously did not cause Labour voters to flock to the Conservatives.

By the summer of 2005, though damaged by the continuing furore over Iraq, Tony Blair was still the biggest and most impressive beast in British politics. He had seen off four Conservative leaders and two Liberal Democrat leaders and led his party to an unprecedented three successive election victories.

At that point, the Conservative Party, accustomed to power, and rightly uncomfortable without it, changed course, plumping for a smooth, fresh-faced PR man, the 39-year-old whizz kid David Cameron. Personable, fluent and charismatic, a young leader with young children, including a dearly loved, severely disabled son, Cameron impressed voters. He was new, attractive, the eloquent representative of a fresh Conservative generation. That was very significant because the UK is not at heart a socialist country. It is really centrist – a social democratic or even 'wet' Tory country. Of course, it is a huge generalisation, but most people want free enterprise and fairness, the chance to get on and protection if they don't, a country that stands up for itself but engages with others.

Cameron was to make two strategic decisions at the outset that came to define his leadership, not merely in Opposition but in government. One was made in order to get closer to Blairite New Labour and the other, taken for reasons of personal self-interest at the time, was to place him at loggerheads with moderate opinion. That first decision was to embrace the fight against climate change, show support for environmentalism, and demonstrate a new, more progressive Conservative approach. This meant not merely posing with huskies and introducing a lighter blue-green logo. It entailed also offering to support Tony Blair in developing his school academies programme against scores of Labour MPs and councils almost atavistically opposed to it. Cameron camped on Blairite ground. I am not arguing that these nuances of political positioning made an impression on voters. They simply signalled a shift and an attempt to embrace the most positive features of New Labour, just as Blair ten years earlier had accepted trade union reform and Conservative tax and spending levels. Cameron surprised Blair at PMQs by offering to support his school reform policy and also made a telling jibe in positioning himself as the heir apparent to Blair, saying, 'He was the future once.'

The second decision was fateful and ultimately disastrous. In bidding to become leader, Cameron promised Eurosceptic Tory MPs that he would take the Conservatives in the European Parliament out of the principal and largest centre-right group, the European People's Party. That group was regarded by many right-wing Tories as pro-EU federalism and therefore unsuitable. In the European Parliament, influence is exerted by operating within alliances. Though the EPP was more pro-European than the Conservative Party, successive leaders – including Thatcher, Major, Hague, Duncan Smith and Howard – had all thought it made sense to be part of it. Cameron, thirsting to be leader and enticed by the prospect of securing the votes of some of his colleagues, was happy to make the commitment to quit it.

Once elected, he denounced the UK Independence Party

(UKIP) as 'racists, fruitcakes and nutters' and declared that under his leadership the Conservatives would stop banging on about Europe. Rather, he would focus on the economy, the environment, family policy, public services, the concerns of millions of people across the land. Yet having pledged to withdraw from the EPP, he had to honour the pledge. There was no obvious alternative so ultimately the party ended up loosely co-operating with a number of hard-right, nationalist parties, some of whose members appeared racist, homophobic or both. In Opposition, it was moderately damaging to Cameron. Tony Blair pilloried him for caving in to right-wing headbangers, and mainstream European Conservatives, notably the Christian Democrat Chancellor of Germany, Angela Merkel, were infuriated and horrified by such a crass misjudgement on Cameron's part. The harm might have been greater if Europe had been central to the political debate at that time, or if Cameron had sought to place it there. Wisely, he did not, choosing to concentrate instead on building a domestic narrative. Speaking effectively in the Chamber, just about holding his own with Tony Blair, served him and his party well at that stage.

Cameron was helped too by the new leadership of the Liberal Democrats. Charles Kennedy had been succeeded by Sir Menzies ('Ming') Campbell. Talked about as a possible leader when Charles Kennedy was elected in 1999, Campbell had decided not to put his name forward but he served with distinction as his party's Foreign Affairs spokesman from 2001 to 2006. In that role, he was excellent. Knowledgeable, urbane, fluent, he was widely seen as a statesmanlike figure even by those who disagreed with him. But as leader, he bombed. He appeared to lose confidence, suffer stage fright and be ill at ease with the welter of domestic issues he had to address.

At Prime Minister's Questions, he raised the plight of old people, prompting the Tory MP Eric Forth to heckle 'Declare your interest!', causing MPs to burst out laughing. It was a cruel jibe but, sadly, it highlighted the truth that he seemed so lacking in vim or energy. He was yet another example of someone who had done well in addressing a single brief based on knowledge, understanding and insight but could not hack the much bigger task of leading a party. Tony Blair was the leader of experience; Cameron the zestful young pretender. Campbell was neither fish nor fowl. Rather, he was old-fashioned, passé, a nicer version of Michael Howard. After just over eighteen months, Campbell stepped down as leader and was replaced by the young, thrusting, personable Nick Clegg just months after Tony Blair had resigned and been replaced by Gordon Brown.

How did this trio perform? Rarely has a leader enjoyed such an auspicious start or so speedy a descent as Gordon Brown. No one can know for certain whether Tony Blair would have been able to lead Labour to a fourth successive election victory any more than one can prove that Margaret Thatcher would have achieved that feat for the Conservatives if she had not been dumped by her party in 1990. What was clear, however, by 2007 was that a lot of voters had wearied of Blair who, a year earlier, under pressure from Gordon Brown and many Labour MPs, had promised to quit. When Gordon Brown was effectively crowned party leader and Prime Minister – there was no candidate for the leadership against him – the omens were overwhelmingly positive. He and the Labour Party enjoyed very high poll ratings and were in a commanding position. Brown looked very strong, whereas both Cameron and Nick Clegg appeared to be vulnerable. Yet at this point everything went wrong for Brown. First, as when any serving Prime Minister is replaced – in the last three decades, the examples are Thatcher to Major, Blair to Brown and Cameron to May – there was feverish speculation about a possible early election, about whether it would or should take place. There was a growing expectation in Parliament that Brown, buoyed by brilliant poll ratings, would take the chance to seek his own mandate. Ministers themselves seemed to feed the speculation and, at any rate, did nothing to dampen it. The idea was out there for weeks, unconfirmed but also undenied.

At the Conservative Party Conference in October, George Osborne unveiled a plan to reduce inheritance tax sharply and it was well received, certainly in the media and apparently in the polls. The Conservatives received a boost. At this point, weeks late, Gordon Brown suddenly announced that there would be no early election as he wanted to get on and govern, developing his vision and programme for the country. When asked if new, less favourable polling had caused him to drop the idea of the election he had appeared to be planning, Brown bluntly denied that his decision had anything to do with the polls. Politicians, media and public alike did not believe a word of it. Cameron taunted Brown that he was running scared. Almost overnight, he suffered a reputational hit from which he never recovered.

In the Chamber at PMQs, Brown was nowhere near as formidable as some, myself included, had expected. Once again, the contrast between specialist and generalist was stark. As Chancellor of the Exchequer, whatever people thought of his record – largely a matter of political taste – Gordon Brown reigned supreme in the Chamber. He knew his brief backwards and regurgitated his key achievements with rapier-like speed. He mastered, even monstered, successive Shadow Chancellors from Peter Lilley to Francis Maude, from Michael Portillo to Michael Howard, from Oliver Letwin to George Osborne. None of them was able to lay a glove on him and, needless to say, neither could any backbencher from either side of the House. Yet at PMQs he looked less self-assured and was far from convincing. He could not anticipate the range of subjects that would be raised and, inevitably, could not produce the conclusive responses that he had been accustomed to churning out at will as Chancellor. What's more, unlike Tony Blair, who was versatile – long, short, serious, funny, boastful and self-deprecating – Gordon Brown did not carry a bag of different tools. Rather, he had one weapon – a sledgehammer – and used it almost indiscriminately. David Cameron taunted and teased him and he would often be visibly agitated, the more so as the government's problems mounted. To me, Gordon Brown was the better brain, the more sophisticated thinker and the more principled public servant. Yet Cameron looked far more at ease, was quicker on his feet and, in Chamber combat, simply superior.

Brown as Prime Minister was also hit by the global financial crisis in 2008. In fact, Brown led a multilateral response that limited the damage and paved the way for a kind of economic recovery, but he received no credit for that. Indeed, when in a slip of the tongue he said that the government had 'saved the world', he was mercilessly ridiculed. Rather, the issue became whose fault the crash was and who was best placed to steer the economy in the future. The Conservatives, supported by the right-wing press, blamed Brown for past excesses of spending and borrowing. This was economically illiterate and the Opposition under David Cameron had never spelled out which large budgets should be cut. Yet in the blame game, Brown came off worse. He sought to argue that inadequate regulation of financial services was partly to blame – and the Conservatives had advocated more comprehensive deregulation – but that case never took root in the public mind. In any event, he had been Chancellor for a decade before serving as Prime Minister and had been no stranger to lighter regulation of financial services. Much of the blame for that could be laid at his door. Cameron and George Osborne developed a telling narrative that you should not give the keys to the guy who crashed the car. Exaggerated, simplistic, flawed as an argument it was, but it was effective. Gordon Brown was damaged.

Compounding his problems, in May 2009 the *Daily Telegraph* exposed the parliamentary expenses scandal. That scandal embroiled Members of all parties. Both Brown and Cameron had made honest mistakes in their own claims.

Those mistakes were comparatively minor and of themselves did no great reputational harm. The problem was that Brown was Prime Minister and Labour was in office. When such a scandal erupts, it is a safe bet that the government of the day will suffer more than its opposition. Gordon Brown was rarely, if ever, flippant. He was the most serious-minded of leaders and, by all accounts, a total workaholic. He had wanted to be Prime Minister for well over a decade but he did not give the impression of enjoying it at all. In adversity, Tony Blair would produce a self-deprecating joke, a smile and then plough through the problems he faced. Brown could not do that.

In those closing years of the Labour government, the political clash was overwhelmingly between Brown and Cameron. It was always difficult for the third party to secure much attention, unless a big issue arose on which it differed fundamentally from the two largest parties, as with Iraq under Charles Kennedy. So it was hard going for Nick Clegg. He was fluent, telegenic, appealing and, if people knew who he was, they generally liked what they saw. He did not, however, cut through to the mass electorate until the 2010 election campaign itself. Then he was helped modestly by rules on balanced coverage and massively by the staging for the first – I hope not the last – time of three television debates between the party leaders. Brown and Cameron were known quantities, the former experienced, the latter fluent and versatile. Clegg was largely unknown. He performed extremely well – 'I agree with Nick' – not merely in terms of eloquence and knowledge, but in coming across to voters as reasonable, fresh and worth a chance. In the euphoria following Clegg's initial apparent triumph, the Liberal Democrats polled at 30 per cent and more. His strength did not evaporate but it lessened sharply in the days ahead. Nevertheless, Nick Clegg held the balance of power in a hung Parliament. What followed was to be first the making, and later the breaking, of his time as a political leader.

* * *

As the leader of the largest party after the 2010 election, it was no surprise that David Cameron became Prime Minister. There was surprise and some unease among right-wing Tory MPs that he opted to seek a fully fledged coalition government with the Liberal Democrats. He argued, with justification, that a so-called 'confidence and supply' agreement would be potentially unstable and suggest a less than full-hearted commitment to work together. Cameron preferred the big, evidently statesmanlike gesture of a formal coalition. Nick Clegg assented and became Deputy Prime Minister. In return for offering the stability of a coalition majority of 77 seats, Clegg expected a commitment from Cameron to a referendum on electoral reform but, fatefully as it transpired, he did not insist on the Liberal Democrat policy – its headline manifesto commitment – to scrap tuition fees or even limit their increase. In return for a share of power, Clegg ceased to be an opposition leader, sitting instead on the government front bench and having no opportunity to question the Prime Minister in the House of Commons.

David Cameron had already proved himself in Opposition to be the most capable Conservative leader since his party had lost office. In government, unsurprisingly, he grew stronger for a number of reasons. First, even though he had failed to win outright, he had achieved a stable government in financially the most testing of times. Although Labour was vitriolic towards Nick Clegg, the Liberal Democrats had long preached co-operative politics and were now practising it. The significance – both symbolic and practical – of having Clegg and George Osborne at his side was immense. Secondly, just as 'time for a change' had worked against the Conservatives in 1997, so it damaged Labour in 2010 and beyond. The media and public sense that it was time for a new beginning was palpable, and Cameron and Osborne began to ram home their message that austerity was the only way out of the deficit. After May 2010, Harriet Harman, Labour's deputy leader, served as Acting Leader of the Opposition until Labour had concluded its leadership contest over the summer. The party turned inward and by the time Ed Miliband became Leader of the Opposition in September 2010, the Conservative economic narrative had become firmly embedded in the public mind.

In the Chamber of the House of Commons, Cameron was not assailed by both Labour and Liberal Democrat leaders but by only one of them, namely Ed Miliband. Prime Minister Cameron had one core message, which translated as 'we're fixing your mess'. He repeated the mantra that the Conservatives had 'a long-term economic plan' to slash the deficit, committing to eliminate it by the end of the 2010–15 Parliament. Labour, he argued, created the deficit and had neither the will nor the ability to tackle it. Furthermore, he established early ascendancy over Ed Miliband at PMQs and in other set-piece clashes between them. He ridiculed Miliband as the man who had knifed his elder brother, David, the initial favourite for the job, in order to lead his party. This was clever as he combined it with pointing out that Miliband had not had majority support among either MPs or party members but had won through the votes of the trade unions. This fact allowed Cameron to characterise and demonise Miliband as a left-wing stooge. Far from being fresh or interesting, was the message, this man is just a typical Labour leftie, an attack he could not begin to make against Tony Blair. Cameron was assisted in his portrayal of Miliband by the fact that Ed had worked for Gordon Brown and was well known, like Ed Balls, to be more a Brownite than a Blairite. In the Commons, therefore, Cameron repeatedly slated Miliband as an old 'tax, spend and borrow' Labourite, a claim he reinforced when Ed Balls, a bright, trained economist but also a protégé of Gordon Brown, became Shadow Chancellor in 2011.

Ed Miliband started on the defensive in that he suffered the fate of every Labour leader in my lifetime with the sole, albeit only partial, exception of Tony Blair. The media were against him and out to get him. As always, there was not so much as a pretence of being fair or even-handed. The biggest-selling newspapers – other than the *Daily Mirror* – were hostile, parodying him as Gromit from *Wallace & Gromit* as his eyes and look were thought to bear a resemblance. That was the calibre of the attack. Sure enough, the newspapers generally sell far fewer copies than twenty years ago. Millions of people get their news online. Yet even then the right is well-represented and the sheer cacophony of anti-Labour, anti-Miliband noise did not help him.

In my experience, Miliband was thoughtful, highly intelligent and very resilient. He was not, however, a natural in the Chamber. He had never been a great platform speaker and, at first, he was not particularly adept in debate. David Cameron, on becoming Conservative leader, had said that he wanted to bring an end to 'Punch and Judy politics', preferring a more serious, mature, respectful approach. No doubt it seemed the right thing for a leader to say and, at a stretch, he might have believed it at the moment that he said it. Of course, he forgot about it as quickly as he had thought of it, opting for abusive attacks on Gordon Brown, Miliband and later Jeremy Corbyn. Miliband himself, a man interested in policy and ideas, started out by saying that he favoured a more restrained and policy-based exchange with the Prime Minister. The odds were always against such an approach. The shape of the Chamber lends itself to adversarial politics. Prime Minister's Question Time is framed as a theatrical clash of the titans, a boxing contest in which one beats the other. That was also both the expectation and the thirsty desire of MPs on both sides, cheering their own leader and cat-calling the other side.

Ed Miliband began on a sober, restrained note, not merely in debating Afghanistan and Libya but on the domestic front too.

Once big issues and controversies came to the fore, exchanges became more coarse.

Measured over the five years that they squared up to each other in the Chamber, there is no argument that most of the time Cameron got the better of their exchanges. He was more fluent, quicker on his pins, had the numerical advantage in seat numbers and, of course, the benefit of thorough briefing which, as a natural speaker, he was able to deploy to maximum effect.

Yet Cameron's dominance was never complete or uninterrupted. When riots took place across England in August 2011, I agreed to the Prime Minister's request to recall Parliament. It is often said that disorder brings a shift to the political right, as people crave order. Naturally, in the Commons David Cameron was quick to condemn rioting, looting, arson and murder, and to underline his support for the police. He performed very competently. Yet Miliband did too, also condemning violence but expressing real concern that an absence of hope had helped to spawn such an unusual outbreak, the first of its kind since the poll tax riots of the late 1980s and the Brixton and Toxteth riots over unemployment at the beginning of that decade. To his credit, Miliband made a serious speech that struck a chord with many who felt that the country was too divided between the haves and the have-nots. The poor were suffering grievously and paying more than their fair share for the economic downturn precipitated by selfish and reckless bankers.

Again, and for a short period, very successfully, Ed Miliband took on News International, castigating Rupert Murdoch's company for its phone-hacking and helping to force the abandonment of its bid to acquire BSkyB. Others, including Cameron, eventually fell into line with the Opposition on the matter but it was Miliband, for whom the ground had long been prepared by the campaigning Labour MP Tom Watson, who seized the initiative. Subsequently, Miliband developed a policy to freeze crippling gas and other utility prices and it resonated with the public, outraged by the rip-off perpetuated by effective monopolists. At first the Conservative government lambasted him for pursing a Marxist policy, before adopting a similar policy itself.

Yet these sorties by Miliband, though they undoubtedly shaped him in the public mind as someone who understood their problems and instincts, were never enough to put him in a commanding position. Even when Labour defeated the government over Syria in 2013, the result was used to attack Miliband for shifting position for partisan purposes. Labour did forge ahead in the polls but never established an unassailable ascendancy.

* * *

Though none of us was to know it at the time, the Prime Minister's decision to provide for a referendum on Scottish independence in September 2014 was not merely a bold constitutional gamble. It proved also to be significant in terms of domestic electoral politics across the UK. Of course, voters opted by 55 to 45 per cent for Scotland to remain in the UK. Conservative, Labour and Liberal Democrat parties all supported the No to independence campaign but Labour's stance came back to bite the party. The SNP ruthlessly pilloried Labour for being just another English establishment party and by November 2014 I recall an experienced Scottish Labour MP telling me that a political earthquake was brewing in Scotland, with dozens of Labour seats set to be lost to the Scottish Nationalists. Labour had long enjoyed dominance in Scotland with approximately 40 seats, mostly rock-solid and largely taken for granted. In the general election of 2015 there was a massive swing to the SNP and Labour lost all but one of its seats to them, which triumphed in 56 constituencies, leaving one each to Labour, the Conservatives and the Liberal Democrats.

Alongside this seismic shift there was a parallel development. In the 2015 campaign, Ed Miliband had stressed that he was seeking an overall majority but did not rule out governing with the SNP. The Conservatives pressed ferociously the message that Labour would be prepared to rupture the UK to achieve power. The charge was essentially nonsense because if Scotland departed the UK – which the referendum had decided, with Labour support, it should not – that would wreck the chance of a majority Labour government in Westminster. Yet perception is key. In a great many English marginal seats, the spectre of Miliband governing in cahoots with the SNP's Nicola Sturgeon was alarming. David Cameron had even suggested weeks earlier that Labour's readiness to deal with the SNP was despicable.

On 7 May 2015, against the predictions of the pollsters, the Conservatives won a small overall majority, the first such Conservative victory since John Major's in 1992. More particularly, it was a devastating defeat for Ed Miliband, whose seat tally slumped from 258 to 232. There was compelling evidence to suggest, therefore, that the independence referendum had, paradoxically, both preserved the Union and paved the way for a resurgence of Scottish nationalism, hugely damaging Labour's electoral fortunes in the process.

To my mind, Ed Miliband was a gutsy and thoughtful leader who nevertheless was unable ever to appeal to floating, notably former Conservative, voters as Tony Blair had done. Miliband was at heart judged to be a metropolitan leftist and the man who slayed his brother to help himself to a political prize called party leadership. Personally, I do not buy the argument that you can't trust someone who competes with a sibling. Politics is not, or should not be, about hereditary entitlements. Yet the public never took to him. Authentic, principled, robust under pressure he was – but, fundamentally, David Cameron was more popular and judged to be a better national leader.

In that 2010–15 Parliament, Nick Clegg as Liberal

Democrat leader was transformed into Deputy Prime Minister, and he readily agreed that he must be accountable to the House by having to appear at a Deputy Prime Minister's Questions. Relentlessly attacked by both Labour and anti-coalition right-wing Tories, Clegg displayed a steely resolve both to stick to his guns in supporting and seeking to shape coalition policy. He had conceded on tuition fees and lost on electoral reform when voters decisively rejected the idea. Yet on other fronts he was more successful. He pushed for a pupil premium policy that would boost education spending in disadvantaged areas, argued to take more people on lower incomes out of tax and persuaded David Cameron to legislate for equal marriage. Inevitably he had to play second fiddle to the Conservatives. He had not won the election. There was not a Liberal Democrat government. Rather, he sustained a stable if not especially progressive administration for five years. He did so patriotically, loyally and with determination and, to me sitting in the Speaker's Chair, he grew consistently in confidence, competence and stature. Yet there was a terrible price to pay. The Liberal Democrats had alienated both their left-of-centre voters and, perhaps, millions of people who disliked the Conservatives' policies and wanted an alternative in 2015. Clegg and his party were tarred as the Tories' helpmates and suffered a crushing defeat, plummeting from 57 seats to just 8. Clegg held his own seat at the election but lost it in 2017.

There was an irony about David Cameron's success in 2015. Five years earlier against a tired government, he had failed to win outright. Now, despite austerity and against pollsters' predictions, he gained 24 seats and was able to govern alone. Right-wing Conservative MPs had long distrusted Cameron, fearing – rightly – that he preferred governing with Nick Clegg to depending upon them. In 2010 Cameron had been committed to a referendum on the EU Lisbon Treaty if the Conservatives formed a majority government. They did not and, therefore, he was neatly and conveniently freed from that commitment. Now in 2015 he led a single-party government, he was pressed by Eurosceptic MPs to resurrect the referendum plan, and he agreed.

I confess that as a Remainer myself I could see an argument for a referendum, though it was risky. The issue was one of constitutional significance. The three main parties all wanted the UK to remain in the EU and, therefore, a general election was not a means by which to ascertain whether people wanted to remain or leave. Moreover, as a large minority, probably at least 40 per cent and possibly 50 per cent according to the polls, wanted to leave, UK membership of the EU was frankly unstable. We were not wholehearted members of the Union but neither had we expressed a desire to exit. There was something to be said for resolving the issue once and for all.

Cameron pressed ahead with his EU Referendum Bill and Labour felt that they had to support it, or risk being accused of trying to deny the public a say. There was no threshold requirement built into the legislation – a straight majority would suffice. That was eminently defensible. Less so was the government's decision, supported by a majority in Parliament, to restrict the vote to eighteen-year-olds and above. It was in line with the voting age for elections and, therefore, consistent, but it meant that young people who would be most affected had no say. If they had been able to vote, the result would probably have gone the other way.

The fact remains that in over a decade as leader of his party, David Cameron had never made a passionate, principled, progressive case for UK membership of the EU. He was forever tactical, desperate to ward off the UKIP threat by sounding appropriately Eurosceptic and to placate his own right-wing backbenchers. When the referendum came, he had achieved next to nothing in his much-vaunted renegotiation of our membership terms. The new Labour leader, Jeremy Corbyn, backed Remain but was lukewarm. Several prominent Tories, led by Boris Johnson and Michael Gove, campaigned to leave, and the Conservative press did so with zeal. Those who felt left behind in modern Britain, and who opposed large-scale migration, blamed the EU and the establishment who supported UK membership and they turned out at the ballot boxes to back Brexit. So David Cameron led the country into a referendum of his own choosing and was the handmaiden, if not the architect, of our departure. He led the UK out of the EU by accident. It was not a triumph of statesmanship.

Over six years as Prime Minister, David Cameron led a government that reduced the deficit and, to his credit, introduced equal marriage. Painful austerity measures hit the poorest hardest, hurting women in particular. Living standards stagnated. Health and education services struggled and the UK prepared to leave its biggest market and the power bloc it had joined over forty years earlier. As Leader of the Opposition, Cameron had got the better of Gordon Brown. As Prime Minister, he had outperformed Ed Miliband in terms of personal ratings and in leading the Conservatives to victory in 2015. When Jeremy Corbyn was unexpectedly elected Labour leader in September 2015, Cameron soon found the measure of his opponent, getting the better of him in the great majority of their exchanges. At times he showed a so-called Flashman tendency, appearing almost to bully, and certainly to abuse both Miliband and Corbyn, succumbing to sexism when riled too, telling Labour's Angela Eagle to 'Calm down dear' and getting a cheap laugh from loyalist Tory MPs for telling his arch-critic, Conservative MP Nadine Dorries, that she was 'frustrated'.

What did he achieve? One coalition government after which voters were poorer. That was followed by an election victory and almost immediately preparations for a referendum that he did not have to call, the result of which profoundly divided the country and that seems set to leave citizens poorer, politics nastier, racism given a new lease of life and the United

Kingdom more vulnerable and less influential than at any time of my life. I am reminded of the verdict of the man he worked for and would consider a friend, Norman Lamont. Cameron was 'clever, but not profound'. That is true. In the pantheon of great leaders, the name of David Cameron will never feature. In a list of opportunist lightweights, it will be at the top.

* * *

When Ed Miliband, shell-shocked by defeat, resigned as Labour leader in May 2015, Harriet Harman, his deputy, once again accepted the mantle of Acting Leader. As in 2010, she did not seek the leadership. Once the candidates were known, it seemed initially a safe bet that either Yvette Cooper or Andy Burnham would succeed Miliband. Jeremy Corbyn was nominated as a candidate by the requisite number of Labour MPs, several of whom did so simply to allow him to put his case. He appeared to be merely the left-wing Campaign Group standard-bearer, putting up to make the pure socialist case but without the slightest expectation of winning. That was my reading of the situation and, I suspect, his. Yet the seeds of his victory had unwittingly been planted. Ed Miliband had introduced a new £3 membership subscription and several hundred thousand new members had been recruited to the party. Many were left-wing, anti-cuts, idealistic students tired of, and plain hostile to, Labour's cautious approach to Opposition. They wanted principled, uncompromising resistance to the Cameron government and the promise of a radical Labour alternative. Jeremy Corbyn was their obvious candidate. He appeared to be what he was: a conviction politician and an unbending left-wing ideologue. He was sincere, true to himself and – in the age of the practised soundbite and the scripted speech – a natural and authentic figure, telling members exactly what he thought. Having won a landslide in his party, he had to prove his mettle in Parliament and in the country.

In starting out as leader, Corbyn faced three apparently insurmountable obstacles. First, he was up against a now experienced Prime Minister who had just won his own mandate whereas he, Corbyn, had not only never served as a minister but never in over thirty years sat or even aspired to sit on his party's front bench. He had been a career-long protest politician and a serial left-wing rebel – in 500-plus parliamentary votes – against his own leadership. Secondly, fewer than 10 per cent of his MPs had voted for him and large numbers bitterly resented being led by someone whom they judged utterly ill-equipped for the task. Thirdly, the mainstream media were almost universally hostile to him, though he did enjoy greater support on our increasingly vocal social media.

In the Chamber, Corbyn began by appealing for a kinder, gentler politics, characterised by respect and a willingness to co-operate. He also set out to adopt a less aggressive and strident tone at Prime Minister's Questions than had become the established norm. He began questions by quoting from people who had written to him, often in response to his open request for voters' suggestions of subjects that they wanted him to raise. Initially, it was interesting because it was different, and it ensured that he was noticed. Many voters disapproved of the noise, the tribalism, even the frequent juvenility of PMQs. Yet he soon ran into trouble. His questions were often too long. He would lose the House or, at least, cause it to lose patience. David Cameron rammed home the charge that Corbyn was an extreme left-winger, mocked his mildly shabby appearance and did all he could to demonise Corbyn and his closest ally, John McDonnell, as a threat to the very fabric of our democracy.

At the 2017 election, however, against all the odds, Corbyn sharply improved Labour's position in Parliament as the party took 262 seats, 30 more than under Ed Miliband in 2015. The tragedy at Grenfell Tower, the government's internal divisions over Brexit and his own self-confidence and credibility from the election all contrived to make him stronger. Yet that advantage was lost by internal divisions and, in particular, the damaging row over anti-Semitism in the Labour Party. In my experience, he is genuine. He is not anti-Semitic. I have found him decent to the core. Yet he had certainly shared platforms with people who are hostile to Jews and he had been very slow to get to grips with the poison of racism in his ranks. He has shown resilience by the bucketful but the obstacles to him becoming Prime Minister remained formidable.

For just under ten months, Corbyn was up against David Cameron, and then he faced Theresa May. His fellow Opposition Leader was the Liberal Democrat Member for Westmorland and Lonsdale, Tim Farron. I have known Farron since he entered Parliament in 2005 when he beat the Conservative Shadow Cabinet Member, Tim Collins. Farron was straight-talking, decent, as pro-European as his predecessor as leader, and a committed Christian. In Parliament, Farron was never as crisp a performer as Clegg or Ashdown had been, and he did not enjoy the public popularity of Charles Kennedy. After the 2016 referendum, however, he had a distinctive message of being pro-EU. In the run-up to the 2017 election, he committed to a second referendum on the final EU-UK deal or, indeed, to a plebiscite if there was no deal. This appeared to give his party the prospect of a new lease of life, forged out of the distinctiveness of being the only major UK-wide party offering the chance to stop Brexit. Yet for all his energy he did not rouse voters. A Christian uncomfortable with homosexuality and abortion, he was bogged down by questioning over those issues not in Parliament but on the hustings. He never seemed at ease and did not gain the foothold in the country that he needed. Many observers expected that Remain voters would shift their support to the Liberal Democrats. It did not happen on any scale. The Liberal Democrats were still paying the price for their spell in government and added only four seats, securing twelve MPs at the 2017 election. Tim Farron promptly resigned as leader and was succeeded by Sir Vince Cable who, having lost his Twickenham seat in 2015, won it back in 2017.

Cable is intelligent, measured and responsible. He too had demanded a 'people's vote' on any deal with the EU and made it clear that he opposed Brexit and would like to stop it. Yet for all his experience, weight, sincerity and moderate brand of politics, he had made little impact as leader of his party. He was far more effective as his party's Shadow Chancellor before the 2010 election and more influential as Business Secretary in the coalition government. As leader, he seemed unable to rise to the challenge.

* * *

That leaves for consideration Theresa May. What may be said of her as Prime Minister and a party leader?

As we all know, she was a dark horse candidate to become Prime Minister. After the 2015 election, no one would have expected David Cameron to be resigning as Prime Minister thirteen months later. Most commentators reckoned that he would step down some time before 2020, hoping that his friend and Chancellor of the Exchequer, George Osborne, would succeed him. The referendum result destroyed David Cameron's political career and it appeared also to destroy George Osborne, not least as Prime Minister May promptly sacked him as Chancellor. I say 'appeared' to destroy George advisedly. He soon took on a substantial portfolio of outside interests, including in early 2017 amid some controversy the editorship of the London *Evening Standard*. In stepping down as an MP, presumably because he expected Theresa May to return at the June 2017 election with a large majority and no job for him, he decided to plough his furrow outside the Commons. Ironically, if he had remained an MP, he might have toppled Theresa May. In politics in the UK, you are only a player if you have a seat in the Commons. He didn't after June 2017, and the rest is history.

As we have seen, Andrea Leadsom felt obliged after a misjudged comment about Theresa May not being a mother to withdraw from the leadership contest, allowing May to become Prime Minister without the burden of having to traipse round the country for two months in pursuit of the votes of party members. Although no one said or even necessarily thought at the time, I believe that that absence of a contest was highly significant. Theresa May is decent but as wooden as your average coffee table, a worthy public servant but as dull as ditch-water, courteous to everyone but lacking in an ounce of small talk with anyone, honest but lacking in any original convictions, as capable as the next politician of reading a script but devoid of any spontaneity or natural fluency, let alone charisma. If she had had to perform on the stump at party hustings, those failings might have been exposed and Andrea Leadsom could well have become party leader and Prime Minister. They weren't and she didn't.

Theresa May impressed at first with her decisiveness. She had always kept her own counsel under David Cameron, holding down the difficult job of Home Secretary amid its inevitable plethora of controversies and not courting the limelight. She had never been seen as right-wing or left-wing, simply solid, safe, sensible. As Prime Minister her speedy dismissal of Messrs Osborne and Gove – the latter later returning when she felt she needed him – was thought reasonable and her elevation of Boris Johnson to Foreign Secretary, David Davis as Brexit Secretary and Liam Fox as International Trade Secretary bold and risky, but also canny. She was signed up to deliver Brexit and effectively recruiting its principal cheerleaders to assist her in doing so. It was either naïve, presumptuous or both for the Prime Minister to believe that she could trigger Article 50, the starting gun for a two-year countdown to exit, without a parliamentary vote. The Supreme Court ruled otherwise and it was an embarrassment – no more than that – for her. A short Bill was rushed through Parliament and in late March 2017 the Article 50 notice was served. Most MPs had voted for that to happen, though at that stage – tellingly and perhaps disastrously – the government had not set out its preferred vision of Brexit. Nor did anyone know what Theresa May thought.

In Parliament, however, the polls, and the media, she enjoyed a prolonged honeymoon. She had signalled to MPs before and after she took office that she did not intend to call an early election. That would be a recipe for instability. In November 2016, in a conversation in Speaker's House on wider issues, she told me the same. I believed her. To this day I am convinced that she did not plan to go to the polls. Cautious by nature, knowing that constitutionally she did not have to do so, and keen to build her own record after first delivering some form of Brexit, she was instinctively disinclined to rush to the country. The next election would be, she suggested, in May 2020.

Some senior Tories, almost certainly including the Chief Whip, Gavin Williamson, and the Party Chairman, Patrick McLoughlin, persuaded her to seek her own mandate. The party was at least twenty points ahead in the polls and she was far more popular than Jeremy Corbyn, whom she appeared regularly to outgun, not least by simple repetition of core messages. 'Brexit means Brexit', 'strong and stable', and so on were her mantras.

Yet it was a mistake to go to the voters with a campaign designed around the personality of a Prime Minister so patently lacking one. A stilted monotone, a resistance to meeting individual voters spontaneously and a horror, verging on meltdown, when confronted by any unexpected questions from a journalist at a press conference did not bode well for the campaign or her leadership. Perhaps worst of all, the Conservative manifesto contained proposals to require millions of people to pay for dependants' social care. A case could be made for shifting the burden away from the general taxpayer to the family members with assets of their own. However, no ground had been laid. No public debate had been conducted. No one had had any wind of such an imminent prospect. It was also bound to hit lots of natural Tory voters. As a vote-loser, it could scarcely be better devised by Theresa May's political opponents. So the manifesto was denounced in the media and Theresa May performed dreadfully from start to finish.

By contrast, Jeremy Corbyn, for all his weakness in Parliament – at the despatch box and as a former maverick opposed by most of his colleagues – was authentic, natural and accustomed to performing well at mass gatherings. When the election was called, the expectation was that Theresa May would win a landslide of at least 100 seats, possibly up to 150. That lead, if it was ever real, evaporated throughout the campaign and, as we know, Theresa May lost the small majority she had. It was the cobbled-together 'confidence and supply' agreement with the DUP that kept the Prime Minister in office. When she stood on the steps of Number 10 Downing Street, she set out an almost Blairite vision of wanting to govern for all, not just the privileged few. Social mobility was her driving purpose. Yet since serving as Prime Minister in June 2017 and for the remaining two years of my Speakership, one issue dominated government, Parliament and political discourse: Brexit.

It was tough for Theresa May. She had not voted for it but felt that it was her democratic duty to deliver it. In her determination to prove to the right-wing media and her formidably organised European Research Group of Brexiteer backbenchers that she would do so, she ruled out membership of the single market, wavered about what a customs union or partnership might mean and had absolutely no idea of how to tackle the issue of the Irish border. It was two years after the referendum, seventeen months after triggering Article 50 and thirteen months after the 2017 general election before her government issued a White Paper on the approach to Brexit. Moreover, her so-called Chequers proposal was scorned by many of her own MPs, several of her ministers and in September 2018 by the entire EU Council of Ministers. Yet still she resisted any suggestion that the final deal or 'no deal' outcome of negotiations should be put to a people's vote.

In my personal dealings with Theresa May, she was always proper and courteous. There was no trickery about her. Where David Cameron, William Hague and Michael Gove had schemed against me, she did not. She was altogether more grown-up than that. Sadly, however, she was stubborn when flexibility was needed and, lacking a natural majority and in hock to the DUP, she appeared frozen, politically boxed in, almost paralysed and unable to chart a clear and safe course for the UK.

Theresa May is not a bad person. She works exceptionally hard and wants the best for her country, while lacking a clear sense of what that is. Rudderless, without imagination, and with few real friends at the highest level, she stumbled on, day to day, lacking clarity, vision and the capacity to forge a better Britain. In a contest as to who has been the worst Prime Minister since 1945, it is hard to choose between Anthony Eden and Theresa May.

10

How to Be a Good MP

What does it mean to be a 'good' MP? How should a newcomer to the House go about achieving that accolade?

The truth is that there is no professional qualification needed to be a Member of Parliament, no formal job description and no explicit contract with voters. Every MP does the job as he or she judges best, but it makes sense to think about the audiences a Member should aim to impress: constituents, the party he or she represents, and the House.

When I came into the Commons in 1997, I was told of Members who were thought to be 'good constituency MPs' because they sat for hours in the library replying by hand to constituents' letters. A few may still do so but the phenomenon is much rarer today. Although such a personal touch is impressive in one sense, it was easy and perhaps even efficient when a Member received fifteen letters a week from local residents, as the former Cabinet minister Shirley Williams told me was her lot when she entered the House in 1964. It would be vastly more challenging and a poor use of time to work like that in 2020, when a Member receives hundreds – sometimes even thousands – of constituency communications every week and can harness more staff and, crucially, technology to assist. The key imperative for a new Member settling in now is to set up a good office with capable staff and a clear delineation of responsibilities between them: who does the diary, who leads on casework and who researches policy issues to produce briefing papers for use in the MP's questions, speeches and articles as well as to draw on in constituency visits and media interviews. It is good to get back to every constituent within a working week – more quickly if possible. Good MPs know that they have to see things from the voters' point of view. Most people contact their MP infrequently, asking his or her opinion or seeking help. They want an answer and a prompt answer at that.

A Member should be visible – staging regular surgeries, visiting schools and hospitals, attending community groups and ensuring that that visible presence is reflected in the local media. Inevitably, I cannot know from the Speaker's Chair which colleagues are especially active and visible in their constituencies though I do get an inkling of it from the frequency and passion with which they refer to situations in their areas. In the 2015 intake, for example, Rebecca Pow, the Conservative MP for Taunton Deane, name-checked her constituency almost every day, citing people she had met there, initiatives she had seen and examples of good practice in agriculture, schools, the environment or health care that she wanted to commend to the House. Similarly, Emma Hardy, the new Labour MP for Hull West and Hessle, was tireless in bringing graphically to our attention the plight of some of her most disadvantaged constituents.

As in any career, familiarising oneself with the workplace is a prerequisite of success. Members should start by getting a feel for and understanding of the shifting culture of the Chamber, which is smaller and more intimate than you would think from watching proceedings on television. The acoustics are good and 99 per cent of the time Members don't have to shout to be heard. Even raised voices are unnecessary and can grate. A conversational tone is fine. To a new MP, my advice would be to spend time there during the daily Question Times and debates, even if only an hour a day. It will pay dividends. A Member will see how Question Time works, watch and

listen to colleagues and practise asking questions. As we have
seen, the House – and the Speaker – can be intolerant of long,
rambling questions, and the House can also vent its frustration
with a Member who repetitively and unimaginatively trots out
the party line – particularly if the Member is plainly reading
from a whips' office crib sheet. A Member who performs as an
attack dog against the other side of the House can irritate colleagues, as I can personally testify having done it myself in my
first few years in Parliament. Someone who pipes up on every
subject, has little original to say and takes too long to say it,
drives the House to distraction. In my last Parliament, I noticed
Labour's Geraint Davies and the Conservatives' Vicky Ford
fall into this trap. Both conscientious Members, they did not
always detect when the House had heard enough from them.
By contrast, MPs who asked probing questions succinctly and
made pithy speeches went down well. On the Conservative
side, Sir John Redwood and Sir Desmond Swayne were commendably concise. For Labour, Emily Thornberry and Yvette
Cooper were textbook inquisitors.

Let me raise the elephant in the room. I have often met
highly intelligent, capable, principled and public-spirited
people who fear that they are not cut out to be MPs because
they are not good public speakers, don't enjoy communicating
on their feet or both. How important is it to be an effective
public speaker to be a good MP? The answer is that it helps,
but it is not essential. What's more, styles vary and times
change. Tub-thumping oratory, often honed in public-school
debating societies and at the Oxford or Cambridge Union,
is not altogether an invisible relic of the past but it is rare
these days and not always effective. For example, the Attorney
General, Geoffrey Cox, a distinguished QC by background, is
extremely articulate, has a deep baritone and a talent for rous-
ing oratory. Yet in the Chamber in 2019, it didn't quite work.
It was too showy, too theatrical, too much of a performance,
whereas Dominic Grieve, one of Geoffrey's predecessors as

Attorney General and also a QC, seemed much more easily to command the attention and respect of the House. Dominic is equally fluent but his style is measured, reasonable, almost clinical, rather than ostentatious or flamboyant. The same is true of Sir Oliver Letwin, a former philosophy don, who chats his case conversationally with the House, displaying a mastery of his subject and unfailing courtesy to anyone who challenges him. Jess Phillips, the Labour MP for Birmingham Yardley, is altogether more chatty and conversational in tone than Cox or other traditionalist debaters and yet she is unmistakably clear and passionate. Aside from those I have mentioned above, Ken Clarke, Hilary Benn, Chris Bryant, Joanna Cherry, Stewart Malcolm McDonald and Sir Edward Leigh are all first-class communicators though with differing styles. Ken is authoritative, passionate and humorous. Joanna is analytical, lawyerly and able to respond to any critique. Stewart can please a crowd effortlessly and Hilary radiates sincerity with every word.

As it happens, none of the current House tops the list of the greats. For me, the best speaker I heard in over two decades in the House was Tony Benn, captivating and even mesmerising, though I often disagreed with him and I rarely heard him refer to his own constituency. He was very much Westminster's representative in Chesterfield, rather than Chesterfield's representative in Westminster. The best debater – quickest-witted, sharpest and most formidable in argument – was the late Robin Cook. He was simply brilliant, though at his best Ken Clarke ran Robin a close second.

Some colleagues love being on their hind legs and have a mental filing cabinet of questions to ask at all times. Labour's Barry Sheerman, MP for Huddersfield for over forty years, is a prime example. He sometimes refers to his constituency, notably when advertising the merits of the University of Huddersfield or lamenting the detrimental impact of Brexit on industry, jobs and living standards. For two terms the chair of the Education and Skills Select Committee, he speaks with knowledge and understanding of schools and the FE sector alike. He sees it as part of his role to challenge the government across the field of policy. A similar approach is taken by Philip Hollobone, the independent-minded Conservative Member for Kettering, who is eloquent, matter-of-fact and admirably succinct in his questioning of ministers. Another strong performer on the Conservative benches, demanding improved road infrastructure, longer prison sentences for violent criminals and an end to the 'nanny state', is Philip Davies, Member for Shipley. From the moment he was elected in 2005, he made it clear that he had no desire to be a minister, preferring simply to be the voice of Shipley. Philip is outspoken and controversial, notorious to critics for talking out Private Members' Bills, but he operates within the rules of the House and is a highly skilled MP.

Oratory and the ability to rouse an audience will always have a place in politics. In my experience, they are not crucial to success in Parliament. Clarity, sincerity and integrity are the pre-eminent factors, together with the ability to maintain a laser-like focus on the subject at hand. On the whole, a Member is more effective for having a specialism: with few exceptions, a jack of all trades, however eloquent, tends to suffer a lower standing in the eyes of the House.

Dozens of colleagues perform well, either in the Chamber or in Committees, or both. There is, however, just a sprinkling of backbench colleagues on both sides whose passion and determination in pursuit of their chosen issues have been truly exceptional.

Stella Creasy, the Labour MP for Walthamstow, is one of the most outstanding parliamentarians of her generation. By background a psychologist, Stella has an academic approach to her work – finding evidence, analysing it, marshalling an argument based upon it and then, with the fire and indefatigability of the successful campaigner, pressing for the policy change she seeks. She has been active on several fronts but, for me, the most striking have been her efforts to tackle loan sharks preying upon the most vulnerable people in our society, and her fight to ensure that women in Northern Ireland can receive abortions on the NHS in England. As a pointer to the need for persistence, Stella devoted five years to the first of those causes. She toiled from 2010 to 2015 until she persuaded the government to restrain the payday lending industry and, since 2018, has argued for action to prevent spiralling credit card debt. By contrast, her abortion initiative was taken just after the 2017 election through an amendment to the Queen's Speech for which she garnered over one hundred signatories. I selected the amendment for a debate and a vote, but no vote was necessary. The Chancellor, Philip Hammond, seeing that several Tories were backing Creasy, bowed to the inevitability of defeat and promptly announced that the government would guarantee publicly funded abortions for women from Northern Ireland travelling to England. It was a triumph for Creasy and testament to her prescience, skill and political reach as a campaigner. A common thread in studying what makes a good MP, particularly a backbencher who lacks the great administrative machinery that a minister can call upon for support, is persistence, and she demonstrates it.

Another way to be a good MP, making an unforgettable mark, is to pursue with relentless zeal one issue for decades. In my time as Speaker, the most remarkable examples have been two Conservative politicians of divergent views and career trajectories. Aside from being just two months apart in age, they also share a commitment to putting principle before personal power. Bill Cash and Ken Clarke, the former an arch Brexiteer, the latter a staunch pro-European, are polar opposites. I have lost count of the number of times I have heard people tell me that they can admire democratic politicians of whatever hue who fight for what they believe in, even if in doing so they damage their own careers. I identify with that. After all, politics is public service and MPs should do what they judge to be right. Of course, politics is also a team activity and a Member can legitimately decide in some circumstances to put the team before his or her views. Moreover, not every Member has the certain and unwavering view on a subject that Cash and Clarke represent.

For the most part, the two MPs have pursued their approaches to the EU very differently. At the time of writing this book, Bill Cash had served in Parliament continuously, as the MP for Stafford and then for Stone for over thirty-five years, of which all but two years has been as a backbencher. His spell on the front bench was in Opposition under Iain Duncan Smith's leadership from 2001 to 2003, so Cash has never served as a minister. Sometimes a Member can reach a view as a result of a blinding revelation, a phenomenon or discovery that made the scales fall from their eyes. So it has been with Cash. He entered Parliament in 1984 after an early career as a solicitor and, in common with the vast majority of Conservative MPs – naturally including Ken Clarke, already then a minister in the Thatcher government – he voted for the Single European Act 1986 which provided for the biggest extension of qualified majority voting in the history of the European Union. In other words, it allowed for far more decisions on policy matters to be decided by a majority vote of EU member states, rather than simply leaving each country to decide its own policy. At the time, like the Prime Minister, Margaret Thatcher, Cash believed that the Act was necessary in order to realise the vision of the single market, then widely regarded as Europe's free-trade area and strongly championed by the Tory Party. Later, however, Cash concluded that the Act had been used to undermine the sovereignty of Parliament, allowing vast numbers of decisions to be made without the approval of the House of Commons. As a lawyer, a constitutionalist and a Conservative, Cash was offended by that. Thereafter he resolved to wage guerrilla warfare against the

Maastricht Treaty in the early 1990s – tabling 240 amendments to the Bill that implemented it – and, indeed, against the subsequent Amsterdam, Nice and Lisbon Treaties. He fought vociferously against any further transfers of powers to the EU and inveighed against the Blair government's initial plan to join the European single currency. For many years, Cash argued for reform of the EU to make it a looser association of sovereign states. Only in more recent years, as the prospect of such an acceptable arrangement diminished, did he argue for an in/out referendum in which he campaigned to leave.

Cash has made his mark in the Chamber, where he is an almost invariable presence and contributor to debates on Britain and the EU. Yet he has also served on the European Scrutiny Committee for over twenty years, studying thousands of EU directives and regulations and making recommendations to Parliament. No one Member can claim responsibility for bringing about the 2016 EU referendum – there were many staging posts and government decisions that led to it. Yet if I had to identify a single parliamentarian whose zealous, repeated and inexhaustible campaigning on the EU made David Cameron shift tack, it would be Bill Cash, the MP who refused to go away. For better or for worse, depending on your views on the EU, Cash has been a far more influential MP than vast numbers of colleagues who have served as ministers, even at Cabinet level, but not delivered any dramatic change.

Ken Clarke has been an outstanding MP in a very different way. Now seventy-nine, Clarke entered the House just shy of his thirtieth birthday. Inspired by Rab Butler and Iain Macleod, he was of a generation of Tories who saw the UK's future as inextricably intertwined with the then Common Market. He was from the outset a passionate pro-European but he pursued what would be viewed as a conventional career for an intelligent, capable and ambitious politician. His approach, while serving his Rushcliffe constituents, was to join the government as a whip under Ted Heath, before becoming a minister in the 1970–74 government and rising through the ranks under the premierships of Margaret Thatcher and John Major. Throughout his time serving in those administrations, Ken Clarke remained a committed pro-European, supporting the Single European Act and later the Maastricht Treaty. He consistently made the case within government and publicly for the UK's EU membership.

For well over a decade after the Conservative defeat in 1997, he sat on the backbenches where I sat and listened as he broached a range of issues from Europe to the economy, from the NHS to Iraq. Back in government after the 2010 election until 2014, Clarke was again highly effective from the front bench as Justice Secretary. Since becoming a backbencher again he has returned to the fray with vigour, expressing his opposition to the EU referendum, his passionate belief that the UK should remain at the heart of Europe and his utter conviction that a hard Brexit would be disastrous for the UK. He has not served on committees or, apparently, made the hugely detailed study of EU directives and regulations undertaken by Bill Cash. Rather, he has been a good MP in a different way. A Chamber person par excellence, he has consistently spoken in EU debates prior to and following the referendum, exhorting colleagues to recognise the benefits of the status quo and the perils of the UK seeking to negotiate trade deals on its own against others with greater clout. Moreover, he was the only Tory MP who voted against the invocation of Article 50, judging that the UK government had no clear idea what Brexit meant or how it envisaged the country's future outside the EU.

The striking characteristics of his parliamentary performances, which are of the highest rank, were twofold. First, Clarke argued with evidence rather than by advocacy, and was only too happy to hear and respond to dissenting interventions from colleagues. Secondly, and this is perhaps why he is so popular in Parliament, Clarke always played the ball, never the man or the woman. He could tease an opponent but spite or abuse was no part of his repertoire. As this chapter seeks to demonstrate, there are many ways to be a good MP. Ken Clarke, who retired at the 2019 election, was not a good MP. He was outstanding.

* * *

Sometimes a Member, even a representative of long standing, can quickly acquire a greater profile or recognition from one issue or cause. The issue may have been consciously sought or arrived at by chance. My Buckinghamshire colleague Dame Cheryl Gillan is a good example. She discovered, to her grave dissatisfaction, that provision for adults on the autistic spectrum ranged from poor to non-existent. More particularly, whereas there were statutory obligations to children with autism, there was nothing comparable by way of duties to adults. Cheryl, a hugely conscientious and determined Member, piloted a Private Member's Bill, the Autism Act, through Parliament in 2009 to plug that gap. She worked on a cross-party basis and, crucially, with interest groups in the sector to frame a suitable piece of legislation. Of course, it is no panacea for the problems faced by autistic adults but it does require local authorities to develop policies and options for them. To this day, Cheryl Gillan takes a close interest in the subject.

If authenticity and persistence are key to success as a Member, a personal connection with a subject can be a potent factor in the mix. The tragic and horrific fire which engulfed Grenfell Tower and cost seventy-two lives broke out on 14 June 2017, a mere six days after the general election. The newly elected MP for Kensington, Labour's Emma Dent-Coad, an established political campaigner in the area, was quick off the mark in pressing for rehousing of survivors, a full public inquiry and preventative action for the future. Yet no

MP has spoken with greater force or passion on the subject than David Lammy. The MP for Tottenham might not seem the obvious candidate to lead a parliamentary charge on the issue but he was and is. Many of the victims were ethnic-minority Britons and, tellingly, Lammy and his artist wife had mentored, employed and encouraged a young woman called Khadija Saye, who died in the fire. It was raw, close to home, inescapably personal to Lammy. That fact, combined with his passionate, angry eloquence in laying bare the sheer avoidable horror of what had happened, carried real weight. On police resources, seizure of documents for investigation, the possibility of criminal charges, health assessments and bereavement counselling for survivors, and finance for safe cladding, Lammy was indefatigable in questioning ministers. I am sad to say that Theresa May, Sajid Javid – Housing, Communities and Local Government Secretary at the time – and then middle-ranking minister Dominic Raab were matter of fact, even cold, in response. I do not suggest that they did not care, but they showed no empathy whatever. I felt embarrassed for them as they gave such a poor account of themselves whereas David Lammy was exactly the articulate, truth-seeking, progress-chasing parliamentarian that Grenfell folk and the public alike wanted to hear.

Another intensely personal cause, also led by Lammy, was justice for the 'Windrush generation' deported from the UK under the 'hostile environment' immigration policy pioneered crassly by Theresa May. The *Guardian* newspaper exposed the scandal in 2018 and Lammy rightly took up the cudgels on behalf of those victims. That he did so as the son of Windrush-era migrants lent added potency to his demand to establish the full truth, secure justice and obtain compensation. I granted him an Urgent Question in April 2018 and another in July. In May, June and September, he spoke to the House of the contribution of Windrush migrants to the life of the UK, charting their journey from discrimination to acceptance to

widespread public respect. He was visibly and audibly outraged that as part of Theresa May's hostile environment for
illegal immigrants, people who had every right to live in the
UK, and who in many cases had done so for decades, suddenly
faced a hostile state questioning their presence and then forcing them out of the UK to go to countries in which some had
never set foot, let alone lived. It was intolerable and no MP
said so more devastatingly effectively than David Lammy.

Two good examples of good MPs who are not particularly
good public speakers are Margaret Hodge and Andrew Tyrie.
Hodge served as a minister in the Blair and Brown governments. What I saw of her suggested that she knew her briefs
and was highly competent. Yet as chair of the Public Accounts
Committee she made a much bigger impact. Articulate in
conversation, Hodge is one of those MPs who does not excel
at speaking on her feet. She is adequate in such a situation but
not especially fluent or impressive. However, she is a tough-
minded, painstaking and unsparing inquisitor as Starbucks
senior managers, to give but one example, discovered to their
cost when she and her colleagues grilled them on corporate
tax avoidance before the committee. She selected inquiries of
real public interest and led from the front in challenging witnesses on their records and intentions. Sure enough, she had
her stern critics who felt that she inappropriately harangued
and humiliated witnesses. For my part, I believe that she shone
a light on unethical practices and poor performance, both by
corporate actors and by public agencies such as HM Revenue
and Customs, proving a highly effective chair of one of the
most important committees in Parliament.

Andrew Tyrie was a good MP too. Articulate conversationally, he is no orator. Not only is he not a theatrical performer, he
is not a speech-maker or even strikingly fluent in the delivery
of a scripted speech. Donnish and professorial in manner, he
is lacking in presence. Much of the time, he did not command
the House or put in incisive performances. Yet he understood

economics, finance, pensions and the gamut of issues covered by the Treasury. In my judgement, he would have been a very competent Conservative Treasury or Work and Pensions Minister but, for whatever reason, it was not to be. Instead, Tyrie was elected chair of the Treasury Select Committee in 2010 and held the post for two Parliaments until his retirement in 2017. He knew his brief and led the committee in an unshowy but resolute fashion for those seven years. As a knowledgeable and persistent interrogator, he won respect for probing ministers without fear or favour. Moreover, Tyrie provided evidence that a good committee chair can gain respectful attention in the Chamber simply by virtue of his or her reputation as a creditable performer in that role.

Two other good MPs who have made their names as backbenchers warrant a mention. Dr Sarah Wollaston is interesting because she is almost the antithesis of the stereotypical career politician. A hospital doctor turned general practitioner by background, she was chosen by open primary – by local electors rather than just Tory Party members – as the Conservative candidate for Totnes in the run-up to the 2010 election. She had no discernible political footprint and entered Parliament at the comparatively late age of forty-eight. In nine years in the House of Commons, Wollaston has made a greater mark than many politicians do in a lifetime of public service. Her campaigns have by no means all proved successful but she has brought real-life experience, refreshing candour and an impressive communication style. Wollaston argued in her maiden speech that the price of alcohol was too low, encouraged consumption and led to a higher incidence of crime. She went on subsequently to press for minimum unit pricing for alcohol so that booze could not be sold by shops as a loss-leader. The coalition government had signalled a readiness to introduce unit pricing but it backed off, prompting denunciation by Wollaston and others.

On Europe, Wollaston shifted sides, but more interestingly

than most of her backbench colleagues. Lots of MPs supported Remain but later accepted the verdict to leave the EU
and rushed to proclaim their commitment to help deliver it.
Wollaston initially backed the Leave campaign. Suddenly, she
performed a volte-face, declaring that the Leave campaign
pledge to release £350 million extra per week for the NHS was
simply not true, and she promptly switched sides. Convinced
that leaving would harm the economy, she then fought in the
referendum campaign and beyond for the UK to remain. In
December 2017 she voted with Dominic Grieve and nine
other Conservative MPs to guarantee Parliament a meaningful
vote on any deal. Subsequently, as a Conservative, a Change
UK MP, an independent MP and now a Liberal Democrat, she
has publicly, strongly and repeatedly called for a people's vote
on the outcome of the Brexit negotiations.

Though Wollaston has not sought ministerial office, she was
elected chair of the Health Select Committee when Stephen
Dorrell stepped down in 2014 and was re-elected in 2015
and 2017. Though she lost her seat at the 2019 election. Respected by many Conservatives, she is especially well regarded
by Opposition Members who see her as sympathetic to some
of their policy concerns and as the constructive, non-partisan
truth-seeker that she is.

I mentioned that Cheryl Gillan and Margaret Hodge are
much more memorable for their work as backbenchers than
for their contribution, albeit serious and dedicated, as ministers.
The same is true of Labour MP Chris Bryant, one of the most
well informed, articulate and formidable parliamentarians on
either side of the House of Commons. Bryant served as Deputy
Leader of the House and as Minister for Europe under Gordon
Brown. In both roles he was very competent at the despatch
box, but it is as a backbencher that he has stood out. On
numerous fronts, Bryant has been very effective. With Tom
Watson, he was a key driver in exposing the phone-hacking
scandal, using opportunities in the Chamber to publicise the

subject. He is a vociferous pro-European and an outspoken critic of Vladimir Putin. In recent years, he has secured Private Members' legislation to increase penalties for those who assault police officers or other emergency service personnel and argued persistently for better care for the victims of acquired brain injury. As knowledgeable about parliamentary procedure as any parliamentary colleague and more than most, Bryant is both clever and diligent. He is not the best speaker I have ever heard but he is extremely good – knowledgeable, direct, humorous and, essential to a parliamentarian striving to make a difference, not shy of repetition. Stubborn, wilful, determined not to take no for an answer when the right on his side should elicit a yes, he is a superb parliamentarian.

* * *

Most MPs, certainly in the two biggest parties, aspire to be ministers. Their motivation will vary but it usually entails a mix of personal ambition and a desire to do a good job at the highest level possible in government. A minority will be inspired by a particular cause and seek the ministerial office that will enable them to promote it. But most simply have a general commitment to their party's basic philosophy and reckon that they can give effective expression to it in whichever department they are placed. Some of these are visionaries, thirsting to deliver major change. Others see themselves as incremental reformers or, if the situation so requires, efficient administrators of the status quo and communicators of stability. Of my ten years in the Chair, nine saw Conservative or Conservative-led government. Inevitably, therefore, I witnessed far more Conservative ministers than Labour.

For me, a notable change-maker, and also one of the most memorable and underrated figures in British politics, is Harriet Harman. Elected in 1982 as Labour MP for Peckham, she has sat in Parliament without interruption for over thirty-seven years. This makes her the longest-serving female MP and, therefore, the 'Mother of the House'.

Harriet has built an enduring legacy that has improved lives on a number of different fronts. When she entered Parliament in 1982, only 3 per cent of MPs were women. Seeing that her own party, which ostensibly believed in equality, was making progress at snail's pace, Harman led the fight for all-women shortlists for parliamentary elections, enabling Labour to return a record 101 female MPs in 1997. The policy was successfully challenged by a Labour man, so Harman introduced the Sex Discrimination (Election Candidates) Act 2002. This allowed Labour – and any other party – again to facilitate such shortlists and her party proceeded to increase its female representation, which now accounts for 51 per cent of its MPs. This is another reminder of what being a good MP, in this case as a minister, entails. Put simply, it is a case of don't get mad, get even. Persistence, perspiration and perseverance are vital. It is a measure of Harman's success that David Cameron acted sharply to improve his party's female representation in Parliament.

Harriet Harman wanted to feminise the agenda of politics and wanted women in the country to see women in Parliament speaking up for them, understanding their concerns and enabling them to fulfil their aspirations. Every day, looking at my colleagues, calling people to ask questions and deciding who should speak next in debates, I saw a House more representative of the country than when Harman entered the Commons in 1982 or when I joined in 1997.

Harman has also made important contributions in extending maternity and paternity rights and childcare, after decades of resistance on traditionalist grounds to such an approach, and on tackling domestic violence. Increasing sentences for that crime, making breach of a family court injunction a criminal offence, setting up a specialist squad of domestic violence prosecutors in the Crown Prosecution Service, establishing

Independent Domestic Violence Advocates to help victims, introducing Domestic Homicide Reviews after each domestic violence death and outlawing the provocation defence to murder – these were all precious milestones in the drive against violence in the home.

Finally, on the policy front, Harman piloted the Equality Act 2010 through Parliament. This measure, to which she had to fight resistance in the Cabinet, covered positive discrimination for recruitment on grounds of race – for example, for the police; action against age discrimination; a positive duty on all public authorities proactively to combat inequality and discrimination; gender pay transparency; positive duties to tackle disability discrimination and a law to protect breast-feeding in public. The simple premise of the legislation was that all prejudice and discrimination was abhorrent and it was a public policy imperative to tackle it, both structurally and for individuals. No one drove the agenda with greater energy or persistence than Harman.

In the Chamber, Harriet was a highly competent, if not outstanding, speaker. Her style was matter-of-fact rather than rhetorical or flamboyant, but she was invariably both clear and fluent. A trained lawyer with a sharp brain, she had also been battle-hardened by decades of speaking up, for example, for gender equality long before it was fashionable to do so. The result was both that she knew her arguments backwards and I never saw her fazed or flummoxed by any hostile intervention. I rarely saw her openly patronised by an opponent – though I think that had been a regular occurrence in the 1980s – but woe betide anyone who took that tack with Harriet. She could and would swat such critics like flies. She had a great combination of rigorous, serious point-making and gentle humour. Standing in for Gordon Brown at Prime Minister's Questions, she denounced William Hague when he foolishly ribbed her about wearing a stab vest in her constituency when she went on patrol with the local police. Her conclusive rejoinder was that if she was inclined to seek sartorial advice, the last person she would ask was 'the man in a baseball cap'. My sense was that Harriet consciously eschewed the Oxford Union debating style beloved of many Tories and of some Labour politicians of an earlier era. She was businesslike, efficient, focused and succinct.

Another visionary minister was Ed Balls, the trusted lieutenant of Gordon Brown who was appointed in June 2007 as Secretary of State for Children, Schools and Families. Unquestionably bright but previously regarded by many as a backroom Machiavelli, the new appointment gave Balls the chance to break free of that casting and to show what he had to offer on a wider set of issues of interest to millions.

The central thrust of his approach was to bring together schools and children's policy for the first time in the Children's Plan – marketed under the strapline Every Child Matters – and to raise the education and training leaving age from sixteen to eighteen. He sought to offer not merely the academic route to success but vocational opportunities too, setting out a series of national targets for improved performance for children and young people. Ten years on from the increased spending on schools ushered in by Tony Blair, Balls developed a New Deal programme of capital expenditure to construct new and improved school buildings across the country financed by the Private Finance Initiative. Balls was never lacking in self-confidence and relished the chance to pit his wits against Conservative and other opponents. He was forceful in debate, knew his own mind and, in my experience, was never intimidated by anybody. Yet he was not a top-notch speaker in the Chamber, not least because he lived with a stammer that he publicly acknowledged in 2008. In common with many people living with such a challenge, Balls would often speak fluently for several sentences before eventually juddering to a halt. His brain would be working more quickly than his mouth could get the words out, and it hampered him. Needless to say, it was no indictment of him but it often meant that a stream of eloquence would be abruptly halted.

If Harman and Balls stand out as transformative radicals, there were other exceptionally able Labour ministers notable for their fluency, competence and steel but who were more managerial. Douglas Alexander and Hilary Benn will both be best remembered for their tenures in government as Secretary of State for International Development. In that field of policy, much of the tone had been set earlier in the New Labour years and the priority to accentuate work on the Millennium Development Goals was obvious to them. Both approached the task with energy, understanding and focus but neither recast the department's approach fundamentally, believing rightly that their task was to use DfID in conjunction with the NGOs – Oxfam, Save the Children and so on – to deliver better.

Margaret Beckett was likewise an immensely competent figure throughout the Blair years. If there is a policy to associ-ate with her, it is the introduction of the National Minimum Wage. It was a long-standing Labour pledge, rather than her personal idea, but she implemented it competently and totally out-argued the Conservatives, including (I am embarrassed to say) me at the time, who foolishly predicted that it would wreak economic havoc.

Jack Straw was one of a handful of ministers who served in Cabinet throughout the Blair and Brown governments from 1997 to 2010. A good parliamentarian in the sense that he relished debate and attended keenly to his opponents' argu-ments, engaging with and seeking to rebut what he saw as unjust criticism, I always felt that Straw was highly regarded by colleagues across the House. He was without doubt also very much a man of government, a team player – some would say an upmarket party hack – always wanting to be in the min-isterial equivalent of the First XI. He was one of those people always content to do whatever job his leader requested. A four-year spell as Home Secretary was followed by a five-year stint as Foreign Secretary, just over a year as Leader of the House of Commons and a shade under three years as Lord Chancellor and Secretary of State for Justice.

As Home Secretary, he took two initiatives of particular note – incorporating the European Convention on Human Rights into British law with the passage of the 1998 Human Rights Act, and ordering the Macpherson inquiry into the circumstances of the death of Stephen Lawrence. The inquiry report concluded that the Metropolitan Police Service was 'institutionally racist' and made several recommendations that have led to real changes in London's police force. Fifteen years later, Straw himself said that ordering the inquiry was 'the single most important decision I made as Home Secretary'.

Straw was a devoted party man, capable in debate, skilled in transitioning seamlessly from service under Blair to service under Brown, and one of the great survivors of modern politics. I found him personable and engaging. Yet, while I applaud his tenacity and note what the late Barbara Castle described as his 'low cunning', I struggle to think of a great cause that he personally devised and championed. A consummate managerialist, Straw was no visionary.

Deploying the visionary versus managerialist categorisation used above in relation to Conservative ministers, Michael Gove definitely sits – rather, he dances ostentatiously – in the first category. Highly intelligent and well read, he is a conviction politician who delivers change and is also easily the most outstanding debater on the Conservative front bench.

Appointed Secretary of State for Education in May 2010, Gove made a dreadful start with his botched announcement of cancelled school building projects and his Shadow, Ed Balls, roasted him royally for that mixture of incompetence and arrogance. Thereafter, Gove recovered and established himself as the most brilliant member of the government. That is not a verdict on the merits of his education reforms – which were controversial, to say the least – but on his ability in devising, implementing and communicating them, at least in the Chamber. He came to be known for pioneering free schools, for overhauling the curriculum and for introducing more rigour into exams. I emphasise communication 'in the Chamber' with good reason. Just as Ed Balls, his predecessor, was not by any means a favourite with the public, neither was Gove. For all his fluency, courtesy and even charm, he was not telegenic, appeared to go out of his way to antagonise the educational establishment and did not poll well. To the public he was a polarising figure disliked by teachers and viewed, therefore, more widely with unease, suspicion, even distrust. In the debating Chamber, Gove rallied the support of his party with supremely capable performances, making a powerful pitch for his own policy and teasing, ridiculing and denouncing Ed Balls. Later, faced by Blairite Shadows in Stephen Twigg and Tristram Hunt, Gove delighted in seeking to expose divisions between them and their leader, Ed Miliband, or the Parliamentary Labour Party. Tory MPs lapped it up and always wanted more. Gove's manner in dealing with opponents oscillated between rank denunciation, gentle sarcasm and oleaginous flattery. Of the latter, there was too much. He supped excessively at that fountain and it could come across as patronising, false or both.

In Gove's subsequent role as Justice Secretary, which he held for only just over a year, his ambition was to deliver penal reform and a much greater focus on effective sentencing policy, crucially prioritising rehabilitation of prisoners. In my view, it was a great pity that he was not able to see through that vision but was replaced by the hapless Liz Truss, who achieved nothing of note and simply horrified the legal profession by her shocking unwillingness to stand up for the judges when they were denounced by bigots in the media. As Environment Secretary since 2017, brought back by Theresa May after she sacked him from Justice the year before, Gove has been hyperactive on several fronts: banning products with microbeads, outlawing sales of ivory products and increasing sentences for animal cruelty.

Flawed though he is, Gove was nevertheless an outstanding Secretary of State in my view. First, and most importantly, he was not merely holding the office, but wielding power. He had a vision. For better or worse, he was determined to use his power to make change happen. Secondly, he was not merely a master of the big picture but knew the detail too and communicated as well from the government front bench as anyone I heard in my twenty-two years in Parliament. We are not best friends, and never will be. Yet I am happy to salute Gove as a fine minister and parliamentarian.

* * *

If Michael Gove was a notably strategic and visionary minister, so too was George Osborne. As Chancellor of the Exchequer from 2010 to 2016 he enjoyed two notable advantages. One was that he had served as Shadow Chancellor for five years from 2005. He took the opportunity to establish himself – in the Chamber, in the media and in the City – and give detailed thought to the approach he would take at the Treasury. Even though the economy was in a very different and much worse position by the time he took office, that time was well spent. The other advantage throughout his tenure was that his strong personal and political alliance with his boss, Prime Minister David Cameron, remained rock solid. If Cabinet colleagues sense friction between the Chancellor and the Prime Minister, they can play off that to strengthen their departmental hand at the Treasury's expense. There was no such chance and George Osborne remained impregnable, despite fluctuating poll ratings, throughout his six years at the helm.

As Chancellor, Osborne pursued austerity policies aimed at reducing the budget deficit. On taking office, he moved quickly to set up the Office for Budget Responsibility and commissioned a government-wide spending review, concluding in autumn 2010 and setting spending limits till 2014–15. Yet by March 2015 the annual deficit had been cut only by about half of the initial target, so the debt-to-GDP ratio was still rising. In addition, the national debt increased more during the coalition government's five-year term than during the previous thirteen years. The economy deteriorated after 2015, not least on account of uncertainty in the run-up to the EU referendum. In July 2016 the UK still had a budget deficit of 4 per cent, a balance of payments deficit of 7 per cent of GDP and, apart from Italy, the worst productivity among the G7 nations.

Of course, when Theresa May became Prime Minister she immediately sacked Osborne as Chancellor and he left Parliament at the 2017 election. Now is a suitable time to consider his strengths and weaknesses in Parliament. It is sometimes suggested by critics that the Cameron government was relentlessly tactical rather than strategic, clear about the next move but less so about a guiding mission. In the case of the Chancellor, there is ground for arguing the opposite. He often made short-term mistakes – the 'pasty tax' and cuts to tax credits, soon reversed – but was clear and consistent in his overall approach. His objective was to slash the deficit, take people at the bottom end out of tax and liberate the supply side of the economy to generate wealth. In line with clarity on strategy, there was clarity in messaging. In the summer of 2010, as mentioned earlier, the Conservatives exploited Labour's distraction of its own leadership contest to move to frame the terms of the political debate about the economy. Osborne repeatedly rammed home the message that Labour's recklessness in spending and borrowing had brought about the crash. This was a far cry from the earlier Conservative pledge to stick to Labour spending totals. The new Chancellor's message was that Labour had presided over boom and bust. In addition, he and his ministerial colleagues contrasted

Labour's apparent fecklessness with the new government's commitment to its 'long-term economic plan'.

In the Chamber, George Osborne proved to be a fast learner. Initially, as Shadow Chancellor, he had a slightly squeaky, high-pitched, almost childlike voice. Before long, the voice had deepened, the tone was better judged and he was far more effective. Osborne was no orator and he didn't need to be. He simply looked and sounded increasingly authoritative at the despatch box, knowing his arguments very well, sticking to clear basic messages and ridiculing his Shadow, Ed Balls, at every turn for Labour's record of so-called boom and bust. Osborne's image as rather haughty, arrogant and sneering did him no favours. The public did not appear to like him, but they trusted him.

* * *

Andrew Lansley, who entered Parliament in 1997 as the Conservative MP for South Cambridgeshire, served as Secretary of State for Health from May 2010 until September 2012. Even though he had been Shadow Secretary of State for Health for almost six years before then, nothing could have prepared him for the sustained and tumultuous controversy that he experienced in assuming the health portfolio in government.

In Opposition, Lansley had pledged that under a Conservative government there would be 'no top-down reorganisation of the NHS'. Such a structural overhaul would be complex, bureaucratic, expensive and a distraction from the necessary focus on patient care. Yet in January 2011 he published the Health and Social Care Bill, containing planned reforms that would allow GPs to take over management of the NHS from Primary Care Trusts. The purpose of the reforms was to prepare the ground for GP groups to take control of NHS budgets.

Leaders of the British Medical Association (BMA), the

Royal College of Nursing (RCN) and both Unison and Unite unions argued that the extent of the reforms, and the rush to introduce them, risked damaging the care of patients. Lansley was widely and ferociously attacked for his plans, including being denounced in a hip-hop track. Eventually, amidst the unrelenting chorus of criticism, the government announced in April 2011 that there would be a pause in the progress of the Bill so that the government could 'listen, reflect and improve' on its proposals. Later that month, the RCN conference overwhelmingly backed a motion of no-confidence in Lansley. A year later the Secretary of State's claim that clinical staffing levels had gone up by nearly 4,000 was met with howls of derision and in June 2012 a BMA conference called for Lansley's resignation. Many doctors felt that the policy was wrong and that it directly breached the pledge that there would be no 'top-down reorganisation' of the NHS in Conservative hands. Lansley did not accept that his policy represented such a change, believing that it empowered local doctors, but he was never able to persuade more than a tiny proportion of GPs of his case. Ultimately, his Bill was heavily amended to reflect criticism of it but, politically, Lansley was irreparably damaged. In September 2012, the Prime Minister moved Lansley out of the health brief to the more tranquil role of Leader of the House of Commons, his last role in government before being appointed to the House of Lords.

What can be said of Lansley's tenure? Lansley is an intelligent man and, as befits a former civil servant, he had long been viewed in the House as a man with a voracious appetite for detail. Yet on health, though he could talk for ever about his policy, he either did not foresee the scale and intensity of opposition that he would encounter or thought that he could ride it out. One of the criticisms of him was that his reorganisation would cost money, and he never had a satisfactory answer to that charge.

For my part, knowing him and observing from the Chair,

I did not believe that his intention was to privatise the NHS. Such a policy would be totally unsaleable in this country and politically suicidal. That said, and fluent though he was, he was by a country mile the most appallingly deficient – no, let me put it more bluntly, the most disastrous – communicator of a hopelessly flawed policy that I encountered in twenty-two years as a Member of Parliament and ten years as Speaker.

There were two aspects to that chronic failure. First, until heavy revision of his Bill became inevitable, he exuded a remarkable and deeply damaging conviction that he was right about his NHS reform and everyone else was wrong. This jarred. It grated. Ultimately, it provoked fury among the medical profession. He might have got away with that – Nye Bevan had faced such hostility more than six decades earlier – if the public had been on his side. He could not because they were not. Secondly, in Parliament, Lansley was not able to inspire the House. Indeed, to say that he was a boring speaker is a monumental understatement. Lansley was staggeringly, mind-blowingly, insurpassably boring – completely failing to convince anyone, and driving listeners to a grisly combination of fatigue and exasperation unequalled by any other member of that or any Cabinet I can recall.

* * *

One of the most talked-about ministers in Theresa May's government – indeed, one of the very few to provoke much discussion – was Boris Johnson, Foreign Secretary from July 2016 to July 2018, before becoming Prime Minister in July 2019. I shall hereon refer to him as 'Johnson' and explain why. He gets much greater slack than he deserves partly because of the near-ubiquitous use of his first name only, lending a patina of cosiness and hail-fellow-well-met that helps him to evade the kind of scrutiny offered to colleagues with less memorable first names. Even though Johnson has been a prominent public figure since his first election to the House of Commons in 2001 – and very high-profile as Mayor of London from 2008 to 2016 – he has served in government only in that one, albeit senior and prestigious, role.

As context in looking at how Johnson fared, it is salutary to bear in mind two points. First, although Theresa May appointed him to one of the great offices of state, she simultaneously created two new departments, namely the Department for Exiting the European Union (DExEU) – to be headed by David Davis – and the Department for International Trade (DIT), whose Secretary of State was to be Liam Fox. So the Prime Minister – ingeniously or foolishly depending upon your point of view – appointed a triumvirate of vociferous Brexiteers to deliver Brexit. Yet before that set of appointments, the Foreign and Commonwealth Office would have been the lead department on Europe policy. After it, the Foreign Office was merely one of three departments involved, and no longer in the forefront, its role having been ceded to DExEU and DIT. So, Boris Johnson's formal role in the Brexit negotiations was as near to non-existent as made no difference. The second point was that as a newspaper columnist over many years before he entered the Commons and during his parliamentary career as well, Johnson had frequently attacked other countries and leaders in colourful terms, causing many to fear that he could prove a major liability in government. At one time he was accused of bigotry, after using the words 'piccaninnies' with 'watermelon smiles' when describing Commonwealth citizens. He championed British colonialism and referred, apparently disparagingly, to gay men as 'tank-topped bumboys'. Many years later, in the EU referendum campaign, he was closely associated with the campaign advertisement which implied that staying in the EU would risk the UK becoming home to 70 million Turkish citizens – widely viewed as a discreditable and racist claim – and he also argued that Brexit would release

£350 million per week to be spent on the NHS, which not one person now seriously believes.

On becoming Foreign Secretary, Johnson will have seen at once that he was not to be the lead minister, after Theresa May, on Brexit. Indeed, he was almost completely sidelined from the negotiations, the policy formulation, the process of translating the referendum result into practice. No stranger to pursuing and gaining headlines, it was obvious to me that that marginalisation caused Johnson to strive mightily to get his point of view across. Hence in scarcely coded articles and speeches he was at pains to emphasise the need for a clean, no-nonsense, 'pure' Brexit as apparently envisaged by the Prime Minister in her January 2017 Lancaster House speech in which she set out her 'red lines' for the Brexit negotiations with Brussels. Furthermore, he made light of the Irish border issue, implying that it was being used by the EU as an obstacle to a full Brexit when, in his view, it need not be. He even appeared to cast doubt on whether the 1998 Belfast Agreement, which secured peace, was necessary any longer.

In relation to wider foreign policy, I cannot think of a single concrete positive achievement of Johnson's two-year tenure. However, his cavalier approach to his role, an almost innate incapacity or disdain for precision, triggered a human crisis which remains unresolved.

On 1 November 2017, Johnson told the Foreign Affairs Select Committee that Nazanin Zaghari-Ratcliffe, a British citizen serving a five-year prison sentence in Iran after being arrested on holiday on suspicion of training BBC Persian staff, had been 'simply teaching people journalism'. Her contention was that she had been on holiday there – no more, no less – and her husband in the UK had corroborated that story. Three days after Johnson's remarks to the select committee, the High Council for Human Rights in Iran – presumably so-called precisely because the regime does not respect such rights – doubled Zaghari-Ratcliffe's sentence, quoting

Johnson's words as evidence against her. Johnson's Shadow, Emily Thornberry, and Zaghari-Ratcliffe's local MP, Tulip Siddiq, both criticised the Foreign Secretary's remarks and urged him to retract them. However, Johnson dug his heels in, insisted that he had been misquoted and simply stuck to the mantra that nothing he had said was responsible for or justified the regime's incarceration of Zaghari-Ratcliffe. At the very least, it was blindingly obvious to me that Johnson had been clumsy, inept and undiplomatic where a decent Foreign Secretary should be calculating, coherent and cautious. What a mess he made of the issue, compounding the misery of a British citizen to whom morally he had a duty of protective care.

In March 2018, in the course of Foreign Office Questions, Johnson referred to the Shadow Foreign Secretary, Emily Thornberry, as 'Lady Nugee', a reference to her husband, the High Court Judge Sir Christopher Nugee, whose name she did not take, any more than Yvette Cooper had ever called herself 'Yvette Balls'. My judgement was that the Foreign Secretary's comment was 'inappropriate and sexist' and I intervened to say so with some force. Johnson then apologised, lamely bleating that he had meant no harm.

The above examples of clumsiness, together with his journalist's penchant for a graphic phrase or description, frequently landed Johnson in hot water. His comparison of Muslim women wearing the burqa with 'letter boxes' and 'bank robbers' justifiably provoked outrage in some quarters, as did the suggestion that Theresa May's EU withdrawal deal was a 'suicide vest'. Many people reckoned that he was dead meat in any future Conservative leadership election. I myself was not at all convinced that he would attract the votes of enough Tory MPs to reach the shortlist of two candidates for Conservative Party members to choose from in a nationwide ballot. In fact, of course, he did, topping the poll in all three rounds of the parliamentary contest. The belief that he was the candidate most likely to deliver Brexit in autumn 2019 was a big factor in his success. Conservatives were extremely anxious both that that objective should be delivered for its own sake and for fear of suffering electoral carnage at the hands of the Brexit Party if it was not. Still bigger was his apparent public appeal which, Tory MPs believed, would enable them to hold their seats in an election in which Boris Johnson would lead the party to victory over Labour under Jeremy Corbyn.

During the leadership contest, diplomatic telegrams that revealed the critical view of the British ambassador in Washington, Sir Kim Darroch, of the Trump administration were leaked. The Prime Minister, Theresa May, the Foreign Secretary, Jeremy Hunt, and other ministers condemned the leaks and rushed to commend our ambassador, a highly respected career diplomat doing his job in offering candid impressions to his own government. Sure enough, Boris Johnson deprecated the leak but in a live television debate he stopped short of supporting Sir Kim. When the latter, denounced by President Trump, quickly resigned it was suggested that lack of support from Johnson was a factor in that resignation. There was some criticism of Johnson but it washed off him very quickly and, of course, in the ballot of Conservative Party members he convincingly defeated his rival, Jeremy Hunt, by 66 per cent to 34 per cent, becoming Prime Minister on 24 July 2019.

As it happens, I like Boris Johnson. He can be charming and witty. He has never been other than courteous to me. We played tennis in January 2017 at his official country residence, Chevening, and he took his 6–0 6–0 6–0 defeat with very good grace. He is not stupid, but highly intelligent, very well read and a fine conversationalist. However, he is careless with words and facts and, even by the standards of a profession in which self-regard is not uncommon, he is disproportionately preoccupied with whatever serves the cause of advancement for B. Johnson. As a debater, he is undistinguished and, as a public speaker, though humorous, he is often downright poor

– hesitant, unable to string sentences together fluently and about as likely ever to warrant the description 'captivating orator' as Bertie Wooster or his chum Gussie Fink-Nottle. Apart from those notable limitations in a man who has since become Prime Minister, he is, at his occasional best, a passably adequate politician in an age not replete with them.

* * *

For me, one of the great Cabinet disappointments of the Theresa May years was Amber Rudd. Intelligent, quick-witted, articulate and mainstream, Rudd had always struck me as a committed but moderate Conservative. She served very competently as Secretary of State for Energy and Climate Change under David Cameron before being promoted to Home Secretary by Theresa May when the latter became Prime Minister in July 2016. Later, she was also given the role of Minister for Women and Equalities. Once again, in both roles, she exhibited energy and purpose. When she was forced to resign in April 2018 as Home Secretary when the Windrush deportation scandal was exposed, I was one of a very large number of people who felt considerable sympathy for her. She was carrying the can for a scandal whose seeds had been planted by her predecessor as Home Secretary, Theresa May.

Given that May was flailing in Number 10, I was surprised to hear on the Westminster grapevine that Amber Rudd was very keen to return to the government front bench under her premiership. In fairness, it could be said that she wanted to help and reckoned that she could be a voice for a 'soft' Brexit and compassionate Conservatism within the Cabinet. In fact, though when she came back into the Cabinet as Secretary of State for Work and Pensions she strove to improve the controversial and flawed Universal Credit policy, I saw precious little evidence that Rudd was exerting any wider influence. It was often suggested in the media that she might resign in protest at Brexit policy, but neither she nor her fellow pro-Europeans in the Cabinet did so. This was disappointing to many back-bench pro-European Tories who wanted more support for EU customs union membership or even a second referendum on Brexit. Rudd hinted publicly at such possibilities from time to time – and was more visible and audible in the media on these matters than any of her like-minded Cabinet colleagues – but she did not follow through by supporting Dominic Grieve, Justine Greening, Sam Gyimah or others. Put simply, she was the noisiest of the Brexit sceptics in the Cabinet but it was all gong and no dinner – she made a racket but no sacrifice until her belated resignation from the Cabinet in September 2019. In stepping down as Minister and relinquishing the Conserva-tive whip, she objected to Boris Johnson's Brexit policy and the withdrawal of the whip from twenty-one decent, rebellious colleagues. She was right about that but took far too long to see and reject what had been staring her in the face for years.

All of the above can be defended on the grounds that Rudd was bound by collective Cabinet responsibility. That said, we are dealing here with the biggest policy issue facing the United Kingdom since the Second World War, and one might hope that senior politicians who hold a particular view might consider putting principle before power. My critique of Rudd is that she was much given to sounding off in the media and outspoken denunciations of, for example, Boris Johnson and any idea of a no-deal Brexit but, when the crunch came, she folded feebly. She backed Jeremy Hunt over Boris Johnson and made public her view that 'no deal' was unacceptable, but within less than two months she performed the most cringe-making about-turn as soon as it became obvious that Boris Johnson would be Prime Minister within days. After months of giving the impression that she would absolutely resist a cliff-edge Brexit, Rudd suddenly signalled that, though it was highly undesirable, it could not be discounted. She would support Boris Johnson if he became Prime Minister and, she signalled, other colleagues should do likewise. In other words, she wanted to stay in the Cabinet. To put it mildly, it was not brave, but careerist and self-serving. It was the type of approach that makes people contemptuous of politicians. I felt embarrassed for her and, frankly, saddened.

Eventually, Rudd did find the government's position simply untenable, and to her credit resigned from the Cabinet on 7 September, surrendering the Conservative whip in Parliament in protest at Boris Johnson's policy on Brexit, and to a great extent redeemed herself.

Of the Liberal Democrats in the coalition government, Jo Swinson, though a comparatively junior minister, was outstanding in the Chamber. I would not call her a visionary. It would be premature – she was simply too junior a minister to have the chance to set out a vision – but her communication skills were impressive, even inspiring. Appointed in September 2012 as Parliamentary Under Secretary of State for Employment Relations and Consumer and Postal Affairs, she retained her role until her defeat in East Dunbartonshire in 2015. A strong and long-standing supporter of gender equality, Swinson nevertheless opposed mandatory gender quotas for companies, arguing that the key to progress was persuading businesses to see for themselves the commercial benefits of hiring and promoting more women. That would in turn promote the confidence on which continued female progress would depend.

As a minister, Swinson worked to promote fathers' rights in regard to parental leave. Her approach was to introduce new legislation which allowed parents to divide parental leave between themselves with the clear objective on her part of encouraging fathers to spend more time with their newborn infants.

She was equally keen to promote employee ownership, by establishing a FTSE-compliant UK Employee Ownership Index, supporting a simplification of regulations for companies seeking to promote such ownership. More controversially, she backed a scheme that would allow companies contractually to offer employees shares of up to £50,000, exempted from capital gains tax, in return for waiving some of their employment rights. Philosophically though it is the Conservatives that have laid claim to be the party of share ownership, Swinson argued that the roots of the policy lay in the liberal utilitarianism of the eighteenth-century thinker Jeremy Bentham. The theory, of course, was that giving employees a direct stake would improve productivity and lower staff absenteeism.

Jo Swinson was a notably competent performer as soon as she entered the House in 2005. Although her party secured 62 seats at the election that year – its highest total in decades – their numbers were still modest. Jo took the opportunity to get stuck into debates in the Chamber and by the time she became a minister, she was an extremely accomplished and engaging contributor. Some Members blossom in office, others shrink. Jo Swinson fell firmly into the former category. Knowledgeable, articulate, personable and courteous, to me listening from the Chair she was one of the government's, and her party's, best communicators. Her career was interrupted by defeat to the SNP's John Nicholson in 2015 but she was re-elected in 2017 and quickly became deputy leader of the Liberal Democrats and then leader in July 2019, succeeding Vince Cable. People who thrive as ministers tend to develop an authority which permeates their speeches and questions when they leave office. Jo Swinson is a fine example of that genre. Unfortunately, she lost her seat at the 2019 election, and therefore resigned as leader of her party.

For me, the other Liberal Democrat star of the coalition government was a man called Steve Webb. I readily acknowledge that beyond his Northavon (later Thornbury and Yate) constituency, and the pensions industry, he is not a household name. A product of comprehensive school and Hertford College, Oxford, Webb initially worked at the Institute for Fiscal

Studies, where he specialised in research into poverty, taxation and the benefit system. In the mid-nineties, he became a Professor of Social Policy at the University of Bath. Elected for the previously safe Conservative seat of Northavon in 1997, he was known in the early months of his membership of the House of Commons as Professor Steve Webb, and his name appeared on the Order Paper accordingly. This can only have been done with his knowledge and approval. Accordingly, it provoked some teasing. Dennis Skinner, the fiery left-wing Labour MP for Bolsover, was known to heckle, 'Ey up, this one's clever. He's a Professor.' The reader could be forgiven for thinking that Webb was pompous or boastful. Nothing could be further from the truth. Rather, it was his title immediately before he became a Member of Parliament and, properly proud of it, he began using it as it seemed appropriate. However, he quickly stopped doing so and any observer could tell on hearing Webb that he was highly intelligent and personable. His reputation in the Commons was as a mildly left-of-centre Liberal Democrat with slightly more Conservative views on social issues, possibly born of his strong Christian faith. Nick Clegg was once reported to have been overheard saying that he couldn't stand Webb. Ironically, that blunt and unpleasant remark about a man by no means generally disliked probably helped to secure his chances of becoming a minister, given that he was undeniably bright and able.

Appointed Minister for Work and Pensions in the Conservative-Liberal Democrat coalition government in 2010, Webb must have known that he had given a hostage to fortune the previous month. In a letter in April 2010, on behalf of the Liberal Democrats during the election campaign, Webb had said that he regarded 'index-linked [pension] rights as protected'. However, that was a campaign pledge in an election that the Liberal Democrats did not win. Instead, they became junior partners in a Conservative-led coalition. In July 2010, as a minister in that government, Webb announced plans to link private-sector pension payments to the Consumer Price Index (CPI) instead of the Retail Price Index (RPI), which would inevitably reduce the value of index-linked pensions.

Perhaps more importantly, as a minister Webb led big changes to the pensions system, including the pensions triple-lock guarantee and auto-enrolment, which automatically placed staff into a contributory pension scheme unless they opted out. It was estimated that 600,000 people were auto-enrolled by the end of 2013 and that by 2014 there was an additional £11 million per year invested in UK pensions.

The above is a brief description of Steve Webb's record as a minister. It was progressive and creditable but no more so, perhaps, than the output of other competent ministers. In itself, that record does not tell you why I have included him in a relatively small group of ministers judged exceptionally noteworthy. What made him so in my mind was his outstanding performance over five years in the Chamber. Webb did not launch *ad hominem* attacks on political opponents, as some politicians do. He always played the ball, rather than the man or the woman. He was unfailingly clear, fluent, able to communicate often complex detail in terms everyone could understand. Very obviously, Webb was in total command of his subject and that inspired confidence and respect. In that coalition government, no minister came across to me as better informed or more authoritative. I remember once telling Webb just how impressively he had performed and he took the compliment graciously. Yet I felt that outside the pensions industry Webb – who was never a glamorous, swashbuckling, self-promoting character – never really received full political credit for his knowledge, talent and competence.

* * *

Success in Parliament does not demand immersion in a set text or an approved manual. Such a tome does not exist. A

Member has a moral duty to vote, enforced by the party if he or she neglects to fulfil it. On arriving in the House, a Member will receive plenty of advice from seasoned colleagues as to what works, what does not and what 'good' looks like. Yet, for all that, it is for the MP to decide. It is generally wise to specialise in a small number of subjects but not to be so narrow as to neglect issues that may be of great interest to constituents or to close down the Member's own chances of committee service or ministerial preferment. It unquestionably helps to speak well, but we are no longer in the era of Nye Bevan or Iain Macleod, let alone Gladstone and Disraeli. A good point briefly made in lay person's terms often finds a more appreciative audience than a long, rhetorical oration for which, quite literally, the media and colleagues do not have time. Members can speak up for their principles and air constituents' grievances in the Chamber. A lucky few who succeed in the Private Members' Bill ballot even get the chance to change the law, as Cheryl Gillan did for adults on the autism spectrum. Often, however, a Member will find it more rewarding to sit on a select committee, becoming closely familiar with the policies, expenditure and administration of a particular government department and scrutinising its work.

At any one time, only about eighty MPs are government ministers. That can be rewarding too if a minister enjoys the role, values his or her boss, the Secretary of State, and reckons to be making a difference. Yet it is not always fun. It can be a hard grind. A minister cannot vote against the government on any issue without resigning and is unable to pursue constituency issues on the floor of the House.

Of course, a Member can be 'good' in different roles at different times. Indeed, versatility or flexibility is perhaps the trustiest guide to contentment in Parliament. A minority of Members set out to be career backbenchers – the late Paul Flynn from Labour and the Tories' Philip Davies being excellent examples of dedicated MPs who never wanted to be ministers. Most colleagues welcome the chance to serve in government, contributing either to the making of policy or to its delivery and communication. Yet they may do so only for a few years at most, so a shrewd Member will not view it as the only goal or source of professional contentment. Members probably do best, and are happiest, if they can cope with the vagaries of events, Shakespeare's slings and arrows of outrageous fortune, be they chances of office or the disappointment of losing it. My mother used to say to me as a young man, 'Try to live for the day, dear, and enjoy it.' In Parliament, part of being a good MP is to enjoy the journey for its own sake, as whether or where one finally arrives is uncertain. That uncertainty is part and parcel of the life of politics.

11

The Brexit Imbroglio

On the morning of 24 June 2016, standing outside 10 Downing Street, David Cameron announced his resignation as Prime Minister. He had campaigned vigorously for the UK to remain in the European Union during the referendum on our continued membership, but his much-vaunted commitment in 2013 to renegotiate the relationship between the UK and the EU had yielded precious little. As a result of that failure, the fact that he never previously made a positive pitch for the EU, and the misguided but prevalent hostility to immigration, the naysayers prevailed.

Some critics carped at his decision to step down. It was pointed out that he had pledged in Parliament that whatever the outcome, he would continue to lead the government. That did not strike me as much of a criticism. In the run-up to and during the referendum campaign, he could hardly have made it a confidence vote in his leadership, and would have been accused of bullying or petulance if he had. More seriously, there is an argument that he should have stayed put and followed through on the voters' verdict. I am one of the last people on the planet to defend David Cameron, but I don't criticise him for resigning. He had personally led the Remain campaign in the most important constitutional plebiscite for over forty years, and lost. He decided without delay to depart, with dignity and grace, so that a successor could lead the country to a different future. There was no dishonour in that.

In one sense, it might seem strange that Theresa May wanted to be the Prime Minister who delivered Brexit. After all, she had voted Remain and never given any clue that she had contemplated doing otherwise. I could not recall her making a powerful speech in favour of Remain – she did not – but neither had anyone else in the parliamentary party. Equally, she had never supported Brexit. In truth, bar the 'Nasty Party' 2002 speech she made challenging Conservatives to address their negative public image, she had made no very distinctive speech about any subject, anywhere, at any time in the nineteen years since she had been elected to Parliament. Personally I could not possibly have stood for office to implement a policy that I instinctively opposed and judged to be damaging to this country. But there is a perfectly respectable and democratic argument that says, 'Brexit is the public choice. It must be implemented sensibly. I, Theresa May, as a practical person of government rather than an ideological warrior, will strive to lead the government in implementing the voters' verdict.'

On becoming Prime Minister, May moved to assuage the concerns of Tory MPs and voters who could reasonably doubt her commitment to deliver Brexit. First, she coined the tautology 'Brexit means Brexit'. Although it was derided by many, notably Remainers, it achieved its objective of reassuring the vociferous right wing of the Tory Party that she meant to deliver. Several Brexiteer Conservative MPs who did not vote for her as leader rushed to tell me privately how encouraged they were that May, whom they had never rated or thought ideologically on their wavelength at all, was impressively determined to deliver the goods.

She sacked the fervent Remainer, George Osborne, and appointed three die-hard Brexiteers to key posts: Boris Johnson, David Davis and Liam Fox. She appeared to be reaching out to the right and simultaneously tasking this trio to stand and deliver.

Before the summer recess in July 2016, there was some

uncertainty as to when the government intended to invoke Article 50, the trigger for a two-year countdown to Brexit. Many people, myself included, assumed that over the summer recess the Prime Minister and her Cabinet would craft a plan covering the divorce bill, the rights of EU citizens living in the UK and the outline of the type of relationship they wanted with the EU in the future.

When Parliament returned from the summer recess on 5 September 2016, I received my first big post-referendum shock. The Brexit Secretary, David Davis, delivered an oral statement to the House to provide an update on the working of his new department. To say that the statement was underwhelming, uninformative and unimpressive would be an understatement. It pains me to write this because I have known David for thirty years; he is a highly intelligent guy and I was genuinely pleased for him that nineteen years after he last served as a minister, he had been propelled into the Cabinet to implement the Brexit for which he had honourably campaigned. What's more, when I say that the statement was unimpressive, I don't even mean his delivery of it. He is not a natural speaker – much better on the media than in the Chamber or on the conference platform – but he looked chipper, spoke confidently and seemed delighted to be at the despatch box. My point is simply that to the evident astonishment of Members across the House, he had nothing new or substantive to say.

Decoded, Davis was merely reiterating the 'Brexit means Brexit' mantra. Listening to him and observing how he was received by colleagues in the Chamber, my sense was that MPs thought that he begged several questions. By what means did he expect to achieve it? And by when? He said that he would be guided by 'some clear principles', but it was a stretch to call his statement a set of principles. Rather, it was an extraordinarily banal and threadbare series of slogans and statements of the obvious that advanced understanding not one iota. If the government had rejected any pursuit of consensus (when the referendum was won by so narrow a margin), had resolved not to put the national interest first, had stressed a desire to maximise uncertainty and had said that parliamentary sovereignty would not be restored, Davis would have met with horror and incredulity. What he said to the House did not amount to a strategy or a positive vision: it was merely a set of broad aspirations.

Davis was questioned that day by eighty-five backbench MPs, and stood at the despatch box for over two hours. Yet at the end I had not the foggiest idea how the government planned to deliver Brexit.

Of all the contributions that afternoon, two resonated with me in particular. Stephen Gethins, the SNP spokesperson, wondered aloud 'Was that it?' And then Ken Clarke, the Father of the House, delivered a withering verdict. He said that he understood the Secretary of State's difficulties, and encouraged 'him and his colleagues to take as long as they possibly can to work out a policy. I look forward to hearing from him again when the government have found something they can agree on that indicates what Brexit actually means.' Frankly, to him and to me, sitting in the Chair and listening intently to every word, the position was as clear as mud.

At the Conservative Conference in autumn 2016, the EU-related passages of Theresa May's speech were largely unspecific. The exception was the bald statement 'Article 50 – triggered by the end of March'. If that left us with any clue, it was presumably that the government would have a much clearer idea by then, almost six months later, as to what it would seek by way of agreement with the EU.

From October to December 2016 there were two further Ministerial Statements to the House on Brexit – the first by Theresa May and the second by David Davis. But we were given no further indication as to the strategy that the UK would adopt. For my part, it was baffling. Of course, leaving an institution to which the UK had belonged for over four decades was not a cinch. Extricating the UK from the web of legal, political and economic relationships would take time, and there was more than one way of doing so. Perhaps, I mused to myself, there was no agreement within Cabinet as to the route to follow?

Seeking to allay the growing anxiety that the British government was drifting in its approach, the Prime Minister opted to deliver a major speech on the subject on 17 January 2017 at Lancaster House. In summary, it was a manifesto for a clean or 'hard' Brexit. She wanted out of the single market and out of the customs union. When out, she would aim to negotiate a comprehensive free trade agreement with the EU. It was the speech in which she painted her famous – or perhaps infamous – red lines. In underlining a determination to leave the single market, Theresa May was motivated by visceral opposition to freedom of movement. Some will argue – as I do – that freedom of movement has brought great benefits to the UK. To the Prime Minister, however, it brought undesirable and unpopular immigration. She would not defend it because she simply didn't believe in it. Forced to choose between the economic benefits of the single market and the obstacle it presented to control of the movement of people, she consistently and wrongly sided with the anti-immigration lobby.

The speech was meaty and substantial, but neither wise nor deliverable. If we left both the single market *and* the customs union, the idea that the negotiation of a fuller free trade agreement with the EU would be straightforward struck me as utterly implausible. It also flew in the face of the evidence of how long it takes to negotiate a trade deal – seven years on average. I was relieved to hear the Prime Minister commit to a vote for Parliament on the final deal but, as it soon turned out, that commitment was less full-blooded than it seemed. If Parliament rejected the deal negotiated and the two-year countdown to Brexit had concluded, a 'no' vote to a deal could just mean leaving with none. That prospect came into sharp focus towards the end of 2018, when the government eventually initialled a deal with the EU.

Against the government's wishes, the Supreme Court ruled to my delight that MPs and Peers must give their consent before the government could trigger Article 50 and formally initiate Brexit. This was a setback for the Prime Minister but no more than a temporary irritant. The government introduced its European Union (Notification of Withdrawal) Bill – in other words, the triggering of Article 50 – and secured its passage in March 2017 within six weeks. The Bill contained two clauses and a total of just 66 words. Parliament thought it was doing its democratic duty and, procedurally, government and Parliament were totally in order. Politically, however, it was folly bordering on insanity. After all, the most important duty of Parliament is to hold the government to account. Approving this Bill did no such thing: it gave the government a blank cheque to pursue Brexit as it wished. In retrospect, it may well be seen as the gravest legislative error of my lifetime.

For months, through the autumn of 2016 and the first quarter of 2017, Theresa May had insisted that she would not seek an early general election, rather to my relief. I had dreaded the possibility of an early election, having intended this to be my last Parliament after standing again in Buckingham in 2015. I had expected to step down as Speaker in the summer of 2018, having done the nine years I had said in 2009 was my intended maximum. But I came to feel I should stay another year: a swathe of Brexit legislation was on its way, and much of it would be complicated. It did not seem the time to vacate the Chair and make way for a relative novice, or indeed a government stooge. There was enough instability already.

As we all now know, the Prime Minister returned from her walk in Wales over a bank holiday weekend and announced her decision to seek the agreement of Parliament to a general election on 8 June. Explaining her change of mind, she cited opponents of Brexit, in particular the SNP, claiming that they were threatening to try to block the UK's departure from the EU – although her clear lead over Jeremy Corbyn in the polls must also have been a factor.

In 2015, I had been re-elected with a majority of 22,942, my biggest victory in Buckingham. My small campaign team had canvassed door to door but it was a slow process and very inefficient. In 2017, for the first time in thirty years that I had fought general elections, I resolved not to knock on doors at all, bar one afternoon on a housing estate called Buckingham Park. Ironically, after no doorstep canvassing, I was re-elected by a majority of 25,725, a margin almost 3,000 greater than two years earlier.

If the election went well for me, it went spectacularly badly for Theresa May. True, she did not lose. Nor did Labour win. Morally, however, she lost, and she must have known it. Her manifesto was shocking. The campaign was dreadful. She performed badly and came to be known as the Maybot, a reference to her wooden, stilted and robotic style when speaking or answering questions. By contrast, Jeremy Corbyn performed well, showing that he was authentic, relaxed and able spontaneously to engage with people. The Liberal Democrats, meanwhile, were squeezed. Despite Tim Farron offering a distinctive alternative on Brexit – namely opposition to it and a call for a referendum at the end of the negotiation – his party increased its tally only from eight to twelve seats and the best-known Liberal Democrat, Nick Clegg, lost his Sheffield Hallam seat to Labour. The Conservatives fell from 330 seats to 317 and Labour rose from 232 to 262. Theresa May had lost her overall majority, her stock was badly damaged, and the party was furious.

The day after the election I was astonished by the content and tone of Theresa May's post-mortem broadcast. Obviously she did not look full of the joys of spring, but she showed no contrition whatsoever towards her own party or her defeated colleagues. Far more seriously, she displayed not an ounce of recognition that the loss of her majority had implications for her and her capacity to deliver her Brexit policy. She apparently took the rather bald view that both main parties had undertaken to deliver Brexit, and that was that. To her mind, Parliament had no choice but to go along with whatever Brexit she negotiated. Over the following two years, it became gradually clearer that she thought Parliament had no right to do otherwise, and was duty-bound to vote through 'her' Brexit. Constitutionally, that view was questionable. Politically, it was naïve, indeed almost barking mad, to suppose that opposition parties could be expected to agree to whatever she negotiated.

Those eleven days between the general election and the State Opening of Parliament on 19 June presented a window of opportunity for the Prime Minister to change tack and to signal a desire for a cross-party, united approach to negotiation with the EU. She flunked it. Driven apparently only by a desire to stay in office, Theresa May simply struck a 'confidence and supply' agreement with the Democratic Unionist Party. That meant that they would prop up the government – supporting it in any vote of confidence and voting for its Finance Bills – so that it was 'supplied' with the proceeds of taxes to allow it to spend money. She had called the election in pursuit of a bigger majority to push through her preferred Brexit deal, but in failing in that quest had suffered a double blow: the loss of numbers to support her and a loss of credibility. Nevertheless, she resolved to soldier on and to bulldoze Brexit through Parliament with Conservative and DUP votes only. She had no regard at all for the views either of the Opposition or of the 48 per cent who voted Remain.

* * *

Month after month after month passed without any clear or detailed outline of what type of relationship with the EU the government envisaged. Parliament, the media and the EU thirsted for a sense of what the future trade relationship might look like. Put very simply, the choice was between Norway and Canada. Under the Norway model, the UK would opt to remain close to the EU in terms of regulation, enjoy good market access, but sacrifice sovereignty and face a cash cost. Under the Canada model, the UK would cut loose from the EU and seek a free trade deal which offered greater freedom, but fewer rewards. What the EU did not want was for the UK to think that it could have the big benefits of one and the small costs of the other. Having one's cake and eating it was not on offer – though Theresa May appeared to want just that.

Here there was an unreality, indeed a dishonesty, in her approach. She just would not recognise the trade-offs entailed by Brexit. If the UK insists on full control of its trading arrangements, it will not be in a customs union. If a country makes that choice, as Theresa May did, there is a price to be paid. It will not have frictionless trade with its neighbours. If it wants total regulatory freedom, it will not be in the single market – the one market for UK goods and services that is bigger than any other. If that is the chosen course, British industry will be hit, jobs will be lost, living standards will be adversely affected and the quality of life will be damaged. To pretend that you can have everything – all the benefits and none of the costs – is a gross deception and downright irresponsible.

Inevitably, a growing chorus of demands for clarity led to a White Paper on the government's most important policy priority. Entitled 'The Future Relationship between the United Kingdom and the European Union', this paper quickly became known as the Chequers Plan because it was finalised at a meeting of the Cabinet held at Chequers on 6 July 2018. The plan aimed to keep the UK in a close relationship with the EU and stated that the new relationship would be 'broader in scope than any other that exists between the EU and a third country'. This would be done by establishing a new association agreement.

This was a crucial moment in the Brexit imbroglio. The Cabinet apparently endorsed the White Paper, but two members of the triumvirate appointed to deliver Brexit, David Davis and Boris Johnson, disagreed with it so fundamentally that within days they left the government. It was later suggested that control of the White Paper had been seized from DExEU by Downing Street – a view supported by the fact that the DExEU Permanent Secretary, Olly Robbins, had left the department to work directly for the Prime Minister. It was an extraordinary way to run the government. Yet a major clash within government was one thing. A major clash with Parliament later beckoned. That was another thing and, for the government, far worse.

Davis was replaced by a friend and protégé of his, the rising Brexiteer Dominic Raab. It fell to Raab to present the Chequers Plan to the House amid scenes of chaos and confusion as, in a departure from the usual etiquette, copies of the documents were not available to MPs, as he had expected. He described the White Paper as a 'detailed proposal for a principled, pragmatic and ambitious future partnership between the UK and the EU'. He did his best to sell the plan as a prospectus for free trade, but it faced coruscating criticism from large numbers of Tory MPs – especially those hailing from the vocal Brexiteer wing of the party, who felt it failed to reflect the referendum result and amounted to a 'betrayal' of Brexit. The Prime Minister robustly championed the plan as the basis of a deal with the EU but the response from Brussels was disconcerting: Michel Barnier, the EU chief negotiator, and Donald Tusk, President of the European Council, suggested that it was a modest step in the right direction but certainly not the basis of a deal. Aside from any other consideration, it did not address the issue of the Irish border.

After months of negotiation, the Prime Minister announced

on 13 November 2018 that she had struck a deal with the EU and would present it to Parliament. Two days later the Brexit Secretary, Dominic Raab, who had been in post for just four months, resigned in protest at it, objecting especially strongly to the 'backstop' provision – indefinite membership of a customs union to prevent a hard Irish border. The deal, known as the Withdrawal Agreement, still had to be formally approved at a special meeting of the European Council in Brussels on Sunday 25 November. The following day, Theresa May came to Parliament to make a statement in which she announced the deal and submitted herself to questioning by MPs. Her statement was twelve minutes long. It was followed by nearly two and a half hours of rigorous, intense, often painful questioning from colleagues on both sides of the House.

Opposition from Jeremy Corbyn was predictable, and could be discounted by the Prime Minister. The same could even be said for the hostile reaction of the SNP leader, Ian Blackford. What was astonishing, however, was the staggeringly hostile reaction to the Prime Minister's deal from her own benches. Of the first fifteen Conservative MPs I called to question her, not one supported the agreement. Absurdly, Conservative sources later briefed the media that this was somehow my fault – that I had deliberately let the exchanges run for an hour without calling a supportive colleague.

The facts are simple. I called Members from both sides of the House and from all strands of opinion, including prominent Brexiteers and Remainers. I could not possibly have anticipated the uniformly negative reception in that first hour. First, I am not psychic. Until Members spoke, I could not know for sure what they would say. Secondly, in over twenty-one years in the House of Commons, I could not recall a major government announcement – the culmination of two years' work and negotiation – receiving such a comprehensive thumbs-down.

In total, 124 MPs questioned the Prime Minister, of whom

96 were critical. I had never seen such a mauling. True to form, May was monotonous, unimaginative and robotic in her responses. I did not feel embarrassed by her but I did feel embarrassed *for* her. It was a damning indictment of two years of procrastination, mixed messages and confused thinking. Yet, outwardly, the Prime Minister appeared unperturbed, convinced that she would be able to get her unpopular deal through the Commons in the face of compelling evidence that she would not.

MPs on both sides of the House demanded publication of the legal advice on the Withdrawal Agreement and the House passed a motion to that effect. The government did not oppose the motion but said that the convention that legal advice to ministers was not published should take precedence over it. This line of defence was totally unacceptable to all of the opposition parties and to a number of government backbenchers who, as committed parliamentarians, held that a motion instructing publication was binding, and must be respected. It certainly *was* binding, as I made clear from the Chair. Despite the motion, and my ruling, the government still refused to publish the legal advice. The House then passed a motion declaring the government in contempt – but, perhaps foolishly, applied no sanction, and the government, the first in recorded history to be held in contempt, behaved as though nothing had happened. From Theresa May downwards, ministers were unapologetic, insouciant, seemingly relaxed about their own disgraceful behaviour in ignoring the express instruction of Parliament.

After much procrastination, the government scheduled five days of debate on the Withdrawal Agreement. In deference to colleagues, and in acknowledgement of the seriousness of the issue, I decided that I would aim to chair every minute of the debate from start to finish. Over the first three days, I sat in the Chair for a total of thirty-four hours, sustained by occasional sips of water, a packet of extra-strong mints and some cashew nuts. The Opposition speakers were firmly opposed to the deal; government backbenchers sharply divided. The Prime Minister had achieved the singular feat of uniting Brexiteers and Remainers alike against her deal, and this prompted her to panic and pull the remainder of the debate and a vote on the Agreement. In doing so, she admitted that her rationale was that she would not win that vote. Instead she promised that she would extract legal assurances from the EU that the UK would be able to withdraw from the backstop, and that it would not be indefinite.

As Speaker, I declared that this arbitrary postponement when so many colleagues – 164 of them – had spoken, others had applied to do so, and all had anticipated the vote the following day, was deeply discourteous, but I had no power to insist that the debate and vote went ahead. It was infuriating for the House, but the government controls the business. Each day, if it does not move – i.e., start (or continue) – a debate, the debate does not happen.

Although the Prime Minister had bought herself a bit more time, she inevitably faced huge pressure to extract the legal undertakings she had promised. The government could perfectly well have opted for one of three courses of action to follow the deferral of the vote. They could have rescheduled the debate for the following week so that the vote would take place before Christmas . . . but they didn't. They could have asked me to agree to a recall of Parliament on 2 January so that the vote would take place earlier in the following month . . . but they didn't. Or they could have confined the debate in the week commencing 7 January to two days, fulfilling the earlier commitment to five days of debate and the prospect of a vote on 8–11 January, depending on when that two-day period began . . . but they didn't.

Instead – deliberately, bare-facedly, shamelessly – they pulled the debate for a full month, resuming only on 9 January and providing for a full five days' debate so that the vote would take place only on 15 January, exactly five weeks after it was supposed to occur. Be under no misapprehension. The Prime Minister did not propose another five-day debate for Parliament's benefit. Colleagues were itching to conclude the debate and have the vote, as previously promised and scheduled, before Christmas. She proposed a more elongated timetable for her benefit. At first, I reckoned that she wanted more time in order to persuade EU leaders to hand her a rabbit that she could pull out of a hat. In fact, on reflection, I doubt that even that was her main motivation and, if it was, it failed – as most serious commentators had predicted. Rather, in the most staggering show of irresponsibility, she was deferring the vote for as long as possible in order to run down the clock and then tell MPs that to avoid crashing out of the EU without a deal, the so-called 'no-deal cliff edge', they had no realistic option but to vote for hers.

On the second day back from the Christmas break, 8 January, the government tabled its Business of the House motion prescribing a five-day debate. Having had an earlier such motion amended against their wishes, the government whips tried to avoid that by including in the motion the word 'forthwith' (such motions are not debated and have typically been deemed by the Speaker to be unamendable). However, this struck me as profoundly undesirable in this case, even hazardous – it would suit the hard-line Brexiteers thirsting to leave the EU without a deal; and might also suit Theresa May, as it chimed with her run-down-the-clock strategy (the latest iteration of her kick-the-can-down-the-road strategy). However, I sensed that it would not suit a majority of MPs who desperately wanted to decide on the PM's deal and then to explore alternatives if it was rejected.

Dominic Grieve tabled an amendment on the evening of 8 January that would require the Prime Minister, if her deal was defeated the following week, to bring forward her new Brexit plans within three days rather than three weeks. Late that

evening a senior Clerk called my office to seek my agreement
that the amendment should not be published on the Order
Paper the following day, as she thought it could not be put
to a vote: the government's motion did indeed use the word
'forthwith' – clearly on Clerks' advice – and was therefore
in her view unamendable. I disagreed and instructed that it
should appear on the Order Paper the next day.

At our daily briefing on 9 January, looking down at his
papers rather than at me, the Clerk of the House referred to
the amendment but said that, of course, it could not be voted
on because of the wording. Again I disagreed and told him
that I was selecting it. Ashen-faced and as shaken as if he had
just learned of an appalling tragedy, the Clerk looked up open-
mouthed and stared at me in disbelief. No Speaker had ever
made such a ruling, he said. It went against precedent.

We were, I said, in unprecedented times. The notion that a
minority government should be free to exert unfettered control as part of a scandalous time-wasting plot was absurd. That
such a plot was intended to blackmail the House to accept a
deal it didn't want, or else suffer the indescribable calamity of
a cliff-edge Brexit, was not merely ridiculous. It was disgusting
and obscene.

Chairing International Development Questions in the
Chamber later that morning, I was approached by the Government Chief Whip, Julian Smith. Shaking with rage, he
banged his fist on the table to the right of my Chair and said,
'You will not dictate what happens here!' I replied that I had
simply selected an amendment. If he didn't like it, he could
instruct his colleagues to vote against it. He snarled that I was
'out of order', and stood there for some minutes seeking to
engage me in further conversation but I declined. He wanted
to know how the government could register its view about my
decision. The fellow had just done so, in the rudest and most
threatening way. Complaining bitterly, he eventually stalked
off.

After Prime Minister's Questions, over twenty Conservative MPs raised Points of Order in which they queried my selection of the Grieve amendment. No doubt some were doing so of their own accord, but it was obvious to everyone in the Chamber that the government whips were stirring up as much trouble for me as they could, orchestrating the protest which featured several of the usual suspects, in other words government toadies whose response to a whip instruction to jump would be 'how high?'. With a couple of honourable exceptions, Points of Order from Conservatives were openly hostile, whereas those of Opposition MPs were almost uniformly supportive. The Leader of the House, Andrea Leadsom, whose near-pathological hatred of me was well known, joined in, demanding to know if the Clerks and I had been in agreement on the matter. I side-stepped that because their advice was, and always had been, private. Nevertheless, I explained my reasoning that nothing in or about the government's motion explicitly ruled out an amendment and I judged that the House should be able to vote on the one proposed by Grieve.

In a stunning display of hypocrisy, Andrea Leadsom then demanded that I publish the Clerks' procedural advice – it was oral, not written, so there was nothing to publish – and provoked Opposition derision as she and her colleagues had long resisted publishing their legal advice on far bigger matters than the selection of an amendment. I resolved to stay calm and courteous throughout the hour or so that Points of Order lasted. If some of the nastier and more bigoted critics – Leadsom was a prime example – thought that they would force me to back down or even to break down, they were deluded. They could have gone on for the rest of the day for all I cared and I would not have budged an inch.

When the vote finally came, the Grieve amendment was passed by 308 to 297. I had facilitated the House to decide what it wanted and it decided for Grieve and against the government, seventeen Tory MPs voting for the amendment on top of almost all Opposition MPs. Theresa May, the Chief Whip and Andrea Leadsom looked foolish and desperate.

Sure enough, Leadsom gave interviews denouncing me, as did many Tories. Other MPs backed me 100 per cent, including my erstwhile Speakership rival, the former Labour Cabinet minister and Leader of the House, Margaret Beckett. As I had said in the Chamber, 'If we were guided only by precedent, manifestly nothing would ever change.' The following day, Leadsom again verbally attacked me in the Chamber. I replied and stressed that I was not the cheerleader for the executive but the champion of Parliament.

The hysteria on the government benches and in parts of the media was as silly as it was short-lived. From 9 January, there followed a straightforward rerun of the five-day debate scheduled before Christmas and arbitrarily pulled on 10 December when May realised she would lose. Frankly, there was no need for five days' debate. Governments almost invariably offer less, not more, time for debate and the 'generosity' in this case was not for the benefit of MPs. It was a cynical manoeuvre to play for time and hope to win colleagues round.

The ploy was doomed. The Opposition was virtually unanimous in rejecting the May deal and hordes of Tory MPs, mainly Brexiteers but Remainers too, signalled that they would vote it down on 15 January. It was duly rejected by 432 to 202, the 230-vote margin representing the biggest defeat of any government policy in parliamentary history. It was an utter humiliation for Theresa May as 116 Conservative MPs voted against her, together with the Unionist MPs from Northern Ireland. After this cataclysmic result the Prime Minister and other party leaders rose to offer their immediate reactions. Theresa May accepted that it was clear that the House did not support the deal but added, somewhat acidly, that the vote told us nothing about what it *did* support. Given the enormity of her defeat, the rejection of what she had negotiated over two years with the EU, it would be reasonable to expect a

Prime Minister, either immediately or very soon, to resign. Yet it became obvious that she had no intention of doing the honourable thing.

My impression was that the Prime Minister was angry, not with herself for any mistakes made, but with the House. It was as if she thought that Parliament had misbehaved and needed to learn to do as it was told. Her tone was not a gracious acceptance of defeat but a sullen defiance of those she thought had improperly obstructed her.

She did, however, say she would hold meetings with her colleagues, with the DUP and with 'senior parliamentarians from across the House' – though curiously, despite prompting, she repeatedly declined to refer to the Leader of the Opposition – to identify what would be required to secure the backing of the House. She also intended to honour the House's decision on the Grieve amendment that I had controversially selected on 9 January. This required the government, in the event of defeat, to make a statement about the way forward and to table an amendable motion by Monday 21 January. I was so glad that I had selected that amendment. Without it, the government would have had three weeks, rather than three working days, to respond. For people who thought that the government was deliberately running down the clock with a view to browbeating MPs to back its poor deal with the EU, such a prospect would have been infuriating.

Over the next few days, those cross-party meetings began. Jeremy Corbyn at that stage was refusing to meet the Prime Minister until she had agreed to rule out a no-deal Brexit. Other senior MPs from a variety of parties did so but were taken aback by Theresa May's inflexibility and lack of humility. A common refrain was along the lines that 'her door might be open but her mind is closed'. On the surface, it seemed very odd. She had been trounced by the House, including by a huge number of her own MPs. However, the truth was that for all her talk about the national interest, the Prime Minister's priority was to hold the bulk of the Conservative Party together. She dare not defy the right wing of her party, the European Research Group, by entertaining opposition ideas. That group of MPs, led by Jacob Rees-Mogg, was almost certainly a small minority both in Parliament and in the country as a whole but it was entirely in tune with the views of the elderly and extreme Conservative Party membership.

On 21 January the Prime Minister made a further statement to the House as she had promised. Once again, she reiterated her opposition to a second referendum, refused to rule out 'no deal' and rejected a customs union option. She pledged to table a so-called 'take note' motion for debate and potential amendment the following week.

So, on 29 January, the merry-go-round resumed once again. The 'consultations' with senior parliamentarians had achieved zilch, as the Prime Minister was not prepared to alter any of her red lines. So the House had before it the government's 'neutral' motion, which simply noted the November draft deal. To that motion, fifteen amendments were tabled and I selected seven, most of which were rejected.

Yet the Prime Minister derived succour from the final vote of the evening. Sir Graham Brady, the Conservative MP for Altrincham and Sale West and chair of the 1922 Committee – in other words, chair of the Conservative backbenchers – had tabled an amendment requiring the Northern Ireland backstop to be replaced with 'alternative arrangements' to avoid a hard border. He and other signatories to the amendment – many of whom had rejected her deal previously – would support the Withdrawal Agreement subject to that change. This amendment was passed by 317 to 301.

There was a supreme irony here. The deal, including the backstop, had been agreed in November with the EU. Theresa May had regarded it as acceptable. Indeed, she had commended it to Parliament. It was not someone else's deal. It was *her* deal as much as it was the EU's deal. Yet now she whipped Conservative MPs to vote for Sir Graham's back-bench amendment so that she could go back to Brussels and ask the EU to remove that part of the deal to which twenty-eight countries had signed up. No sooner had the government won the vote on the Brady amendment than the EU made it clear again that the Withdrawal Agreement would not be renegotiated and that the backstop would remain part of it. The Brady amendment was a unicorn, a mythical creature. To a beleaguered Prime Minister, however, it kicked the can down the road again and bought her another breathing space.

Perhaps at this point it is as well to pause and recap. In December the government pulled a debate three-fifths of which had taken place in order to avoid defeat at the end of it. The matter was postponed for five weeks to allow the government to secure legally binding changes. They did not materialise. Then the government was defeated by a record 230 votes on 15 January and the Prime Minister again pledged to return to the EU to secure . . . yes, you've guessed it, legally binding changes. They did not materialise. On 29 January, sixty-four days after Theresa May first commended the deal, including the backstop, to the House, she said that she would go back to Brussels to secure . . . yes, you've guessed it, legally binding changes. That night Conservative MPs cheered, more from relief than delight, but the message sounded like a badly cracked record.

I began to think that this charade could not continue. If in February there was no change, the House would have to reach a determination – back a deal or extend Article 50 to allow more time to reach a satisfactory outcome, including asking the electorate to give their verdict.

Earlier in this chapter, I recalled the furious protests from Conservative MPs when I selected an amendment by Dominic Grieve. The protests were predictable but containable. Naturally, I have to be able to defend my rulings. I could, I did and I would do so whenever necessary. My approach was sometimes innovative and reforming, notably in this case, and I was comfortable with the inherent reasonableness of the options I was offering to Parliament. I admit that I was anxious to innovate and to challenge usual practice in order to support Parliament. By contrast, the government of Theresa May, notably since it became a minority administration after the snap election of 2017, regularly broke with convention not to support Parliament but to stifle it. This was done in order artificially to sustain its own position.

As I have said, the government was a minority administration. It no longer had a majority on Brexit issues or much else besides. Its reaction to its diminished status over the previous eighteen months had not been to co-operate with the House of Commons but to try to subjugate and control it. Theresa May arbitrarily prolonged the parliamentary session over two years so that there would not be a Queen's Speech in the meantime on which she could lose a vote. She packed Public Bill Committees with Conservative majorities that did not reflect the parliamentary arithmetic. The government frequently refused to vote on Opposition motions that it expected to lose, and then refused to implement them when it was defeated. When MPs and judges were branded 'enemies of the people' by right-wing newspapers, the Prime Minister and her Cabinet offered no defence of parliamentary democracy or an independent judiciary. Perhaps most shamefully of all, as mentioned earlier, the government was held in contempt of the House and shrugged it off, giving not a fig for what a majority of MPs thought.

All governments try to control Parliament. A healthy tension has always characterised the relationship between the executive and the legislature. But this was not a healthy tension. It was far worse. Led by a robotic Prime Minister with not an ounce of empathy, a very inexperienced and incompetent whips' office, and the most substandard Leader of the House in my two decades and more in the Commons, the government regularly displayed, to the embarrassment of some of its senior MPs, its total contempt for Parliament. Its behaviour – not once, not twice, but repeatedly, week in and week out – was shabby, undemocratic and profoundly dishonourable.

Throughout my tenure as Speaker, I met people, sometimes constituents but frequently not, who asked me what I would do to promote a policy that they liked or to stop a policy that they disliked. Naturally I explained that as Speaker it was not my role to do that. I was the referee or umpire, not a player. Ordinarily, they would accept the point, though sometimes rationalising their desire for help by explaining that what they wanted was not party political, but ethical, or in some other way vital to the public interest. My reply would be the same. My task was to facilitate the House and, above all, to champion the legislature to challenge the executive.

Nowhere has that been more true than on Brexit. For the first seven years of my Speakership, the executive was pro-EU and, of course, so were most MPs. Nevertheless, Members on both sides of the Commons wanted to question the Prime Minister of the day and Foreign Office ministers on UK policy towards the EU and, as on every subject, my guiding principle was to hear, wherever possible, all the voices. Let every MP question the minister. In Parliament, the rights of minorities matter. It falls to the Speaker to protect them, be they minority political parties such as Plaid Cymru and the Greens or minority voices within parties, for many years the so-called Eurosceptics in the Conservative Party and, on a much smaller scale, in the Labour Party. That is why when I revealed in February 2017 that I had voted Remain in the referendum, the attempt to 'convict' me of bias failed miserably. The rebellious questioning and speeches of the Eurosceptic backbenchers – not to mention their votes against the party line – could be a real nuisance to the government and sometimes make them deeply unpopular. That, however, was a problem for their whips, charged with enforcing party discipline. It was not a problem for me. My attitude as Speaker was that if a Member had the urgent need to raise a question or stage a debate, I would give it the go-ahead. Following the 2016 referendum, however, the flow of Urgent Questions from the Brexiteers almost completely dried up for at least two years. I don't say that as a criticism of those MPs. Their side had won. They were no longer challenging the government at that point, but supporting it.

In more recent times, the source of Urgent Questions has changed. Frequently, it has been Remainers, from Anna Soubry to Tom Brake, who have submitted UQs on the government's Brexit plans and I have granted them because they needed to be put. I can honestly claim to have been completely even-handed and impartial as between Brexiteers and Remainers. Where MPs are called to question ministers delivering oral statements, it has long been my practice almost always to call every Member who wanted to ask a question, so by definition no one of whatever opinion was disadvantaged. Where Urgent Questions are concerned, I had granted them to Remainers and Brexiteers alike, on merit. My view on the policy was irrelevant to my judgement on procedure.

* * *

The Prime Minister refused to accept that her deal was dead. She sought concessions from the EU on the Irish backstop but was rebuffed. She then worked furiously to win round rebellious Conservative MPs, ducking another so-called meaningful vote until she reckoned she could win it. Exactly eight weeks after the 230-vote slaughter of 15 January, the government tabled a second meaningful vote motion for debate and decision on 12 March. It contained a number of legal changes that the government considered to be binding and which had been agreed with the European Union after intensive discussions. However, although the whips had converted some rebels, the government was again heavily defeated, this time by 149 votes, rendering the defeat the fourth most severe for any government in recorded history.

Despite the second serious setback at the hands of Parliament, the government seemed curiously mulish and unmoved. Once again, the idea that the Prime Minister might resign did not seem to occur to her. Equally, there was no sign that she would drop her red lines and strive to forge a compromise with the Opposition. Instead, there was briefing to the media to the effect that the trend was 'in the right direction' and it became abundantly clear to me that the Prime Minister had no intention of changing tack. Rather, Theresa May and her colleagues were gearing up for yet another go at getting her deal through the Commons in the coming days.

The prospect of a 'repeat' vote gravely concerned me – and, I knew, concerned other MPs – for two reasons. First, there is a long-established convention in the House that the same, or substantially the same, question cannot be put twice in the same session of Parliament. Yet the government, blissfully unaware of or blithely indifferent to this convention, was openly talking about bringing back the motion on 'the deal' and again urging MPs to support it. This would be disrespectful to the House of Commons and an abuse of its procedures.

Secondly, put bluntly – though I did not use this word to the House, as I did not wish to raise the temperature any higher than necessary – it smacked of bullying. My suspicion, shared by colleagues on both sides of the House and on both sides of the Brexit debate, was that the government aimed to browbeat, harangue, intimidate and threaten – in other words, bully – MPs into voting for a deal they did not want. That was wrong and, as Speaker, I felt I should stand up for the right of MPs individually and the House collectively not to be so shabbily treated by the executive.

I decided that I would make a statement to the House on Monday 18 March, giving my ruling on the matter and affording the government the chance to consider its plans. Naturally, I consulted the Clerk of the House, Dr John Benger, beforehand. He readily acknowledged the convention but was wary of it being used to prevent the government seeking to pursue its chosen policy. To me, it was either a strong convention, there to avoid time-wasting and in place for the protection of the House, or it wasn't. John was concerned that if I used it to thwart the will of the Prime Minister the government would be so infuriated that it would mobilise against me. So be it, I concluded. Most Members did not want the government's proposition to be brought back. A strong convention allowed me to stop it returning and that is what I chose to do.

Addressing the House immediately after Work and Pensions Questions, I reminded Members that the 24th edition of *Erskine May* (the bible of parliamentary procedure) stated on page 397 that 'a motion or an amendment which is the same, in substance, as a question which has been decided during a session [of Parliament] may not be brought forward again during that same session'. It went on to state that 'attempts have been made to evade this rule by raising again, with verbal alterations, the essential portions of motions which have been negatived. Whether the second motion is substantially the same as the first is finally a matter for the judgement of the Chair.'

I emphasised that the convention was very strong and long-standing, dating back to 2 April 1604. One of the reasons the rule had lasted so long was that it was necessary to ensure the sensible use of the House's time and proper respect for the decisions that it took. Decisions of the House mattered. They had weight. In many cases, they had direct effects not only in Westminster but on the lives of our constituents.

I summarised the chronology of events relating to meaningful votes on Brexit, explaining how proceedings to date had been orderly. I pointed out that it had been strongly rumoured that a third, and even possibly a fourth, meaningful vote motion would be attempted. My conclusion was that if the government wanted to bring forward a proposition that was different from the one rejected by the House on 12 March, that would be entirely in order. What the government could not do was to resubmit to the House the same proposition, or substantially the same proposition, as that of the previous week, which was rejected by 149 votes.

My statement was followed by no fewer than thirty Points of Order. I was happy to deal with all of them – I was happy in my mind that the ruling was correct, and felt I had been clear and upfront about my reasons for making it. What's more, the government had time to consider its own approach in light of what I had said.

The government did indeed consider how to proceed. Ten days later the Minister for the Cabinet Office, David Lidington, and the Attorney General, Geoffrey Cox, came to see me at their request. They were a tad sheepish, probably knowing how ridiculous it was that the dysfunctional operation of the government whips' office and the Leader's office, represented respectively by Julian Smith and Andrea Leadsom, meant that neither was communicating with me, forcing these two ministers to do so instead if they were to be able to submit a motion for debate that would be judged orderly by me. Smith and Leadsom, real amateurs in their roles, were out of their depth. I advised Messrs Lidington and Cox that they had options: they could 'prorogue' or discontinue this session of Parliament and stage a State Opening, thereafter allowing them to put the Withdrawal Agreement to the House as it would be a new session; they could attempt to repeal the provision in the EU Withdrawal Act 2018 that provided for a meaningful vote on the Withdrawal Agreement; or they could table a new proposition.

They decided to pursue the latter course and came back later that day with a motion Cox had drafted that would invite the House simply to support the legally binding Withdrawal

Agreement, but not mention the Future Partnership Declaration, the non-binding but path-finding 'political declaration' on future relations between the UK and the EU. This was in spite of the fact that ministers had previously said that the two were indissolubly linked. Whatever the rationale, it was in vain. Despite a huge whipping operation, the government still lost by 58 votes. The formulation was different, but even in improvised form, the government's Brexit deal had been put to Parliament for a third time and still been soundly defeated.

Over and over and over again, on 15 January, 12 March and 29 March (the day we were supposed to have left), the executive told the legislature what it wanted and the legislature said no. Thirty-three months after the referendum, and despite two years of toil to produce a Brexit plan that she thought honoured the 2016 plebiscite and protected the UK economy, Theresa May was thwarted by Parliament. She thought that her deal was a sensible, pragmatic, reasonable British compromise. It was not. It was a mess of potage which predictably won the votes only of mainstream, dependable, government-supporting loyalists on whom every executive depends.

Fatally, however, it failed to appeal to those who felt most strongly about Brexit. The committed Brexiteers scorned it as a fudge, a labyrinthine mess, a sell-out that would tie the UK in knots and bind the country to the EU long into the future. To them, the keepers of the holy Brexit faith, it was BINO, Brexit In Name Only. And the half a dozen hardcore Remainers on the government benches looked at the deal and judged it to be straightforwardly inferior to the current deal that the UK enjoyed as a member of the European Union. They would not vote for a deal that they reckoned would leave the UK poorer, weaker and less secure than it is today.

Naturally, I know my colleagues from all parties and all shades of opinion. It is hard to be a rebel – so much easier to keep your head down and stick to the party line. Yet the easy course is not what a Member of Parliament should take unless he or she also thinks it is the right course. The rebels did not. They thought that the easy course, the course of conformity, was the wrong course. Whatever my personal views, I admired, both as Speaker and as a human being, every one of those rebels who did what he or she thought was right, daring to be different, opting to defy the diktats and heavy-handedness of the party machine.

* * *

Either side of the government's defeat on 29 March, and almost in parallel with ministers' persistent efforts to secure approval of 'the deal', Parliament was striving to find a way forward. For weeks, some Members on both sides of the House had floated the idea that the House could stage what are called 'indicative votes' on different Brexit options to establish which had support and which did not. A successful amendment in the name of Sir Oliver Letwin first secured time for debates and votes on 27 March.

No fewer than sixteen motions were tabled and it fell to me to select which of them should be debated and voted on. Of the sixteen, I was able quite easily to whittle down the motions chosen to eight, on the grounds of how many colleagues had signed them and the breadth of support they enjoyed. As always, I wanted to be scrupulously fair to Brexiteers and Remainers alike, selecting for example both a revocation of Article 50 motion proposed by the SNP's Joanna Cherry and a no-deal Brexit motion from Conservative backbencher John Baron. Of the eight motions, none was carried but four fared respectably, including Ken Clarke's motion supporting a customs union.

A second round of indicative votes took place on 1 April. I was keen to help the House try to reach a conclusion and saw no merit in selecting again a proposition that had been massively defeated before – a no-deal Brexit motion, for example – or choosing what had come to be known as a 'unicorn', a mythical creature that had no credibility. I chose four credible motions but again, none was passed.

Ministers and backbench loyalists were delighted, and in some cases gloating, that nothing won and, true enough, it was not a good look for Parliament. But nor was it a disgrace. The government had had years to negotiate its proposal and spent four months trying to bulldoze MPs into backing it. Backbenchers had had two days to put motions to the House, no voting system that would guarantee a victor and the deliberate non co-operation of Cabinet ministers who were whipped to abstain on every vote. Despite these constraints, MPs came closer to success than the Prime Minister had ever managed.

Subsequently, a cross-party coalition of MPs featuring the Conservative Sir Oliver Letwin and Labour's Yvette Cooper was able to command the support of the House to suspend Standing Order 14, which stipulates that government business shall have precedence at every sitting. More controversial was the takeover of the Order Paper, that is to say the agenda and timetable of Parliament, by MPs who were not members of the government and were acting against its wishes. Naturally, the government thought it was quite wrong and said so loudly from the Prime Minister downwards. It was even suggested that to overturn the right of the government to decide what was debated each day was unconstitutional. I disagreed. Government control of the Order Paper has certainly been the norm since the early twentieth century but, before then, it certainly was not. Standing Orders of the House are not the property of the government but, rather, as the title implies, that of the House. It can keep them, amend them or scrap and replace them wholesale as it wishes. The Clerks shared my view that if colleagues from different parties in the House wished to propose a suspension or disapplication of a Standing

Order, they should be free to put such a proposition to the House. They did a number of times and lost. Then they did so in April 2019 and won.

I accept that some who thought this wrong did so on principle. Yet, to a great extent, the so-called constitutional row was really a proxy war between Brexit protagonists. Brexiteer rebels like Sir Bill Cash and Sir John Redwood were opposed to Cooper-Letwin as they thought that those members should not be free to propose legislation that might block a no-deal Brexit. By contrast, Labour, the SNP, the Liberal Democrats, Change UK MPs, Plaid Cymru, the Green MP Caroline Lucas and Conservative MPs who either wanted the UK to remain in the EU or, at least, to avoid a no-deal Brexit, were cheering Cooper-Letwin on from start to finish.

The procedural takeover was unusual, but it was certainly not unconstitutional. I was completely satisfied that it should be allowed to proceed if a majority wished it to do so. My role as Speaker, again, was to facilitate the House and I did so in that situation as I always tried to do over a decade in the Chair.

* * *

Many Brexiteers, in Parliament, the media and the country at large, were angry that the UK did not leave the EU as scheduled on 29 March 2019, or even, as repeatedly promised by Boris Johnson, on 31 October 2019. Their beef was that the 2016 referendum was a binding instruction to Parliament. They pointed out that through Article 50, the two-year countdown to Brexit was triggered with overwhelming support from MPs of the two major parties. They insisted that those parties had since failed to deliver the will of the people and that many of their MPs have actively conspired against that will, i.e. to stop Brexit. Indeed, some would even argue that in championing Parliament over the government, I as Speaker sided with Parliament against the people. It is a serious charge and it deserves a serious answer. There are several parts to that answer.

First, although the referendum was not legally binding, the public narrowly voted for Leave yet, ever since, debate has raged as to what Leave meant. To some, it meant leaving the customs union and the single market; to others, it did not. To some, it meant leaving without a deal; to others, it did not. To some, it might mean leaving with May's deal or Johnson's deal; to others, it does not. In short, there was a preference to leave but no consensus, either in 2016 or in 2019, as to what Leave would look like.

Secondly, Theresa May secured Parliament's support for a snap election in 2017, arguing that such an election would enable her to provide the 'strong and stable leadership' needed to deliver Brexit. She claimed that 'every vote for the Conservatives will make me stronger when I negotiate for Britain' with the EU. In other words, she would be stronger with a bigger majority. Yet she lost her majority altogether. The 2017 election did not reject Brexit, but it did not endorse it either.

Thirdly, delivering Brexit would never be about waving a wand or passing a law, but about concluding a negotiation and securing Parliament's support for its outcome. The UK government decided with the EU that Leave would be a two-stage process – finalising a withdrawal agreement and then concluding a future partnership. To this day – not least because the government has created the impression that if Johnson's deal is approved, and the implementing legislation is passed, the Brexit box will have been ticked and politics can immediately focus instead on all the issues neglected for the last three years – much of the public is blissfully unaware that years of trade and other negotiation lie ahead. Yet the two stages of the process are inextricably bound up with each other. People want to know what the overall deal is before deciding if it is better or worse than what we have now.

Finally, and crucially, the UK has a parliamentary democracy, admired and imitated around the world. The duty of

MPs is to do what they think is right for the country. Three years on from the referendum, we know far more than we could have known in June 2016 about the 'deal' on offer, its likely effect on our economy and the implications for our standing in the world. If Parliament judges that the balance sheet of Brexit will be positive for the UK, it can support it. If, however, Members of Parliament, whose professional task is to scrutinise legislation and policy to judge what serves the public interest, think that the Brexit deal or any other form of Brexit will make the British people poorer, less secure, or both, they have no obligation whatsoever to vote for it. They can revoke Article 50. Or, alternatively, they can legislate for another referendum to ask the voters, before the country proceeds with such a fundamental and lasting change, whether they want that change or prefer to remain in the EU. As Speaker, my job was not to presume to know the 'will of the people' but to facilitate the will of Parliament.

The British public may have been perplexed, even infuriated by this long-running saga but they were certainly not uninterested in it, not least as reflected in the People's Vote marches and the six-million-strong petition to revoke Article 50. Many were gripped by the parliamentary drama, as indeed were citizens across Europe. In October 2018, the month before the publication of the Prime Minister's deal, around 230,000 people regularly watched the BBC Parliament channel. Five months later, in March 2019, I'm told that figure had increased to 1.75 million. Later still in the year, the number of viewers soared to 2.75 million. I saw it myself on the streets, too – as Speaker, I had got used to being recognised when I was out and about. People often called out 'Order!' and sometimes asked for selfies. However, this increased dramatically in 2019 and I seemed to be stopped every few minutes when I stepped out of Parliament. The number of requests to do foreign media interviews rose sharply, and our internet-savvy kids (aged fifteen, thirteen and eleven at the time) could not help but notice the clips of me doing the rounds. Oliver, Freddie and Jemima delighted in introducing me to YouTube videos and then greeting me, randomly, by singing the memes of 'Mr Peter Bone', 'Bambos Charalambous' and 'Thangham Debonnaire' as they fancied. When Sally and I proposed that they get on with their homework, tidy up or load the dishwasher, they took to shouting '*Orderrr*', 'Division!' and 'Clear the Lobby'. Inevitably, the noes had it (three kids against two parents) but, let's just say (as I load the dishwasher and Sally tidies their rooms) that they did at least do their homework.

* * *

I have described above what I did in my role as Speaker while all this was playing out. What did I actually think, though? As mentioned earlier, I told Reading University students in February 2017 that I had voted Remain, prompting squeals of synthetic outrage among a tiny minority of colleagues and some media. In March 2018 the same fraternity sought to generate a hue and cry over a car sticker alleged to be displayed in my windscreen saying 'Bollocks to Brexit'. Actually, it was in the windscreen of Sally's car, and she had got it from the indefatigable Steve Bray, otherwise known as 'Mr Stop Brexit', who had protested persistently – come rain, snow or sun – outside Parliament since the EU referendum result. Displaying it in her car was her prerogative and the idea that it constituted a disgrace was pompous nonsense. However, in truth, I made a mistake at that time. My office was dealing with a barrage of press enquiries following the *Newsnight* bullying allegations and, foolishly, we didn't bother to counter that story, thinking it trivial. Unfortunately the myth of the sticker in John Bercow's car persisted and was often referred to in press articles and online comment.

Eventually, I was presented with an opportunity to correct the record. One day in January 2019 towards the end of Points of Order, Adam Holloway MP stood up. Looking puce and wagging his finger at me, he declared indignantly: 'We've all noticed in recent months a sticker in your car making derogatory comments about Brexit . . . this is a serious point about partiality. Have you driven that car with the sticker there?' I responded, with elaborate but superficial courtesy, telling him that I had the highest regard and affection for him but that he had made a factual error: the sticker was on my wife's car. 'I'm sure the Honourable Gentleman wouldn't suggest for one moment that a wife is somehow the property or chattel of her husband. She is entitled to her views. That sticker is not mine and that's the end of it.' The exchange between us went viral on Twitter and Sally and the kids were enormously tickled by it.

The simple truth is that, since the mid-noughties, I have supported UK membership of the European Union, recanting my earlier opposition. I was not a Remainer because I somehow did not believe in my country, or in the power of the British Parliament to make laws, or in the talent and capacity of my fellow citizens to prosper. My reason for supporting British membership of the EU is threefold: power bloc, trade bloc, progressive legislation.

As Winston Churchill said, Europe is 'where the weather comes from'. The EU is a global player because it so effectively combines and amplifies the collective might of its twenty-eight (for the moment) members. Its large and prosperous market makes the EU a global rule-setter, since any foreign company that wants to produce at scale must adopt EU standards, and any country that wants seriously to boost its trade must respect the interests of EU members. This clout allows the EU not just to stand up to other global players, including China and the US, in enforcing its high standards, but also to the largest multinational corporations.

In 2008 the UK introduced the world's first legal framework for binding carbon emissions targets with the Climate

Change Act. It then drove the same change in EU climate change policy, and, with Britain at the helm, the EU in turn used its clout as a global standard-setter to bring this reform to the entire world. By leading the European Union on climate change, Britain was able to give a lead to the world. The same principle of amplified British power applies to standing up to Russian aggression, combating terrorism, defending human rights, and far more besides. Our place in the EU lets us set the global weather.

If Churchill understood the importance of a collective Europe as a power bloc, Margaret Thatcher understood its importance for trade. In 1988, she said: 'How we meet the challenge of the single market will be a major factor, possibly the major factor, in our competitive position in European and world markets into the twenty-first century.' She was right. Two-thirds of UK exports are today either to the EU or to countries with whom the EU has a preferential trade deal. Britain has built its international competitive advantage in services on the single market of which it was itself an architect. Knowingly to leave that market and then to have to spend years negotiating access to it is, to me, an act of wanton self-harm which we may rue for decades if it is not stopped or reversed.

Yet the EU is not just a market. It is a club of democracies that share fundamental values of human dignity, freedom, equality and solidarity, and this is encapsulated in the 'social dimension' of the EU. The EU has secured rights for citizens across the board: non-discrimination protections, parity for part-time and agency workers, access to paid annual holidays and parental leave, to name just a few. To extreme advocates of massive deregulation to create a minimal state, such regulation is viewed as a cost, a nuisance, a bureaucratic burden on virtuous employers. However, to my mind, it is part of the DNA of a decent society and a contributor to the quality of life that we value. Above all, by securing co-operation between

European countries that not so long ago were riven by near-continuous conflict, it has brought about a golden era of peace and prosperity.

Brexit is the most chronic threat to the British national interest. That threat flows directly from the decision of David Cameron to opt for a referendum. A case could be made for resolving uncertainty by putting the issue to a national vote, though in practice we now know for a fact that it has done nothing of the kind. The issue is as high-profile as ever and more toxic. The argument *against* a referendum was stronger. There was no mass demand for that referendum in the country. Worse still, it was called by David Cameron not out of principle, but as a tactic to appease Tory Eurosceptics and to neutralise UKIP. It was a massive, reckless and disastrous gamble. Leading Britain out of the European Union by accident is scarcely a proud legacy for any Prime Minister.

Some say that the verdict of the British people must be respected. True enough – when I received hundreds of letters and emails of complaint from constituents in the first few weeks after the 2016 referendum, saying the Leave outcome was not valid or should be reversed, I gave them short shrift. It was a legitimate referendum and we must respect the result, I replied. I am not embarrassed to have sent such replies. In retrospect, however, I think it would have been far better for the plebiscite never to have been held. A binary choice on a complex issue at very short notice was supremely unwise. Predictably, it has unleashed turmoil that could have been avoided. Wrong-headed and often downright dishonest arguments were made for Brexit and hysterically plugged day after day by our biggest-selling newspapers. It was a commentary on David Cameron's deep-seated arrogance that, against that backdrop, he fondly supposed that he could prevail.

Yet now, more than three years later, the situation is starkly different. We don't have idly to speculate on what might happen. We can observe the damage already done to our economy, our politics – consumed by this one subject almost to the exclusion of all else – and our international standing. Democracy is not about one vote, once. It is a dynamic process. What's more, the vote was a vote for departure, not a vote for a destination. The idea that we threaten the fabric of British democracy if we offer people a choice to vote on the outcome of a two-year negotiation is absurd. Surely the time has come to go back to the people – and this time, that must include the people who have to live with the result the longest, namely sixteen- and seventeen-year-olds. Offer them the choice: leave with the deal on offer, or remain. To put 'no deal' on the ballot would be utterly irresponsible of any government given the cataclysmic harm it would inflict. If people vote to leave, that's it. The verdict on a specific proposal will be clear and must be heeded. On the other hand, if the British people decide to remain, that proves two points. Second thoughts are often better than first . . . and it was right, in light of the known facts, to seek the consent of the people.

Meanwhile Theresa May has suffered a political disaster and tragedy, her entire premiership defined by an issue and a policy that for the previous two decades of her career as a Member of Parliament had never been a priority for her. It is hard to overstate just how dreadful, how diabolical and how disastrous Theresa May's leadership was. She began with no clear plan for Brexit. After nine months, she had a plan – the Lancaster House approach – but no basis for thinking that it would secure Parliament's or the EU's agreement. She nevertheless invoked Article 50 in a spirit of blind optimism. Three weeks later, she moved to call a general election she had said repeatedly for months she would not seek to call. She endured the excruciating embarrassment of having her political judgement – the terms of the manifesto – and her zombie-like campaigning style cruelly exposed. After polling day, she then behaved, without a natural majority, as though she enjoyed the command it would have given. She negotiated a deal with the EU which was rejected by eye-watering margins and then spoke and acted as if the EU had a duty to change what twenty-seven member states had agreed with her – not imposed upon her. She treated the House with utter contempt and disdain when she needed its support. She displayed the worst communication skills I have ever seen in any British Prime Minister in my lifetime.

On top of all that, I came to feel that even her word counted for little or nothing. For example, she had said that she could not be the Prime Minister who led the UK into European elections – the implication was that she would resign if that scenario arose. Yet just before the Easter recess, when asked about it, she ducked the challenge by saying that the way to avoid it was to back her thrice-rejected deal. Her performance was off-the-scale awful – toe-curling, cringe-making, spine-chilling and medal-winning in the infliction of self-harm.

Of course, after the third defeat of 29 March, Theresa May did not get to put her deal to the House of Commons again. Instead, the EU offered a further extension to 31 October, Donald Tusk imploring us to use the time 'wisely'. Further weeks passed with nothing on the deal tabled in the House because the Tory rebels were holding firm and the government simply did not have the votes. In what should have struck her like lightning as excruciatingly embarrassing evidence of the hopelessness of her political standing, the EU elections in the UK went ahead on 23 May. The Prime Minister had sworn that she could not entertain such a prospect but it happened all the same. Both the Conservatives and Labour fared badly, the former haemorrhaging votes to the newly formed Brexit Party under the leadership, both charismatic and demagogic, of Nigel Farage. His party won 29 of the 73 seats, amassing 31.6 per cent of the vote. The Conservatives won only four seats, polling fifth behind the Brexit Party, the Liberal Democrats, the Greens and Labour. It was the Conservatives' worst electoral performance since 1832.

On 24 May 2019, the day after the EU elections in the UK but before the declaration of the results, the Prime Minister stepped out into Downing Street to announce that she would resign as leader of the Conservative Party on Friday 7 June, remaining in post as Prime Minister only until the election of a new Conservative leader by the summer. Her statement earlier in the week of what she called a new and bold offer to Parliament had apparently satisfied no one: in a long series of clumsy, ill-judged and maladroit moves on Brexit by Theresa May over the previous three years, it was a strong contender to be ranked the worst of the lot.

Her resignation announcement was a long time in the coming, delivered with extreme reluctance and only because it must have ultimately become obvious to her that it was inevitable. No one, bar the most devoted loyalist, wanted her to stay, and she had run out of cans as well as road to kick them down.

Three features of her resignation speech struck me. Theresa May talked about the need for compromise, making the point as though that is what she had offered, although she had done nothing of the kind. She had cobbled together a policy that satisfied neither Brexiteers nor Remainers. More than two and a half years after the referendum and over eighteen months after her failed general election gamble, she agreed to talk to other parties but offered no meaningful concessions at all. She had a very strange idea of compromise, amounting to saying to others, 'You make concessions and I will consider whether I can accept them.' Yet it was not Jeremy Corbyn or Vince Cable who needed to get a Bill through Parliament.

A second feature of the speech was the attempt to describe a policy legacy. It was laughable, for there was none. Theresa May had not merely failed on her Brexit agenda, she had failed on almost everything else she had pledged to deliver. She had failed to tackle the 'burning injustices', failed to counter the explosion in knife crime, failed to address the rise in racial attacks and failed to devise a policy to meet the challenge posed by the crisis in social care.

Finally, a Prime Minister who had become notorious for her absence of empathy and her robotic reiteration of vacuous mantras, suddenly displayed raw emotion about giving up the leadership of the country she loved. There were tears in her eyes and a lump in her throat. I could understand how upsetting it must have been for her but, candidly, I could not feel much sympathy. There was no such emotion over the victims of Grenfell Tower, those affected by the Windrush scandal or the daily misery endured by the homeless and those dependent on the foodbanks that have mushroomed alarmingly across the UK over the last decade. She was tearful only when adversity affected her.

As I write, the saga is unfinished. Elected in July 2019 to succeed her as leader of the Conservative Party and, therefore, Prime Minister, Boris Johnson did negotiate a different deal with the EU. That deal included the removal of the backstop. Yet it will undoubtedly entail new bureaucracy, has already provoked Unionist consternation, and strikes me as far inferior to the status quo. I cannot predict with any certainty whether the UK will leave the EU, still less the detailed consequences for the UK if we do. My instinctive hunch is that the conduct of the referendum, the shaping of Brexit policy by the May government thereafter, and the handling of the departure will be pored over by academics and others more closely than any other decision of government, including the decision to go to war in Iraq, since the Second World War. Although I have no inside knowledge causing me to predict it, I firmly expect that the administration of Brexit will be the subject of a long, detailed and unsparing public inquiry. Time will tell if I am right.

Epilogue: The Next Decade

Serving as Speaker, and living inside the most famous Parliament in the world, was the greatest privilege of my life. It never palled. From start to finish, I relished the experience. Yet nothing is or should be for ever. A decade or so in post was enough. As 2019 beckoned, I knew that I wanted out as soon as I could responsibly leave. In January, I reckoned that I would leave by the summer recess in July. From April, when the EU granted an extension to our membership to 31 October, Sally and I agreed that I should continue until then, when either the UK would leave, with or without a deal, or Parliament would vote to seek a longer extension, pending either a general election or another referendum.

Contrary to the view of my critics that I was determined to cling on indefinitely, I felt no such desire. Rather, it was a matter of duty. To walk away in the middle of the biggest political challenge of the post-war period felt irresponsible and unfair both to the House and to whoever succeeded me as Speaker. As it turned out, the 31 October deadline was missed and the matter was still unresolved when I stepped down, but I could not postpone my departure indefinitely. The Brexit imbroglio seemed to be reaching its endgame, one way or another, and it was time to say thank you, hand over to someone else and say goodbye. Time to stop living in a company flat in a palatial house. Time for the Bercow family to live in the Bercow family home.

There were two reasons to go. First, and more important, someone else with new ideas and energy should have the chance to take Parliament forward. Secondly, even though I loved the role of Speaker as much as ever, I wanted while young enough, at fifty-six, to do something else, finding a work-life balance which suited me and my family. Constitutionally, I did not have to leave the Commons, thereby ceasing not only to be Speaker but to be a local MP, but I did so without hesitation. The House does not want an ex-Speaker hanging around and, potentially, proving an irritant to the new incumbent. In any case, I wanted to be free to take on new roles. Naturally, I knew that some people would regret my departure and others would rejoice at it.

As mentioned in the Prorogue, I first stated my intention to stand down both as Speaker and as an MP on 9 September 2019. My statement was followed by spontaneous Points of Order from twenty-nine Members wishing to record their appreciation of my tenure. Obviously I had not anticipated such a warm reaction, but there was no shortage of time that day and I naturally gave colleagues free rein to say what they wanted to say. Beginning with Jeremy Corbyn, they were extraordinarily generous and many were lavish. The House can be cruel but it can also be kind. At their best, Members rise above past conflicts and resentments, showing themselves to be gracious. I appreciated in particular the contributions of Michael Gove, Anna Soubry – whom I greatly admire but with whom I had previously clashed ferociously – and Peter Bone, an arch Brexiteer who strongly disagreed with some of my rulings but still offered me a glowing tribute. It was big of him.

On 31 October, my last day in the Chair, the Leader of the House, Jacob Rees-Mogg, chose to pay fulsome tribute to me, notwithstanding our recent differences on matters of procedure. He was followed by another thirty-eight colleagues whose kind words I will always treasure, none more so than those uttered by Iain Duncan Smith. I had not been loyal to him when he was Leader of the Conservative Party but he had it in him to look at me afresh as Speaker and to offer his unstinting support. That meant a lot.

As soon as I had announced my departure, the focus inevitably turned to possible successors and I resolved to keep out of their battle. It was for my colleagues to choose, which they did on Monday 4 November, whittling down a field of seven candidates before finally electing the Labour MP for Chorley, Sir Lindsay Hoyle. My advice to Sir Lindsay, who had served dedicatedly under me as Deputy Speaker for nine years, is simple. First and foremost, stand up for backbenchers: they are more than three-quarters of the House. You are there to champion the legislature, not to bow to the executive. Secondly, challenge the Clerks who advise you on procedure. They are capable but cautious, sometimes absurdly so. Remember always that they advise, but you decide. Thirdly, don't settle for the status quo. Strive for improvements in the running of the Chamber, the management of the Parliamentary Estate and the quality of Parliament's engagement with the public. If my successor ever wants further advice or a listening ear I will be happy to oblige in private. However, I have no intention of giving a running commentary on how my successor is doing.

I hope to contribute usefully in the House of Lords. I have acquired some experience over more than two decades in the Commons and would welcome the chance to speak up periodically, whether on constitutional issues or on other issues dear to my heart. In all likelihood, I will pursue a portfolio career. Having worked largely self-directed for so long, and at least to some extent determining how I spent my time, it is hard to imagine wanting to work full-time for one person or organisation. Instead, I want to pursue a range of activities which interest me. I aim to speak, to consult and to lecture, either in the UK or abroad as I am passionate both about communication and about higher education. For thirty-four years since I graduated from the University of Essex, I have thought about the place at some point every day. I was beyond excited in 2017 to be asked to serve as its Chancellor, and I hope to devote a little more time to doing so in the period ahead. I would like to work to promote businesses' sense of corporate social responsibility and am keen to back charitable causes, of which the dearest to me is the promotion of social mobility. It is a searing indictment of successive governments that although the UK remains one of the richest countries on earth, we do not live in a meritocracy. The opportunity to get on in life is still skewed disproportionately in favour of those who went to the right school or have parents with money, contacts or both. Perhaps 'twas ever thus, but I salute and want to support those able hard-workers from disadvantaged backgrounds who strive to reach the top in whatever walk of life – be it politics, the media, business or the professions.

Finally, I want to enjoy more sport, especially to find the time to play and watch more tennis, usually accompanied by my good friend, multi-sport enthusiast and fellow Fed-head, Ed Guest. As I have mentioned, my all-time sporting hero is Roger Federer, the greatest player in the greatest era of the greatest sport ever devised. I have derived enormous fun and stimulation watching Federer play at Wimbledon, the O2, in Paris, in Basel and in Geneva, but high on my bucket list is a visit to the Australian Open in Melbourne.

Passion and exuberance are key to my experience of sport. When I am watching tennis, I always enjoy it and am totally relaxed if I don't much mind who wins. By contrast, watching Federer in a tight match, I am excitement and tension personified. In fact, Sally sometimes says that I have insufficient faith in my hero as he usually turns things around. I plead not guilty to that. Rather, it is that I know that no one can win all the time. I have indeed seen Roger turn matches around from very precarious positions but if he has an off day, or plays someone performing out of his skin, he may lose. Terrified that he might, and grumpy if he does, characterise my mindset.

My second sporting passion is football. I have supported Arsenal since the age of eight and, since 2012, I have been a season ticket-holder with our now sixteen-year-old son, Oliver. I rarely miss home games and will try in future to support the team at more than the half a dozen away games per season that I have managed to attend in recent times.

There is nothing to beat live sport. Never more so than when Arsenal are desperately clinging on to a one-goal lead or trying every which way to find an equaliser with just five minutes to go. Occasionally, before a match starts, I will make or take a phone call, but during a match? Never. Watching Arsenal is like watching Federer. I switch off from work and from any other problems or challenges, focusing 100 per cent on the match. It might seem a strange way to relax, but I reckon that every football fan will understand when I say that it works for me. I wouldn't be without it. Having waited for years to acquire those season tickets, I will never give them up.

* * *

As I contemplate the next decade for the United Kingdom, the challenges for Parliament strike me as falling into two broad categories: those which are issue-specific and those which are thematic or focused upon values.

The most immediate, and therefore pressing, issue is physical. Parliament is a magnificent set of buildings but they are ancient, dilapidated and in dire need of comprehensive overhaul. MPs and Peers have accepted that a thorough restoration and refurbishment of the Palace of Westminster is required. The estimated cost is approximately £4 billion though I confidently predict, from my limited experience both of builders and of public-sector contracts, that the ultimate price will be much higher. It is reckoned that the work can get under way only from around 2025 and take up to ten years, though given the natural tendency of large construction or renewal projects to overrun, and the additional consideration that exploratory works will uncover previously undetected hazards, the time-scale could be longer. The main issue to date has been whether the work could be done while parliamentarians remained in situ. The judgement, prudent and inevitable, is that both the Commons and the Lords need to relocate and I very much doubt that that judgement will change. Although the project is intended to make the Palace of Westminster safe rather than to create something new, there are some MPs and commenta-tors who would like to see a Continental-style, semi-circular and consensus-oriented Chamber. For all that I am an enthusi-astic change-maker on many fronts, I am instinctively, perhaps almost romantically, a small 'c' conservative on this point. Crit-ics contend that the adversarial layout of the Chamber, with government on one side and Opposition on the other, breeds adversarial politics. If it were, say, a semi-circular horseshoe, tempers would be less likely to fray and constructive debate more likely to take place. I am sceptical that the atmosphere would necessarily change or even that it should. There are big differences, philosophically and practically, between right- and left-wing views of the world and even between those views and those of determined centrists. Those differences should be played out in our democratic legislature. My overall outlook is that we should keep the best and improve the rest. Let's fix what's broken and add a legacy benefit in the process of restoration and refurbishment: improve disabled access, build a top-quality visitor centre to showcase Parliament's story and provide new, superior archive facilities to replace those which are now fast deteriorating.

Some critics who lament the state of British politics reckon that the source of poor governance and of disengagement from politics is the first-past-the-post electoral system. Of course, the Liberal Democrats, and their predecessors, have long inveighed against a system that gravely disadvantages them, just as the Conservative and Labour Parties have defended the status quo, which has generally protected them. To be fair, the disillusionment with the present system runs wider. Many people argue that the status quo has never represented at all accurately how people vote in elections but that it now fails even by its own yardstick – namely to deliver a decisive result and strong government. The trend of the last four decades of falling support for the Conservative and Labour Parties was reversed in 2017, but the distribution of votes nationwide meant that the Conservatives, who had the larger share of the vote, failed to achieve an overall majority. Importantly, two of the last four general elections have produced hung Parliaments. The 2010 result spawned a coalition – welcomed by some and derided by others – which at least allowed for stable government over five years. The 2017 outcome led only to a confidence-and-supply arrangement with the fifth largest party, the Democratic Unionist Party, whose parliamentary representation is confined to Northern Ireland. In parliamentary terms, it is legitimate. In practical terms, it has led to instability and a concern that, on Brexit, the DUP does not speak for Northern Ireland, which voted to remain in the EU.

I am sceptical that a move to proportional representation would transform our politics for the better. It would produce a mirror image of how people voted, which the blunt instrument of the 'winner takes all' method we now use does not. However, it would empower smaller parties, almost certainly allow extremists of right and left to gain a foothold in Parliament, and institutionalise coalitions, deal-making, horse-trading, not merely over policies but personnel. In other words, post-election decisions would be not merely about what policy to implement but about who would be in power to deliver it. This is the norm in a great many democracies. It is workable and it may prove to be popular. That said, I am far from certain that it would be better than what we have in place now, let alone that it would be a panacea for our problems. For all that, I have a hunch that if the next election produces a stalemate or, alternatively, it dramatically excludes or under-represents a big share of public opinion, the debate about electoral reform might ignite once again.

If the means of composing the House of Commons is an issue, the make-up itself does not pass without criticism. It is true that the House elected in December 2019 is more richly diverse and representative of modern Britain than any of its predecessors. There are now 220 women MPs, the highest number ever; 65 ethnic-minority MPs, or 1 in 10, compared with 1 in 40 just ten years ago; there are now 45 openly LGBT MPs; and more who went to state school – as our own children do, I am proud to say. Nevertheless, if you believe as I do that Parliament should more closely reflect the population as a whole, there is no ground for complacency and much work to be done. In particular, the parties still tend to attract a disproportionate number of middle-class candidates. Alongside efforts to promote diversity of gender, ethnicity and sexuality, the UK Parliament could still benefit from having more representatives who had worked in more junior and middle-ranking occupations. People with experience of low pay, tough working conditions and the challenge, for example, of raising a family while struggling on benefits, could all add invaluable perspectives to parliamentary debate and the scrutiny of legislation. The parties need to be bolder and more imaginative if they are to reach out to people from such backgrounds and to persuade them to choose politics as a career.

Shortly I want to ponder some of the defining characteristics of the UK, the challenges the country faces and the implications for Parliament in the decade ahead. However, before doing so, let me focus on a clear and present threat to our political culture and the reaction of the major parties.

A resurgent wave of populism in the UK, the US and elsewhere poses an existential threat to liberal democracy. It is of potential interest to all who care about our political health and of consuming concern to all who cherish parliamentary democracy. Angry outbursts on social networking sites, simplistic sloganeering – whether by Trump in the USA or Farage in the UK – and the narrative of betrayal and treason are a sinister threat to representative democracy. Trump has lobbed vile abuse at female and minority ethnic opponents, rubbished whole areas of the US in venomous terms because they are governed by Democrats, impugned the integrity of professional judges and lambasted as 'fake news' stories that criticise him. His approach is not to offer arguments, but to spread bile and to cast as enemies of the United States people who hold and express views that differ from his own. It is part of a hyper-narrative that aims to portray him as the faithful protector of Americans against those seeking to weaken the country and to drag them down. A similarly abrasive tone is adopted in the UK by Nigel Farage, aided and abetted by the more bellicose parts of the media that seek to vilify anyone who resists the shrill, nationalistic, pro-Brexit and anti-immigration message peddled by the hard right. Frankly, pop-up populism is no substitute for the serious debate, analysis and scrutiny of issues that are the business of a parliamentary democracy. If elected politicians don't stand up for Parliament and parliamentarianism, no one else will. The role of a Member of Parliament is to make judgements on difficult and complex issues in order to serve the national interest, not to pander to prejudice.

I would make this case with total conviction even if the 'populists' in the UK enjoyed majority support. As it happens, however, the truth is that more often they do not. When subjects are debated, alternatives posed and nuances explained, only a minority of voters sign up to extreme policies. For example, 'What do we want? Brexit. When do we want it? Now!' might be a suitable chant for use at a street demo and it's a legitimate expression of opinion. It is not, however, a reliable guide to the intricacies of policy that government and Parliament must determine. The unfailing instinct of the populist is to declare that the answer to a problem is obvious and to impugn the integrity or even patriotism of anyone who disagrees. The tragedy of 'populism' in recent times is that it has ceased to be the exclusive preserve of fringe groups and has become mainstream. In the UK, Theresa May herself played with fire by her trashing of Parliament and her appeals over its head to electors, opportunistically and rather desperately attempting to portray herself as a friend of the people against the supposedly self-serving machinations of MPs who disagreed with her. This was unworthy stuff and has since been followed by Boris Johnson and a number of his ministers behaving in a similar fashion.

For my part, I defend, indeed I robustly champion, not the right but the duty of politicians always, everywhere and without fail, to speak and vote as they think best for the country. If that is popular, good. If not, they should do it anyway, explain their reasoning and be great persuaders. That is the responsibility of a politician in a parliamentary democracy.

Of course, populist clamour, be it for Brexit or against immigration, for large-scale public ownership or against austerity, has increasingly found expression within the major political parties. Throughout my tenure as Speaker, I belonged to no political party. My task was to referee the parliamentary disputes between the party combatants. Inevitably, I have closely observed all of them and formed some thoughts about the state of the three UK-wide parties.

The Conservative Party is the most successful party in the history of the UK and of the Western world as a whole. It has displayed an infinite capacity to adapt to the changing mores of society and to the different challenges of each era, positioning itself as the best party to govern in the national interest at that time. Since the Second World War, most of its electoral success was achieved by retaining core support of voters of the right and centre-right and persuading so-called floating voters in the centre ground to support it as the party best equipped to facilitate prosperity and security. Under Margaret Thatcher, it shifted to the right to address the particular circumstances of the late 1970s and the 1980s – powerful trade unions, inefficient state industries, high marginal tax rates, an unmet yearning among council tenants to own their own homes and concern about the threat posed by the Soviet Union. It is only fair to record that the Thatcher governments were often more pragmatic than their ideological advocates – or even than Lady Thatcher herself in later years – suggested. Furthermore, none of her three administrations ever recommended leaving the European Union. The party's success has been achieved by garnering broad-based support as the political force that encourages individuals to prosper, uses the nation's wealth to provide public services and help for those who need it, and defends the country against crime at home and threatened aggression from abroad. The party always had a hard-right contingent – anti-European, sometimes anti-immigrant, xenophobic, even racist. I know because, to my shame, I briefly consorted with such types myself more than thirty-five years ago. The key point is that these people were members of the Conservative Party but they were not the majority of it and, crucially, they did not run it.

Opinions in today's Conservative Party about immigration and race are very mixed. Many who know him believe that Prime Minister Boris Johnson is a social liberal, a genuine internationalist and a crusader for a global Britain which, free from the alleged shackles of the European Union, will trade freely and co-operate effectively with nations across the world. We shall see. As yet, we do not know. What we do know is that the members of the Conservative Party are disproportionately in favour of a no-deal Brexit by comparison with the wider electorate. What we do know is that Conservative members harbour a much greater concern about, frequently amounting to an antipathy to, Islam and the possibility of a Muslim Prime Minister than voters as a whole. What we do know is that, although the Conservative Party's membership has been in long-term decline, tens of thousands of new members have joined in the last three years, often former UKIP members with a view to electing a committed Brexiteer as leader. In short, the 150,000 or so old, white, middle-class, anti-EU and strongly right-wing Tory Party members have been buttressed by extreme Brexiteer entryists. Their mission is to ensure a Brexiteer leader, a Brexiteer parliamentary party and the conformity or deselection of those MPs who hold a different view.

There is no denying that a substantial share of the electorate is attracted to a Brexiteer, anti-immigration, hard-line policy platform. Frustrated by, almost despairing of, Theresa May and seeing UKIP as both extreme and poorly led, such voters flocked to Nigel Farage's banner as the leader of the Brexit Party in the local and European elections in 2019. Boris Johnson was clearly determined to win back those voters for the Conservatives and to repel the Farage threat to his chances of leading a majority Conservative government. Preventing punters peeling off to the right, i.e. the Brexit Party, is judged necessary by the Prime Minister, yet it carries a risk. Keeping or regaining right-wing voters means mouthing mantras and messages that may alienate other voters whom the Conservative leadership wants to recruit to build an election-winning coalition. Younger, urban, professional people who see the Conservative Party as their natural home as the party of free enterprise and opportunity are often more pro-European, relaxed about immigration and focused on education, health, social care and the environment. A hard-right song resonates with some voters but it repels others. At its best, the Conservative Party has framed a much wider narrative and appealed to voters across ages, socio-economic groups and parts of the UK. A shrill, populist, anti-Europeanism will appeal to those who subscribe to ideological right-wingery but could turn off voters in droves in Scotland, Wales, London and elsewhere. What's more, if the Conservatives deliver either a no-deal or a hard Brexit and that is followed by a prolonged economic downturn marked by job losses, falling tax revenues, lower living standards and declining public services, the party could pay a heavy electoral price. That punishment would be entirely deserved.

There is one remaining factor for the party and voters to consider. Divided parties lose elections, unless others are still more divided. At the very least, divided parties risk real reputational harm. I was horrified in 2019 to see Dominic Grieve subjected to a vote of no confidence by the Beaconsfield Conservative Association, which had clearly been infiltrated by extreme Brexiteers who wanted rid of their local MP. Let me be clear. I have known Dominic Grieve for over thirty years. We were parliamentary colleagues for over twenty years. We are not personal friends, simply professional acquaintances. Grieve is a serious, intelligent, learned, articulate, patriotic, outstanding parliamentarian speaking and voting for what he judges to be in the national interest. What's more, he is undeniably a genuine Tory to his fingertips, always has been and always will be. He is not someone who can be accused of having shifted his views. Instead, it is the Conservative Party on the ground that has become so extreme. If it cannot tolerate someone of his calibre – or, for that matter, Nicholas Boles, who has jumped ship in response to its lurch to the right – that is a damning indictment of the party. The point has much wider application – be the target Grieve, Boles, David Gauke, Antoinette Sandbach or anyone else targeted for deselection on grounds of ideological impurity. In the national interest, I earnestly hope that Boris Johnson will stamp on intolerant cliques who plot to oust good MPs who dare to dissent from their leadership.

To date, however, as mentioned earlier, he has instead withdrawn the whip from distinguished Conservatives who have dared to defy him. It has not been an encouraging debut.

A parallel threat faces the Labour Party. It is a matter of

public record that its membership has dramatically increased since 2015. Some of that increase derives simply from opponents of austerity spontaneously joining the party under the £3 per member system in solidarity with Labour and Jeremy Corbyn. Some of it is the left's answer to UKIP entryism into the Tory Party and has apparently occurred on a much bigger scale. Certainly, the election of Jeremy Corbyn as leader in 2015, the most left-wing leader in decades, was a shock to the Labour establishment, unwelcome to most Labour MPs and roundly condemned by the overwhelmingly right-wing media. Many observers predicted the electoral annihilation of the Labour Party in the 2017 election. But a dire Tory manifesto, chronic performance by Theresa May and authentic on-the-stump salesmanship by Jeremy Corbyn confounded the critics. Although he did not win, Labour increased its seat tally by thirty and deprived the Conservatives of victory. Moreover, some of its left-wing policies, notably on railway nationalisation and abolition of tuition fees, were popular. However, three years on, Labour is in big trouble.

I can well understand why Jeremy Corbyn sought to preserve constructive ambiguity over Brexit. Many of his voters in the north and the Midlands want out of Europe and he sought their votes. By contrast, most of his supporters in Scotland, London and the south-east are opposed to Brexit and he wanted them too. Brexit will not be the biggest political issue indefinitely but it was at the 2019 general election. The constructive ambiguity was perhaps sustainable until the government's third defeat on the EU Withdrawal Agreement on 29 March 2019. At a stretch, it could have been upheld until the EU in April granted an extension to Article 50 until 31 October. Once Boris Johnson embraced the notion of Brexit on 31 October with or without a deal, in his words Brexit 'do or die', Labour's stance had to change. Most party members, including many of Corbyn's left-wing backers, wanted Labour to adopt a more explicitly pro-European position. They yearned either for revocation of Article 50 or for a commitment to a second referendum and full-blooded Labour support for the UK to remain in the European Union. If Labour had taken that approach and led a principled campaign to stop Brexit, it would have offered a distinctive alternative to the Johnson government. However, such an approach itself contained risks and, in any case, it was not to be.

Just as the Conservatives should be able naturally to accommodate moderate MPs out of sync with their leadership, so Labour should too. By that, I am not talking about people like Kate Hoey who appear to have scant commitment to any Labour policies at all, but I am talking about people who disagree with the leadership but are fundamentally Labour to their core. In my view, deselecting MPs for mere ideological deviation is not only undesirable, it is dangerous to the party that promotes or permits it. For what it is worth, however, I am not one of those who think that Labour can win elections only by adopting the approach of Tony Blair. I admire what he did to make Labour electable and to win three successive elections. However, times change. Labour doesn't need to ape the Tories on the public finances. After all, public services are under massive strain and in-work poverty is shocking. The public appetite for further austerity has evaporated. Voters are persuadable that a new approach is required and a left-of-centre pitch for power is entirely credible. It will have to be led with passion, costed in detail and supported by a united party that is as hell-bent on winning as the Conservatives will be.

As for the Liberal Democrats, their fluctuating fortunes are testament to the proposition that there are no final victories or defeats in politics. The late Harold Wilson is often recalled for his adage that a week is a long time in politics. If that be so, a few years can seem like a lifetime. The Liberal Democrats went from being coalition government partners to suffering electoral slaughter in 2015, leaving them with a mere eight seats from the fifty-seven enjoyed in the previous Parliament. The 2017 election saw only the most feeble improvement in their tally to twelve, but in 2019 the party enjoyed excellent local election results, gaining 700 seats, and a strong European election, taking sixteen seats and finishing an astonishing second ahead of Labour and the Conservatives. They were boosted further by the defection from Labour of Chuka Umunna and victory in the Brecon and Radnorshire by-election. After an uncertain start to his leadership in July 2017, Vince Cable made worthwhile gains and helped to position his party unmistakably as utterly opposed to any Brexit and equally committed to giving voters a final-say referendum between Brexit and Remain. His successor from July 2019, Jo Swinson, is a highly capable and energetic leader, but the 2019 general election was a massive disappointment to her personally, and to her party. With only eleven seats in parliament, it is hard to see a Liberal Democrat recovery any time soon under our existing electoral system.

This is a memoir. Inevitably, it has focused on the past – past milestones, past controversies and past reforms to improve the workings of Parliament. The one exception came in Chapter 5, where I sketched out three priorities for further reform in the running of the House of Commons as a legislature: namely, establishing a House Business Committee, changing the way we handle Private Members' Bills and creating a trigger mechanism by which MPs, rather than merely the government, can recall Parliament when it is in recess. Those reforms are worth making. They would improve our parliamentary democracy. Yet I recognise that they are mainly of interest to, and set to be determined by, the inhabitants of the Westminster bubble. As I draw to a close, I want to look well beyond this bubble, and reflect more widely on what British public life – and the challenges that change could offer to Parliament and politics – may look like by the end of the next decade.

Let me begin by acknowledging that there will be probably be a great deal of continuity between now and 2030 as well as substantial change. In explaining that continuity, I want to set out what I believe to be the 'hardware' aspects of the United Kingdom as a nation-state and the British as a distinct people. Put another way, I am intrigued by the force of the fundamentals – geographical and demographic, economic and commercial, cultural and social – which make us who we are and which largely explain why we are different from other nations. I think those fundamentals are very strong. Most have deep roots. They explain the character of our core political institutions and their stability over the centuries, including Parliament. That stability suggests that they are destined to be similarly effective in the next decade despite whatever might transpire as a result of the B-word.

Thereafter, I want to look at the 'software' – how people live their daily lives. Here I want to signal what I think will be very radical change induced by what in some circles is called the Fourth Industrial Revolution but which I think is even more dramatic than that, a transformation far closer to the discovery of a Second New World.

Let us start with the hardware of our geography and demography. The United Kingdom is a small island nation at the edge of north-west continental Europe with a very distinctive relationship with water. Our climate is mild and wet. We have a large number of comparatively narrow rivers that are not that distant from each other. They were, even centuries ago, relatively straightforward to bridge. We thus had more internal mobility and movement than other European countries that had more extreme climates, much larger mountain ranges and far wider river systems. This relative ease of internal transportation also led to fewer linguistic differences within the UK than elsewhere.

Then there is the sea. The UK is a modest-sized country with a surprisingly long coastline due to its configuration and the large number of small islands within it. The coastline

of the UK is actually 12,429 kilometres long. There are
only eleven other nations plus Antarctica and Greenland
that can boast longer coastlines. In Europe, only Norway,
which has double our coastline, and Greece have more, and
if we were to count the whole British Isles then we would
overtake the Greeks by a wide margin. Britain has a longer
coastline and hence more exposure to the sea than Mexico,
Brazil, India, Chile and South Africa, all of which one might
instinctively deduce had longer coastlines than we do.

The next hardware feature of the United Kingdom concerns
its extraordinary demography. The first point is that there are
a lot of us. The UK is the 78th largest country in the world by
size but has the 21st largest population and the 50th greatest
population density. If that 50th does not sound striking then
it is worth recalling that many of the other 49 are very small
states indeed, such as Monaco. There are actually only five
countries in the world with populations that are bigger than
the UK that have higher population densities, and they are in
Asia, namely Bangladesh, India, Japan, Philippines and Viet-
nam. The only three European nations with higher population
densities than ourselves have much smaller populations:
Malta, the Netherlands and Belgium.

The second point is that there are not only a lot of us but
that we are exceptionally urban. A little more than half of our
citizens live in cities of 150,000 people or more. The equivalent figure in Germany, Spain and Poland is less than 30 per
cent. In Italy, it is just about 20 per cent. In France, it does
not reach 15 per cent. The only other European nations that
are similarly urban, but even then at only 40 per cent on this
metric, are Russia west of the Urals, Belarus and Ukraine. So,
we are a country of cities surrounded by the sea.

The third point is that we are dominated by our capital city
to an extent that we often do not notice. London is larger than
the next eighteen UK cities combined. It is the third largest
city in the widest notion of Europe after Moscow and Istanbul,

and it is rapidly catching both of them up. It is also eight times (and rising) the size in population terms of Birmingham, our second city in the United Kingdom.

It is worth focusing on that more than we do. London is eight times the size of Birmingham. Yet Paris is only two and a half times the size of France's second city, Marseilles. Berlin is just twice the size of Hamburg. Rome, Madrid and Warsaw are less than double the size of Milan, Barcelona and Lodz. Indeed, there are only three examples of countries that have populations of 50 million plus where the gap between the first and second cities is even wider than in the UK now. This trio are Ethiopia, Philippines and Thailand. In many ways, the UK has a Third World internal population distribution. We are a country of cities but overwhelmingly one overarching city that is surrounded by the sea.

Now let us look at the economic and commercial hardware. The UK is the fifth largest economy in the world, with a very similar GDP total to France, so much so that exchange rate movements can switch over the ranking of the two economies at almost any time. This is really punching above our weight. The UK has 0.85 per cent of the world's population yet 3.34 per cent of the world's GDP. This is still likely to be true come the year 2030 with the only question being whether both the UK and France are overtaken by India, which has the seventh largest economy and plainly the potential to expand more.

The UK economy is also astonishingly open. In 2016 it was the second largest recipient of foreign direct investment on the planet after the United States. In the same year, it was the third largest source of foreign direct investment on the globe after the US and China. This is phenomenal.

Finally, London has a remarkable standing in financial services. Only New York can dispute its status at the top of the financial premier league. Frankfurt and Paris are an extremely long way behind. This has also been true for a very long period. London has been among the world's top three financial centres since the reign of Henry VII more than five hundred years ago. To illustrate its importance, afford me an example. If you were to draw a line on a map from just west of Kensington to just east of Canary Wharf, that would be about ten miles. Then move up and down that line for a mile and you would have a rectangle representing 20 square miles. That box involves an effective control of more capital than not only every other square mile combined in the UK itself, or every other square mile combined in the EU, or every other square mile combined in all of Europe, or of Europe plus Russia, but more than every other square mile combined of all the rest of Europe and all the territory of the former USSR. This twenty square miles in London beats in terms of capital the 11,041,420 square miles of the rest. Once again, whatever the next decade might have in store, it is hard to see that this is about to end.

In this overview of the hardware of the UK, we must never forget its cultural and social features. The UK has an amazing story to tell in terms of education. According to the QS Index, the barometer in this field, this country has four of the top ten universities in the world and 16 of the top 100. If one were to assimilate the various aspects of education then they would constitute our second largest export industry after financial services. By contrast, within that same QS Index, France has two of the top 100 universities in the world (with its best ranked 43rd), while Germany has three (the top one being placed 64th). This country also has an outstanding record in terms of science with the second largest number of Nobel Prizes in this field awarded to it after the United States. We are also something of a cultural superpower, whether it be in music, film, theatre, literature or sporting events. Ours is the international language and our time-zone has many advantages to it. While our manufacturing sector might not be as large proportionately as some of our neighbours, it has a focus on very high-specification fields such as aerospace.

We are a major international centre for venture capital and technological innovation. We are also these days, as Napoleon prematurely snorted, 'a nation of shopkeepers' in that we have 5.75 million businesses (mostly sole traders or micro-firms) or one for every ten adults. The same number in the United States is one for every fifteen adults.

Once again, these hardware features have a lengthy history to them and look very well established. They are unlikely to have disappeared or even to have been seriously diminished by 2030. All of which is an argument for comparative continuity. The public which our House of Commons will need to represent a decade or so hence will continue to be shaped by similar geographical and demographic, economic and commercial, cultural and social forces as it has been in the past and is so today. This is by no means a reason for arrogance or complacency. Rather, it is an attempt to understand why we have been the sort of nation and the kind of people that we have been. Moreover, it explains why that in turn has expressed itself through our key political institutions of which the House of Commons is clearly central. In short, those institutions are obviously different from those of many other democracies. Our hardware largely explains what is our British exceptionalism.

* * *

What then of the prospects for our national software, or the way in which people live their lives? This is obviously hugely important, and technology and technological change are at the heart of it. I suspect that over the past two decades or so since I entered the House of Commons there has been more change in national software triggered by the arrival of the internet, mobile phones and sophisticated portable computers than almost any law enacted by Parliament. To state this is not to marginalise the House of Commons but to keep political life in perspective. Politics is led by technology, if change is dramatic enough, not the other way round. When I was studying eighteenth-century British history at school we did not spend much time memorising all of the names of Prime Ministers and Cabinet members (although Lord Hague might well have done). Instead, entirely rightly, we concentrated on the people, the inventions and the dates associated with the Industrial Revolution because that is what mattered from 1750 to 1850.

An assessment of the national software to come over the next decade is difficult for three reasons. First, I am by no means a tech guru. None of what I write here is due to primary research. There is no chance of my appearing on the front cover of *Wired* magazine, which, I am told, is the ultimate accolade for a tech entrepreneur. Indeed, on a daily basis, as anyone who has ever worked with me will know, I struggle with even elementary technology. The sentence 'Mr Speaker does not really do tech' would, as an understatement, rank alongside 'Donald Trump is not really a shy, retiring or modest individual'. Nevertheless, I also hope that in my time as Speaker I have taken a keen interest in advancing technology inside Parliament even if I do not necessarily fully comprehend where it came from, what it is and precisely how it might operate.

Secondly, even those with far more impressive qualifications than mine have found it hard to distinguish between the trendy and the transformational. To take one example, William Thomson, the first Baron Kelvin, was a Victorian mathematician and scientist widely viewed as the greatest British figure in his field since Isaac Newton, near to whom he is buried in Westminster Abbey. But even he once said in a public address: 'Radio has no future. X-Rays are clearly a hoax. The aeroplane is scientifically impossible.' History is littered with other examples of eminent howlers.

Thirdly, failure is to a degree inevitable here because the best that even the finest mind can do is to extrapolate from those technologies that are known to exist or are on the horizon, and estimate what the impact would be if they were to improve further and be adopted for other uses. What we cannot do is anticipate technologies that have not been invented but which might be wholly disruptive. This means errors will occur. When the first travellator was seen in Europe in 1900, it caused an absolute sensation. It was widely predicted that no one would be walking on pavements by 1920. When I was a child in the age of the *Apollo* astronauts many people thought that by the year 2000 people would fly from London to Australia in but a few hours and that there would be colonies of human beings living on the Moon and perhaps even Mars. None of those predictions proved accurate. At a slightly more mundane level, at one stage in the early 1990s it seemed as if the future of storage data rested with the CD-Rom and the transmission of it via the fax machine, only for the internet, smartphones and then the emergence of the 'cloud' to make a total mockery of such assumptions. The dear old fax machine was usurped by email, then the likes of Twitter, WhatsApp and Snapchat. Our national software will doubtless come under the influence of amazing innovations that have not yet seen the light of day.

Despite this, if we look at what we can see, it is reasonable to assume that national software will be very different in 2030 than it is today. The transformational impact of technology will surely be enormous. More data has been created in the past five years than cumulatively in the whole of human history before that point. The rate of new data emerging is becoming even faster. Moore's Law, the observation that the number of transistors in a dense integrated circuit will double every two years, may not prove to be an absolute but it probably will hold true for at least a few more years.

We should hence anticipate a wave like no other. It will come in many forms. It will arrive through the coming of autonomous vehicles, whose impact will probably be felt first and most profoundly in commercial transportation rather than private cars. It will come via artificial intelligence, robotics and machine learning. This will be reinforced by developments in augmented and virtual reality, a space that is presently dismissed as merely about games and entertainment but whose potential is much wider. It will be hardened by the fintech revolution and cryptocurrencies, which mean that we will soon reach a moment when having a bank hold your money securely and in a form that is determined by a government, when you could do that as easily yourself and in a type beyond the reach of party politicians or central bankers, is as irrational an act as continuing to pay for landlines.

It will be cemented by the evolution of an internet of things that would allow a mobile phone in London to adjust the air conditioning, heating and such like in a second home in, say, Portugal. It will express itself in the continued rapid advance of e-commerce in the UK (the nation that already does the highest percentage of all trade online in the world) at the expense of bricks-and-mortar stores. It will perhaps find its most fascinating expression in developments in the life sciences and MedTech that will enable all of us to know far more about our health ourselves than we could ever imagine.

These are simply the spheres in which we have a sense of what might happen. It does not allow, as I noted previously, for all that is to come, which is a mystery as of now but may not be by 2030. In all of this, the existence and expansion of a wider array of social media tools still will amplify the message. Politics and political institutions such as Parliament will surely feel the impact.

* * *

I will now attempt to assess what the challenges might be to Parliament and politics come 2030. It is insane to aspire to do so in detail. The best that one can do is to identify themes likely to be linked to changes in national software and contemplate what they might mean for the House of Commons.

The first broad theme that I can identify is that of speed. In a world where free software allows citizens and consumers to demand that their desires and requirements are met close to instantly, a similar sense of immediacy will be expected from their Parliament and parliamentarians. As issues emerge, the expected response time will be ever shorter. To be told that a major development will be discussed in Parliament a few days or a week later would be deemed manifestly insufficient. A society with the technological means to act at considerable pace will expect better than that.

Which means, I suspect, that much of the agenda of the House of Commons will have to be shaped on at most a daily basis. The Urgent Question and the SO24 debate will become the norm. Other devices such as general debates, setting aside four or five days for debate after the Budget and even Opposition half-day debates, might well be considered too rigid. The choice of which ministers and departments should face oral and written questions might no longer be done by rotation but on an instant analysis of what seems to be the most relevant today. If Parliament does not respond at the speed that its electorate wants then it risks rendering itself redundant. The House of Commons of the future will, I suspect, because of the enduring power of the hardware factors that I outlined earlier, probably look quite similar in 2030 as 2020 (the green benches are pretty safe, I reckon) but its timetable may well have to be much more fluid and flexible than now. In that spirit, one senses that the arrival of remote electronic voting cannot be deferred for ever. For my part, I am a convert to the idea of electronic voting in the House of Commons – which would save us hours every week and hundreds of hours a year – and to the right to vote online in elections.

The second broad theme is that of access. The House has, in my view, been quite imaginative in its efforts to allow individuals with strong views to transmit them to us by various means, whether that be through e-petitions or evidence submitted to inquiries, but as the pace of technology develops it is reasonable to hypothesise that the avenues of access will have to become much wider by 2029.

The third broad theme is that of specialisation. If the rate of data accumulation is to be what it is reasonable to think that it will become, it will be impossible for any individual or institution to have sight, let alone any concept of command, over all of it. Specialisation will become the norm as we all seek to master strands of knowledge and accept that vast swathes of it will be beyond us. What are the implications of that for the House of Commons? This is, of course, speculative, but it could be a shift in legislative scrutiny away from the Chamber as a whole towards its committees. Public Bill Committees may be abolished in favour of more select committees which are also larger in size and which develop discreet sub-committees functioning beneath them. Debate in new forms would be the primary responsibility of the whole. Legislation would be the main function of the parts.

The fourth broad theme is that of transparency. This refers not only to the 'end products' of the House of Commons but also how they are derived. Although we have made some progress in what may be described as the demystification of Parliament in recent years, there will need to be more done in this respect by the end of the next decade. There are not many people in emerging technology who think that the line 'our product is complicated to understand' constitutes much of a sales pitch. The process by which we do our business and the language with which we address each other has to be consistent with what I strongly sense will be another communications revolution within a decade.

Finally, Parliament will need to recognise and respond to

what is in many ways the most stunning development in all this: the shift in a society from one that is structured as a solid to a liquid. The group (whether it be a social class, a political party or a pressure group) is being displaced by the network (a much looser and more freewheeling structure). Intermediary institutions are being placed under pressure everywhere as technology permits the interested individual to do without entities that sit between themselves and the resources that they want access to, whether that be banks, high street shops or conceivably even doctors and hospitals. Direct engagement looks like it will become the name of the game and that engagement may be on a highly individualised basis.

The casework that almost every MP finds crushing at times today is likely to become much greater. The House will thus have to think about its technological response to all this and how it can allow MPs to be as reactive to their more sophis-ticated and multi-channelled constituents as they need to be. If not, then Parliament will risk being seen as another one of those unnecessary institutions that an engaged public senses it no longer needs. We may live in an era in which it is thought to be a smart move from time to time to 'cut the cost of politics'. In all candour, unless we receive a blessing and a bonus in terms of vast cost savings via technological development that has not been revealed to us, I struggle to conceive of how we can provide the level of personal service in 2030 that is likely to be asked of us without having to spend more. If we are candid about that, however, we might find there is a consensus for making the investment.

Before reaching what I hope will be viewed as a confident conclusion, I want to enter a caveat. I have talked about national hardware and national software but not noted the role of national values. This is not an omission that should be allowed to stand, especially when we live in an age where at home and abroad we can witness what were once thought to be deeply entrenched values being rejected. Values are to future progress what Wi-Fi is to so much modern technology – the essential prerequisite. There is no uniquely right set of values, of course, although there are some that are uniquely wrong.

I could easily have spent this entire chapter musing about values but I want instead to mention three. The first is an outlook on life that is internationalist in sentiment. This is not intended as a clever or a coded attack on the stance that might be taken towards the relationship between the UK and the European Union. There are many different forms that an internationalist outlook on life can have. There are Remain advocates who have little interest in the world beyond their own continent just as there are Leave adherents who are absolutely sincere in their enthusiasm for a Global Britain.

What is vital, nonetheless, is that an international approach of some kind is central to this country. We are, as I observed earlier, a mere 0.85 per cent of the global population now and that figure could well be closer to 0.75 per cent at the end of the next decade. While we can congratulate ourselves in punching above our weight in many areas of life, it is also the case that 0.85 per cent is too small a share of humanity to assume that we hold any majority, let alone a monopoly, on wisdom. There is no room for post-imperial delusions or simple isolationism. We are part of something much bigger than ourselves. This should always inform our thinking.

The second value we should cherish and which we surrender at our true peril is civility in our discourse with each other. This is under threat as referenced in the last chapter, from simplistic populists who reckon that the only legitimate viewpoint is their own. One of the less desirable aspects of the technological revolution is that it has created new channels for hate speech and for the deliberate manufacture of distortion and falsehood. It has stoked a climate of conspiracy, of rage and of violence. Yet democracy is not about decibel levels. Honest disagreement and courteous discussion are not acts of betrayal, evidence of an elite acting in its own interests or a contradiction in terms. They are the essence of what real democratic discourse is about. This cause would be assisted, in fairness, if we were all a little more honest about the opportunities but also the limitations of politics. In the real world, ministers act with imperfect information, often unappealing options and too little time. We would do better to recognise this and not treat every twist and turn in political life as if a crisis. The consequence of excessive criticism between democrats has been to legitimise *anti*-democrats. Civility in our discourse is not merely a matter of manners but has a material impact on our lives.

My final value is the importance of respect between generations. In this instance, I am at least as much concerned about respect for the young as for the old. If one is really to have faith in the future then one has to have faith and trust in those who will build it. That value has been central to my approach to the role of Speaker which I was honoured to hold. It has been the essence of how I have chosen to spend my available time as Speaker when not in Westminster. It has led me to champion the fantastic Education Centre and to hold my 'Skype the Speaker' sessions with schools across the country. That interaction was among the most inspiring of the work that I did.

In a similar spirit, I am immensely proud of the fact, mentioned in Chapter 7, that I have chaired every single one of the now annual sessions of the UK Youth Parliament from 2009 to 2018 and that I have spoken at every annual conference of that organisation over the past decade. I find it utterly fantastic that so many young people have such a passion for debate and for democracy that they want to be part of such a network. Finally, while I seek to talk and listen to a very broad range of audiences in my travels across the United Kingdom, I have a strong disposition to speak to and take questions from students. A belief in the young as well as a reverence for the old is to me the most underestimated of values. Values as the hidden wiring that makes the machinery of democracy work are also underestimated. It would be a bad, mad, sad world in which reasoned argument in institutions such as our Parliament were to be marginalised by an alternative, far inferior, form of public life in which 'debate', in so far as that term could be deployed at all, consisted simply of a ceaseless stream of crass Twitter slogans.

If we are truly to give young people a voice, we need to give them a vote. If young people aged sixteen and seventeen can join the army, have sex and pay taxes, they should be able to vote. I earnestly hope that Parliament will legislate to enable them to do so.

Obliging oneself to think a little more deeply about what I have described here as our national hardware has been a very rewarding exercise. It makes me feel less disturbed about the seeming turbulence of our contemporary politics whether that be at home or abroad. Fundamentals are exactly that, fundamental. We forget about our geographical and demographic, economic and commercial, cultural and social fundamentals at our peril. There is much there of which we should be proud.

Similarly, when compelled to consult with others who are more familiar with the technological advances which we will probably witness, I personally feel comfortable with the Bill Gates quote that we tend to overestimate what technology will achieve in the next three years and underestimate what it will achieve in the next ten. As a father of three still relatively young children, I do not look forward to 2030 and its likely technological landscape with fear or horror – quite the opposite.

I am also confident that Parliament and politics will rise to the challenge. To do so, we will need to recruit a diverse range of individuals with commitment, intelligence and a determination to preserve, protect and promote the values essential for democracy in the UK to flourish. National hardware plus national software plus national values will determine the UK of 2030.

Postscript

As we saw, on 29 October 2019, Boris Johnson persuaded Parliament to vote for a general election to be held on 12 December. It was mildly ironic because rumours abounded that supporters of a People's Vote were by then far closer to a potential majority than many people recognised, not least because a number of prominent ex-Tory ministers were moving in favour of it. However, the Liberal Democrats and the SNP both scented advantage to them in having a general election. Although there is a widespread view that the 2017 Parliament had run its course and that an election was timely, I frankly disagree. The Parliament still had up to two and a half years to run. MPs were holding ministerial feet to the fire and resisting a No Deal Brexit. They could have continued to do so for a while longer if they had so wished.

Instead, all the major parties opted to fire the starting gun for a pre-Christmas poll. The Conservatives published a minimalist manifesto with no hostages to fortune, learning from the calamity of Theresa May's approach two and a half years earlier. The Prime Minister fronted his party's campaign by reiterating the simple and simplistic slogan 'Get Brexit Done'. Predictably, it resonated with millions of voters suffering from Brexit fatigue, who believed that the saga of our EU departure had dragged on unresolved for too long. Johnson, not normally renowned for sticking to his script, was remarkably restrained throughout the campaign. He dodged the toughest broadcast interviewer, Andrew Neil. Media appearances were tightly controlled and mostly soft-focus. Of course, there were gaffes, notably when he refused to look at a photo of a four-year-old boy lying on the floor in an NHS hospital and instead pocketed the reporter's phone. Another day, he hid in a fridge as he sought to avoid a TV interview with *Good Morning Britain*. Yet these were judged by the predominantly right-wing media to be minor mishaps. Most importantly, Johnson practised ruthless message discipline, repeating relentlessly the mantra 'Get Brexit Done' and scaremongering about the prospect of handing Jeremy Corbyn the keys to Number 10.

The story of the election is that the Tory message was hugely successful in scores of Labour seats in the Midlands and the north of England, as well as a handful in Wales. The Conservatives won by a majority of 80 seats, losses in Scotland massively outweighed by the gains in England. The Tory total of 365 seats starkly contrasted with Labour's 203, a net loss of 59 seats from 2017 and the party's worst election performance since 1935. In what had been framed by the Conservatives and most media alike as the Brexit election, Labour's stance to renegotiate and then stage a second referendum did not widely appeal in its own heartlands. Moreover, Labour canvassers reported deep hostility to Jeremy Corbyn for being too left-wing, failing to tackle anti-Semitism in his party and lacking a credible, appealing message. Ironically, individual Labour policies were popular, such as free care for the elderly and slashing rail fares, but the overall narrative was not. Specifically, the manifesto was thought to be an overly detailed wish-list that could not be delivered. At his count in Islington, Jeremy Corbyn immediately declared that he would not seek to lead the Labour party into another general election but, instead, pave the way for an orderly transition to a new leader. The Liberal Democrats were squeezed by the bigger parties and their leader, Jo Swinson, lost her seat. Besides the Conservatives, the other big victor was the SNP, who won 48 seats, making a total of 13 gains on 2017, profiting at the expense of all three UK-wide major parties.

What are the implications of this result? The Conservatives had the parliamentary numbers to pass the first phase of Brexit – the withdrawal legislation – without difficulty. The second phase of Brexit, however – negotiating a trade deal with the EU – will be less straightforward. Boris Johnson has repeatedly committed to achieve that deal by the end of 2020 and moved to stop Parliament seeking any extension to the transition period. But the trade deal will not be shaped by him alone. It depends also on the EU. If the UK government settled for close regulatory alignment with the EU, which it insists it won't, the deal could potentially be done on time. If the Prime Minister wants greater freedom from the EU's rules and regulations, so-called regulatory divergence – as he has consistently argued – the prospect of a No-Deal Brexit at the end of 2020 will be firmly back on the table. As for the single biggest trade deal outside the EU, with the United States, all the evidence suggests that that will be a hard-grind negotiation, requiring not months but several years and potentially demanding unwelcome concessions by the UK to American commercial interests.

The election result, and the delivery of Brexit, will also have implications for the UK government's relations with Scotland and Northern Ireland. Of course, the Nationalists lost the 2014 independence referendum by 55 per cent to 45. That poll, by common consent of the then Conservative–Lib Dem coalition government and the Scottish executive, was a once-in-a-generation test of public opinion. During the election campaign of 2015, Scotland's First Minister, Nicola Sturgeon, appeared to accept that the referendum was definitive, signalling that she had no plans to seek another referendum and that only a 'material' change of circumstances would warrant a further poll. At that election, the SNP increased its Westminster representation more than nine-fold, from 6 to 56 seats, leaving Conservatives, Labour and Liberal Democrats with just one seat each. In the 2016 EU referendum Scotland voted by 62 per cent to 38 to remain in the EU. At the 2017 general election, the SNP fell back to 35 seats but in December 2019 the party rallied strongly to win 48 out of 59 seats, once more dominating the Scottish political landscape. Nicola Sturgeon has now served notice that she demands the right to another Scottish independence referendum. Constitutionally, such a referendum is the prerogative of the UK Parliament to grant or not as it thinks fit. Boris Johnson has emphasised that he will not agree to such a referendum. In short, the irresistible force of the SNP has met the immovable object of the Johnson government.

The Scottish Nationalists may opt to hold an 'indicative vote' on independence, i.e., non-binding, though my hunch is that they will do so only if they are super-confident of winning it. In practice, the phoney war between Westminster and Holyrood is likely to continue not just for months but for years. Yet, for better or for worse, Scotland's place within the Union is more fragile and precarious than ever.

The same could be said for Northern Ireland. The pro-Brexit Democratic Unionist Party lost two of its ten seats, including that of its Westminster leader, Nigel Dodds. Sinn Féin took seven, the SDLP won two and the Alliance Party secured one. The DUP now represents a minority of Northern Ireland's Westminster seats after enduring an unprecedently bad election. It is also a matter of record that Northern Ireland voted in the 2016 EU referendum to remain, and the fact that the DUP backed Brexit against the majority wish of the province's electorate damaged its standing with voters. Under the terms of the Johnson Brexit deal, goods from Northern Ireland as well as the Republic of Ireland will face new paper checks and this may prove deeply unpopular. Any goods going from Britain into Northern Ireland will be subject to an EU Customs Code, effectively an Irish Sea trade border. The Unionists remain firmly opposed to the Johnson Brexit deal but have no leverage at Westminster. Nationalists of every hue are against Brexit in any form. The Unionists want above all to remain in the UK. By contrast, Nationalists who are growing in numbers would prefer a united Ireland and the prospect of it is undoubtedly greater than before the Brexit imbroglio began.

The irony of all of the above is that an avowedly unionist party – the Conservatives – has won its biggest majority for three decades in circumstances which could trigger the break-up of the union of the United Kingdom of Great Britain and Northern Ireland. Sure enough, truth can be stranger than fiction.

Acknowledgements

First and foremost, I want to thank my wife, Sally, and our three children – Oliver, Freddie and Jemima. Sally strongly encouraged me to pen an account of my atypical, even odd, political career, and to get it done while in office. That led to me rising at the crack of dawn, both of us spending some time on the book at weekends, and a dedicated focus in parliamentary recesses over the last eighteen months. Throughout, Sally has been unfailingly supportive. Astonishing though it may seem in 2020, I write longhand and Sally willingly typed the bulk of the manuscript, offering advice on style and substance in the process. Our lovely children never complained and always encouraged me to put my thoughts on the record. I will always be grateful for their support.

In Speaker's House, we were lucky to be served for ten years, loyally and extraordinarily effectively, by our Slovakian nanny Renata. She, her husband Peter, and their two young children have become good friends to our family.

Sadie Smith, Tom Tweddle, Jade Knight and George Blake all served me superbly in a professional capacity. Yet, voluntarily and in their own free time, they helped with typing, research and fact-checking. Capable and dependable, I cannot praise them too highly.

My former parliamentary colleagues Dr Julian Lewis and Chris Leslie read and constructively commented on extracts from the book and I salute them both. Tim Hames and Steve Richards read the first draft and made invaluable suggestions on its structure and content. For the title of the book, credit goes to Fiona Vandersluys, Julian's partner.

However, my most profuse professional thanks are due to my agent, Andrew Gordon, of David Higham Associates. Recommended by Steve Richards, opting for Andrew was the best decision I made. Clear-thinking, calm and wise, he also had fifteen years' experience as an editor before crossing the professional floor to become a literary agent. That editing experience was precious as Andrew laboured to convert my overlong stream of consciousness into a coherent and uncluttered narrative. He is a brilliant professional whom I would recommend to any author.

The book completed, Andrew helped me to find a fantastic publisher in Alan Samson at Weidenfeld & Nicolson. Hugely experienced, Alan was quick to support me and he and the team – Cathy Dunn, Ellie Freedman, Susan Howe, Steve Marking, Fiona McIntosh, Lucinda McNeile, Paul Stark, Maura Wilding and Zoe Yang – have done an outstanding job in preparing and promoting the book. On top of his prowess as a publisher, it is a commentary on his good taste that, like me, Alan is an Arsenal season ticket-holder.

Picture Credits

The author and publisher would like to thank the following for permission to reproduce their images:

Bercow family pictures Plate 1 (top, below), 2 (top right, centre left), Plate 8 (below), Plate 9 (top, below), Plate 10 (top, below), Plate 15 (below)

david@hoffmanphotos.com Plate 2 (below right)

Getty/Anadolu Agency Plate 5 (top), Getty/Dan Kitwood Plate11 (below), Getty/David Levenson Plate 4 (top left), Getty/Peter Macdiarmid Plate 4 (below left), Plate 7 (top), Getty/Mirrorpix Plate 3 (top right), Plate 6 (below), Getty/WPA Pool Plate 12 (below), Plate 13 (top), Plate 14 (top right), Getty/Oli Scarff Plate 13 (below)

PA Images/PA Archive Plate 8 (top)

Shutterstock/Glenn Copus/Evening Standard Plate 6 (top left), Shutterstock/Everett Collection Plate 11 (top), Shutterstock/Vickie Flores/LNP Plate 7 (below), Shutterstock/Gerry Penny Plate 12 (top), Shutterstock/Rob Pinney Plate 14 (top left), Shutterstock/Tim Rooke Plate 4 (top right), Shutterstock/Mark Lloyd/Daily Mail Plate 6 (top right), Shutterstock/Ray Tang Plate 6 (below left), Shutterstock/James Veysey Plate 15 (top)

©UK Parliament/Catherine Bebbington Plate 3 (below), ©UK Parliament/Jessica Taylor Plate 14 (below), Plate 16 (top, below)

Index